THE NINE O'CLOCK WHISTLE

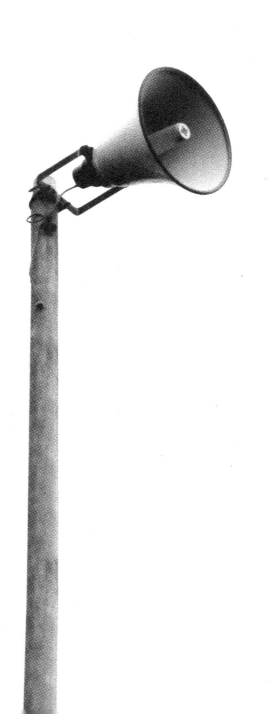

The
NINE O'CLOCK
WHISTLE

STORIES OF THE FREEDOM STRUGGLE FOR CIVIL RIGHTS IN ENFIELD, NORTH CAROLINA

**WILLA COFIELD,
CYNTHIA SAMUELSON,
AND MILDRED SEXTON**

INTRODUCTION BY DAVID CECELSKI

University Press of Mississippi / Jackson

Margaret Walker Alexander Series in African American Studies

The University Press of Mississippi is the scholarly publishing agency of
the Mississippi Institutions of Higher Learning: Alcorn State University,
Delta State University, Jackson State University, Mississippi State University,
Mississippi University for Women, Mississippi Valley State University,
University of Mississippi, and University of Southern Mississippi.

All photos are courtesy of the authors unless otherwise noted.

www.upress.state.ms.us

The University Press of Mississippi is a member
of the Association of University Presses.

Copyright © 2025 by Willa Cofield, Cynthia Samuelson, and Mildred Sexton
All rights reserved
Manufactured in the United States of America

∞

Library of Congress Control Number: 2024951249
Hardback ISBN: 9781496852380
Epub Single ISBN: 9781496852373
Epub Institutional ISBN: 9781496852366
PDF Single ISBN: 9781496852359
PDF Institutional ISBN: 9781496852342

British Library Cataloging-in-Publication Data available

*To the courageous Black people of Enfield
who between 1963 and 1965
risked life and limb to create a better world.*

CONTENTS

Maps xiii
Foreword. xv
Acknowledgments. xvii
Introduction. xxi

PART I: THE NINE O'CLOCK WHISTLE
Willa Cofield

1. **Preface to Part I: Blowing the Whistle** 3
2. And Some Fell on Good Soil 5
3. Early Beginnings 5
4. The Entrepreneur 7
5. Sundays. 14
6. The Cofields 15
7. Grandmama and Grandpapa George. 26
8. My Early Love Affair with School. 30
9. Attending Brick Tri-County High School 35
10. **Following My Star** 43
11. Reaching for Young Womanhood at Hampton Institute 43
12. Teaching in Halifax County. 56
13. The Brick Rural Life School: Doing Common Things
    in an Uncommon Way 59
14. My Year at the University of Pennsylvania. 68
15. Resuming Life in Enfield 71
16. Living the Dream of Teaching in My Hometown. 75
17. **Politics Change My World** 81

18.	Reed Johnson Runs for Town Commissioner	81
19.	Inborden Students Challenge Segregation	85
20.	The Protest Spreads	90
21.	*North Carolina v. Robert Blow* and *North Carolina v. Marie Davis*	96
22.	The March on Washington Sparks Events in Enfield	98
23.	Ninety-Day Boycott of Enfield's White-owned Businesses	105
24.	Danger Signals at Inborden High School	108
25.	**Breaking the Back of Racism at the Ballot Box**	114
26.	The Halifax County Voters Movement	114
27.	The Principal Turns Up the Heat	120
28.	The Voter Registration Campaign	124
29.	County Registrars Stage Voter Registration Slowdown	131
30.	The May 30 Primary	138
31.	**The Political Becomes Personal**	141
32.	No Contract for You	141
33.	The Community Shows Support	145
34.	The Literacy Class	149
35.	The KKK Burns Crosses	152
36.	The Hearing in Eastern District Court	157
37.	Six Black Children Integrate the "White" Enfield School	165
38.	The Second Hearing of *Johnson v. Branch*	173
39.	NEA to the Rescue	178
40.	Halifax County Board of Commissioners	181
41.	My Interrogation by NEA Panel	185
42.	The Third Hearing of *Johnson v. Branch*	187
43.	Judge Larkins Rules on *Johnson v. Branch*	189
44.	Building a New Life	191
45.	The Fourth Circuit Court of Appeals Reverses Ruling of District Court	196
46.	The Settlement	200
47.	**Ending Notes**	203
48.	My Legacy of Struggle	203
49.	Epilogue	205
50.	The Whistle Today	212

PART II: NEXT IN LINE
Cynthia Samuelson

51.	**Preface to Part II**	217
52.	Growing Up in Enfield	217
53.	Dixie Street	220
54.	St. Paul Baptist Church	224
55.	Grocery Stores	226
56.	Inborden School	227
57.	Introduction to the Arts	231
58.	Confidence and Optimism	233
59.	**Southern Racism Exposed**	236
60.	*Brown v. Board of Education*	236
61.	Emmett Till	238
62.	Rosa Parks	239
63.	Montgomery Bus Boycott	239
64.	Little Rock, Arkansas	240
65.	Greensboro Sit-Ins	242
66.	Freedom Riders	242
67.	Jackson, Mississippi Sit-In	243
68.	Sixteenth Street Church Bombing	245
69.	**Racism in Enfield**	246
70.	The Doctor's Office	247
71.	Harrison Drug	248
72.	The Friendly Grill	248
73.	Rose's Five and Dime	249
74.	The 9 O'Clock Whistle	250
75.	The Public Library	250
76.	The Park	251
77.	**Fighting Racism**	253
78.	The Klan	253
79.	The Boycott, Picketing, and Jail	254
80.	People Who Joined the Fight	256
81.	John Salter	257

82. JV Henry..259
83. Robert Blow..259
84. TT Clayton...260
85. The March on Washington..261
86. Retaliation..262
87. Enfield after the Sixties..264
88. School Integration...264
89. The Public Library..264
90. Downtown...265
91. Population and Demographics..266
92. Black Officials..267
93. Highway 301 and Interstate 95..267
94. Dixie Street..268
95. Farming..269
96. Impact of the Sixties on My Life....................................271
97. Mentors May Not Support You..271
98. You Must Overcome Obstacles..272
99. Do Not Hate Anyone...273
100. Life Isn't Fair...275
101. Perception Can Become the Reality.....................................276
102. Change the System...277
103. Get a Good Education..277
104. Overcome Adversity..278
105. Let No One Intimidate You...281
106. Be Yourself...282
107. You Can Learn from Anyone...283
108. They Walked the Walk...286
109. Willa Cofield Johnson...287
110. Lillie Cousins Smith..288
111. Ira D. Saunders...289
112. William "Bill" Jones..291
113. Going Home...293

PART III: THE IMPACT
Mildred Bobbitt Sexton

114. Preface to Part III 299
115. **My Family** 301
116. My Paternal Grandparents. 301
117. My Father's Military Service 303
118. My Parents' Wedding 304
119. My Birth and Birth Place 304
120. Places Lived and the Births of My Brothers and Sisters. 305
121. **My Grade School Days** 308
122. Inborden School: Segregated Beginnings .308
123. Dawson Elementary School: A Family Legacy 309
124. Back to Enfield and Inborden Elementary School 310
125. My Neighborhood. 311
126. Protection of Children 311
127. Hannon Street 313
128. Caring Community. 315
129. My Intermediate Years 318
130. Seventh and Eighth Grades 319
131. My Hometown of Entrepreneurs 320
132. Black Businesses 321
133. **My High School Years** 324
134. Starting My Teens: 1960–61 324
135. News of Current Events: 1961–62 328
136. The Protests Begin: 1962–63. 329
137. The Nine O'Clock Whistle 332
138. Picketing and Threats: 1963–64 333
139. A Time of Courage 334
140. **My Life Continues** 337
141. North Carolina College: 1964–68 337
142. My Return to Enfield: 1968–70 339
143. Integration of Enfield Schools: 1970–71 341
144. Black Soldiers in the 1960s. 343

145.	True Integration: 1970–74	343
146.	**My Professional Career Blossoms**	346
147.	My Tenure in Hampton City Schools	346
148.	Conclusion	347
149.	**Epilogue**	349
150.	Enfield Today	349

Notes 351

MAPS

Fig. M1. Locating Enfield in North Carolina / Grassroots Media Productions.

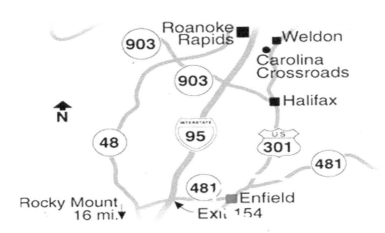

Fig. M2. Locating Enfield in Halifax County / Grassroots Media Productions.

MAP OF ENFIELD

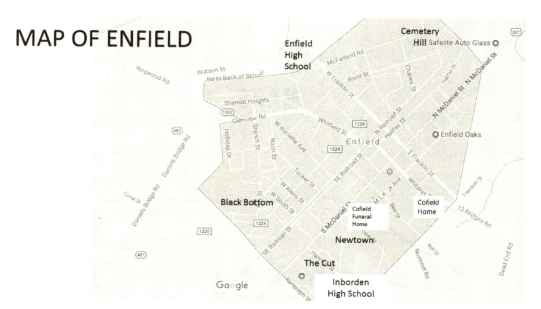

Fig. M3. Map of Enfield with Black neighborhoods encircled / Grassroots Media Productions.

FOREWORD

Almost sixty years after Cynthia Samuelson and Mildred Sexton sat in Willa Cofield Johnson's English classes at Inborden High School in Enfield, North Carolina, the three women joined to write this book. Here in separate memoirs, they recount their pre-1960s lives, their involvement in the civil rights movement, and the lasting impact that participation made in the years afterward.

Their memories form the spine of the recently produced documentary *The Nine O'clock Whistle*, where photos, archival materials, and the observations of other commentators bring the story to life. The book, however, goes beyond the film, providing an in-depth look at the Enfield story impossible on the screen. The book, for example, includes details about Willa's legal suit against local and county officials, as well as the pioneering work of the Halifax County Voters Movement.

The authors believe that the book and documentary will help the Enfield story become an acknowledged part of the historical record of the civil rights movement. They chose to use the storytelling format to make the contents accessible to a broad spectrum of people, especially young ones. Teachers may find using the film and the book together an effective strategy for helping their students understand the civil rights movement.

It is the authors' fervent hope that many people will learn about *The Nine O'clock Whistle*, especially how Black people in Enfield silenced the whistle, contributing to the great struggle for civil rights, liberating their own hearts and minds, and, ultimately, changing the world. Finally, by learning how people in Enfield confronted the racism that pervaded their community, the authors hope that readers will look at problems in their own community with new eyes.

ACKNOWLEDGMENTS

Many people generously supported the completion of this project. In the late summer of 2017, it seemed that our efforts to produce the film *The Nine O'clock Whistle* would not succeed. With some sense of urgency, Willa Cofield called her former Inborden High School students and asked if they would join her in writing a book of stories about the impact of the 1960s upon Enfield.

Several students responded, but the small group that began to hold a conference phone call every Sunday evening included Cynthia Samuelson, Mildred Sexton, Marshall Harvey (Fig. A1), and Evon Anderson Hughes (Fig. A2). Throughout the fall, we talked about two hours and shared memories of what had happened in Enfield fifty-four years ago. To our deep sorrow, both Evon and Marshall passed away before we completed the project, but they both left us with unforgettable stories about their years at Inborden High School.

Many other Enfield residents and former Inborden students contributed to the project by telling us their stories, providing photos, or supplying information. They included Doris Johnson Daniels, Jennie Ward, Rev. Albert Gee, Beverly Gee Hamlin, Cornelius Tillery, Geraldine Marrow, Bud Albert Whitaker, Rev. Harry Carroll, Barbara Shaw Simmons, Beverly Bailey Herbert, Jannie Burnette, Victor Marrow, Karl McWilliams, Mrs. Addie Clarke Bobbitt Draughan, Larry Bobbitt, former mayor of Enfield Kai Hardaway, and former North Carolina Representative Thomas Hardaway.

We are deeply grateful to Dr. Elwood Watson, professor of history at East Tennessee State University, and Dr. Crystal Sanders, professor of history at Emory University, for reading early drafts of our manuscript and encouraging us to continue working. Former Rutgers University professor William Jones, retired master teacher, not only shared his teaching strategy of "talking to the text," but gave hours of close reading and commenting on our stories.

Librarians at the Enfield Library, the Halifax County Library, the Halifax Community College Library, and the Plainfield Library provided helpful assistance in searching for relevant photos and documents. We thank Dr.

Fig. A1. Evon Anderson Hughes (November 23, 1946–January 1, 2019) / 2017 Grassroots Media Productions.

Fig. A2. Marshall Harvey (December 8, 1945– February 13, 2022). / Courtesy of the Harvey Family.

Jonathan Dembo, Special Collections Curator in the Joyner Library at East Carolina University Library, for help in accessing old issues of newspapers and materials in the Special Collections. We thank Professor David Dennard, retired professor of African American Studies at East Carolina University, for reading the manuscript during his Christmas holiday.

From Santa Rosa, California, former colleague and trusted ally Mary Ann Michaels provided invaluable editorial support and loving attention to our writing. Karen Riley, coproducer of *The Nine O'clock Whistle* documentary, continued her invaluable commitment to sharing the story of Enfield's 1960s encounter with the forces of social and political change. Throughout the writing, Linda Holmes, author and friend, provided guidance and direction on countless occasions to encourage us and share her deep knowledge of the perils, obstacles, and sometimes joy of publishing. Angenetta Robinson made an invaluable contribution in preparing the manuscript. Annette Alston, author and comrade at the People's Organization for Progress, gave encouragement and helpful advice.

We offer sincere thanks to Dr. Katherine Charron, professor of history at North Carolina State University, for her close reading of the manuscript, helpful suggestions, and facilitation of the publishing process. We thank Dr. Everett Ward, former president of St. Augustine's College, who read the manuscript with careful, appreciative eyes and gave helpful insights regarding its relevance and value. We are deeply grateful for Dr. David Cecelski's major contribution to getting the book published, reading and commenting on the manuscript, writing the introduction, and his general upbeat, encouraging support.

We hold the deepest reverence for John Salter's efforts to break the back of racism in northeastern North Carolina and apologize for not calling him Hunter Gray, the name he used long after his work in the South. In addition to being a committed freedom fighter, John Salter was also a scholar who recognized the historical value of preserving records. The Hunter Gray Papers at the Wisconsin Historical Society proved an invaluable source of newspaper articles, legal papers, and reports that John regularly sent to his Southern Conference Educational Fund (SCEF) sponsors. Years ago, John made certain that Willa had access to this rich and diverse treasure trove.

The following Seeking Educational Equity and Diversity (SEED) staff members were vital in helping create Willa's mindset and will to take on this project: Peggy McIntosh, Emily Style, Brenda Flyswithhawks, Gail Cruise-Roberson, Emmy Howe, Jondou Chen, Nancy Livingston, Judy Logan, Patricia Badger, Cathy Nelson, Dena Randolph, Kim Wilson, Raquel David-Chen, Ana Reyes, Bob Gordon, Carol Alm, Gladys Hughes, Lori Kawabara, Odie Douglass, Andre Larue, Manuel Penaloza, Cathy Orihuela, Donald Burroughs, Hugo Mahibir, Marcia Lovelace, and Chris Dunlap.

Former colleagues at the New Jersey Department of Education's Office of Equal Educational Opportunity (OEEO) Rebecca White Johnson and Marcellus Smith provided reassurance and encouragement. Marcella Simidiris of the People's Organization for Progress also gave her enthusiastic support. Thanks to Rev. Philip Hess of the United Church of Christ of Plainfield, NJ for his early efforts to find a publisher.

Special thanks to Rodney Pierce, Dr. Karla Solomon and the Enfield-Roanoke Rapids Alumnae Chapter of the Delta Sigma Theta Sorority Inc., and Rev. Alvin Harmon and the First Baptist Church of Enfield for helping bring the story of the Enfield civil rights movement to a younger generation.

We apologize to all those who contributed to the completion of this project whose names we may have unwittingly overlooked. Lastly, we thank our families for their forbearance and tolerance, and for putting up with us as we were immersed in the many tasks that writing the book required.

INTRODUCTION

David Cecelski

The Nine O'Clock Whistle is the story of the civil rights movement in the small town of Enfield, North Carolina. It is the memoir of three extraordinary Black women told, one by one, in their voices: first, Willa Cofield's, then Cynthia Samuelson's, then Mildred Sexton's. Their story is an important, untold chapter in the African American freedom struggle, and it is deeply moving, gracefully rendered, and utterly unforgettable.

Willa Cofield is now ninety-five years old. She has had a long and accomplished life as a scholar, teacher, and human rights activist. During the 1960s, she was a high school teacher in Enfield and gave herself heart and soul to the African American freedom struggle. She was fired for her activism in 1964, and the federal lawsuit that she filed to challenge her dismissal was a landmark moment in America's civil rights movement.

Cynthia Samuelson and Mildred Sexton were two of Willa Cofield's students at Inborden High School in the early 1960s. They grew up in Enfield during the Jim Crow era and joined the civil rights movement there when they were teenagers.

Like Dr. Cofield, their mentor and now dear friend, they seem to remember every little detail of life in Enfield. Whether it is the lilt of the people's voices, the dust on the streets, a child's first solo at church—or Cofield and her five-year-old daughter standing on a front porch and watching a seventeen-foot-high cross burning, unflinching and undaunted—it is all here. In the pages of *The Nine O'Clock Whistle*, a whole town, a whole age, a people's whole struggle for freedom comes to life.

I have been a historian of America's civil rights movement for most of my life, but I still found *The Nine O'Clock Whistle* revelatory. The story of this grassroots struggle for freedom and justice has never been told previously, and indeed the saga of Black activism in the broad swath of Black Belt counties that make up northeast North Carolina is largely unchronicled and, in most cases, forgotten. It is one of the most conspicuous gaps in our understanding of the civil rights movement across the American South. Many students of history will know that Ella Baker grew up only twenty-five miles from Enfield, and several historians, including myself, have made passing reference to the Halifax County Voters Movement.

But that is just the tip of the proverbial iceberg. In the 1960s, civil rights organizers who visited that part of North Carolina often compared its oppressiveness and fierce resistance to Black civil rights to what they had encountered in the Mississippi Delta and other parts of the Deep South. Thanks to these three women, at least the story of the civil rights movement in Enfield will not be lost.

The Nine O'Clock Whistle is a book that speaks to our intellect, but also to our hearts. Indeed, there are moments in these pages that have gotten so deep under my skin that I believe that I will always carry them with me. I cannot imagine, for instance, ever forgetting Mildred Sexton's richly textured narrative of Enfield's African American neighborhoods when she was a girl. As she guides us through the streets, you can breathe in the sense of community, the safety she felt there, and the love she received there.

I found other scenes in *The Nine O'Clock Whistle* unforgettable in a very different way. How can one ever forget the civil rights gathering where Inborden High's students erupted in what seemed like a never-ending chorus of "We Shall Not Be Moved" and other freedom songs? Or the night that the town's black citizens first refused to vacate Enfield's downtown streets after the "Nine O'Clock Whistle" rang? Or the time, that same night, when white authorities turned the town's fire hoses on Black protesters, pounding children and their mothers and fathers against sidewalks and storefronts?

That last scene will of course bring back memories of the far more famous moment, just a couple months earlier, when Bull Connor turned the fire hoses on Black protesters in Birmingham, Alabama. The most significant difference was that, in Enfield, as in so many small towns in the South, no national television cameras captured the scene in a way that would sear America's soul.

I suspect that that every reader will find their own parts of *The Nine O'Clock Whistle* that move them especially deeply. As for myself, I found that even some of the book's smallest moments and briefest asides caught me off guard. One that I am remembering now, for example, is Cynthia Samuelson's account of the day that she discovered a carload of armed white men following her home. She was only seventeen years old at the time. Like so many of the incidents recounted in *The Nine O'Clock Whistle*, it is a tiny moment, but captures something profound about the civil rights movement in Enfield as a whole. I will not give the story away here, but suffice it to say that it speaks volumes about how Enfield's African American community prepared its children for just such moments and how the older generation stood vigilant, always ready to protect its young. Samuelson tells the story matter-of-factly, and in only a few sentences, but I found it wondrous, and in a way quite beautiful.

The Nine O'Clock Whistle is the kind of book that only comes around once in a very long while. The voices of these African American elders are tenderhearted, but they brook no foolishness. (Two of the authors are retired public school teachers, after all.) In their words, we see Enfield's civil rights movement through the knowing eyes of the women they are today, but also through the eyes of the young woman and girls that they were in the 1960s.

We learn of one town's struggle for racial justice but, through that story, also come to meet some of the central figures in the civil rights movement throughout the American South. We walk side by side with civil rights demonstrators in Enfield's streets, but Cofield, Samuelson, and Sexton also show us an African American community that had been laying the moral, spiritual, and intellectual groundwork for those protests for generations.

The book's account of the role that Black teachers and historically African American schools played in Enfield's civil rights movement is especially compelling. In the pages of *The Nine O'Clock Whistle*, teachers such as Cofield and Lillie Cousins Smith, who was Cynthia Samuelson's mother, are revealed to be part of a long tradition of Black educational leaders who, despite being under constant surveillance, and never having the resources available to their white counterparts, proved to be—to quote Matthew—as wise as serpents and as gentle as doves in their defiance of white supremacy.

Here, as vividly as I have ever seen, these three women—scholars, teachers, elders—help us see and appreciate the *subversiveness* of African American education in the Jim Crow South. Their narrative compels us to look anew at those Black teachers and their schools as a wellspring of the African American freedom struggle in the American South. In so doing, they help us see the past more clearly, but also give inspiration to all those who are struggling today to speak the truth in classrooms throughout, in James Baldwin's words, these "yet-to-be United States."

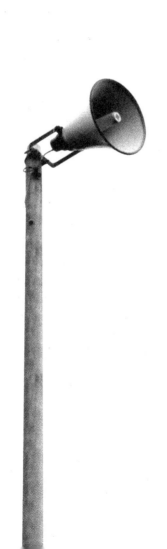

PART I
THE NINE O'CLOCK WHISTLE
Willa Cofield, PhD

Fig. 0.1. Willa Cofield, Inborden High School teacher and community activist, 1964. / John Salter Collection.

1. PREFACE TO PART I

Blowing the Whistle

During the plantation era in the South, a bell rang morning, noon, and night to order the work day of the slaves. Even today vestiges of the practice can be heard in Enfield, North Carolina, when the noon siren signals the whole town that it is time for lunch. The siren also is used to alert the all-white volunteer firefighters and emergency responders that there is a fire or an accident on Interstate 95. After World War II, Enfield officials began blowing the whistle at nine o'clock on Saturday nights as a signal for Black people to leave the downtown area. Violators of the curfew were subject to arrest. The sound of the whistle reached every corner of the town. Unfailingly, when it blew, it commanded everyone's attention.

The curfew whistle underscored the rigid segregation between the Black and white communities that had existed since plantation days. Like many other segregated towns, Enfield had a Black Wall Street. Enfield's Wall Street was one block long, and although the street sign said it was Franklin Street, everyone I knew called it Wall Street. I feel certain that the name reflected a time when Black entrepreneurship flourished in Enfield. A large two-story building and a pink stucco house dominated the block. In the 1940s, Mr. Hudson moved his shoe repair shop from Whitfield Street to the first floor of the wooden structure on Wall Street. Most days, he could be seen peering over specked glasses and clinching the stub of a cigar in his mouth as he shuffled between the work counter and the cash register (Fig. 1.1). A taxi business occupied a room on the first floor, and during World War II, Dr. Winston Bryant, recently graduated from Meharry Medical College, practiced medicine in one of the upstairs units. Cary Pittman, who had once built dozens of Rosenwald Schools and numbered among the most prominent of Halifax County Black people, often parked his car in front of the hulking structure.

Fig. 1.1. Black-owned businesses like Mr. Hudson's Shoe Shop provided gathering spaces for the Black community, ca. 1938. / Courtesy of Library of Congress.

Fig. 1.2. Mae Cofield with young baby, Willie Mae (a.k.a. Willa Mae), near Henry Cofield's grocery store. / Willa Cofield personal collection ca. 1928.

In the pink stucco house at the end of Wall Street, Dr. George DuBissette ran a community hospital.

During my early childhood, I heard many tales about the hospital. They intrigued me, for I was born in the DuBissette Hospital in the fall of 1928 (Fig. 1.2). Sometime after I was born, the Ku Klux Klan threatened Dr. DuBissette. Finally, they burned a cross in front of the small building and drove him from the town. Many years later, his daughter remembered that as a young child, she had sat in the back seat of the family car as her father sped over the burning cross and fled to safety, never to return to Enfield.

2. AND SOME FELL ON GOOD SOIL

3. Early Beginnings

Despite the meanness of the town, I had a safe, secure, and happy childhood. I grew up feeling the love of parents, grandparents, and other kin. Both my parents came from large families, blessing me with many aunts, uncles, and cousins. My first cousin, Andrades, and I were almost the same age, and for a while both our families lived close to each other on Dixie Street. As toddlers, when our parents would not let us visit, we played on our individual porches, calling out to each other as we skipped, jumped, and pranced. Midyear, my third-grade class became so crowded that the principal sent my half of the room to fourth grade. Andrades, who attended a different school, never forgave my principal for skipping me to the fourth grade, for it meant I was a year ahead of her in school.

Curtis Junior, my second favorite cousin, was only two years older than I, but a gifted storyteller with a wild imagination. He thrilled me with tales of his adventures. One summer at an unusual overnight stay with other cousins at our grandfather's house, Curtis Junior and Miss Margaret, our grandfather's second wife, both told stories about their adventures working for white people. After Miss Margaret talked about working for rich people in Tarrytown, New York, Curtis told of working in the home of the Randolphs, a white Enfield family. Curtis said that he could not enter the house through the front door. He could only open it to white visitors. After his employer added cooking to his responsibilities, he quit.

Curtis Junior assured me that he knew the conductors on the trains that passed through Enfield daily. He said that often they let him ride to the next stop alone and without a ticket. One day he offered to take me on a train trip to Halifax, the next stop after the northbound, steam-powered train left Enfield. Following his directions as well as my four-year-old mind and body permitted, I packed a small tin box with a sweater, and the two of us left the backyard, followed Pope Avenue for two hundred feet, and cut through a big field clearly visible from the back porch of my Dixie Street home. Fortunately, my mother saw us as we took a shortcut through the weed-infested lot, and she yelled for us to come home. I was so disappointed, having looked forward with so much excitement to the twelve-mile train ride to Halifax.

I knew nothing of the Depression, even though it certainly circumscribed our lives. I felt part of a prosperous, influential, and respected family in the community although our house had no indoor plumbing and three bricks propped up one corner of our kitchen stove. To bring in extra cash, my parents sometimes rented out two of the three bedrooms in our house. Once I begged to attend the PTA Summer Camp at Bricks, but my parents decided that they could not afford the six-dollar-a-week fee.

I measured our prosperity by other things. We owned a telephone, the only family in the neighborhood with this convenience. We always had a working car. My mother grew gladiola and beds of verbena in our backyard. My father always worked hard. In the summer, he drove to the sandpit and brought home a truckload of sand, which he dumped in the backyard for us to build sand castles and make mud cakes. On one exciting, unforgettable day, my parents came to the Enfield Colored Graded School before dismissal time with the happy news that they were taking my two sisters and me to the circus. As we exited the big Ringling Brothers Circus tent, my mother and father bought red, white, and blue batons with shiny rhinestone caps for my two little sisters. Our home was peaceful. I never heard my mother and father argue. My father complained about money shortages sometimes, but my mother always tried to convince him that things would work out. If he began disciplining us at mealtime, Mama quietly suggested that we should be permitted to complete our meals before we heard his criticisms. My parents enforced a strict code of behavior. I could not do things because my friends could do them. I had few visiting opportunities in my neighborhood. Friends could come and visit me, but I usually had to find entertainment within the confines of my own house and yard.

In the summertime, my father bought bushels of peaches and tomatoes for my mother to can. Sitting around a large tin tub on the screened-in back porch, we all helped with the peeling. Both parents seemed to enjoy these family projects. Everyone could sample the peaches as they peeled. After we peeled the last peach, my mother spooned the fruit into large, galvanized pans and added sugar to let the peaches sit overnight and form a syrup. Early the next morning, Mama washed and sterilized clear Mason jars, gently simmered the peaches on top of the kitchen range, then filled the jars for winter eating.

Fig. 4.1. Young Thomas Cofield celebrates a trip to Norfolk, Virginia, with a visit to a photographer's studio, ca. 1920. / Mae Cofield Family Collection.

4. The Entrepreneur

My father certainly earned the title of entrepreneur, starting many businesses while still a young man (Fig. 4.1). Cofield Funeral Home grew to be the shining star of his business investments. I was the oldest child, and I liked nothing better than following my father around the big storage and work building next to our house on Dixie Street. When Dad built caskets, I loved watching him and handing him the hammer or holding a piece of white pine lumber while he sawed. I watched intently as he stretched gray fabric over the exterior of the long pine box, put in straw to create a nice bed, and finished by covering the inside of the upper lid with ruffled, white satin.

Often my father let me ride along when he went on out-of-town trips for monthly reports and collections from the Cofield Mutual Burial Association agents (Fig. 4.2). I still remember the warm greetings that the two of us received at the home of Mrs. Hargreaves in Halifax, Mrs. Ida B. Johnston in Roanoke Rapids, and Mrs. W. T. Edmonds in Weldon.

Fig. 4.2. Agents and staff of the Cofield Mutual Burial Association meet. Augustus Cofield (left) and Thomas Cofield (right) kneel in front. Reed Johnson is partially seen standing at extreme left, ca. 1955. / Photo courtesy of Eloise Wilkins; J. B. Harren, photographer.

Mrs. Mary Pullen lived in Enfield and brought her monthly report to the funeral home. My sister, Sylvia, loved to tell the story of one of Mrs. Pullen's visits during Sylvia's tenure as the Cofield daughter helping in the funeral home (Fig. 4.3). At the end of the month, Mrs. Pullen came to the office to give her monthly report of Cofield Burial Association members who had paid their dues. Soon after Mrs. Pullen settled into her seat on the other side of the desk, the telephone rang, and Sylvia answered in the way my father taught all of us: "Cofield Funeral Home. May I help you?" At first, Mrs. Pullen glared stonily at Sylvia from her chair on the other side of the desk. Then, as Sylvia continued speaking to the phone caller, Mrs. Pullen took a small fingernail file from one of her bags and began cleaning her fingernails. Ending the call as quickly as she could and turning to Mrs. Pullen, Sylvia politely apologized for the interruption. "Sorry, Mrs. Pullen, can we get started on your report?" Continuing to file her nails, Mrs. Pullen looked coldly at Sylvia and said, "I waited for you. Now you can wait for me."

There were kind people around us who helped my parents: Harry Lewis did odd jobs in the store and washed the hearse and funeral cars. Little Bud rented the small bedroom in our house and drove a taxi cab. Jew clerked in the grocery store. My mother prepared meals for Little Bud and Jew as another source of income.

When I was about five years old, we moved from the Black Bottom section of Enfield to New Town, and we lived there until I was ten. For the rest of his

Fig. 4.3. Willa's sister, Sylvia, served her tenure as receptionist at Cofield Funeral Home, ca. 1944. / Mae Cofield Family Collection.

life, I heard my father say, "I'm going to the corner." We all knew that he was headed to the strip of buildings located in New Town at the corner of Dixie Street and Pope Avenue. Dad had purchased the property from Mr. Ira Wood, a white Enfield businessman under circumstances that I never learned. The purchase included a store, café, barber shop, storehouse, and four green clapboard houses. We moved into one of the green houses, sharing the backyard with the funeral home, storage building, café, and barber shop. The shed that housed the hearse and funeral car also boasted two-by-four crossbars where my childhood friend, Lillie Mason, and I played skin-the-cat (Fig. 4.4). My father improved the house facing Pope Avenue and made it the Cofield Funeral Home. The store and café looked very much like a saloon in an old western movie. People often sat on the crude wooden benches against the exterior wall to chat or to observe anything that might be happening on Pope Avenue or Dixie Street.

The store served as the hub of public life in New Town and The Cut, a cluster of Black neighborhoods on the southeastern side of the town (Fig. 4.5). At the front of the store on the Dixie Street side, my father cornered off a space big enough to hold a large iron safe, a desk, and a swivel chair. Here he kept credit records and held private conversations. People bought their groceries at the store—frequently on credit. In those Depression days, it was very important to be able to buy staples like flour, meal, lard, fatback, sugar, and coffee when people didn't have the cash. "I'll pay you Saturday," promised many customers.

Fig. 4.4. Playmates, Willie Mae (Willa) and Lillie Marie, celebrate the new baby, Sylvia, 1934. / Mae Cofield Family Collection.

At midday, after the twelve o'clock whistle blew, some people bought their lunch at the store: a small tin of sardines, a few saltines; a slice of cheese and a slab of souse with crackers; or a can of delicate Vienna sausages. My father kept a bottle of vinegar and hot peppers on the counter, so that customers could spice their meal to taste. Customers stood at the counter and ate their snack from a piece of slick wrapping paper. Many people loved soft drinks: Pepsi Colas and Royal Crown Colas were among the top sellers. In the morning, the combination of a package of freshly baked sweet rolls, oozing in sugar, and a Pepsi Cola made a popular snack. A pack of cigarettes cost twenty cents and a single cigarette a penny. Snuff and Prince Albert chewing tobacco ranked as hot sale items. The store offered several brands of snuff: Navy, Sweet Society, and Tube Rose counted among the best sellers.

Neighborhood children ran in with a nickel or even a penny and looked carefully at the candy counter before making their purchases. Some knew

Fig. 4.5. In the heart of New Town, Cofield's Grocery, Café, Barber Shop, and Funeral Home anchored the neighborhood and provided economic stability for the family. / 2017 Grassroots Media Productions.

exactly what they wanted and hardly needed to look. For a penny, they could buy a Baby Ruth, three Mary Janes, five chocolate Silver Tips, or a B-B Bat. A nickel permitted the purchase of a small bag of these sweets. At the front of the store, a large bunch of bananas swung from the ceiling, and in several strategic locations, long glue fly traps helped keep the store relatively free of flies. A cane-bottomed chair near the back door offered people a place to sit and enjoy a cold soda. One happy day, my father cut an opening in the lower wall separating the store and the café and slid in an ice cream box, making it possible to scoop ice cream from either the store or the café. Orange popsicles, bars of vanilla ice cream dipped in chocolate or orange ice, ice cream sandwiches, and Dixie cups of plain vanilla or chocolate ice cream filled the deep wells of the box.

Long before television, many regulars came to the store at the end of the day to buy a soft drink, to talk, and hear the latest news. Mr. George Arthur, who had attended elementary school with my father, worked at the peanut mill. He could always be counted on to take a seat in the circle of men who surrounded the big coal heater. You could hear his favorite saying, "Lord, today!" punctuating the conversation as the men commented on the critical state of Black people or the poor economy. The men spoke of the need for change, and I shivered as I heard them agree, "Somebody is going to have to die." During the baseball season, customers lined up and rooted for the

Brooklyn Dodgers or the New York Yankees. I listened with pride when my father spoke. I could tell that the other men looked up to him and respected his opinion.

My father showed that people could not run over him (Fig. 4.6). On weekends, the store offered fresh fish, which were trucked in from Norfolk, Virginia. The fish arrived about four o'clock in the morning—long before the store's seven o'clock opening. The driver always left the large wooden box of ice-covered trout, butterfish, and croakers right at the front door. One winter, my father began noticing a decrease in the number of fish in the box. As the weeks passed, it became clear that he was not receiving a full order of fish. Before complaining to the seafood distributor, he decided to get up early and watch from the front window of the store to see what happened after the deliveryman left.

At four o'clock promptly, the fish truck drove up and the driver deposited the box at the store's front door. The truck driver jumped into the cab of the truck and headed back to 301 Highway. Ten minutes later, someone came from The Cut walking toward the store carrying a basket. My father immediately recognized the individual. Sure enough, as the man approached the box, he took a screwdriver from his pocket and began prying off the top of the wooden box. My father opened the door with his shotgun drawn and yelled, "I've caught you! You're the one who has been stealing my fish!" The man was completely flabbergasted and had to admit that he was the one. After that incident, no one tampered with the store's early deliveries.

Even during the Depression years, the store's business prospered, adding to my sense of security and well-being. When the store added a refrigerated meat counter, everyone could see that the business was growing. In addition to cured and salted meats, the store began selling sausage, pork chops, bucket steak, spare ribs, and neck bones. On the first Sunday morning after the new counter arrived, my ecstatic father reported to my mother, "The cash register showed sales of $30!" After that, on Sunday mornings we always had bucket steak with rice and gravy for breakfast.

My father began early preparing me for work in the store. Indeed, soon after my tenth birthday, I began clerking in the store. My dad taught me how to make change and use the cash register. I had watched him so much that I knew how to approach customers, how to open a can of sardines, and how to fill orders for groceries. Often, I was in the store by myself. My father didn't mind if I ate a piece of candy, but I don't remember being highly attracted to those delicacies. What fascinated me was the bottles of bright red, maraschino cherries that lined the top shelf near the cash register. No one ever

Fig. 4.6. Thomas Cofield, ca. 1935. / Mae Cofield Family Collection.

bought them. My curiosity finally overcame my fear of being caught, and on one of the occasions when I was in the store alone, I climbed on top of the counter, furtively opened one of the jars and plucked a red, juicy cherry from the very top. After I took this risk once, I repeated it several times, always careful not to open the same jar. This curiosity also led me to discover a beautiful Humana doll, my sister's future gift from Santa Claus, that my parents had hidden on top of the tall case of light bread and pastries.

One Sunday afternoon my father invited a white labor union organizer to speak at the First Baptist Church following the regular church service (Fig. 4.7). I remember Dad begging people to stay and listen to this important visitor from a labor union who would instruct them on how to register and vote. Several people did stay, enough to fill the pews at the front of the sanctuary.

But no sooner did the white labor man mount the platform and begin to speak, than the double doors at the back of the church opened to reveal Chief Sykes and another policeman. Suddenly, the atmosphere in the sanctuary changed from expectation to uncertainty and fear. My father stood and hurriedly strode to the back of the church. We could not hear the conversation, but nobody was listening to the speaker either. The doors closed and my father returned to the front of the church with everyone's eyes on him. With clear embarrassment written on his face, he apologized to the audience and the speaker, saying that the meeting could not be held as planned.

Everyone, including the visitor, swiftly left the church. My father gathered my mother, sisters, and me and took us home where we stayed only briefly. He then drove thirty-six miles to Wilson, where he went to the home of the union organizer. My mother, sisters, and I sat in the car while my father talked to the union man who never got a chance to tell Black people in Enfield how to register to vote.

Fig. 4.7. First Baptist Church, 1978. / Willa Cofield personal collection.

5. Sundays

We took church and religion seriously, although during the first years of my life, I don't think my father attended church regularly. I suppose he was too busy running the store and funeral home, and he made my mother responsible for our Christian education. But always, we were taught to be respectful to others, especially older people, and to follow the Golden Rule, to treat others as you would like to be treated. My mother demanded that we greet people who sat on their porches on Dixie Street. Saying "Good morning" was insufficient. Mama insisted that we include the individual's name in the greeting. Older people paid close attention to how children addressed them, and if I forgot, they told my parents.

I learned the twenty-third Psalm in Miss Fanny Hunter's first-grade class, and I think my parents taught me the Lord's Prayer. I believe that they taught the prayer to me on our drive to visit my mother's parents, for the imagery of approaching Draper's Crossroads (which is where we turned off the main road on the way to my grandparents' farm) still colors "the Power, and the Glory, forever. Amen." On Sunday mornings, before breakfast, my father always read a chapter from the Bible. He loved the twentieth chapter of Ecclesiastes, his mother's favorite:

The heavens declare the glory of God, the firmament showeth his handiwork. Day unto day uttereth speech and night unto night showeth knowledge.

There is no speech nor language where Thy voice is not heard.

My mother loved the Psalms. After the reading of the Bible, everyone said a Bible verse and then we all said the Lord's Prayer together. At school, throughout the time I attended elementary and high school, we began each day with a similar devotion: a patriotic song, Bible verses said by every student and the teacher, and the Lord's Prayer. I followed the same order during my years as a teacher in North Carolina public schools.

On Sunday evenings, my family often visited my grandparents. My mother's parents lived about eight miles from our home on a farm near Draper's Crossroad, and my father's parents lived in Enfield on North Railroad Street. Both houses had large front porches with rocking chairs. My parents always showed love, respect, and kindness toward their parents.

6. The Cofields

My Grandpapa Henry and Grandmama Grace Cofield raised a brood of nine children, eight of them boys—Bennie, Harry, Curtis, Thomas, Augustus, Nathaniel, Junius, and James—and one girl, Julia (Fig. 6.1). Junius and Julia were twins. The fourth son, Thomas, was my father. The Cofields lived in a two-story house on North Railroad Street with a horseshoe drive that curved through the front lawn. An ancient cedar stood near the street and a huge oak tree shaded the front porch. When we went to visit on Sunday evenings, I usually had a chance to play with Andrades, my first cousin, who lived next door to my grandparents, although her house faced a different street. When we left, my heart always skipped a beat as my father made the sharp right turn onto North Railroad Street. A huge, uncovered ditch lay perilously close to the dirt road, and I always feared that we would fall into that big hole in the earth.

Occasionally, when I was very young, my mother and father let me spend the night at my grandparents' house. One night when it was hot and uncomfortable in the upstairs bedroom, Aunt Julia took me downstairs where we sat in a rocking chair and watched a big silver moon shining over the peanut factory across the railroad tracks. Somehow, in my mind that memory is linked with the song, "When the moon comes over the mountain," leading me to believe that Aunt Julia sang that song as we rocked together in the early morning hours.

Fig. 6.1. Grace Cofield with her nine children. Henry Cofield, her husband, avoided photographers whenever he could, ca. 1916 / Mae Cofield Family Collection.

The living room held large Victorian furniture upholstered in black leather with heavy mahogany arms and legs resting on large claw feet. My sister Sylvia once reminded me that a spectroscope lay on the table in the living room with double pictures, which became one picture when you looked through the lens. I vaguely recall my disappointment that the photos displayed military scenes of World War I. I remember that the staircase banister provided the swiftest means of coming downstairs from the second floor, and when no adults were in sight, we children almost always chose it.

Grandpapa Henry had been born in Enfield to Anna and Henry Cofield in 1872—just seven years after the end of the Civil War (Fig. 6.2). Aunt Julia told me that before Enfield had electricity, the streets were lighted with gas lamps. She said that every evening Grandpa Cofield rode his horse around in the twilight, lighting gas lamps on the streets of Enfield. The salary he made

Fig. 6.2. Mostly white Enfielders downtown at the turn of the twentieth century, ca. 1895. / Brick School Collection.

as a lamplighter was not enough to support his large family, so he engaged in whatever work that he could find. Grandpapa Cofield knew many ways of putting food on the table. A skilled hunter, he trapped all kinds of animals, dried their skins, and sold them. Aunt Julia thought that he sold the skins to Nels Pender, who dealt in many forms of merchandise in his shop at the corner of Bryant and North Railroad Streets. Years later, I remember the Nels Pender shop as a virtual junkyard or a mammoth outdoor flea market.

My father always gave great credit to his Grandmama Lucy, Grace's mother, for the family's survival. He said that Lucy Bradley, who was a cook in the Parker family, provided food for her daughter's family on a regular basis. He said someone went to Grandmama Lucy's house every day. Aunt Julia said that as a child she loved to spend nights with Grandmama Lucy, who lived in a small, one-room cabin that stood in the backyard of the white family that she cooked for, although she owned a much nicer house on Cemetery Hill. The little house stood on the Parker property well into the 1980s (Fig. 6.3). Aunt Julia said that on visits to her grandmother, she never thought that the house was small. As a young woman, Lucy had managed a grist mill on a big farm in Dumpling Town and lost her left hand in an accident at the mill. My father said that the mill stood right in the fork where the Tillery and Halifax Roads intersect. He said that the family who owned the farm had a lot of orchards and grapevines. Aunt Julia said that even though her grandmother had only one hand, no one could drive a buggy like she could.

Fig. 6.3. Willa's great grandmother, Lucy Bradley, lived in this cabin when she cooked for a white family, ca. 1985. / Willa Cofield personal collection.

Everyone in our family knew the classic story about my paternal grandfather, Henry Cofield, whom I called Grandpa Cofield. During the lean days of the late 1880s, Henry Cofield left his wife Grace and his nine children in Enfield, and he and his sister Julia went to Savannah, Georgia, where Henry worked in the pine tree industry. The logging camp where he worked was far from any town. The men were responsible for tapping the pine trees and gathering the thick resin which was then used in a variety of ways: in ship building, making asphalt, and as turpentine. The men worked long hours in the deep forests near the Savannah River.

The laborers were paid on Christmas Eve at the end of a year's work, and because the camp lay so far from town, a company store supplied most of their needs. The employers set up accounts, and the men bought snacks, cigarettes, chewing tobacco, snuff, sweets, and other items to relieve the tedium of work and isolation, all to be paid for at the end of the year.

My grandfather noticed how frequently some of the men visited the company store. In return for a modest sum, he offered to prepare simple meals for them. When they were too tired to walk to the store, they called upon Henry's services. The work was hard and dirty, so Henry offered to wash their grimy overalls and shirts, so that they could maintain some modicum of cleanliness.

On Christmas Eve, the men gathered in the clearing in front of the commissary to receive their pay. Both employer and employee understood that the amount owed to the company store would be deducted from the employee's paycheck. The white boss told the excited crowd of men, "There is one man here who only owes the company store two cents. His name is Henry Cofield."

Henry promptly answered, "You got that wrong, Sir. I don't owe you anything." The employer replied, "Yes, you do, Henry. One day you were deep in the woods, and you gave me a post card to mail to your wife, Grace. I put a stamp on it, and you owe me two cents."

With the same type of grit that he had demonstrated in Georgia, Henry Cofield started his grocery business as a vendor with a booth in a building in downtown Enfield, one of only two Negroes in the market. Daily, he faced taunts and jibes from white vendors who resented his presence. Aunt Julia believed that these white competitors tried to entrap him by planting stolen clothes in his storehouse. She credited her mother Grace's sharp intuition with suspecting some foul play and early one morning, warning her husband to inspect the barn. After discovering a large box of clothes in the barn, Henry immediately went to the police station and reported the clothes, which had been taken from a local dry-cleaning firm.

To escape that hostile environment, Henry opened a store at the corner of Bryant and Railroad Streets, opposite Nels Pender's flea market business. At first, the store sold meal that Henry had ground from the corn he raised. Later, the store stocked potatoes and other vegetables from Henry's garden, as well as produce grown on local farms. The store also sold cheese that came in round hoops and crackers packed in tin cans.

In 1910, in a small building behind the grocery store, Henry Cofield, together with some friends as partners, opened a funeral home. By the 1930s, the partners had disappeared, leaving behind only a sign on the front door, saying "Cofield, Bullock, and Johnson." The chief work of the business was to build and sell caskets. Aunt Julia remembered coming home from school one day and seeing men at work on a casket. She asked her father, "Who's dead?" He answered tersely, "George Washington." Innocently, she said that she went home and told her mother, "George Washington is dead. They're building a casket for him at the funeral home."

In those days, a horse-drawn hearse transported the body from the funeral home to the home of the deceased for an overnight wake and the next day carried it to the church and graveyard. The Cofield home site included a large garage in which Julia's brothers sometimes parked the hearse. Aunt Julia said that when she and her brothers saw the reflection of passing trains in the windows of the hearse, they would say to each other, "Look at the haints!"

In further conversation about the funeral home as it was in those days, Aunt Julia said, "They didn't embalm bodies then. The first embalmer that I know anything about was my brother, Nathaniel." In the mid-1920s Nathaniel studied embalming at Reynaud School of Embalming in New York City. His photo hung in the Cofield Funeral Home throughout my childhood. It showed a group of somber individuals. Uncle Nathaniel was the only person of color. I think that there was one woman in his class. Nathaniel came home to work in the family funeral home. His tenure in the business was fraught with conflict. He ultimately died of tuberculosis in 1942. My mother liked him very much, citing the tender affection he showed to me as an example of his gentleness. Far from earshot of my father, she said that he was the best one of my father's brothers.

Grandpapa Cofield was small in stature but possessed an iron will and great drive. He ruled his household with a firm hand. He did not like to be late. On Sunday morning, rather than wait for other family members, he walked to New Bethel Church by himself—about two miles—and when they arrived, he had already made a fire in the big stove and the church was warm and toasty. He did not like small talk and lingering visits. One of the family stories described a trip that he and Grandmama made to see relatives in New York City. Once my grandfather saw that everyone was in good health and apparently doing well, he was ready to go home.

My mother loved to talk about Grandpapa Cofield. Many times, she recalled his moderation of a church meeting. When the church sanctuary filled with noisy voices, Grandpapa shouted at the top of his voice, "Let's have otter (order) or mink one!" Mama would laugh heartily as she told this story over the years, always repeating it as if no one had heard it before.

Grandpapa had been a force at New Bethel Baptist Church. The book, *Who's Who Among North Carolina Baptists*, said that he was a deacon, trustee, and superintendent of the Sunday School. I think he may have been a founding member of the church. At least, I heard my mother tell stories about his work in turning the building around so that it faced Plant Street rather than Dennis Street. The book, which was published in 1940, also commented on his worldly possessions, noting,

> Mr. Cofield is active in church, civic and business affairs.
> In all community activities he is found a willing worker.

He owns his own home, fourteen tenant houses in the town, a thirty-acre farm, and other valuable holdings.[1]

Next to New Bethel Church, my grandfather loved the Enfield Fire Department, a voluntary company that fought fires that frequently threatened Enfield homes. At that time, many communities in the South relied upon Negro fire companies for protection from fires. So prevalent was the practice in North Carolina that Negro fire companies organized a state association. As a young child, I remember the fire company association meeting in Enfield. My nephew found a photo of the men attending an Enfield conference years later. My childhood memory focused on the tournament with people crowding the downtown streets to watch the firemen—who wore black caps, bright red shirts, and crisply pressed white pants—engage in foot races, hose handling, and other fire-fighting skills.

Henry Cofield strongly supported the state association, traveling to many North Carolina towns for the annual state convention. In Enfield, the peanut mill owners helped sponsor the trips to the conventions. These trips were like vacations, with overnight stays in host members' homes, local parades, and meetings to hear invited speakers. Aunt Julia drove my grandfather to the firemen's conventions that were held in cities around the state.

The era of Negro fire companies ended in the early 1930s. Once town budgets began providing substantial financial support to municipal firefighting companies, Southern towns replaced these volunteer, all-Negro companies with all-white, municipally supported fire departments. The Enfield Fire Fighters were forced to shut down when supporters of the all-white municipal fire department stole the equipment of the Negro unit, making it impossible for them to continue fighting fires. People in the town began to depend on the better-equipped, publicly supported, all-white group.

Grandpapa loved the Halifax County Sunday School Convention and faithfully attended its late summer meetings. On the last night of the three-day convention, children from throughout the county competed in a speaking contest. My parents prepared me to enter the contest when I was very young by teaching me one of Robert Louis Stevenson's poems.

The Swing
Robert Louis Stevenson, 1850–1894

How do you like to go up in a swing,
Up in the air so blue?

Oh, I do think it the pleasantest thing
Ever a child can do!
Up in the air and over the wall,
Till I can see so wide,
River and trees and cattle and all
Over the countryside—
Till I look down on the garden green,
Down on the roof so brown—
Up in the air I go flying again,
Up in the air and down![2]

As I grew older I learned other poems, and for several years I joined other children on the front bench of local churches to compete in the speaking contest. The summer that I was in fourth grade, my parents could not attend the convention at White Oak Church in a community about eight miles from Enfield. Instead, they taught me my recitation and sent me along with my grandfather. When the judges announced the contest winner and I did not hear my name, I could not hide my disappointment, and tears began running down my cheeks. One of the adults pointed out my distress to my grandfather, and soon after, one of the judges returned to the podium and announced that there was an additional winner of the contest. She called me to the front of the church and gave me a quarter. When I went home, I happily showed my quarter to my parents and told them I had won fourth prize. I didn't think they needed to know that I had cried and Grandpapa had interceded in my behalf, but, of course, they found out. Although my memory has faded, I am certain that I finally won first prize at the Halifax County Sunday School Convention's speaking contest. The desire to win was too intense for me to give up without capturing this prized honor.

Grandpapa Cofield also farmed. He had a horse and a wagon and grew cotton, sweet potatoes, and corn on several acres of farmland on Railroad Street. I remember well a large garden in a fenced-in area behind his home, a mulberry tree near the chicken pen, and a black walnut tree in the backyard. I will never forget the summer that he planted sweet potatoes on a vacant lot on Dixie Street in The Cut. I remember this well because he asked me to help him harvest the sweet potatoes, one of the pleasant memories of my childhood. I loved digging in the fine soil and finding the big red potatoes. It seemed more like searching for eggs at the Sunday School Easter egg hunt than work. I saw Grandpapa at least once a week when he drove his wagon to our house to pick up slops to feed his hogs. I was thrilled when I became old enough to sit on the wagon seat and ride with him to Franklin Street, where he pulled over and let me off. I bounced and skipped the two long blocks home, feeling a bit grown-up and proud that both Grandpapa and my mother trusted me to walk home alone.

I have very few memories of Grandmama Cofield, although I was eight years old when she died. When I was about four years old, Tit, a young neighborhood boy, took me for a visit to her house. My grandmother gave me a beautiful tin plate, which I clutched to my chest as we walked home. It was a very windy day, and the wind blew the plate from my hands and into a drain on the side of the street. Neither Tit nor I could retrieve it. I thought that this was probably an event that I had imagined until I asked my mother about this childhood loss a few years before she died. She told me that it had happened just as I remembered it.

Grandpapa made certain that all the family knew of his strong disapproval of women who smoked or wore pants. As a student at Brick Junior College, Aunt Julia once came home straight from gym class without changing from her gym suit, which would be considered extremely modest by today's standards. She said, "He had right much to say about it, and I never let him see me in pants again." She said that it was common for farm girls to wear pants but Aunt Julia never thought of herself as a rural person. However, she said that after her husband, Joseph Exum, gave her a pants suit one Christmas, she changed her mind. Whenever Grandpapa saw me in pants, he always made a wry comment, but by my time, pants as female attire had become so common that he sometimes just glared at me without saying anything. On the other hand, when my father's youngest brother, James, married, he was careful to let his new wife, Elizabeth, know how Grandpapa felt about women who smoked. All the children loved Aunt Elizabeth, and one summer, when she stayed with them while my parents and I made a trip "up North," they informed her if they saw Grandpapa headed toward our house. They did not want Grandpapa to catch her smoking.

Uncle Harry enjoyed telling a story about his father that I heard many times. He always filled his narration with raucous laughter and foot stomping—if he was seated. He said that when the children of Grace and Henry were growing up and before they moved to the two-story house across from the peanut mill, his father had a practice of buying a barrel of salted herrings, which he kept on the back porch of their house on Cemetery Hill. Grandpapa assigned Harry the job of fetching a dozen salted herrings from the barrel on the back porch each evening and soaking the fish in a dishpan for the next morning's breakfast. Even when I was a child, fried herring with pan-fried corn bread was considered a bountiful breakfast. When the barrel was relatively full, the job of retrieving the fish from the barrel was not difficult. "But," Uncle Harry said, "as the barrel of fish got lower and lower, the water got thicker and slimier and the task of pulling them out got nastier and nastier." Finally, as the last few fish remained in the barrel, he was forced to lean over the side, move his hand around in the black, smelly water and literally fish for the slippery herring. "When I got the last one out, I was so happy, but," he continued with much laughter, "don't you know that the very next morning, Papa had a whole new barrel of herring for us to eat!"

I also learned from my father that Grandpapa had wanted each one of his children to learn a different trade, barbering, shoe repair, or carpentry. Early, he worked with them to establish a business enterprise, H. C. Cofield and Sons. This business operated a grocery store, sold wood and coal, and invested in rental property. After my grandfather's death, my father, Thomas, served as executor of his father's will. Over the years, I heard the instructions my grandfather had given my father repeated many times: Grandpapa asked him to help each of his brothers and the one sister. Years after my father's death, my nephew, Thomas, produced Grandpapa's will at a family gathering. The words that he read sounded exactly like what my father had said on so many occasions. Not everyone felt that they had received adequate help, but my father obviously had considered the responsibility a trust and undoubtedly did the best that he could.

When they were growing up, Uncle Harry, according to my father, frequently helped his mother with the cooking. He became a skilled cook and grew up to operate several cafes in Enfield. In the early 1950s, he and his son opened the Little Palace Restaurant on Highway 301 (Fig. 6.4). I have met many Black people in the Northeast who, traveling south in the days of racial segregation, had stopped for a memorable meal in Uncle Harry's Little Palace Restaurant.

Although the Cofield women of my parents' generation generally conformed to the traditional women's role of taking care of the house, the garden, and the children, there were exceptions. In the summer of 1937, Uncle Harry's wife, Lillie Belle, attended the Apex Beauty College in Brooklyn, New York (Fig. 6.5). After graduating, she returned to Enfield, and in two new rooms attached to Harry's café, she opened a beauty salon. Her business thrived for the next three decades, inspiring many other Black women to follow her example. Aunt Julia actively participated in the management and operation of Cofield-Exum Grocery Store. Other wives, including Reather, wife of Augustus Cofield, Maderlin, wife of Curtis Cofield, and my own mother, Mae, helped their husbands from the sidelines and even occasionally worked in their husbands' business operations.

Part I: The Nine O'Clock Whistle 25

Fig. 6.4. Three friends, Doris Johnson Daniels, Doc and Cleveland Lowe, stop at Uncle Harry's Little Palace Restaurant, ca. 1960. / Courtesy of Doris Johnson Daniels.

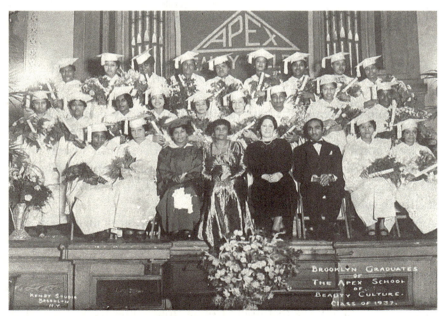

Fig. 6.5. Lillie Belle Cofield (extreme left in first standing row) graduated from Apex Beauty College in Brooklyn in 1937. Madam Sara Spencer Washington (seated in the center in the shiny, satin gown) was founder of the Apex empire of beauty company, schools, and products. 1937. / Courtesy of Elaine Hardy Holland.

Fig. 7.1. Mary Harvey McWilliams (1869–1943), "Grandmama George," ca. 1935. / Mae Cofield Family Collection.

Fig. 7.2. Grandpapa George (1860–1954), early 1930s. / Mae Cofield Family Collection.

7. Grandmama and Grandpapa George

On our Sunday evening visits to the farm home of my mother's parents, George and Mary McWilliams, we usually found my Grandpapa sitting on the front porch in his rocking chair. Grandpapa George had a bushy white mustache and his nose had little pocks from the 1914 smallpox epidemic. Near his rocking chair lay a fly swatter and a walking stick, an improvised tobacco stick or the branch of a young sweet gum tree.

    My father usually parked the car between the two-story main house and the separate kitchen-dining room structure. The small separate house held two rooms: a kitchen and dining room. A big chimney with a fireplace served both rooms. A shelf near the kitchen door held fresh pails of water with a dipper. Nearby stood a covered well that supplied drinking water for the family and the farm animals that drank from a trough attached to the well. A wooden duct carried buckets of fresh water to the container where the horses and cows drank.

During those Sunday evening conversations on the front porch, my grandfather liked to talk about his life. I sat swinging my feet on the edge of the porch and drank in every word:

I was five years old when the Civil War ended. I was a little boy and didn't understand exactly what was going on, but I heard the bells ringing and remember men in white vests coming into our yard. They told us that we were free. One of the older women yelled, "Go tell old Doc Batchelor he can pull his own fodder!"

He said that his mother, Mariah, put him out to work when he was twelve years old. He said that he made up his mind that someday he would own his own farm and not have to answer to any boss. I wondered how anyone only twelve years old could have such grown-up thoughts, but I didn't dare ask. "I met your grandmother, Mary, at Wayman's Church, where folks who had been slaves learned to read, write, and figure. They had a singing class, and I loved to sing. You know why most folks can't sing? You have to mess your face up to sing. You have to be willing to look ugly."

Grandpapa said that as soon as he could he started buying land and married Mary and they raised fifteen children—seven boys and eight girls. "Clearing new land and working from sunup to sundown, we put together this farm. Our goal was to leave each one of the children one hundred acres of land."

Grandmama never came to the front porch to join in the conversation but sat quietly in her bedroom at the back of the house. So, after talking to Grandpapa a few minutes, my mother usually drifted off to spend the rest of the visit with her mother. A short, cheerful woman with long white braids that she wrapped around her head, Mary McWilliams was much younger than her husband. "When we married, he was much older, but each year he got closer to my age. To hear him tell it," she said, "we are now about the same age."

She loved quilting, and her room held a dozen or more shoe boxes with quilt pieces ready to be assembled in some new pattern. In the winter, Grandmama and her visitors sat in comfortable rocking chairs that faced a whitewashed fireplace. Mama had given her mother a set of bright yellow and white water glasses in a white wire container that sat on the bureau as a constant reminder of my mother's generosity.

Mary liked to spend time with her adult children and sometimes came to stay with our family in Enfield. Although I enjoyed seeing my mother in such good spirits, on these visits Grandmama liked to spend time patching my dresses that I then had to wear to school. She seemed not to understand that although we were poor children, no one wore patched clothes to school. She was a very practical parent and told my mother, who was busy polishing my two little sisters' white shoes, "If you bought them black shoes, you wouldn't have to polish them."

I finally got to ride on the train one Christmas when Grandmama went to visit two daughters and a son who lived in Richmond. I was about six years old, so the year would have been 1934. Somehow my parents decided that I should accompany my grandmother on the one-hundred-mile train ride to Richmond, Virginia. Uncle Jesse, my mother's brother, would ride with us to Richmond, then continue his journey to New York City. When we arrived in Richmond, we walked into the huge waiting room which held a dazzling Christmas display showing a holiday village with houses, trees, skaters, snow, churches, stores, and miniature people that was, by far, the most beautiful thing that I had ever seen.

In the summertime, my grandfather often turned to my father and told him to go into his bedroom, look under his bed, and get a watermelon that he had brought in from the field. My Grandpapa cut the big, green watermelon into long slices and lined them up on the side of the porch. Everyone took a slice and for the next few minutes there was little talking.

My grandparents never let us leave their house empty-handed. Long before we left, Grandpapa gave us a basket and said: "You, children, take this basket and go down to those apple and pear trees. Pick the good fruit from the ground, first, and if you don't have enough, climb the tree and pick enough fruit off the tree to fill the basket."

We'd grab the basket and bolt down the little path, past the green figs and sage bush, jump over the battered wire fence, and run into the orchard. I loved Grandpapa's apples. They were yellow and tart and speckled. No one else grew banana-flavored apples. We picked peaches from the orchard and pears from two trees that stood in the field between the house and Draper's Road. In summer, we visited Grandmama's garden and loaded the trunk of our car with white potatoes, green beans, squash, and onions. In the fall after the frost made them sweet, we cut collard greens that Mama cooked with cured pork.

Sometimes I spent several days visiting my grandparents. On these visits, I helped my grandmother gather vegetables for the midday meal, and I followed her into the dark smokehouse for cured pork. One summer Grandpapa planted the garden far from the house in a field near Mr. Ocie Davis's farm. I remember walking with Grandmama to see if there were new potatoes under the green potato vines. When we got to the field, she took the garden hoe and very gently pulled the fine soil back. Bending over each plant, she removed a few potatoes, then carefully covered the smaller ones for future harvesting. When we had enough for our meal, we put them in a tin pan and headed back to the house. Stopping at the well, Grandmama dropped the big bucket to the bottom, bringing up a pail full of clear, cold water which she poured over the small potatoes. While the two of us sat under a tree and peeled the potatoes, I secretly chafed as she used a knife and insisted that I use the side of a spoon. Another kitchen assignment I liked better was to shake a quart jar half-filled with thick cream that my grandmother skimmed from the milk until the rich cream turned to butter. It took quite a long time, and I usually required help, but it was magical to see gold flecks appear in the cream and finally turn into a mass of butter.

One afternoon a terrible storm came up. Grandpapa said that we should all go to the storm shelter in the front yard. Grandmama, who suffered from rheumatism and walked slowly, decided not to join us. Grandpapa grabbed my hand and we ran through the howling wind to the little log and mortar building in the front yard. We hurried over the red clay floor and sat on a wooden bench against the back wall. By now the rain was pelting the windows at the front of the shelter. While the thunder and lightning crashed, I huddled close to Grandpapa. He smelled like the cured tobacco that he had been grading down at the pack-house and little gray hairs sprang from his arms.

Like many Black farmers of their time, my grandparents tried to live at home, that is, they lived on what they produced and rarely bought things from the store. In addition to growing vegetables and fruit, they raised hogs, chickens, guineas, turkeys, and ducks. They hauled wheat and corn to the mill to be ground into flour and cornmeal. Grandmama made butter from the milk that the cows produced. They made molasses from sugar cane and cider from late-summer apples. When they built the big house near Plumbline Church, Grandpapa used trees from his own land, setting up a sawmill to cut and finish the lumber and building a kiln to make the brick for the chimneys.

Grandmama sewed their clothes and made quilts for the beds. She made soap by adding lye to leftover kitchen grease and boiling the mixture in a big iron washpot in the yard. Grandpapa cured hams and pork shoulders in the smokehouse. Logs from scrub oak and pine saplings supplied fuel for fireplaces and stoves. They bought few things from the store.

Grandpapa George loved to fish. After I learned to drive, he'd ask me to take him to Bellamy's Lake where he fished for bass and catfish. My younger brother hated these trips. He said that Grandpapa had ten fishing poles that my brother would have to untangle and tie to the side of the car. When we got to Bellamy's Lake, Grandpapa laid them out on the bank of the lake and told my brother to watch them to see if a cork bobbed. According to my brother, Grandpapa never caught anything.

In the summer of 1954, Grandpapa got sick. I stopped by Park View Hospital in Rocky Mount for a short visit with him on my way home from work. He wanted to go home. He told me to get his hat from the closet. I helped him dress, and the two of us walked out of the hospital together. I drove him home, and one month later he died.

8. My Early Love Affair with School

In 1933 I entered first grade at the Enfield Colored Graded School. Built on land donated to the county by Hunter Pope, a local white farmer, the school housed seven grades with twelve rooms and a large central auditorium. The school had steam heat—a rare thing in those days—and a five-hole, outdoor toilet. One leaky water faucet outside the white clapboard building supplied water for the entire school. The classrooms opened into the auditorium, which comprised the heart of the school. At weekly assemblies, the principal—everyone called him Fessa Davis—talked about good conduct. We did a lot of singing at the assembly programs. I loved to sing "John Brown's Baby Had a Cold upon His Chest" and the "Bonnie, Bonnie Banks of Loch Lomond." We actually had songbooks so that we could sing all the words.

We didn't need the songbook when we sang "Lift Ev'ry Voice and Sing," for we knew the words, and everyone stood, for it was known as the Negro national anthem. The auditorium was also where at the end of each year, Fessa Davis gave prizes to students with the highest marks. I considered it the greatest of all honors: to hear my name called and march to the front of the auditorium in front of my mother and father, and Aunt Julia and Uncle Joseph, not to mention my classmates.

During the morning recess, students who had a penny or a nickel would go to Miss Betty Pittman's classroom and buy candy. The best deal was the B-B Bat, a long, hard, chocolate taffy sucker about the size of a half-stick of butter, covered in waxed paper. If you bought a B-B Bat, before you unwrapped it, you hit it on a brick, so that it splintered into a half dozen small pieces. These you handed out to the four or five little girls who crowded around you. At first when you put the candy in your mouth it was stiff and unyielding, but if you held it long enough, the chocolate became soft, filling your whole mouth with sweet, delicious juice. And each time you chewed on it you received another chocolate thrill. We had no idea that profit from the candy sales paid for our crayons, paper, and notebooks.

The county school board gave the barest possible financial support to colored schools. We had no playground equipment to speak of, but we played ring plays and games: Ring around the Roses, Rabbit in the Pea Patch, Here Comes Uncle Jesse, and Here We Go Gathering Nuts in May. Boys shot marbles or wrestled or chased each other across the playground. Girls loved forming a circle and singing, "Little Sally Walter sitting in a saucer." Pairs of little girls clapped each other's hands and chanted Peas Porridge Hot, which we all called Peas Potteridge Hot.

Sometimes when teachers weren't watching, we went to nearby fields and jumped ditches. Pity the poor kid who couldn't reach the other side of the ditch and had to return to the classroom wet, muddy, and disgraced.

The school had no cafeteria, so the lunchbox was very much in vogue. The preferred lunch consisted of baloney on light bread slathered with mayonnaise, an apple or orange, and a slice of cake. My lunch frequently included my mother's deep brown plum jelly sandwiches. At first, kids teased me about these sandwiches, but after I let my friend Lillie Marie nibble a corner, she'd ask, "Willa Mae, please give me a piece of your mama's chicken shit sandwich."

In fifth grade, I fell in love with school. School filled my life with joy and anticipation. One evening at the beginning of fifth grade, my Aunt Reather, herself a schoolteacher who rented the best bedroom in our house, found me sitting in our small living room staring at my fifth-grade history book. She saw instantly that I was struggling with my homework. Aunt Reather sat down on the piano stool and quietly gave me a study strategy that worked so well that I soon became star of the fifth-grade history class. She told me that I should read each section of the assigned chapter in the textbook separately and then repeat the details of the section aloud to myself. We went over the process a couple of times and then my aunt left me on my own. The next day in history class, I knew the chapter so well that I was able to answer any question that the teacher asked.

I loved the teachers, my friends Lillie and Lou Hazel, Mrs. Bullock's history class, and the almost daily singing of the Negro national anthem. One day, a teacher sent me home after she noticed that I kept twisting my red and white cotton dress from side to side. To her horror, she found my abdomen covered with open chicken pox eruptions. I knew they were there, but I hid them from my mother, who would have made me stay at home had she seen them.

As a young child, I believed that teachers knew everything—the whole book. I believed that the teacher told the truth, and I needed no further proof of validity. I was like the children who bragged that they could point to the truth because it was written in a book. "I can show it to you in black and

Fig. 8.1. Sisters Claudette (left) and Sylvia stand beside Willa, who did not want to be in picture and mistakenly assumed that her unflattering hair style would force her mother to exempt her, ca. 1938. / Mae Cofield Family Collection.

white," they would boast. I pained my parents with my constant rejoinder: "But the teacher said . . ." I admired teachers for, unlike my parents, they had attended college and knew the inside of books, where I was certain education lived and thrived.

I greatly enjoyed taking part in school assembly programs and singing in the school chorus. I still remember my pride in a fifth-grade speech about the history of the United States in an assembly program. I hardly cared that half of my audience seemed unmoved. I really felt that I had reached the mountaintop when I gave the valedictory address that marked my graduation from elementary school. The excitement of my family, the admiration of my younger sisters, as well as the applause from the audience, filled my young heart with joy (Fig. 8.1).

Throughout my schooling, my teachers, who were always Black, sought to make us proud of our people. They spoke often of Roland Hayes, Marian Anderson, and Paul Robeson. One day in my fifth-grade history class—after we had spent weeks studying the American Revolutionary War—our teacher, Mrs. Bertha Bullock, told us to put our books away. Mrs. Bullock was a no-nonsense teacher and she always had perfect order in her classroom. In a firm voice, Mrs. Bullock announced, "There is something very important I must tell you that is not in the history book." We leaned forward in our chairs, not knowing what significant information had been omitted from the history book. Then standing tall and straight at the corner of the blackboard, she said "Children, I want you to know that a Black man whose name was Crispus Attucks was the first man to die in the Revolutionary War." This startling revelation immediately made the American Revolutionary War of personal significance, filling us with pride and instantly becoming the most salient information that we had learned about the American fight for independence.

Once near the end of a school day in late summer, Mrs. Bullock called me to her desk. I was not the kind of student to get in trouble at school because of behavior, so I was really curious when she told me to get my books and take a note she had written to my mother. I don't think I sneaked a look on the short walk from the school to my home, but I was very puzzled about this unexpected communication with my mother. When I arrived home, my mother stopped her work in the kitchen and read the note immediately. Mrs. Bullock thought that I was old enough to join church. She suggested that my mother take me to the revival meeting at her husband's church.

In line with Mrs. Bullock's instructions, my parents dutifully took me to St. Paul Church for the revival meeting, which always went on during the last month in August. I was quite familiar with the revival pattern in our community. All three Black Baptist churches in Enfield held revival services in August. The first Monday night in August, everyone went to the First Baptist Church on the Scotland Neck Highway, where Rev. K. P. Battle pastored. During the second week, we all attended New Bethel Baptist Church in Black Bottom, and the last or fourth week in August, churchgoers went to the St. Paul Baptist Church, which was pastored by Mrs. Bullock's husband, Rev. Frank L. Bullock. Mrs. Bullock urged my parents to have me join Rev. Bullock's church.

Like many other people in our town, I had had exposure to a good deal of preaching by the end of summer. One thing I did not like about the revival service was the ministers' practice of recruiting candidates for the mourners' bench. The minister asked everyone in the church to stand, and after everyone stood, the minister asked all the Christians to sit down. It was a trap designed to identify the sinners, who then were invited to come to the front of the sanctuary and sit on the mourners' bench. Since my teacher had instructed my parents to have me join church, I had no recourse and ended up on the mourners' bench with a few other sinners. At the end of the sermon when the invitation came to take Jesus as my personal savior, I stood up and gave the minister my hand. On the following Sunday, I was baptized in the swamp on Highway 301. My parents showed their independence, however, by having me join First Baptist Church where they held membership and not Rev. Bullock's church.

Fig. 8.2. Willie Mae in 7th grade—Willa Cofield is second row center and Lillie Mason is second row third from the left, 1940. / Mae Cofield Family Collection.

Although I was somewhat neutral about saving my soul, I desperately wanted to succeed in school. When I was in fifth grade, every night I earnestly prayed that I would win the end-of-year prize as the smartest person in the class. Downtown stores contributed the prizes and usually chose hard-to-sell items or other merchandise of low value to contribute to the colored school. I won this coveted prize in fifth grade, and later I was valedictorian of my seventh-grade graduating class (Fig. 8.2).

Two other events made 1940, the year I graduated from elementary school, memorable. First, our class took a field trip to Norfolk, Virginia, and the homeroom teacher, Mrs. Bullock, gave us a party. We rented a bus that my father and uncle had engineered from a flatbed truck and an old school bus and, with Mrs. Bullock as our chaperone, we rode the 120 miles to Norfolk and back. On the way, we toured the Coca-Cola plant in Weldon and in Norfolk visited the offices and production site of the widely read Black newspaper, the *Norfolk Journal and Guide*.

The climax of my elementary years came at the end of the school year, when my homeroom teacher, Mrs. Bullock, gave our class a party. On the day of the party, our classes were suspended, and we spent much of the day decorating our classroom. Cousin Henry McWilliams, the school janitor, covered the blackboard with chicken wire, and Mrs. Bullock sent us out to find flowers. We visited the houses near the school and returned with

Fig. 8.3. Commencement program of the Enfield Colored Graded School, where in 1940, Willa delivered valedictory address, "We Are Going On." / Mae Cofield Family Collection.

bunches of spring flowers. We pushed the roses, daisies, verbena, and zinnias, into each hole. Then we gathered wild honeysuckle vines from the nearby ditch banks and draped long strands over the windows. The drab classroom became a place of beauty fragrant with cedar and fresh honeysuckle. Later that evening when we entered the room for the party, we found our teacher had placed a red paper placemat on each desk, with matching napkin, plate, and cup.

We had never seen such splendor! There were Spam sandwiches, grape punch flavored with diced apples, and Dixie cups of vanilla ice cream. The celebration made a perfect ending to my seven years in elementary school.

9. Attending Brick Tri-County High School

Brick Tri-County High School occupied the central buildings of the former Brick Junior College operated by the American Missionary Association. In 1933, the AMA had closed the college. Fred Brownlee, executive secretary of the AMA, wrote that the North Carolina State Department of Education was encouraging public education for both races throughout the state and was prepared to pay salaries for teachers in a centralized high school for Blacks at Bricks, if the three counties would agree to do the administrative work. The

Fig. 9.1. The Brick Tri-County High School, Bricks, North Carolina, ca. 1920. / Brick School Collection.

agreement was made and the three counties, Halifax, Edgecombe, and Nash, rented the buildings for one dollar a year.

In his book, *New Day Ascending,* Brownlee said that the AMA granted the use of buildings and land, provided partial salaries of several teachers for three years, and helped purchase buses.[3] He said that plans were underway to build a $100,000 school building on ten acres of land that the AMA would deed to the three counties. Although Brownlee confidently noted that the regional high school was an assured success, the regional high school was never built. Years after I graduated, the Brick Tri-County High School burned down, and each county built its own bare-bones school for Black high school students.

White high school students who lived in Enfield attended Enfield High School, but Black high school students had no school within our town. Instead, the county of Halifax, along with Nash and Edgecombe Counties, bused Black high school students to Brick Tri-County High School. The three-story brick building that housed the Brick Tri-County High School looked somewhat impressive from the highway (Fig. 9.1), but when we got close, we could see that the cement walks were crumbling and paint on the doors and windows was peeling. Inside the plastered walls were cracked and dingy. Teachers, students, and parents raised funds to help operate the school. Throughout my high school years, popularity contests, talent shows, ticket raffles, and Friday-night socials helped provide operational money. We often used books that the white schools discarded, and our poorly equipped science laboratory had only one microscope. When teachers scheduled an

Fig. 9.2. Teachers of Brick Tri-County High School. The two teachers with arms folded in the back row are Miss Violet Perry (left) and Miss Gladys Hammonds (right), ca. 1940. / Courtesy of Edna Smith James.

examination, they told us that if we didn't want them to write the test on the blackboard, we should bring a nickel to school the next day, so that they could buy stencils and paper to prepare our test materials (Fig. 9.2).

Having walked to and from elementary school every day, I was happy to begin riding the bus in the fall of 1940 when I entered the Brick Tri-County High School, three miles south of our town (Fig. 9.3). We were more fortunate than earlier generations of Enfield Black youth who had walked long miles to attend Brick School.

One of those students, Fred Shields, talks about that four-mile walk to school in the documentary *The Brick School Legacy*, saying, "If we heard the bell begin to ring when we reached the creek bridge, we knew we could get there on time—if we walked just a little faster."

The County used high school boys, who received a small monthly stipend, as bus drivers (Fig. 9.4). The bus was outfitted with four long, leather-covered benches on which students sat facing each other. There was no back support at all for students who sat on the two center benches, but the outer benches permitted the riders to lean against the sides of the bus. Students rode unsupervised by any adult. When the bus drove over the huge potholes on the long, unpaved drive from the highway to the school, the student passengers were often jostled and occasionally tossed from their seats. At such times, some wit would inevitably quip, "Shake well before using!" When the young driver braked suddenly, the riders cascaded to the front of the bus. No one ever reported these incidents to adults, for the drivers were our friends and classmates.

Fig. 9.3. Principal Joseph Wiley greets students from bus that brought Negro children to Brick Tri-County High School. Ca. 1940. / Amistad Collection.

In eighth grade, I entered an essay contest about cooperation. I had heard Louis Austin, editor of the *Carolina Times*, speak at the Methodist Church in Enfield. He talked about the importance of cooperation in the colored community. I used some of the folksy stories he told in my essay. The teachers asked a few of us to read our piece in an assembly program to encourage other students to enter the contest. Everyone raved about my essay because I had not copied ideas from books, the way other students did. Other kids began to look at me as a smart student. At the end of the year, I tied with Alfreda Lane in having the highest academic average in the school. I also acquired a new name. My English teacher Miss Hammonds told me that although my mother named me Willie Mae, the name Willie was for boys, and I should spell my name Willa Mae.

When I was in tenth grade, the science lab acquired its only microscope through a fund-raising drive. The racism responsible for our poorly equipped school rankled us, and we found many opportunities both in the classroom and outside of the school setting to talk about the racial injustice and unfairness that blighted our lives.

In 1943, during my third year at Brick Tri-County High School, a tiny group of trusted students spent one unsupervised hour each day together in a small room on the school's third floor. Although teachers designed the period for study, conversations about Black history frequently dominated the hour. This group of students finally appealed to the principal to add a course in Black history to the curriculum, and the following semester about twelve of

Fig. 9.4. Some of the boy bus drivers also learned to cook in Mrs. Dorothy Bailey Horne's Home Economics class, 1940. / Courtesy of Judith Horne Johnson.

us studied Black history under the guidance of Miss Violet Perry, who usually taught mathematics. Some twenty years later, Black students all over the nation called upon school authorities to add Black history to the college and high school curriculums. Brick Tri-County High School responded to this need long before the protests of the 1960s, as had Brick Junior College in the earlier part of the century.

A few months before I graduated from high school, Miss Hammonds, our English teacher, and Rev. J. W. Wiley, the principal, suggested that we consider producing a pageant at the commencement program rather than having a graduation speaker. They referred us to a pageant, "Ethiopia at the Bar of Justice," to use as a structural guide in developing our own production.

Following our teachers' prompt, we developed three skits about racial discrimination in employment, military service, and transportation. In each case, we showed the privilege that white people enjoyed, and the unfair discrimination experienced by Blacks. In one scene, a job recruiter sat at a table behind a sign saying, DEFENSE JOBS, WE NEED WORKERS. A line of job applicants swiftly formed. The jobseekers included Verna Cotten, a member of our class who looked white. The recruiter swiftly turned away the darker-skinned applicants and after a few cursory questions, employed Verna on the spot.

Stage assistants then arranged several chairs to represent a bus. A group of students boarded the bus. When the darker-skinned students sat in the front of the bus, the driver jumped up and scolded, "Look, folks, I don't want any trouble here. You know where your place is. If you don't take seats in the back

Fig. 9.5. Miss Violet Perry (left) taught mathematics and Miss Gladys Hammonds taught English grammar and literature, ca. 1943. / Courtesy of Edna Smith James.

of the bus and stop inconveniencing these white people, I'm going to call the police and have all of you arrested!" A third skit depicted racial discrimination in the armed services.

Our families and friends and schoolmates, all Black, enthusiastically applauded our production. The only non-Black person in the room was Mr. E. D. Johnson, the white superintendent of Edgecombe County Schools. At the end of the pageant, Mr. Johnson strode to the front of the room, his face beet red, and asked, "Who is responsible for this play?" We all held our breath. We knew exactly who was responsible, but we also knew that our teacher and principal could face serious consequences, even lose their jobs. After several moments of silence, Miss Hammonds rose from her seat and said, "The children wanted to do this, and I supported them" (Fig. 9.5). Rather than have an embarrassing public confrontation, Mr. Johnson chose the high road and said to the audience, "Well, let's give them a big hand!"

As valedictorian of the graduating class, I had a leading part in developing and presenting the drama. The achievement of academic first place was no accident. I had chosen subjects in which I was strong with the express goal of getting good grades. Mathematics and science challenged me, and I avoided taking any subjects in those disciplines until my junior year. What I gained by getting high grades, I paid for with ignorance. Not until I took biology and physical science in college did I learn the simplest facts about the universe and my own body.

I also knew very little about selecting a college or a field to study. None of us had ever heard of guidance teachers or school counselors. What happened once students graduated from my high school depended on the resources of individual students and their families. I wanted to go to college, but I received limited help from my school in choosing a college and course of study.

Since I was a very young child, my father had often asked me, "What do you want to be when you grow up?" Saying I didn't know drew a sharp rebuke, so I usually mumbled some kind of acceptable answer. But as my high school years ended, the answer to this question became critical. Teachers represented most of the educated people in our community. The only college-educated Black women who lived in Enfield that did not teach were Miss Whitworth, the home demonstration agent, and Nurse Rebecca Rogers, who worked for the Halifax County Health Department. Since I loved schools, teaching seemed a natural and best choice. Deciding what to teach represented the major question to answer. I believed my choice lay between teaching English or social studies. Since I had managed to meet the very high standards set by our strict English teacher, I believed that English represented my strongest subject, and I decided to become an English teacher.

Having heard of my interest in Hampton Institute, one teacher said to me, "My niece says that Hampton is quite challenging. I doubt that you can make it there." I had seen the campus of Shaw University, but the aging Baptist institution failed to impress me. When my father drove young Ruby Jones to Durham to attend North Carolina College, he took our family along. When I saw the campus, it was love at first sight! I talked endlessly about my desire to attend the Durham institution.

Attending North Carolina College remained my intention until my Uncle James married Elizabeth Bias, a Hampton Institute graduate. One morning the two of us talked about my future schooling, and this favorite aunt looked me straight in the eyes and solemnly said, "You are going to Hampton Institute."

I sat at the dining room table and copied my letter of application to Hampton Institute over and over on good stationery paper that I bought at Harrison's Drug Store. So that my writing would be straight, I made heavy lines on another piece of paper and laid a fresh sheet of paper on top of the lined sheet. I tried to make my letters perfectly, just as Miss Gladys Hammonds, our English teacher, had taught us. Even though the letter was handwritten, I saw that the lines were all justified. My letter looked as if it had been framed with wide margins on all four sides. My high school principal, Rev. J. W. Wiley, helped with my transcript. He added the piano lessons I had taken after school to give me additional credits. After waiting a few weeks and taking many trips to the post office, the much-anticipated letter from the Admissions Office at Hampton arrived. I had been accepted. I felt so affirmed and excited!

10. FOLLOWING MY STAR

Fig. 11.1. When Willa entered Hampton in 1944, she lived in historic Virginia Hall, built in 1874. / Photographer Ghana Holmes Smith, 2024.

11. Reaching for Young Womanhood at Hampton Institute

When I entered Hampton in the fall of 1944, the Allied forces had taken an upper hand in the war against Hitler and the Axis forces. On June 6, the Allies launched the Battle of Normandy, the operation that marked the successful invasion of Europe. By the end of the summer, they had also initiated a second attack from the Mediterranean Sea. On August 25, Paris was liberated, and on August 30, German forces retreated across the Seine. There was a clear sense that victory for the Allies was just a matter of time. My family did not feel that they were putting my welfare at risk by sending me to a school close to the naval installations in Norfolk and other military sites in the Tidewater area. A Hampton student, my cousin who lived in Newport News, had traveled to

Southport, North Carolina, with her brother's wife a few days before I was scheduled to leave for Hampton Institute. She called my mother to see if she could come to Enfield and join us for the trip to Virginia. I was ready.

In midsummer, my parents had purchased a green and black steamer trunk, and I had kept it at the foot of my bed for weeks, adding to my college wardrobe as I acquired new clothes. I can still remember two lovely sweaters made of nubby cotton, one green and the other a coppery tan. I had a long, dark green corduroy coat that nicely matched a blue and brown pleated plaid skirt. My mother had ordered a white cotton dress with little navy blue dots and a drawstring, lacelike, upper bodice from the Montgomery Ward catalogue. It looked what we called dressy, and I saved it for very special occasions. I also had a blue dress of light wool fabric that had a front placard which hid the full-length zipper. A light green plaid jacket of a loosely knit woolen fabric was another favorite item in my college wardrobe. My mother had bought me a red suit for Easter that spring. I wore it with black patent leather, baby-doll shoes. That was an outfit that also made it into the steamer trunk. My Uncle Joseph and Aunt Julia had given me a double strand of small pearls as a graduation gift. I carefully packed the pearls to take with me to my new life.

My cousin Alice was full of stories of Hampton Institute, having just completed her first year in the tidewater college. Listening to Alice, who loved to talk, I decided that Hampton was an almost magical place. She talked of dances and outside patios, which put my head into a spin. I had never participated in anything like that beyond the Junior-Senior Prom at Brick Tri-County High School, where we cleared chairs from the auditorium and decorated the big, empty space with crepe paper and freshly picked honeysuckle vines. I couldn't imagine the glamor that I would soon be exposed to. I felt that Hampton must be like some of the Clark Gable movies that I had occasionally seen from the balcony of the segregated theater in downtown Enfield. Once I got to Hampton, I concluded that Alice must have been talking about Clark Hall, a popular site for college dances. The building had outdoor patios on the second floor, but I never saw anyone venture onto them at a dance or at any other time.

On the morning of our trip to Hampton, I felt very sad, despite the prospect of future dancing at night on outside patios. My mother and father sat in the front of the car. Alice and I occupied the backseat. The steamer trunk lay in the car's trunk along with other items that the letter from Hampton said I should bring. Saying good-bye to my two sisters and my brother proved harder than I had expected (Fig. 11.2). In fact, I had been so filled with the excitement of leaving for college that I had never thought about the fact that I would not see

Fig. 11.2. Willa's sisters and brother (left to right): Claudette, Sylvia and Ruel. Ruel grew up to manage the Cofield Funeral Home (1967–1978) and to administer several schools, including Inborden Middle School. / Mae Cofield Family Collection.

them for months. As my father pulled the car onto Highway 301, suddenly, as I looked at my brick-siding home, I burst out crying. The trip to Hampton and dancing on the outside patio became less appealing to me. I was ashamed of myself, but I was bawling. My parents assured me that I would like Hampton and that I would be coming home for the Thanksgiving holiday, but I could not be comforted. I didn't know about college. Perhaps I would be happier in the home that I knew. I slumped down in the back seat, and I cried and cried as if my heart would break. The crying did not stop until we arrived at Hampton's campus. I dried my eyes and followed my parents into the administration building to pay my bills and get on with my college education.

Later, my mother told me that when the college official greeted us, he asked her if she was the student. Only in the last years of my mother's life did I understand how much she had wanted to attend college when she was a single young girl. My mother had spent one year at Brick Normal and Industrial

Fig. 11.3. Mae and Thomas Cofield made educating their children a top priority. Ca. late 1960s. / Mae Cofield Family Collection.

School, and it had been her dream to go to college (Fig. 11.3). She never forgot this encounter and cherished the memory that a Hampton admissions officer had thought she might have been entering college.

During my first days away from home, I learned that many other students were awed that I planned to major in English, assuring me that it was a very difficult subject and convincing me that I should seek another major. No one I met had ever heard of my hometown, and when I told them I was from Enfield, North Carolina, they inevitably asked: "Where is that?" At the reception for new students, for the first time I sampled frappe, the wonderful ginger ale and sherbet drink that accompanied many social events at Hampton. At the orientation session for women, I learned how to make a bed with the squared ends of the sheets tucked under the mattress. At the end of my first week away from home, I was amazed to discover that although the school would provide laundry service, with clean sheets and towels every week, I would have to wash my own personal clothes. In discussing the latter revelation with other classmates, seventy-three years later, we were all amazed to realize that in 1944 when we entered Hampton, none of our families owned a washing machine.

I loved my years at Hampton and being a part of the wonderful mix of Black students who came from all over the United States. In my junior year, six male students from Africa enrolled in Hampton. We referred to the school as our home by the sea. Indeed, on clear days we could view ships navigating Hampton Roads, the famed waterway on the Chesapeake Bay. The dark halls and assembly rooms spoke to me of earlier times in the history of our people when a college education was a rare thing for a Black person to acquire.

As a freshman, I lived in Virginia Hall, where Booker T. Washington, who had become one of the most influential men of his time, had dusted a room so thoroughly that he gained admission to the school. Booker T. may have known how to handle the demands of a school like Hampton, but I had few organizational skills and little time management ability. When I registered for classes, I thought having all my classes on three days a week a marvelous arrangement. Thus on Monday, Wednesday, and Friday, I went nonstop, from 7:30 in the morning to 5:30 in the afternoon. On these days I ran with my tongue hanging out from the Academy Building to the gymnasium to my mathematics class in the science building. Tuesdays and Thursdays, when I thought I could do so much studying, I instead spent hours in the snack bar.

Young sailors filled the campus, somewhat compensating for the absence of male Hampton students who had been drafted into the military services. Although the war effort was winding down, men from the United States Navy still came to Hampton to study diesel engines and other technologies. Since the US armed forces were racially segregated in those days, these young men—no women—were all Black. They stayed for three months and then left for assignments at other bases. Their classes and living quarters were separate and apart from college students, but we often attended the same social events. They came to our hospitality hour in the girls' dormitories on Saturday evenings and took us to the movies in Ogden Hall.

One of the favorite pastimes of residents of Virginia Hall was to watch from second floor windows as new companies of these young men marched to their meals in Virginia Hall. Some of the men did not leave the site but maintained permanent residence on the Hampton campus as members of ship's company. I am always pleased to name one of the best-known members of this group: Harry Belafonte. Mr. Belafonte dated my Phyllis Wheatley Society Club sister, Marguerite Byrd of Washington, DC, who was Miss Hampton of 1946 and who became his first wife. When the Navy left Hampton at the end of my sophomore year, they bequeathed the college Armstrong Gymnasium

Fig. 11.4. Lillian Polkinghorne Thornton (third from left) reigned as Miss Hampton of 1947. She is flanked by attendants from each class. / Willa Cofield personal collection.

and new quarters for the Hampton Grill. Hampton male students also began occupying James Hall, the naval students' former dormitory.

When I entered Hampton, I had never seen a football game, never taken a shower—our family only had a bath tub with no shower. I had gone on few dates with young men. Only fifteen years old, I was totally unprepared to make decisions for myself or to live without close adult supervision. I loved the social life, the dances and cultural events staged in Ogden Hall. Homecoming weekend with bands and floats, a midday football game, and crowds of cheering Hampton fans thrilled and delighted me (Fig. 11.4). Later in the year, there were many gatherings in the old gymnasium that were sheer fun. The most popular dance tune in the fall of 1944 was "Hamp's Boogie Woogie." There were several wonderful chords when the band members called out in quick syncopation, "Da DaDa Da Da Da Dah!" and we happy dancers punctuated the musical call with a healthy STOMP!! that rocked the floor of the old wooden gym. The band members repeated the call "Da DaDa Da Da Da Dah!" and following the second STOMP, we dancers took off in wild, no-moves-barred jitterbugging. I can still see one student lifting his feet almost knee-high in a frenzy of joyful abandon. I was not one of the best dancers, but my piano teacher, Clivetta Stewart, once told me that she wished I could transport my sense of rhythm on the dance floor to my fumbling piano rendition of Chopin's preludes.

During my freshman year, I spent many hours in the Grill. Located in Stone Building in the center of the campus, it was the kind of place that my parents would not have permitted me to go to if it had been in Enfield. The walls were painted in graduated shades of orange and brightly painted booths with tables lined the wall. Without having to seek my parents' or anyone else's permission, I often found myself seated in one of the booths with friends, sipping cokes, eating potato chips, and listening to popular tunes on the juke box. Gradually, the stretch of asphalt that bordered Stone Building came to be known as The Block. It was Hampton's center, and young men could usually be found hanging on the Stone Building porch or gathered on the sidewalk in front of the building. Especially after the older veterans returned in the fall of 1946, The Block became a kind of reviewing stand where male students observed and commented on young women students who passed by on their way to one of the buildings on the south end of the campus.

Hampton required all first-year students to attend Sunday evening vespers in Ogden Hall. At first we had assigned seats, and an upper-class student checked to make certain that we were in them. The feature of these programs that I remember most was the singing of Negro spirituals. Usually, two or three students who were music majors led the audience in singing "In Bright Mansions Above," "Ev'ry Time I Feel the Spirit," "Lord, I Want to Be a Christian," or some other well-known song. Myrtle Fentress, a young woman from Norfolk, Virginia, and Clarence Cooper, who, years later, I saw on Arthur Miller's television show, are the only song leaders that I can remember.

Because I had had very little experience in making up my own mind, I became very dependent upon the circle of friends that I formed on B and C corridors in Virginia Hall. I had little confidence in self-reliance or self-direction. Because people marveled at my choice of English as a major, I changed my major to business because my roommate and my close friend were business majors. Brick High School had offered no course in typing; in fact, the school owned only one typewriter. During my two-semester sojourn as a major in business, I learned typewriting, a skill that has served me well since 1944, until this very day.

In the same manner, I applied for membership in the Phyllis Wheatley Literary Society (Fig. 11.5). because my roommate Thomasina's aunt, the famed soprano Dorothy Maynor, had belonged to PWS as a Hampton Institute student. Ms. Maynor had told her niece to follow her example, and I followed Thomasina and submitted my application for membership in the organization. One decision I made alone: I found that I made better grades in English 101 than in general accounting, and at the end of my freshman year, I changed my major back to English.

Fig. 11.5. Members of the Phyllis Wheatley Literary Society basketball team, ca. 1945. / Willa Cofield personal collection.

The fall of 1946 saw radical changes on the Hampton Institute campus. Hundreds of returning veterans swelled the enrollment in our academic classes and gave new life to the trade school. These former soldiers and sailors told stories of their wartime experiences and spoke often of the need for a just society. Many of them brought the traumas of war and manifested alcohol dependency. I never heard of any special classes or programs that addressed their needs beyond informal talks given by the dean of men.

During my first two years at Hampton, student clubs dominated the social calendar, but in the fall of 1946 the college's longtime resistance to sororities and fraternities faded and Greek-letter organizations came to Hampton Institute. We learned that some faculty members had lobbied hard for this change, among them Dr. Marion Capps, a mathematics professor and former eastern regional director of the second oldest of Black women's sororities, Delta Sigma Theta (Fig. 11.6). Almost immediately, Dr. Capps began recruiting young women to the new chapter, Gamma Iota (Fig. 11.7). The mathematics professor interviewed every young woman who had made the honor roll and encouraged her to apply for membership. As a result of Dr. Capp's hard work, Gamma Iota has the distinction of being the first Greek letter organization established on Hampton's campus.

Fig. 11.6. Marion Capps, mathematics professor and sponsor of Gamma Iota, charter chapter of Delta Sigma Theta Sorority, Inc. / Source: yearbook, *The Hamptonian*.

Fig. 11.7. Thirty-seven young women joined Gamma Iota, 1948. Willa stands third from right on the first standing row. / Source: yearbook, *The Hamptonian*.

Dr. Capps asked me to come for an interview and subsequently invited me to join Gamma Iota. Since we were the first chapter on the campus and there were few older Delta members available, we had no preliminary initiation. Thirty-seven Hampton women participated in Delta Sigma Theta's formal induction services and became members on February 8, 1947.

In the fall of 1947 the white Hampton president, Ralph P. Bridgeman, addressed a Rotary Club in a nearby community. Hampton students and some faculty criticized him for the patronizing way he spoke about the vocational prospects of Hampton students. Later in the school year, students threatened to strike, requesting that the board of trustees address a list of grievances, paramount among them the demand that they fire the president. The protest included mass meetings in Ogden Hall, marches to the president's home, and a mock funeral in the center of Ogden Hall Circle complete with a casket, pall bearers, and mourners. My clearest memory of this event is of Alonzo Moron, who became the college's first Black president, ordering the removal of the casket. After the board of trustees' decision to fire President Bridgeman, I attended a class taught by Cecil Lewis in the small cottage that housed English classes. Someone had rearranged the chairs so that they all faced the front of the room in diagonal instead of straight lines. Mr. Lewis began the class by describing the seating arrangement and the times we were living in as dynamic. We students interpreted his remarks as an implicit endorsement of student activism and our demand for change in the leadership of Hampton Institute.

There were many fine teachers at Hampton, including Carl Holman, who later became president of the National Urban League; Clivetta Stewart, a gifted piano teacher; Dr. Charles Nichols, who lectured on American literature; and Mrs. Higginbotham, who taught United States history. I took adult literacy under Dr. Cooper during my last year and found the class surprisingly worthwhile. One day, while we students executed some in-class activity, Dr. Cooper walked around the classroom looking over our shoulders as we completed the assignment. When he looked at my work, he commented, "You have a very steady hand." I have never forgotten this compliment. I continue to take pride in my handwriting, seventy years after this teacher made his casual observation.

Among the teachers in the English department, I was most influenced by J. Saunders Redding, the prominent writer, and Esther Merle Jackson, a drama teacher. Mr. Redding had taught at Elizabeth City Teachers College and had won the prestigious Mayflower Award for his book *No Day of Triumph*. He was very tall and elegant. This gifted teacher and writer had been fired from Morehouse College because of his radicalism. He ran the class, English literature, in a strict, disciplined manner and insisted that we take our schooling seriously. For one thing, he never announced tests. On any day, he shocked our class by walking casually to the blackboard and writing four or five questions that constituted a major test. He required all students to maintain a notebook that contained notes made on his lectures and outside reading assignments. Just as he gave unannounced tests, every class day he asked to inspect two notebooks. No one knew whose notebook he would want to see. To say, "Mr. Redding, I didn't bring my notebook with me today," proved an ineffective excuse, as his unfailing answer, "Oh, that's okay. I will wait while you go to your room and get it." As a result, I, like other students, always prepared for a test in his class, and I always kept my notebook ready for inspection. We were thrilled with the way he pronounced words, baffled by his anti-California bias, and impressed by his way of saying "Be that as it may." Mr. Redding went on to teach at Brown University, his alma mater, and to become the Ernest I. White Professor of American Studies and Humane Letters at Cornell University. His books include *To Make a Poet Black*, *They Came in Chains*, and *On Being a Negro in America*.

My drama teacher, Esther Merle Jackson (Fig. 11.8), impressed me with her sheer passion and enthusiasm. When I took her class in the fall of 1946,

Fig. 11.8. Esther Merle Jackson (at left on second row) taught theater classes and produced plays in Ogden Hall. Reed Johnson (center of first row) starred in the college's 1948 staging of Oscar Wilde's *The Importance of Being Earnest*. / Source: yearbook *The Hamptonian*.

she had just completed studies for a master's degree at Ohio State University and was full of energy and excitement about the possibilities of theater at Hampton. I enrolled in her theater workshop and found myself excited by the schedule of plays and projects that she described on the first day of class. Each student, she told us, would be responsible for a dramatic production.

I volunteered to direct the Christmas skit that the Phyllis Wheatley Society (PWS) would present in Ogden Hall just before we all left for our Christmas holiday. Carl Holman, journalist and English professor, had agreed to serve as a PWS sponsor. Together he and I planned the skit. We decided to use the wonderful "Christmas Song," which Nat King Cole had just released. As the song played in the background, we positioned three young men to represent the Nat King Cole Trio playing on the side of the Ogden Hall stage. Reed Johnson, the new guy I had just met, agreed to play the part of the bass player in the trio. We developed short scenes to dramatize each line of the song. For example, the first scene showed a family sitting around a fireplace roasting chestnuts. It was followed by a scene of carolers wrapped in winter coats, ear muffs, and scarves. The audience loved the production and, standing in the wings on the big Ogden Hall stage, I felt like a Broadway director.

Miss Jackson also produced several outstanding plays during her first year at Hampton. Reed Johnson—the "bass player"—played Earnest in Oscar Wilde's *The Importance of Being Earnest*, and I played the role of Eileen in the Broadway comedy *My Sister Eileen*. The attention that this teacher gave to my mispronunciation of words in the English language proved one of the lasting benefits of my participation in this public performance. I concluded that Enfield boasted few people who consistently spoke standard English, so exposure to the larger culture at Hampton helped in my preparation as an English teacher and as a user of the English language.

After leaving Hampton, Miss Jackson spent long years as a drama professor at the University of Wisconsin in Madison. She earned an international reputation as an expert on American theater, especially on playwright Tennessee Williams. She did not act or direct but took a more academic approach as she inspired drama students.

My friendship with Reed Johnson continued long after my class in theater production. A native of Richmond, Virginia, Reed had entered Hampton Institute in 1941. The war interrupted his education in 1942 when at the age of eighteen, he was drafted into the United States Army. He served in Europe and saw active duty during the terrible D-Day invasion of Normandy. In 1946 Reed returned to Hampton among the great surge of veterans who entered the nation's colleges and universities under the GI Bill. He resumed his study of automotive mechanics with the vague goal of opening a car dealership upon graduation.

Reed reentered Hampton student life with humor, passion, and energy. His strident voice rang out around tables in the dining hall and at football games, where he sometimes sold peanuts to the avid Hampton fans. He impressed the young college women with his tales of prowess in his brief military career and awed them with his striking good looks. Students often described him as the "best-looking dark-skinned guy on the campus" (Fig. 11.9).

Despite the loud lamentations of Reed's male friends who stood on The Block, commenting on everyone who passed and who perceived me as much too young and innocent, Reed and I became a couple. He was the first serious

Fig. 11.9. Reed Johnson's self-assurance and urbane manner captured the attention of seventeen-year-old Willa, ca. 1947. / Willa Cofield personal collection.

boyfriend that I had ever had. Someone told me years later that he had confided to his male friends that he could fool most of the young women some of the time, but he could fool me all the time. The two of us graduated from Hampton Institute in 1948 and Reed taught auto mechanics in the trade school at Tuskegee Institute for one year.

After graduation, I returned to Enfield. I had always wanted to teach, and I thought teaching in my hometown of Enfield would represent the best of all worlds. A white minister who spoke at the Enfield Colored Graded School may have helped shape this dream. In motivating us to make something of our lives, the Baptist minister told us to picture a young man standing in one corner of this auditorium and a young woman in the opposite corner. If the young man desires to get the young woman, he must walk across this room to where she stands, convince her to leave, then he can take her back to his corner. He said, "In that same manner, you must go after an education, get it, and bring it back to your community."

While I was away in college, the building that housed Brick Tri-County High School burned to the ground. Black high school students who lived in Enfield had no school at all. Some students found rides to Phillips High School in Battleboro or Eastman High School, ten miles west of Enfield. Alas, there was no Black high school in Enfield, so I saw no way to fulfill the dream of teaching in my hometown.

12. Teaching in Halifax County

All summer I waited for job offers from Hampton's placement office. The fall school session had begun when I received a phone call. My former Hampton roommate, Muriel Tompkins (later Jones), had turned down a job offer from Mr. William Holmes, the principal of Eastman High School. She suggested that he offer the job to me. Since I had taken some business courses during my freshman year, she thought that I might be able to teach typing and the other courses that he needed to have covered. Mr. Holmes phoned and asked me if I would like to teach business courses at Eastman High School.

I was twenty years old, fresh out of college with no employment. I accepted the principal's offer. My parents were elated, and my father offered his car for my ten-mile commute to the school. At the time, I did not realize the breadth of my father's generosity, for he used the 1948 Pontiac as his main funeral car. On days when the Cofield Funeral Home had funerals, he arranged other ways for me to get to Eastman School. Cars were not manufactured for domestic consumption during the war years, and the auto industry was just gearing up to supply the American market. Soon, however, Dad found a used Pontiac in the community and purchased it for $1,800. I was a bit surprised when he asked me to reimburse him, but I readily agreed to pay him $100 per month, two-thirds of my salary. During the school year 1948–49, I taught English and typing at Eastman High. My sister, Sylvia, joined me for the ten-mile trip and completed tenth grade at the rural school.

Eastman High School was established in 1894 and known as the Johnson Hill School. Its first principal, Mrs. Fanny Myrick, led the school for twenty-five years with no outside funding. When an interviewer asked Mrs. Myrick how the school operated with no help beyond the support of parents, she replied, "We simply worked it up from the ground and prayed it down from the skies."[4] I did not know that Mrs. Myrick had pioneered in the education of Negro children in the Eastman community, but I do remember Mrs. Myrick. She was a tall, stately woman with rich brown skin and lively, flashing eyes.

She lived in the White Oak community, an area served by White Oak Church about ten miles from Enfield. My memory is that she talked very fast and tended to dominate conversations. I remember visiting her home. One of the stories my mother loved to tell described my terrible behavior as a young child at a dinner that Mrs. Myrick served our family. On that visit I embarrassed my mother and father by loudly insisting that I be given a fork instead of a spoon. My mother said it became obvious to everyone but me that Mrs. Myrick did not have a fork to give me, though she kept looking in drawers and opening cabinet doors.

Years before I was born, Mrs. Myrick had approached George Eastman, executive of the Eastman Kodak Company, and asked for help in enlarging and modernizing the school on land Eastman had bought and developed as Oak Lodge Retreat. Eastman deeded three acres of the land to Halifax County and paid one-half the cost of a five-room school. Halifax County, the state of North Carolina, and the Julius Rosenwald Fund shared the balance, with the county contributing $5,000, the state $1,000, the Julius Rosenwald Fund and the community $500. Of course, the grateful community renamed the school. Johnson Hill School became Eastman High School. My mother entered Eastman High in 1924, completing two years of high school there before she married my father.

On the first day that I showed up at Eastman High School, the teacher that I was to replace coached me. I was to teach shorthand and typing and two English classes. She showed me how to record and report attendance for my new homeroom class. She cautioned that I should not record the actual attendance because a truthful report of school attendance would cause the school to lose teachers. The allocation of teachers, she explained, was based upon the number of days students attended school. At the end of the month, I should enter a few absences, but not the actual attendance. Eastman was a rural school, and all the students came from farms in the area. In the fall during harvesting season, most of the children were kept at home to pick cotton and to shake peanuts. Some days the classrooms held only desks. I suspect that in that era Black principals all over the area depended upon selective reporting of student attendance to keep the doors of Black schools open. I dutifully followed her instructions.

I can still remember the names of a few members of the Eastman faculty: elementary school teachers Claudia Brinkley, Mareatha Clark, and Hannah Bogle; and high school teachers Dorothy Boone, Vera McAden, Luther M. Williams, and P. J. Richardson. Edward Francis led the veterans' class, and Miss Howard served as school librarian. Luther Williams, who taught social studies at Eastman High School, later became principal of Inborden High School.

When I became a member of Eastman School's faculty in the fall of 1948, the original structure had become totally inadequate. The dark, smoked classroom walls reflected stains from years of heating the rooms with coal-fired stoves. I remember that the janitor mopped the wooden floors of the principal's office daily. One morning while I sat at a desk in the reception area of the office, Mr. Holmes, the principal, obviously became upset by the way the janitor was mopping the floors. He rudely grabbed the mop from the startled young man and gave him—and me—a lesson in how to mop a floor.

The school had no auditorium, gymnasium, or cafeteria, no room where all the students and teachers could assemble at the same time. Nevertheless, the principal occasionally ordered the opening of folding doors between two classrooms at the front of the building and called all of us together. The first students and faculty to arrive occupied the classroom chairs with everyone else crowding in, filling every bit of available space in the two rooms. During each of the assemblies held during that year, at least one person fainted from the intense heat and lack of fresh air. Mr. Holmes spoke eloquently. It seemed a pity that the school did not have a suitable auditorium where he could display his oratorical gifts. The refusal of the county to build a gymtorium—a combination auditorium and gymnasium—greatly frustrated the principal. Under his direction, the veterans' class began construction of a cinder-block foundation for the building, but funds quickly ran out and work came to a halt.

Soon after I joined the staff, Mr. Holmes began working on a progress report about Eastman School. He hoped to publish the report and use it to raise funds for the gymtorium. Editing the manuscript became my chief out-of-class responsibility. I spent hours poring over letters of solicitation and the text of the progress report, which was entitled "Inching Along." Sometime after Mr. Holmes left, the county board voted to construct a gymnasium/auditorium at Eastman High School.

My life changed in the spring of 1949 when I married Reed Johnson. During the Christmas of 1948, Reed convinced me that we should get married and gave me an engagement ring. Without telling anyone, I went to Tuskegee during the Easter vacation. On Saturday morning after my arrival, Dr. Robinson, a professor in the veterinary science department at Tuskegee and Reed's friend, drove us to Montgomery. Just after Dr. Robinson pinned a lovely corsage of spring iris on my new beige suit, we entered the office of a justice of peace, who read the marriage vows.

I wanted to keep our marriage a secret forever, I think, but my roommate, who was much wiser than I, insisted that I tell my parents. To make certain that we did, this good friend left her home in Norfolk, where we were visiting, and drove with Reed and me to Enfield. Surprised and disappointed, my parents took the news as graciously as they could and welcomed Reed into our family. My father said to Reed, "Why didn't you tell us? We would have helped you."

In the summer of 1949, I took a job at the Brick Rural Life School, where I had been working part-time at night during the winter months. Reed left Tuskegee and used his veteran credentials to find work at the Norfolk naval base. In the fall of 1950, after a few months driving from the Tidewater city to Enfield on weekends, Reed joined the staff of Cofield Funeral Home and soon sought certification as an embalmer.

13. The Brick Rural Life School: Doing Common Things in an Uncommon Way

The Brick Rural Life School, established in 1934, represented the American Missionary Association's effort to continue the excellent programs of farmer education and community outreach implemented by Brick Junior College (1895–1933). Working with a small group of former tenant farmers over a five-year period, the Brick Rural Life School sought to improve the quality of the families' lives and prepare them for farm ownership. The student farm families lived on the Brick farm for five years, each family renting a small homestead.

Mr. Brownlee, executive secretary of the American Missionary Association, wrote that the AMA believed that the tenant farmers "knew more about sharecropping and tenancy than any group of teachers who had graduated from college, no matter how good their training in economics. The Association, therefore, determined to let the tenants work out their own problems. Guidance would be given when requested." He said that classes would be in the homes and in the fields, and students would learn to do the common things of life uncommonly well.[5] The school's director, Neill McLean, a graduate of Hampton Institute and Cornell University and a former agriculture teacher, was soft-spoken, reflective, and sometimes mistaken by visitors to the school as one of the student farmers (Fig. 13.1). He, his wife, Iva, and their four children lived in the home of the former Brick College president.

Fig. 13.1. Neill McLean, director of Brick Rural Life School, wife, Iva, and their children. / Photo by Marion Palfi, Center for Creative Photography.

The school nurtured a cooperative approach to meeting common needs of the student farmers. Ruth Morton, director of AMA schools, said that basic training in building economic security through efficient farm methods and cooperative endeavors undergirded all other phases of the program.[6]

When I began working at the Brick Rural Life School in 1949, a cooperative store, which had been organized in 1938, was on its last legs, but Brownlee wrote that in 1944 the store had revenues of $30,000 (Fig. 13.2). A federal credit union opened in 1938 and operated for at least thirty years (Fig. 13.3). To meet other common needs, the farmers organized a livestock cooperative that promoted variety and quality in stock; a wheat cooperative that put home-grown bread on the table; a molasses cooperative that fostered the cultivation, grinding, and boiling of sugar cane; and a soil control cooperative that sought to increase acreage yield and income from money crops.[7]

Fig. 13.2. The co-op store at Bricks. / Photo by Marion Palfi, Center for Creative Photography.

Fig. 13.3. Officers of the Brick Credit Union that was organized in 1936. / Photo by Marion Palfi, Center for Creative Photography.

During my tenure at the school, the student farmers cultivated their crops by sharing a tractor that they had purchased together (Fig. 13.4). A cooperative cannery invited people in the area to preserve fruits, vegetables from their gardens, and beef from their cattle. One summer in the late 1940s, I helped my mother can butterbeans, string beans, and beef in the Brick Cooperative Cannery. For months afterward, these staples appeared often on our dinner table.

At the end of the public school year, Mr. McLean asked me to become bookkeeper and secretary of the Brick Rural Life School. Two new wings had been added to the former dining hall, and the whole building was newly renovated and renamed Fellowship Hall. It appeared that the site had embarked upon a new era of growth and development. For eighteen months, I worked in a front office surrounded by glossy pink cinderblock walls that contrasted brightly with the muted green walls of Mr. McLean's executive office next door.

Other on-site staff members were Miss Sarah Kyler, who worked with the farm women about matters of diet, sewing, and home management, and Mr. C. Garrett, who performed maintenance chores, cutting the grass, and doing odd jobs. Miss Kyler had worked at Fessenden Academy in Florida before moving to a house on the Brick campus once occupied by Brick College faculty. Mr. C's ancestors had quite probably lived on the Brick farm as slaves when it—and they—were owned by the Garrett Brothers, who moved to Richmond and became rich selling vanilla flavoring. Years ago, I saw a list of

Fig. 13.4. Brick farmers bought and shared a tractor. / Photo by Marion Palfi, Center for Creative Photography.

the enslaved people who had resided on the farm, and it contained the names of many Garretts.

An excellent cook, Miss Kyler supervised the preparation of food for school gatherings. When Fred Brownlee and Ruth Morton of the New York AMA office came to visit, Miss Kyler prepared their lunch of tuna salad and light, homemade rolls. As testimony to her cooking talent, in 1949, Miss Kyler's mayonnaise pound cake recipe won third prize in a national cooking contest. Miss Kyler was devoted to keeping Fellowship Hall clean and would pull out mop and pail and scrub the newly tiled floors in a heartbeat.

During the winter months after crops were harvested, all the student families moved into Benedict Hall, one of the former Brick College dormitories,

Fig. 13.5. Young farmer said he found his wife at Brick's Short Term School. / Photo by Marion Palfi, Center for Creative Photography.

and lived together to attend the Short Term School (Fig. 13.5). The school also welcomed students who lived outside the Brick community. During this winter school, the women prepared meals and the families ate together. The adults held long evening discussions and attended classes during the day. Government officials, college professors, AMA administrators, medical doctors, and other professionals led workshops at the Short Term School. A program for 1936 listed classes in farm business, hog raising, the winter garden, caring for children, canning, citizenship, religion, how to build a brooder house, beautification, and care of chickens. In 1950, my new husband, Reed Johnson, taught a class in auto repair, helping the members of the tractor cooperative overhaul the green tractor's engine.

In the winter of 1950, a white staff member of the Highlander Folk School in Tennessee accepted a three-month residency at Bricks. She led the community women in creating a quilted mural that hung in the reception room for many years. Other people came to the school to share their knowledge, to visit, or to learn about the school.

As bookkeeper, I was not able to attend the Short Term School, but I remember attending two of the evening classes. Fred Brownlee taught a class about religion. I still remember my surprise when my mother, who had accompanied me to the session, answered his opening question: "Who is God?" My mother spoke softly but strongly, saying, "God is love." I also remember being mildly shocked by Mr. Brownlee's characterization of the Bible story of Eve and the apple tree as a ploy of the priests, who wrote the story to discourage common people from obtaining knowledge.

Everyone welcomed the visits of Asa Sims to the Short Term School. He was tall, thin as a rail, and brimming with laughter. A Hampton Institute horticultural teacher, Mr. Sims exhorted the student families to strive for something beautiful in their lives. He told them that if they didn't appreciate the beauty around them, if they thought only of making a living, their lives would have little meaning. With humor, he advised those who thought only of money to go down to the nearby train tracks, lay their head on the rails, and wait for the southbound train. He also led the families in the spirited singing of Negro spirituals. I remember his having a small group of young women sing the beginning bars of "Every Time I Feel the Spirit" over and over until they hit the notes with the right mix of spirit and harmony. Mr. Sims inspired the farm families to landscape their yards, plant and nurture flower gardens, and look forward to the summer visits when everyone could see the beauty that they had created with their own hands.

On one visit in January 1950, Mr. Sims spoke passionately to the families about natural habitats. Before his presentation, I had accompanied him to the woods to gather wild ivy, moss, lichen-covered rocks, broken limbs of sweet gum saplings, and cypress knees—the exposed roots of the cypress tree that grow above ground. We made several trips, each time finding more treasure. With these materials, he created an indoor natural garden on the top of one of the old Brick School tables. During his talk, he used this mini ecosystem display to bring the lesson home that plants and other living things grow best in an environment that supports them.

In his writing about the Brick Rural Life School, Brownlee says that the ideas for the cooperatives and other changes almost all came from discussions held after dinner in the Short Term School. One initiative had been born when a member of the North Carolina Department of Health spoke at the school. The area around the school was—and still is—notorious for the scarcity of medical care. The idea of bringing in a nurse to provide health education and medical assistance evolved in the session with the government official. As an outcome of the visit, the Department of Health agreed to employ a nurse if the people would bear half the costs of salary and clinic expenses. Within six weeks, 360 families in the area had contributed, no one giving less than one dollar or more than five. The State gave its share and Nurse Battle came to the area, providing much-needed medical support to thirteen neighborhoods making up the Brick community. I was a high school student when Nurse Battle came to Bricks and benefited from her counsel when she spoke to my health class.

Brownlee points to a stubborn obstacle that the Brick School student farmers faced: the baffling problem of land purchase. Even the federal government had failed in its efforts to buy land in the area. The original plan for Roosevelt's Resettlement Program had called for the purchase of ten thousand acres of land, including one thousand acres from the Brick Farm. White plantation owners in the area refused to sell and the government officials had turned to the neighboring community of Tillery, where the Resettlement Program was launched in 1935.

During my eighteen months at Brick Rural Life School, there were five student families living on the school farm, and I remember the Tillerys and the Harveys. Alexander Harvey was a highly motivated, dedicated farmer and Martha, his wife, was equally bright and vibrant (Fig. 13.6). At the end of their tenure at the school, the Harveys succeeded in buying a farm, located about six miles west of Enfield on Drapers Road and now visible from Interstate 95. In the late 1950s, the time for small farms ended, and the mechanization and corporate takeover of farm production undermined small, independent family farms. After a few years, the Harveys found themselves giving up farming as a way of life. They moved to Richmond, joining the migration of Black farm families to the North.

One thing is clear: when I worked at the school, I did not understand its political agenda. I knew that the school was racially progressive. I can remember a visitor's description of the site as one of two places in North Carolina where whites and Negroes could eat together, the other being the University of North Carolina. When Ms. Ruth Morton, AMA director of schools and cooperatives, visited Bricks, she occasionally took farm women along with her on trips to Rocky Mount. When Ms. Morton walked on the downtown streets of Rocky Mount, she was careful to carry whatever purchases she had

Fig. 13.6. Former Brick Rural Life School student Martha Harvey (left) and Virginia Wills, Brick School alumna, 1994. / Willa Cofield personal collection.

made. She wanted people to see a white woman walking with a Black woman as equals on a public sidewalk. Such a sight was an anomaly at that time in eastern North Carolina towns.

Now, I believe that if I had known more about the people's struggle for economic justice, I would have better appreciated the school's mission. I did not understand its radical economic ideas. The sponsors of the Brick Rural Life School recognized the intelligence and experience of the tenant farmers who were its students. The school empowered the student farmers through counsel and training and let them make their own decisions. In addition, it taught them efficient ways of organizing their farm business and introduced them to aspects of farm management that as tenants they did not have access to. It showed that they could confront systems of power and make demands. They learned that by working together, they could build credit and buy equipment that none of them could have purchased individually. The school opened windows to another world. The Brick Rural Life School gave many people in this isolated, segregated, deprived community a chance for a better life.

Just before public schools opened in the fall of 1950, I received an invitation to take a job as a sixth-grade teacher at Dawson Elementary School, about six miles from my Enfield home. The offer greatly frustrated me. I was not unhappy with my work at Brick Rural Life School, but I felt lonely and isolated, spending most of my time in the pink office typing thank-you letters to New England churches and preparing financial reports for the AMA. The new job offered the opportunity to work in a traditional school setting, a familiar place to me, and it paid more money, with three months off in the summer. I finally decided to resign from my bookkeeping/secretary position and accept the job offer to teach at Dawson School. Mr. Brownlee and Miss Morton were onsite, and they reluctantly accepted my resignation. But after approaching them, I went home and fretted all night, afraid that I had made the wrong decision. The next morning, I informed them that I had changed my mind and wanted to continue working at Brick Rural Life School. In the interest of furthering my career, perhaps, they politely declined my offer and wished me well on my return to the Halifax County school system.

I spent the school year 1950–51 teaching a sixth-grade class at Dawson Elementary School. I had no experience teaching an elementary class and the work became somewhat daunting. Mr. Clarke, the principal, was very pleasant, and I felt supported in his school. There were aspects of the teaching job at Dawson Elementary School that I enjoyed.

However, I felt demoralized and oppressed when I attended the countywide meeting called by the Halifax County superintendent of schools at Eastman High School. We met in the huge gymtorium, the building that Mr. Holmes had yearned and worked for. I passionately hated this beginning-of-the-school-year meeting. Eastman School, like other Black schools, had no air conditioning, and little air descended from the narrow, high windows to lessen the intense heat. The white superintendent seemed distant, cold, and as unhappy to attend the meeting as we were. The meeting ground slowly and dully through the morning, informing us Black teachers of the things we must do to meet the expectations of our employers.

During my entire tenure in the county system, I only remember one time that we overtly showed disapproval of the authoritarian tone and the racist, patronizing posture of the leaders of the countywide meetings. At a meeting in the middle of the cotton-harvesting season, a white staff person from the North Carolina State Department of Public Schools asked his all-Black audience of teachers and principals to sing "Cotton needs a-picking so bad." as an introduction to his presentation. We refused to join this white spokesperson for the state in singing a song which celebrated the bitter history of our people as cotton pickers. We refused to honor with our voices this difficult, ill-paid work that prevented so many of our students from attending school. Our silence conveyed our disapproval and the flustered speaker swiftly moved to the talk he had prepared for the meeting.

14. My Year at the University of Pennsylvania

In the summer of 1951, I joined my husband, Reed, in Philadelphia, where he was attending Echols College of Mortuary Science. I decided that it would be a good time for me to go back to school and learn more about teaching English. I enjoyed traveling to Philadelphia, looking at the map and helping read road signs. At night, when we finally arrived, I looked with awe at the tall towers and huge stone buildings. I wanted to know everything and annoyed Reed with stupid questions such as "What is in that building?" Soon I found that there were hundreds of such buildings in the city, and I understood my husband's impatient answers to my stream of questions. Through some friends, Reed had found a room in a home on Powelton Avenue, not very far from the University of Pennsylvania campus where I intended to take classes. We had one room for which we paid six dollars a week. Marie, the owner's middle-aged daughter and a Philadelphia school teacher, lived in the large bedroom on the same floor. Unfortunately, not too long after we moved in, Marie became ill and died.

On the first morning after my husband left for his classes, the elderly woman who owned the house came to the room and asked me whether my father was a doctor. Later, I found that she thought that any Black person who could afford to attend the University of Pennsylvania had to have a doctor as a father. By way of preparing me for my visit to the Penn campus, she told me that I should not expect a warm reception, but that people would talk to me.

Hermione and Sheldon Mason lived next door. Hermione, who had suffered a stroke, held her paralyzed arm against her waist and dragged her stiff leg as she walked. She had been a social worker before her illness, but now was housebound and lonely. She welcomed my visits, offering me hot tea, which I had never drunk before, and advice about my studies. I spent many pleasant hours in her bright and clean apartment.

I still remember going into the University of Pennsylvania English Department office and asking for Dr. Shaaber, which I pronounced so that it rhymed with clabber. When the receptionist answered me with the correct pronunciation (Shawber), I was mortified. After reviewing my transcript from Hampton Institute, Dr. Shaaber, the chairman of the department, expressed some concern about my preparation for graduate study. He suggested that I register for two summer classes, a class in poetry and a class in Shakespeare taught by Professor Black. I don't remember much about the poetry class except that it met in Bennett Hall. Almost thirty years later on a visit to the Penn campus, I read in the student paper that Martin Luther King, Jr. had attended the University of Pennsylvania in the summer of 1951 and had attended classes in Bennett Hall, where I had taken the poetry class. With the small number of Black students at Penn at that time, I believe it highly likely that I may have seen or even met him. Professor Black's class proved immensely enjoyable. We read at least three Shakespearean plays, including *Henry II*, parts 1 and 2. The professor read and interpreted the plays himself. I had never heard the English playwright read with such intensity, insight, and delight.

In the early days of the fall semester, I recall moving down a crowded staircase in one of the classroom buildings. A young white man in front of me turned abruptly and his elbow struck me in the middle of my chest so hard that it nearly knocked the wind out of me. He glanced at me and never uttered one word of apology. I might as well have been a sack of peanuts. That summed up pretty much the way I felt at the University of Pennsylvania in the 1951–52 school year—invisible.

Because I had enjoyed Dr. Black's Shakespeare class in the summer, I registered for his class in Elizabethan literature during the fall semester. An immense, tall, ebullient man with silver white hair, Professor Black loved to talk about the South. He said that a quite mystical, romantic aura enveloped the region, that when people hear the strains of Dixie, they are filled with nostalgia and just break out singing spontaneously. Though I never disagreed with him openly, I knew I was not included in his romantic vision of an endearing South. I had great determination, however, and though I had not made the best grades in my summer studies, I was determined that I would do well in Dr. Black's class. At the beginning of the term, he let us know that we were responsible for writing research papers on one of the English writers that we would study. I could tell from his lectures that he greatly admired John Donne, the sixteenth-century mystic poet. I found the professor's comments and enthusiasm intriguing, and selected John Donne as the subject of my research. I hardly remember any of the students in any of the classes, but I do remember one student in Dr. Black's class who had commented about the conundrum presented in conducting research: that to validate the opinions of one commentator required looking at the evidence on which that individual's conclusions rested. She sounded quite erudite. One day as I was leaving class, I heard Dr. Black ask her if she would please select John Donne as the subject of her research. I knew immediately that he did not believe my work would meet his standards.

I also took a class in Victorian literature under Dr. Peckham, who constantly paced the front of the room as he talked and whose lectures I found hard to follow. The challenges I faced in his class were exceeded only by the difficulty of understanding the textbook. The ideas of John Stuart Mills and Thomas Carlyle I found impenetrable. The only other Black student, who taught at Mississippi's Rust College, and I sometimes shared our frustrations about Dr. Peckham's class. One day after class, she went to his office and told him about the difficulty she experienced trying to understand him. Later she told me that he had made no recommendations at all but simply laughed at her comments. Her story discouraged me from approaching him, but I tried to prepare myself for his final examination—part of which involved memorizing dates and authors. That part of his test I aced, and that performance helped me earn a C in his classroom. The course in Methods of Teaching English helped me most. It provided solid strategies for teaching language arts, as they were called, and literature. The class required that we make oral presentations, and I remember rehearsing my presentation so many times that I knew it by heart. My grades at the University of Pennsylvania were not impressive. I can't remember which class it was now, but I made a D in one of my classes. One summer and two semesters at the University of Pennsylvania were enough to convince me that I was not smart at all, that I certainly was not smart enough to obtain a master's degree. I felt ashamed, and I didn't know whom to blame.

On the other hand, Reed successfully completed his classes at Echols Mortuary College in the spring and applied for an interim job at a multilevel parking garage, a bright new convenience in 1952, in downtown Philadelphia. When we parked our car in midtown, we often watched admiringly as the drivers drove the cars down a circuitous ramp. Reed had studied automotive engineering at Hampton and loved cars. His job interview, however, did not go well and he decided to leave me in Philadelphia to complete my spring classes, and he returned to North Carolina alone. I felt a little lonely, but I also experienced a feeling of liberation. I felt free to use as much time as I could on my studies. My days usually began with breakfast at Horn and Hardart's, near 34th Street and Chestnut Avenue in West Philadelphia. I ate alone at the counter and a friendly, personable waitress served me. I ordered the same breakfast each morning: scrambled eggs, bacon, and a toasted blueberry muffin with coffee. After breakfast, if I did not have a class, I went to the library and studied. Although I had completed twenty or more credits, I did not consider my year at Penn successful. I never thought about going back to finish a master's degree. Instead, Reed came up, we packed the car and drove home to Enfield together.

15. Resuming Life in Enfield

Since the town of Enfield offered little decent housing for members of the Black community, in the summer of 1952, my husband and I moved into my old bedroom in my parents' home. My mother ran the household, and my husband and I functioned essentially as older children of the family. Once we had made plans to remodel a house on North Railroad Street, but somehow the plans fell through, and we continued living with my parents. We felt discouraged that we could not afford our own home and live independently. We lived this way for nine years.

My mother and I got along very well, and our living arrangement had many benefits. We paid no rent and really contributed minimally to grocery buying. My mother did most of the cooking, and I worried very little about meal preparation. In addition to my teaching responsibilities, I took an active role in the New Bethel Baptist Sunday School, playing for the junior choir, and helping with special programs. One Christmas my mother and I planned the Christmas pageant carefully, and I decided to become very creative with costuming and church decorations. After weeks of practicing and learning new songs, we gathered curtains, old fur coats, remnants of taffeta, brocade, lace, and other fabrics to costume the cast of two or three dozen youngsters.

I decided that the choir that played a key role in the Christmas pageant should be seen through a background of thin netting. We moved the pulpit furniture to create a stage for the actors and covered the opening behind the pulpit with yards and yards of cheesecloth, which I had dyed a light blue. Two days before the production, my mother and I drove to my grandfather's farm and went into the woods where we found all kinds of vines, running cedar, loblolly pine, and boughs of holly. On the Saturday before our program, the two of us decorated the whole church with evergreens. The church was gorgeous! On the Sunday evening of the presentation, Mr. Harvey, the janitor, built a roaring fire in the coal heater. The church temperature must have been hovering near eighty degrees when we arrived hours before the

Fig. 15.1. Mae Cofield loved growing things. Here she shows off her huge collards, ca. 2000. / Willa Cofield personal collection.

pageant. Mom and I costumed all the youngsters. There were towering turbans and glistening robes for the wise men, fur and leather for the shepherds, and gauzy, tinseled gowns for the angels. The well-rehearsed trios, duets, and the entire choir sang beautifully. Everyone agreed that we had staged a marvelous Christmas program!

Another close bond that my mother and I shared was the cultivation of flowers. Wherever my mother lived, she found a way to grow vegetables and flowers (Fig. 15.1). I often helped her in the flower border in the backyard of the house on McDaniel Street. We spent hours poring over seed catalogues, and whenever we traveled to Raleigh, Norfolk, or Richmond, she and I checked out other people's yards and flower borders. I had learned more about flower culture during my tenure at the Brick Rural Life School. Since many other women and a few men in our community also loved to grow flowers, my mother and I decided to organize a garden club in Enfield to help bring more beauty into our lives.

We held our first meeting at the home of Mr. Willie Williams, a very amiable bachelor whose yard shone with thousands of azalea blooms in the spring. For the next five years or so, the Everblooming Garden Club met once a month in area homes to pursue its mission of bringing beauty to our homes and community.

The Garden Club held several flower shows, where members made floral arrangements and then displayed them at a show to which we invited our friends and neighbors. One fall, after frost had wiped out most of our flower gardens, Mrs. Laura Powell astonished all of us by entering an artful arrangement of wild goldenrod and fleabane daisies. She explained this odd, yet beautiful, creation by saying that as she sat looking through her kitchen window at a field of wildflowers, the thought came that it would be possible to use them for an entry in the flower show. Her bold creation extended our vision and helped us see beauty in common things we had overlooked because they were a pervasive presence in our lives. It was a lesson that Mr. Sims had tried to teach the Brick School farm families.

One distinction eluded our club: we could not win a blue ribbon at the Enfield Firemen's Fair. We were usually beaten by the Inborden School exhibit. After several years of disappointment, I came up with a winning idea: we would display a roadside market similar to the ones I had seen at the Philadelphia Flower Show. During the year that I attended the University of Pennsylvania, I took precious hours from my study schedule and twenty dollars from my slim checking account to buy a ticket to the Philadelphia Flower Show. Besides amazing displays of roses, orchids, and other flowers whose names I could not pronounce, the show featured roadside markets with fruits, vegetables, condiments, and handicrafts that one might encounter on a country road in Pennsylvania in early spring. I convinced members of the Everblooming Garden Club that we should design and build a country road market in our exhibit space at the Enfield Firemen's Fair.

That year the managers of the Enfield Firemen's Fair assigned the Everblooming Garden Club a ten-by-ten-foot exhibit space fairly close to the entrance. The market that we built had a brick floor, a wooden shed, and a fence made of tobacco sticks. Many of the markets in the Philadelphia Flower Show featured a grape-stake fence. I decided that we could get the same effect by tying tobacco sticks together with heavy cord. In the curing process, local farmers hung green bundles of tobacco from these roughly cut sticks. So, we drove a truck to my grandfather's farm and brought back a huge load of tobacco sticks, which we dumped in front of the empty exhibit space. First, we had to remove bits of string from the rough-cut wood. This required care so that we didn't get splinters in our fingers.

Once the sticks were clean, we painstakingly tied them together and created a simulated grape-stakes fence. To protect the wooden floor of the exhibit area, we laid down heavy plastic sheets. Tyler Vaughn, husband of our secretary, Lelia, laid bricks, using a repeating pattern of squares. Instead of mortar, he purchased a bag of sand from Rives Hardware Store and filled in the spaces between the bricks. He then erected a shed-like structure with a roof sloping down toward the front and inserted shelves to simulate the roadside stand.

After the stand was completed, we sent out a call to all our members to bring fresh vegetables and fruit, jellies, jams, and flowers to the exhibit hall to fill the market stand. Caught in the enthusiasm of the moment, the members sent so many plants, containers of fruits and vegetables that the floor space in front of the booth became a sea of produce, shopping bags, plants, baskets, and flowers. We had enough stuff to fill five roadside market stands.

Eliminating what we could not use created a charged atmosphere as each donor expected her item to be front and center. After hours of work, the little exhibit space was filled with dozens of items, including strings of red pepper, pots of chrysanthemums, red Winesap apples, pumpkins, yellow squash, collards, jams, jellies, pickled peaches, handmade doilies, and kitchen towels. Mrs. Louise James had sent her prized elephant ears plant, and no one had the gumption to reject it, so it ended up at the front of the roadside stand, competing with the stand itself as the dominant presence in the market.

Throughout the process of creating the roadside stand, our chief competitor, Eugene Richardson, representing the Inborden School, warily watched us as he worked on his exhibit. After the judging and the blue ribbon shone from the front of our stand, signifying that we had won the grand prize of fifty dollars, he smiled, shook his head, and said, "Well, you really deserve it because you have worked so hard."

Appropriately enough, our final project sought to raise money to build gates for the Cedar Sarah Cemetery, where Enfield Black people found their final resting place. My father beamed with enthusiasm that we had chosen to help improve the cemetery. We sponsored a smorgasbord at the Little Palace Restaurant as our peak fund-raising effort. For the event, my mother made the best beef stew that I have ever tasted, but there were so many other inviting dishes that Mom took most of it home. Without consulting us, my father engaged a mason who built two narrow brick columns at the entrance to the cemetery. Of course, my mother and I, not to mention other members, were truculent and disappointed. I think that this final project ended the short and happy life of the Everblooming Garden Club.

16. Living the Dream of Teaching in My Hometown

During the summer of 1952, when I returned from Philadelphia, Halifax County completed building a school for Black high school students in Enfield. The county had elected to construct six classrooms on the grounds of the Inborden Elementary School, and Mr. Wilder, the elementary school principal, became administrator of the entire complex (Fig. 16.1). Though a very small school, I was certain that it would need an English teacher. It was impossible to talk to the principal, who had gone away to summer school in New York City. My parents, husband, and I decided that we should talk to this man face-to-face, so we drove to New York City, where we found him at the Theresa Hotel on 110th Street. He and his wife had taken a room for the summer. When we called from the Theresa Hotel's lobby, instead of coming downstairs, he invited us to come to their room. I told him of my interest in teaching English at the new high school, and he assured me that if the job was open, as far as he was concerned, I could have it. The rest of our New York visit seemed like a holiday, for we had accomplished the purpose of our journey: I would finally have a teaching job in the town of Enfield.

Getting ready for the new job involved a trip to Richmond, where I shopped at Miller and Rhoads and Thalhimer's department stores. My husband's sister lived in Richmond and took great joy in driving us to downtown Richmond and helping outfit me in suitable teaching clothes. I think I bought five dresses, one for each day of the week. I can still remember a deep turquoise dress with a tucked midriff and a thin, black voile with subtle orange lines and a white pique collar. I intended to be as well dressed in my attire as I was versed in my subject.

When Inborden High School opened in the fall of 1952, it had six rooms—one of which served as a library—five teachers, and three grades, ninth, tenth, and eleventh. Inborden's first graduating class held its commencement exercises in St. Paul Church because the school had no auditorium. Because there were not enough teachers to offer the required subjects, Aaron Wilder, principal, also taught history and social studies. Mamie Ruth Ellis, who had just graduated from Johnson C. Smith, taught science; Ellen and Herbert Mitchell, a husband-and-wife team, business courses and mathematics; and I taught English. Mr. Mitchell coached boys' basketball and Miss Ellis coached the girls' team.

The principal had had difficulty finding a science teacher and Ruth Ellis joined the faculty on the day of the countywide meeting of Negro teachers at Eastman School. Following the long meeting, another teacher, Mrs. Margaret

Fig. 16.1. When Inborden School opened, Black high school students could attend school in their hometown. 1956. / Grassroots Media Productions.

Scott, offered Miss Ellis overnight lodging and a ride back to Enfield. Upon Mrs. Scott's suggestion, the two women stopped at a local drugstore. While the new science teacher waited for Mrs. Scott to speak to the druggist, she observed the young drug store clerk making an ice cream soda for a white customer. Ellis walked to the counter and asked for an ice cream soda.

Somewhat evasively, the clerk answered that she did not have the ingredients to make an ice cream soda. The young teacher pointed to the woman whom the clerk had just served and said, "I want one like you just made for that lady." At this point, the clerk looked at the young Black woman and said, "We don't serve Negroes in here." In utter disbelief, Ruth related this experience to the older teacher. Not surprised, Mrs. Scott assured her, "No, they don't serve us at the fountain." The next morning at our staff meeting, Mr. Wilder told the story. He had heard the incident from the drug store owner, who had phoned to request that he talk to the new teacher and inform her of local customs. Making this small service at the drugstore unavailable to Black people offended and demeaned us. We disliked going to the drugstore for any reason.

I was proud to be a faculty member at Inborden School. Indeed, my work at the University of Pennsylvania had given me a sound set of strategies for teaching both language and literature. During the fall, I usually taught the language arts—the practices of speaking, writing, thinking. Many of my students made frequent mistakes in verb tense and verb and subject agreement.

I worked mightily to make them aware of these mistakes and taught them to use correct forms. Unlike the high school English classes that I had attended, I also required students to do a great deal of writing. I asked that students write short pieces in class and as homework. We had weekly spelling tests and vocabulary-building activities. Sometimes the typing teacher and I worked together to make joint assignments.

I loved the spring semester when I taught literature. We used a series of textbooks that offered a variety of short stories, poems, essays, and plays. Following the practice of my high school English teacher, I required students to memorize poems, passages of Shakespearean plays, and recite them at the front of the classroom. Those were challenging assignments for some students, but most students were able to do well.

Many years later, one of my students demonstrated her lifelong memory of my class in a conversation with Eddie Davis, a former music teacher at Ralph Bunche High School in Weldon who later worked for the North Carolina Teachers Association. Mr. Davis called me at my New Jersey home to tell me of an encounter that he had had with Creola Alston, who at that time was living in a senior residence in Raleigh. He said that he had gone to the residence for a meeting. As he passed through the lobby of the building, he noticed a woman playing the piano. She was still there after his meeting ended, so the former music teacher walked over and complimented her on her playing. He said Ms. Alston told him that she only played for her own entertainment, but she loved music and poetry. She further confided that she had had a high school teacher who instilled in her a love for poetry. She said that one of the poems she learned in that teacher's class is called "Patterns" by Edna St. Vincent Millay. To Mr. Davis's surprise and delight, she recited all the lines of the poem, adding "I learned it in Mrs. Willa Johnson's class."

During the years that I taught at Inborden, the school gained new teachers and space—a science laboratory, additional classrooms, a large building to be used as gymnasium and auditorium. Upon occasion, the latter building also provided classroom space. Classes were large and many students came to school irregularly, especially during the harvest season. Teachers struggled to make the most of the days when students were present. The classroom represented the one area where teachers maintained control. In the Inborden classroom each day, I came face to face with young students, many of them from families I knew well. Often, I was teaching young people whose older brothers and sisters had already sat in my class. These students lived in the small town of Enfield or on farms in nearby communities. In the fall of the year, many could not attend school because their families needed all their hands to harvest acres of cotton, corn, and peanuts. In the farms of the 1950s, laborers performed tasks that machines later took over. Even in the spring, one could see armies of men, women, and children moving through the fields, planting or hoeing young tobacco, peanut, and cotton plants, and in the fall, dozens of workers—many of them very young—gathered tobacco, picked cotton, shook peanuts, and cut down dried stalks of corn.

I remember one student whose father owned a farm in the Dawson community, about eight miles from Enfield, who came to school in September, but did not return until after Christmas. A studious and conscientious student, he was so far behind in all aspects of the class's work that it seemed almost impossible for him to catch up. We teachers understood why he had not attended school and helped him as much as we could. With great effort, he managed to move on to the next grade. That student ultimately graduated from high school and college and became a school principal, justifying our leniency and empathy.

For the next six years, I enjoyed teaching at Inborden High School. In the spring of 1958, I left the school to give birth to my daughter, Tanya. A year later when I was ready to return, I was surprised when the white superintendent raised an objection to my reemployment, for he had never visited my classroom. I received a note from Superintendent Overman, however, informing me that I could not be reemployed because I had violated the policy requiring pregnant teachers to resign in the fifth month of pregnancy. Not only did pregnant teachers have to give up their job, but they also had to resign four months before the baby's birth. Only a letter from my gynecologist saying that the baby had come a full month before the predicted delivery date made it possible for me to rejoin the faculty at Inborden School.

Although sexism was pervasive in our homes, schools, and communities, it had not been named in the late 1950s. Sexism in the 1950s permeated Halifax County schools. Though most teachers in the schools were female, in the late 1950s and the early 1960s, there were no women principals in Halifax County's Black schools, nor did I hear anyone suggest that there should be. Everyone silently accepted the premise that only men possessed the required qualities to administer schools. The Black principals' organization in Halifax County accurately called itself the Schoolmasters' Club, for all its members were men. Male principals enjoyed male privilege, the same privilege that many men enjoyed in their own homes. The social revolution that gave women more control over their lives had not occurred in the midsixties, so most people accepted the second-class position of women as natural. Young women of that day prepared to enter fields such as teaching or nursing—if

Part I: The Nine O'Clock Whistle 79

Fig. 16.2. Willa Johnson sponsored the school newspaper, the *Inborden Reflector*. / Willa Cofield personal collection.

they prepared to work at all. The most desired goal for many women—especially white women—was to marry well and become a housewife. Hollywood movies peddled finding a romantic mate and marrying as a woman's optimal goal in life.

I reentered the job at Inborden High School in the school year 1959–60 upon the invitation of the principal, Luther Williams, whom I had known as a colleague at Eastman High School. I remembered him as a huge, jovial man who fit easily into the warm and friendly social environment at Eastman School. In the early fifties, he and his wife built a house on Whitaker Street near First Baptist Church in Enfield. In the midfifties before our daughter was born, Reed and I built a house in the same block just up the street from the Williamses. We were neighbors. In addition to our daytime work at the school, once a month during the school year, my husband and I joined Mr. Williams and a few other people to play pinochle in our homes.

When I wanted to try a new idea in the classroom or add to the school's out-of-class activities, the principal had offered his enthusiastic support. We both took pride in the school paper that I started, the *Inborden Reflector* (Fig. 16.2). My English class wrote the articles longhand, and students in the typing class prepared the copy for print. After hearing of the National Honor Society, I started a chapter at Inborden High School. The bright students who met the criteria for selection loved the prestige that accompanied membership in the National Honor Society, and becoming a member of the Inborden chapter became a much sought-after goal for many students. I accompanied students on visits to colleges and historical sites to explore the world beyond our small village and to begin seeking admission to college. I worked with students to organize a student council and secured a charter that aligned our school with a national organization of student councils. With my support, students participated in Delta Sigma Theta Sorority's Jabberwock, an annual talent show that the sorority sponsored to award college scholarships. In these endeavors, I had the full support of Principal L. M. Williams.

17. POLITICS CHANGE MY WORLD

Fig. 18.1. When Reed Johnson filed to run for Enfield commissioner, he ignited a fire waiting to be lit. 1960. / Willa Cofield personal collection.

18. Reed Johnson Runs for Town Commissioner

In April 1963, near the filing deadline for the spring primary election, Reed Johnson walked into the Enfield Town Office and informed the clerk that he wished to run for town commissioner (Fig. 18.1). My husband's bold decision to run for a political office in Enfield, where only a handful of Negroes could vote, shocked the town. No one had anticipated such an audacious act.

Fig. 18.2. Word of Reed's filing spread quickly through Black Bottom (shown here in 1977) and other Enfield neighborhoods. / Willa Cofield personal collection.

Fig. 18.3. The Johnsons built this home on Whitaker Street in 1956 (photo ca. 1978). / Willa Cofield personal collection.

Since moving to Enfield, Reed's humor, good cheer, and gregarious nature had made him a popular and well-liked member of the community. He had been known to cross boundaries. Once critical of long speeches at the Inborden PTA meetings, Reed had volunteered to serve as the organization's secretary. Having a male secretary was odd—if not unthinkable—in those days. Reed's hilarious reading of the minutes, however, had become a source of much joy and laughter. But no one had thought he would invade the whites-only area and run for a seat on the Enfield Board of Commissioners.

The announcement created excitement among Blacks and unease among whites. Reed's filing ignited strong political interest in New Town, Black

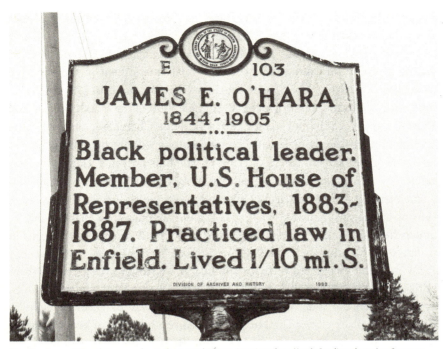

Fig. 18.4. James O'Hara (1844–1905) was the second African American from North Carolina elected to Congress, where he was extremely active and capable. He lived in Enfield during his tenure as Congressman. / Karen Riley, photographer, 2018.

Bottom (Fig. 18.2), and on Cemetery Hill, all the neighborhoods of Enfield where Black people lived. People talked about Reed at Rip McWilliams's barber shop and at Rosalie Cofield's and Queen Pittman's beauty salons. But not everyone took pleasure in the announcement. Soon, we received telephone calls from white men demanding that Reed withdraw his name from the political race. Other callers threatened to burn to the ground our recently built house (Fig. 18.3). On the other hand, Reed's act encouraged Black folks to register to vote, although he had slim chances of being elected.

People said it was the first time that a Black person in Enfield had ever run for political office. Clearly, no one alive in Enfield in 1963 remembered or had ever heard of James O'Hara, a Black man who had lived in the town and served two terms in the US Congress (Fig. 18.4). In 1883, when James O'Hara joined the Forty-eighth Congress, a letter to the *Washington Bee*, a Black newspaper published in Washington, hailed him as "an able man" who belonged to the "younger class of colored men." Before his election, O'Hara had proved his political tenacity, for the Enfield attorney had been an aspirant Congressional nominee in five consecutive elections. A few months later, after observing Congressman O'Hara in the House of Representatives, the editor of the *Washington Bee* noted that O'Hara was "business all the time" and suggested, "he would do more than a half dozen others we have had put together."[8]

Indeed, the Congressman from Enfield was very active in Congress, introducing a resolution calling for a constitutional amendment to the Supreme Court decision that had literally nullified the Civil Rights Act of 1875; introducing a measure to reimburse depositors in the defunct Freedman's Savings and Trust Company; calling for aid for North Carolina Cherokees; and proposing an amendment to provide equal accommodations without discrimination on interstate travel. He sponsored thirteen private bills for relief, claims, or pensions.[9] The astute and active congressman spoke for equal salaries for men and women teachers in the District of Columbia and opposed President Cleveland's veto of a veterans' pension, placing particular emphasis on Black veterans, under the command of General Benjamin Butler.[10] After serving two terms in Congress, he was defeated in the 1886 election and retired to his law practice.

By 1963 the earlier era of Black political activism had disappeared from both the history books and from the collective memory of the community. In 1900, when the state of North Carolina took away Black men's right to vote, Enfield Black citizens had turned to the grim business of keeping themselves and their families alive in a hard time. By 1963, the history of this early period of Black involvement in the politics of the Second District had become remote and invisible.

Very late one night in April 1963, a neighbor called to say that something was burning in our backyard. Jumping out of bed and running to the bedroom window, we saw the backyard lit up by flames shooting into the night sky from a burning cross planted on our lawn. Our five-year-old daughter heard the commotion and looking out the window, jumped on the bed, saying, "There is a missile in our backyard!" (Fig. 18.5).

During the next few days, news of the cross burning spread quickly through the Black community. It was the first cross burning the town had witnessed in over thirty years. The earlier event had closed the fledgling hospital on Wall Street and driven Dr. DuBissette and his family out of town. But no one left town in 1963. The ugly incident instead made Black people angry and motivated them to register. Reed and Lillie Cousins Smith, my friend from childhood and a teacher at Eastman School, began taking carloads of people downtown to register. Alarmed by the numbers of Black people seeking to register, local election officials closed the registration office and announced that the registrar had gone to the beach. Black people began talking about a sit-down on the registrar's porch. But the town officials backed down and reopened the registration office, strategically located in the Enfield police

Fig. 18.5. Tanya, 3, Willa, and Reed Johnson, 1960. / Willa Cofield personal collection.

station. Reed said that people were now begging him to go with them downtown to take the required literacy test and register to vote. His enthusiasm made me set aside my doubts about his candidacy and view it as an opportunity to improve our community.

19. Inborden Students Challenge Segregation

In my classroom, students and I frequently discussed racial matters. We followed the civil rights drama unfolding across the South in the late 1950s and early 1960s with great interest and enthusiasm. I brought in newspapers and magazines and filled the classroom bulletin board with photos of the Freedom Riders, young college students sitting at lunch counters, and Black people attempting to vote. We marveled at these people's assertiveness and courage.

When the students at Inborden High School heard about Reed's candidacy, several of them volunteered to help get people registered to vote. One Monday morning, Milton Evans, an Inborden senior, reported to my English class that he and Marshall Harvey, a sophomore, had seen North Carolina Central College students protesting a segregated Howard Johnson restaurant on a Sunday trip to Durham. His description of the incident electrified the class, and the discussion dominated the entire class period. On the following Thursday after school, twelve Inborden students announced their intention to use the Enfield Public Library, an institution that served only white patrons. Leaving the school grounds in a body, they walked to the tiny library which was housed in a former jail. The librarian on duty told the students that the library did not serve Negroes. On the spot, the young people decided to appeal to the mayor and walked across the railroad tracks to Mayor Shervette's office. Later we learned that the manager of Harrison's Drugstore had noticed the group of students and quietly removed the chairs from the tables, in fear that the students were coming to the drugstore to stage a sit-in. When the students asked to see the mayor, an employee told them that he was unavailable. They made an appointment to see Mayor Shervette later and promised to return.

On the Monday after the library incident, the principal of Inborden High School called the students to a meeting in the science room, where he severely reprimanded them. He told them that under no circumstances should they keep the appointment that they had made to talk to Mayor Shervette. When I heard of this meeting, I went to the principal and questioned him about his talk with the students. He denied that he had told them to cancel the meeting with the mayor. Later, he defended his comments, saying that he had wanted the student group to choose a spokesperson before they engaged in conversation with the city official.

On Friday evening, several adults took many of the same students to a meeting at Quankey Baptist Church near Roanoke Rapids, where Floyd McKissick, the well-known civil rights leader, was to speak (Fig. 19.1). The Durham lawyer, who later became the national director of the Congress of Racial Equality (CORE), talked eloquently and passionately about the Israelites' attack upon the walls of Jericho and how those walls came tumbling down.

On the Saturday evening after McKissick's talk, many of the same students came to a party at our house. My husband wanted to thank them for their efforts to get people to register. We soon learned that these students were in no mood to party. Instead, they wanted to tackle the racially segregated seating at the Levon Movie Theatre in Enfield.

Two students, Marshall Harvey and Ira Dale Sanders, volunteered to go downtown to speak to the theater manager and owner. Tyler Vaughn, an adult, offered to drive them. When they got to the theater, the two students asked Rom Parker, the white owner, to abandon his practice of segregating theatergoers and open the first floor to Black patrons. Rom Parker lost no time in

Fig. 19.1. Floyd McKissick, Durham lawyer and civil rights leader, inspired Inborden students and guided the growing Enfield movement (ca. 1978). / Courtesy of Floyd McKissick, Jr.

informing the two students that he had no intention of letting Black people sit downstairs in the Levon Theatre.

According to the *Enfield Progress*, theater owner Walter Parker said that he and his brother, Rom, had opened the theater on July 7, 1962, after it had been closed for eighteen months, so that the people of the community would have some form of clean, wholesome entertainment on weekends even though profits would be small. "The theater is operated as a private, free enterprise and we feel that we are not violating any city or state law—or even the Constitution of the United States—to operate it as such."[11]

After Rom Parker's rebuff, the students returned to our home, and we all huddled in the living room. Someone suggested that we ask Floyd McKissick for advice. Following this suggestion, I phoned Attorney McKissick, who said that we should put up a picket line and keep it there until they let us sit downstairs.

Fig. 19.2. Inborden students began picketing Levon Theatre on May 27, 1963. / J. B. Harren, photographer. Willa Cofield personal collection.

We followed the Durham lawyer's advice. I pulled out large sheets of orange construction paper and we used black, felt-tipped pens to condemn the racist practices of the Levon Theatre. After completing the signs, we pushed back the furniture in the living and dining rooms, and students walked around in a big circle as though they were picketing. We asked, "What will you do if some white bystander calls you the N-word?" Lillie Cousins Smith, one of the adult leaders known for her own boldness, and whose daughter, Cynthia, was among the picketing role players, called out: "Look them dead in the eye and keep on walking!"

Inborden's baccalaureate service, the first of two graduation events, was scheduled for the next day. Many of the students preparing to picket Levon Theatre were graduating seniors who expected to leave the picket line and join the graduation line at the Inborden gymtorium at 4:30 p.m. All the students planned to attend the annual baccalaureate sermon.

Fig. 19.3. Charles McLean (front), regional director of the NAACP, and Inborden High School students protest racial segregation at the Levon Theatre in the summer of 1963. Cynthia Samuelson personal collection

On that very warm Sunday in May a few hours before the annual service began, fifteen Inborden students made history by walking in front of Levon Theatre carrying signs proclaiming, "WE HAVE ALREADY WAITED 100 YEARS." "JOIN THE FIGHT FOR FREEDOM." "FIGHT SEGREGATED MOVIES NOW." "STAND UP FOR YOUR RIGHTS!" (Fig. 19.2).

On Sunday, May 26, 1963, the line of young students under the marquee of Levon Theatre on Whitaker Street created pandemonium in downtown Enfield. Everybody who could walk, ride, or cycle came to the corner of Whitaker and Dennis Streets to see the young protesters on that Sunday afternoon. Police cars with flashing red lights came early, and the bank parking lot directly across from the theater soon held dozens of cars. Pick-up trucks and cars choked the intersection of Dennis and Whitaker Streets. A police officer stood in the center of the intersection to keep the traffic moving. Drivers of cars passing by filled with gaping passengers drove as slowly as possible to try to comprehend a scene that they had never expected to see in Enfield. White onlookers jeered and called insults. The son of the owner of Beavans' Drug Store cut through the picket line with his aged, dingy Dalmatian dog, but the dog was too old to be a threat. After ninety minutes of walking in front of the theater, the students jumped into cars and scurried to Inborden School for the baccalaureate service.

During the next four weeks, the student protesters continued to picket Levon Theatre. Few Black moviegoers crossed the picket line. No matter what enticing movie the theater owners screened, the upstairs balcony remained empty. After local churches denied our request to use their facilities, my parents, Thomas and Mae Cofield, owners of Cofield Funeral Home, invited us to

Fig. 19.4. Thomas and Mae Cofield invited the protesters to meet in the chapel of the Cofield Funeral Home (ca. 1963). / Mae Cofield Family Collection.

use the chapel of the funeral home (Fig. 19.4). After picketing Levon Theatre, protesters and adult supporters began meeting nightly in the funeral home's chapel (Fig. 19.5). The high-spirited meetings provided a forum for youth and adults to react to the day's events and to plan for the next day's protest. The group met every night during June 1963.

At the end of June, the Parkers closed Levon Theatre (Fig. 19.3). Rather than integrate the seating, they chose to have no theater at all. The *Enfield Progress* reported that the theater owner said that integration would result in the eventual business failure of the firm from loss of patronage by white customers.[12] Thus the white community in Enfield gave up its only theater rather than share it on an equal basis with Black patrons.

20. The Protest Spreads

Both the *Roanoke Rapids Herald* and the *News and Observer* published articles about the unusual events occurring in Enfield. Once the word got out, people from communities already engaged in protest came to town. Floyd McKissick sent a young college student to speak at one of the meetings at Cofield Funeral Home. He not only told us about the protest movement in

Fig. 19.5. Established in 1910, Cofield Funeral Home flourished under the leadership of Thomas Cofield (ca. 1963). / Mae Cofield Family Collection.

his community but also taught us to sing freedom songs, "Everybody Wants Freedom!" and "We Shall Overcome."

The meetings provided a sympathetic audience where many individuals told stories of personal insult and racial discrimination. Many speakers condemned downtown stores for employing only white clerks. They said that these stores depended heavily on Black patrons but employed Black people only as maintenance workers. Some speakers pointed out the all-white police force that in no way reflected the racial composition of the town. Others spoke of doctors' offices, white restaurants, and drugstores. Without exception, all the public facilities in the town segregated their customers based on race.

With the closing of Levon Theatre, the movement participants felt newly empowered, and at one of the meetings in early June, they drew up a list of demands to present to Enfield's board of commissioners. In the following days, they fanned through the town and got hundreds of individuals to sign a petition to present the demands at the town board's meeting. The *Enfield Progress* reported that a delegation of Negro citizens of the town, led by A. Reed Johnson as their spokesperson, appeared before the board of commissioners. On the previous Wednesday evening, they presented a petition "signed by several hundred local citizens of their race, in which they requested certain rights, privileges and facilities," listed below:

- That a Negro police officer with the same privileges as other police be added to the city police force;
- That the city provide sidewalks, curbing and proper drainage for streets in Negro neighborhoods; that these improvements be made first on Dixie Street, a main thoroughfare for children who walk to Inborden School;
- That proper lighting be installed throughout the town of Enfield;
- That the city provide a year-round recreational program for all youth;
- That a swimming pool be built at Oak View Park;
- That an ordinance be passed outlawing segregation in all public places within the confines of Enfield;
- That equal services in street cleaning, garbage collection, etc., be provided for all sections of town;
- That sewerage be extended to all residences within the town of Enfield.[13]

In support of the demands, youthful protesters began picketing downtown stores in early July. The Enfield Board of Commissioners responded by appointing a biracial committee to consider the petition.

A few days later, the commissioners passed an ordinance severely limiting the picketing of downtown stores. Among other things, the ordinance said that picketing should be unattended by noise, shouting, clapping, and singing; that picketing should be limited to the outside five feet of the sidewalk next to the curb; that no more than five persons could picket before any business; that picketers could demonstrate in front of only one business in a block at one time; that signs may not be defamatory; that protesters could not talk to persons traveling on the sidewalk or street; and that no person under eighteen years would be permitted to march, picket, or demonstrate within the town of Enfield. Enfield's town commissioners undoubtedly expected the ordinance to end the protest, for up to this point only students had picketed Enfield's businesses.

The ban on picketing prompted adults in the Enfield movement to take a stand. A few days after the passage of the ordinance, Charles McLean, regional director of the National Association of Colored People (NAACP), visited Enfield to provide support to the growing movement. McLean also wanted to make certain that the movement in Enfield was allied with the NAACP.

While a small group of people had kept the Enfield-Wayman Branch of the NAACP alive over the years, the local organization had witnessed little growth (Fig. 20.1). McLean urged the new crop of activists to join the local NAACP branch, and soon the membership list swelled with new names.

Fig. 20.1. Members of the Enfield-Wayman chapter of the NAACP, ca. 1956. Mae Cofield (far right) and Thomas Cofield (center) stand in the second row. / Mae Cofield Family Collection.

In addition, McLean made certain that the Enfield movement was publicly tied to the NAACP by having us add a line to all picket signs designating the NAACP as our sponsor.

McLean attended our meeting where the town commissioners' recent ban on picketing by youthful protesters was the center of attention. The funeral home chapel was filled with adult leaders, students, and community people. Lillie Smith, Reed Johnson, Tyler Vaughan, Alice Evans, and others spoke against the most recent action of Enfield's commissioners. The remarks from the speakers reflected what we all felt. We had been outmaneuvered. We were frustrated and angry. The ban restricting young picketers threatened to bring an end to our young movement. Virtually all the picketers were under the age of eighteen.

After several speakers condemned the board of commissioners, McLean rose from his seat near the back and strode to the front of the room. In a very passionate and loud voice, he charged: "You are letting these children fight your battle! This is your fight!"

His challenge set a new phase of the movement in motion. The next day, a bright Sunday morning, twelve adults armed themselves with picket signs and walked onto the narrow strip of public land that fronted the Plantation Restaurant on US Highway 301. The protesters' signs derided the owners of Plantation Restaurant for defiantly locking the restaurant's doors when Black people sought to enter and be served. As white onlookers stared and jeered from the other side of the highway, my youngest sister, Claudette Hardaway, Reed Johnson, and I took our places on the picket line.

A few weeks later, the NAACP sent two representatives of its Youth Commandos to Enfield: Robert Blow and Marie Davis, both under twenty years of age. They wore flashy black jackets with the words NAACP YOUTH COMMANDOS in white, emblazoned on their backs. Baby-faced Robert Blow carried far too many pounds, but he was charismatic, likable, and very humorous. While quieter, Marie demonstrated a similar courage and zest to do battle with the racist white people in Enfield. Together, the two young people began organizing the Black resistance in the town.

Governor Terry Sanford sent Capus Waynick to Enfield to build a bridge between the white and Black communities, and Waynick met with Robert Blow. Later Waynick said that he was amazed to find a seventeen-year-old kid leading the revolution. At the end of the day, when Waynick met with a small group of us in my father's office at the Cofield Funeral Home, he told us that he had had no success in trying to talk to Enfield white people. Off the record, he advised us to keep on fighting. When Lillie Cousins Smith asked him if a teacher could picket, he responded that he knew of no North Carolina law that prevented a teacher from picketing. After Waynick returned to Raleigh, Robert Blow and Marie Davis continued organizing to keep the heat on by targeting department stores downtown and the Plantation Grill on the north end of Enfield (Fig. 20.2).

In the summer of 1963, President John Kennedy announced his intent to send a civil rights bill to Congress outlawing segregation in public accommodations. Many businesses serving the white tourist trade that lined the interstate corridor from New York to Miami on Highway 301 began serving customers without regard to race. The owners of the Plantation Restaurant, however, posted a sign on the front door saying WHITES ONLY. Employees were ordered to lock the door if Black people attempted to enter the restaurant.

The Plantation Grill represented a symbol of prejudice and racial hatred to the Enfield freedom fighters. The owner of the Plantation Restaurant and Enfield Motel came from a wealthy family that owned hundreds of acres of farmland a few miles from Enfield. The family's large brick home with its well-kept lawn occupied a prominent site on Highway 481. Black people knew the Plantation Restaurant as a place of employment and the owner as a prejudiced man. The main cook, Buck Brantley, was a deacon at St. Paul Baptist Church and a well-known and highly respected member of our community. Other Black people worked as kitchen assistants or in other low-paying jobs.

During the summer of 1963, the Plantation Restaurant became a focal point to the Black community, an irritating, insulting example of white racism. Every day protesters condemning the restaurant's open display of racial

Fig. 20.2. Enfield protesters targeted the "Whites Only" policy of the Plantation Grill, late 1950s. / Grassroots Media Productions.

discrimination walked back and forth beside the highway, but the WHITES ONLY sign remained intact, and the door stayed locked to Black customers. Finally, some of the protesters decided to use a different tactic.

On a late August afternoon, Reed Johnson, Robert Blow, and about eight other men gathered quietly on Bryant Street on the south side of the Plantation Grill. After brief greetings, they walked west toward Highway 301, but soon turned right and cut between the small frame houses that faced Bryant Street. Stealthily, they approached the back of the restaurant. Reed Johnson, the lead person, opened the restaurant's back door and, to the astonishment of the cooks and kitchen help, the line of men walked through the kitchen and into the dining area of the Plantation Restaurant. The waitresses gaped at the men as they seated themselves. After some confusion and hesitation, the white waitresses offered menus and took orders from the uninvited Black diners. The kitchen help took great joy in preparing delicious food to fill the orders. When the waitresses placed the steaming plates before them, the protesters ate the first meal ever served to Black customers at the Plantation Restaurant.

Despite the exhilaration in our community, the attempt failed to change the establishment's racial policy. Some people said that the restaurant manager broke the plates that the Black intruders had eaten from. The WHITES ONLY sign remained on the door.

A few days after the kitchen invasion, Robert Blow and Marie Davis led forty other protesters to the front door of the Plantation Restaurant. The restaurant stood sixty feet from the highway and until that day, protesters had carefully limited their picketing to an area near the edge of the property. The group of mostly young Black adults waited outside the door, while some sat on the edge of a raised shrubbery box six or eight feet away. Others stood as far away as fifteen feet.

Years later Lillie Smith recalled encountering a would-be protester near the Plantation Restaurant who was leaving the protest site with a protest of her own: Reed Johnson had not let her join the picket line. She had come to the demonstration at the Plantation Restaurant with great expectations and Reed had turned her away. Sister Fenner, who was well known in the community for her belligerent attitude, admitted that she had hidden a weapon of self-defense in her bosom. Reed had turned Sister Fenner away to maintain the integrity of the nonviolent protest in the face of the jeers and racial taunts from white onlookers.

Shortly after the nonviolent protest began, the owner himself emerged from the door and ordered the entire group to get off his property. He threatened to call the police and have all of them arrested. No one left but all waited quietly for the police to arrive. In a few minutes, the Enfield police loaded the petitioners into several police cars and took them to Enfield's jail, where they were charged, indicted with trespassing, and released on bail.

21. North Carolina v. Robert Blow and North Carolina v. Marie Davis

The owner of the Plantation Restaurant, William R. Davis, filed charges against all the alleged trespassers. The resulting legal action became known as *North Carolina v. Robert Blow* and *North Carolina v. Marie Davis*. Two Black attorneys, Theaoseus T. Clayton of Warrenton and William O. Warner of Rocky Mount, represented the defendants in the Halifax County Court hearing. Not surprisingly, the all-white jury found the defendants guilty, and the court ruled in favor of the restaurant owner. To keep the case alive and to avoid paying fines levied by the county court, Samuel Mitchell, a Black Raleigh-based civil rights lawyer, and Floyd McKissick joined Clayton and Warner in an appeal to the North Carolina Supreme Court on behalf of the defendants. The North Carolina Supreme Court heard the cases, *State v. Robert Blow* and *State v. Ellen Marie Davis*, on March 18, 1964.

Attorneys for Blow and Davis argued that the North Carolina state law 14–134 of the General Statutes, making it an offense to "enter upon the lands of another, without a license therefore, making it a misdemeanor," was unconstitutional.[14] They said that the law conflicted with Article I, Section 17 of the Constitution of North Carolina and the Privileges or Immunities, Due Process, and Equal Protection Clauses of the Fourteenth Amendment to the Constitution of the United States. They argued that prosecution of the defendants rested upon the unlawful exercise of legislative power by a private citizen. In other words, the defendants claimed that they had the inherent right to exercise their fundamental freedom to enter the premises of any private business which was open to the public, whether forbidden or not.

Attorney General T. W. Bruton and Deputy Attorney General Ralph Moody represented the State of North Carolina. The state attorneys said that when a person without invitation enters upon the premises of another . . . [and] commits such acts as are reasonably calculated to disturb the peace, he would be liable for trespass. They defended the General Statute 14-134 of the United States. The North Carolina Supreme Court ruled against the protesters, saying that the evidence adduced by the state was sufficient to support the guilty verdict.[15]

Following the court's decision, Samuel Mitchell and Floyd McKissick asked the NAACP for help in making an appeal to the US Supreme Court. A battery of lawyers from that organization—Jack Greenberg, Constance Baker Motley, James M. Nabrit III, Derrick A. Bell Jr. and Charles L. Black Jr.—joined with Mitchell and McKissick to appeal the North Carolina Supreme Court's adverse decision.

On February 1, 1965, the US Supreme Court ruled on *Robert Blow et al. v. North Carolina*. The Court ruled in favor of Robert Blow, Marie Davis, and the other Enfield defendants, remanding the case to the North Carolina Supreme Court for dismissal of the indictments. The Court stated that the Civil Rights Act of 1964 forbids discrimination in places of public accommodation and removes peaceful attempts to be served on an equal basis from the category of punishable activities.

Although the conduct in the present cases occurred prior to the enactment of the Civil Rights Act, the still-pending convictions were abated by its passage. The Plantation Restaurant and Enfield Motel are advertised on billboards for some miles up and down Highway 301. They are further advertised on the radio and in the newspapers. The Court said: "Since these facts make it clear that the Plantation Restaurant 'serves or offers to serve interstate travelers,' it must be held that the restaurant is a 'place of public accommodation' within the meaning of Section 201 (b)(2) and (c)(2) of the Civil Rights Act of 1964. . . . Accordingly, the writ of certiorari is granted, the judgments are vacated, and the cause remanded for dismissal of the indictments."[16]

22. The March on Washington Sparks Events in Enfield

From Reed Johnson's unsuccessful campaign for city commissioner in the spring of 1963 to the picketing of the Plantation Restaurant in August, the town of Enfield had been caught in an unprecedented emotional storm. The protests, marches, and demands for justice had unleashed waves of repressed outrage and hurt in our small community and in hundreds of other Black communities across the South. At the end of the historical summer of 1963, Black leaders of national civil rights organizations proposed a March on Washington. They urged the people who had protested in local communities to bring their cause to Washington to seek redress. The proposal generated great excitement in Enfield. Both young and old expressed their readiness to march on Washington. Everyone wanted to go. Mae Cofield, my mother, firmly announced her intention to board the bus in a meeting at the Cofield Funeral Home. Standing from her seat near the front of the chapel, she said, "Everyone is talking about getting freedom for the children. I want you to know that I want some of this freedom for myself." This determined freedom fighter became one of the first individuals to reserve a seat on Enfield's bus to Washington.

Robert Blow and Marie Davis, the two organizers the NAACP sent to guide us in using nonviolent, direct action, helped fill two big Carolina Trailways buses (Fig. 22.1). Although mostly young people made the trip, Reed Johnson, Lillie Cousins Smith, Tyler Vaughn, Mary Ellen Howington Lewis, Victoria Howington, Jennie Delores Ward, Mae Cofield, Madgie Boone, and a few other adults, accompanied the delegation from Enfield on Wednesday, August 28, 1963. Madgie Boone and Mae Cofield were probably the oldest of the Enfield protesters.

Photographers of the event caught the two women making history, striding together down the Washington Mall. On the evening before the march, a bee stung my four-year-old daughter, Tanya, just over her left eye and by nightfall the eye was swollen shut. Although I had expected to be among the marchers, I did not go to the historical event. Instead, I stayed home, took Tanya to the doctor, and watched the grand spectacle on television. Thousands upon thousands of people from all over the nation marched for freedom on that historic day.

When Reed returned home about midnight, he tried to describe to me the events of the day and the sense of excitement and widespread support that the Enfield delegation had experienced. He said that it had looked as if everyone on Routes 301 and 1 was headed to the March. At the sight of each bus, van, and auto that joined the caravan to Washington, the Enfield contingent's

Fig. 22.1. Enfield protesters at the March on Washington join the fervent singing. / *The Day They Marched*, ed. Doris Saunders (1963).

feelings of anticipation had mounted. As the bus crawled along the crowded highway, the young passengers could hardly contain their impatience at the bus's slow speed and interminable starts and stops.

Lerone Bennett, Jr., a member of the staff of *Ebony* magazine, described the March on Washington in the opening of his unforgettable essay, "The March":

It was the beginning of something, and the ending of something.

It came 100 years and 240 days after the signing of the Emancipation Proclamation. It came like a force of nature. Like a whirlwind, like a storm, like a flood, it overwhelmed by its massiveness and finality.

A quarter of a million people were in it, and of it, and millions more watched on TV and huddled around radios. There had never been anything quite like it. A TV spectacular, a Sunday school picnic, a political convention, an impressive display of Negro unity, a "visible expression of interracial brotherhood," an almost unprecedented exhibition of resolve, a new concept of lobbying, a living petition, a show of strength, an outburst, a call to the national conscience: the mammoth March on Washington was everything they said it was and more; and it moved men and women as they had never been moved before.[17]

Fig. 22.2. Doris Johnson Daniels (1942–2023) joined the Enfield protest and suffered injuries in the downtown confrontation on August 31, 1963. / 2022, Courtesy of Tichanda Thompson.

Fig. 22.3. Laura Cousar, stalwart and courageous protestor, defied Enfield's nine o'clock whistle on August 31, 1963. / Peggy McIntosh, photographer, 1994.

For three hours, they heard speakers demand passage of a Civil Rights Bill and immediate implementation of the basic guarantees of the Declaration of Independence and the Thirteenth, Fourteenth, and Fifteenth Amendments. In Washington, the Enfield participants met young protesters from many parts of the USA. They heard stories of struggle and protest in other communities. They joined hundreds of thousands of people, some of them white, in a clarion call for justice and equal rights. In numerous informal conversations, marchers told their stories of the battles they were waging in their home communities. The brave little band of Enfield protesters found that they were not alone, but part of a powerful surge of people all fired up, ready to change America.

Some of the young Enfield women, including Doris Johnson Daniels (Fig. 22.2), Laura Cousar (Fig. 22.3), and Jennie Ward (Fig. 22.4), heard other demonstrators describe unusual tactics they used when confronting the police in their home communities. To increase the police officers' work, these marchers described an effective response of going limp and lying down in the street. They were assured that this strategy greatly increased and prolonged the work of the police, who then must lift and carry the immobile person to the place of confinement. On the bus back to Enfield, these young women spoke eagerly of their intent to use this new strategy the next time that they were arrested during a protest.

Fig. 22.4. Feisty Jennie Ward brought energy and commitment to the Enfield movement. / Courtesy of Jennie Ward, 2023.

Fig. 22.5. Bud Albert Whitaker joined the Enfield protest at a very young age. He sat on Enfield's board of commissioners from 1991 to 2003. / Peggy McIntosh, photographer.

To the dismay of some occupants of the Enfield bus, one individual, young Bud Albert, remained so fired up from the day's events that he sang freedom songs all the way home (Fig. 22.5). The weary travelers, who had started the trip long before dawn and had spent the day walking, singing, listening, and trying to digest the contents of the historic March, were looking forward to restful sleep on the bus trip home. Bud just could not settle down but continued his musical protest until they arrived in Enfield, a short while before midnight.

The high energy and elevated spirits set the tone for a raucous meeting at Cofield Funeral Home, on the morning of August 31, the Saturday following the March on Washington. With few exceptions, prior to the trip to Washington, the student protesters had respected the town's restrictive picketing ordinance and adults had replaced youth on the picket lines. But the spirit of the day dictated that we abandon this precaution. Previously, Enfield people had been reluctant to go to jail, but on that Saturday morning when Robert Blow asked how many of them wanted to picket and possibly go to jail, dozens of hands—young and old—flew into the air.

Alive in our defiance, I was one of the drivers who transported the youth to downtown stores—Cuthrell's Department Store and Beavans' Drug Store on Whitaker Street and McPhail's Store on Railroad Street. At least two twelve-year-olds, Alice Evans and Deborah Jones, numbered among those who boarded a car in the parking lot for the short ride to downtown Enfield.

In those days, Saturday found the streets of downtown Enfield crowded with people. Whole families came to town for the week's groceries, to buy new clothing, to meander through the shops, to eat hot dogs and drink Pepsi-Colas, and, most of all, to see and chat with friends. My husband said that once, he was a passenger on a train passing through Enfield, and a conductor pointed to the sidewalks of Enfield and told him, "You should see this town on Saturday. It looks abandoned now, but it is jammed with people on Saturday."

On that unforgettable last Saturday in August 1963, the protest lines, filled with young and adult picketers, added another spectacle. The Black shoppers and bystanders understood exactly what the picketers were protesting. When police patrolling the downtown streets became aware of the presence of protesters under the age of eighteen, they began enforcing the local law, handcuffing the youth, and escorting them across the railroad tracks to the town jail. At the same time, several of the officers struggled to arrest non-compliant young women protesters who sank to the ground when the police approached them. These defiant young women found themselves half-lifted then dragged the distance from the picket line to the town jail. Many suffered painful scrapes, cuts, and bruises.

In midafternoon, police began booking all individuals without regard to age. Not very long after the protesters were locked in cells, Thomas and Curtis Cofield, my father and uncle, went to the police station and bailed out the offenders (Fig. 22.6). Those of us in cars waited around the corner and as soon as individuals were released, we transported the offenders back to the staging area at the Cofield Funeral Home on Pope Street. Here they grabbed new signs, boarded a waiting car, and a driver took them back downtown. There they rejoined those who were protesting.

When the police realized that they were arresting the same offenders over and over, the police chief ordered the booking officer to deny bail to all offenders. By six o'clock, the jail was jammed with youthful protesters, older picketers, and many of the adult leaders. Word of the mass arrests spread quickly from the center of town to the Black neighborhoods and into the surrounding countryside. That evening, hundreds of Black people poured into downtown Enfield. They crowded onto the sidewalks in front of Rose's Five and Ten Cent Store and the Bank of Enfield. All eyes were fixed upon the two-story building across the railroad tracks which held the town jail, where dozens of their children, friends, and neighbors stood elbow to elbow behind bars in musty, hot cells (Fig. 22.7).

Fig. 22.6. Thomas Cofield hosted meetings of the Enfield protesters at his funeral home and bailed them from jail when they were arrested (ca. 1963). / Mae Cofield Family Collection.

The town authorities called for additional help, and soon the blue and white cars of state troopers sped into town. Word went out to local whites as well, and the police chief increased his department's firepower by deputizing additional white men. The town officials blew the Saturday night whistle ordering us to leave the sidewalks of Enfield and go home. Instead, the crowd sang out, "We shall not be moved!"

The town's authorities blew the whistle a second time. The singing grew louder and more defiant. We were singing to those who blew the whistle and the white supremacy they represented. We were singing to the clerks in Rose's Five and Ten Cents Store, who made us wait while they served white customers; to the employees and owners of Harrison's Drugstore where we could not buy a coke at the fountain and sit at a table and drink it; to the Bobbitt Brothers, who locked their restroom doors to Black people, even those whose tanks they had just filled with gas. We sang to the many white landowners who insisted that Black children miss weeks from school to pick cotton and shake peanuts. Deep resentment and hurt powered our unmuted Black voices declaring that we would not heed the hated whistle. Not one person left the streets.

In desperation, the town officials brought out the one fire truck that the town owned, and its all-white volunteer fire department repeated what had become common practice on streets throughout the South. They drove the

100 Negroes Arrested In Enfield Race Issue

By ALLEN PAUL

ENFIELD, N.C. (AP)—Police spent most of the day Saturday hauling about 100 Negroes, protesting alleged job discrimination, from a variety store picket line.

Though a major protest march had been planned, Enfield was spared the violence ignited during a similar demonstration a week ago.

Five Negroes took their position on a picket line in front of Rose's variety store shortly after noon. They were the first of those to be taken into custody.

About half of those taken from the picket lines were juveniles. They were released without charges after police took their names. The others were charged with violating a month-old ordinance aimed at racial demonstrations. They were freed under $200 bond each.

The ordinance forbids minors from taking part in protest demonstrations, requires that pickets maintain 15 foot intervals, and limits the number of marchers in a block.

By mid-afternoon, Enfield's small jail was overflowing. Police were arresting one group of pickets after another.

Robert Blow, 19-year-old representative of the NAACP, said the Rose store was being picketed because it discriminates against Negroes in its hiring practices.

He said the new ordinance and weeks of fruitless negotiations with Enfield's Bi-Racial Committee brought the demonstration which resulted in violence a week ago.

Four policemen were injured slightly last Saturday night when they were hit by objects thrown by an angry crowd of about 1,200 demonstrators.

Police fought back with the town's only fire truck and two high pressure hoses.

Gen. Capus Waynick, Gov. Sanford's troubleshooter in racial matters, was unable to break the deadlock between whites and Negroes when he visited here Wednesday and talked to both sides.

JOHNSON

ambassador to the United States, said that, to his knowledge, it was the most rousing reception given by the people of Helsinki to any visitor in three decades.

Visitors in that period have included the Russian victors in two Soviet-Finnish clashes at arms, the winter war of 1939-40 and the 1941-44 skirmishing in which Finland fought as an ally of Germany. Economic circumstances commit Finland to close ties with the Russians in trade. In East-West affairs, the official policy is careful neutrality.

Two years ago Soviet Premier Khrushchev visited Helsinki. He was given a respectful but cool reception by a crowd of 3,000 outside the central railroad station.

Fig. 22.7. "100 Negroes Arrested": The *Rocky Mount Evening Telegram* published a news story about the August 31 confrontation in Enfield. / John Salter collection.

truck slowly through the downtown streets, training the high-powered jets of water on the crowd of people, forcing them against walls, into alleyways, and knocking them down to the sidewalk. They sent many of the protesters to the emergency room of the hospital in Rocky Mount.

Anger and rage spilled over in the Black community into the wee hours of the morning as we tried to assess the injuries and to comfort people who had been hurt. We vowed never to shop again in downtown Enfield, nor to attend the annual Firemen's Fair, which we loved and usually supported in large numbers.

23. Ninety-Day Boycott of Enfield's White-owned Businesses

Reed Johnson led our boycott on Saturdays, the traditional shopping day of many Enfield people. He organized and headed the picket lines in front of McPhail's and Cuthrell's, department stores that depended upon the trade of Black people. From September to December very few Black shoppers ventured past the picket lines and into the shops of Enfield merchants (Fig. 23.1). Cuthrell owned a large department store and two smaller shops in downtown Enfield. Despite the large number of Blacks among its customers, during the post–World War II era, the store had sponsored a float of white students in blackface in the annual fall parade.

Older Black citizens in the community remembered this public insult and revived tales of the incident to help enforce the boycott. As a result, local people began exploring grocery and department stores in nearby towns such as Rocky Mount and Roanoke Rapids.

Almost everyone in Enfield looked forward to the firemen's fair. An exciting week in the middle of the fall harvesting season, the fair grandly displayed exhibits of vegetables and plants cultivated by local 4-H clubs; pies, cakes, and preserved foods prepared by home demonstration clubs; and specimen tobacco, cotton, and peanut plants grown by area farmers. Local civic and community groups competed in exhibit booths inside a large concrete building that had been constructed during the Depression by President Roosevelt's Works Progress Administration (WPA).

A huge fenced-in area behind the building provided a site for a traveling circus featuring sideshows, games, rides, fortune-telling, and picture-taking

Fig. 23.1. Downtown Enfield, 2018. The Ninety-Day Boycott showed how much downtown businesses depended upon Black trade. / Grassroots Media Productions.

booths. My family's photo album contains many pictures of family members taken at the Enfield firemen's fair. The food at the fair was in a class alone. The Enfield firemen always sponsored a tent at which their wives sold the kind of food you could buy in downtown cafes, but the food at the fair people's tent came from a world we had only heard about. Nathan's hot dogs, dripping in mustard and ketchup and sprinkled generously with chopped onions, had a different taste from those served in the Little White Kitchen in downtown Enfield. Big puffs of pink cotton candy, popcorn scooped from the mouth-watering popcorn visible in the bottom of the glass case, and sugary lemonade, which one could sip as she beheld the amazing sights that the fair brought to town. My parents frowned upon spending money on frivolous things that vendors sold at the fair. They cautioned us children not to get caught up in the glitter and glamor. Once when my aunt gave me a dime to spend at the fair, I was laughed at and ridiculed when I got home because I had used half the money to buy a hamburger just like the ones my mother sold in the cafe.

Everyone tried to go at least one night. The evening program usually featured a high dive or some main attraction that enticed the crowd. Once there, people from the town and countryside spent the evening walking round and round the concourse, stopping occasionally to ride the Ferris wheel, buy a hot dog, try their luck at a game of chance, or chat with friends.

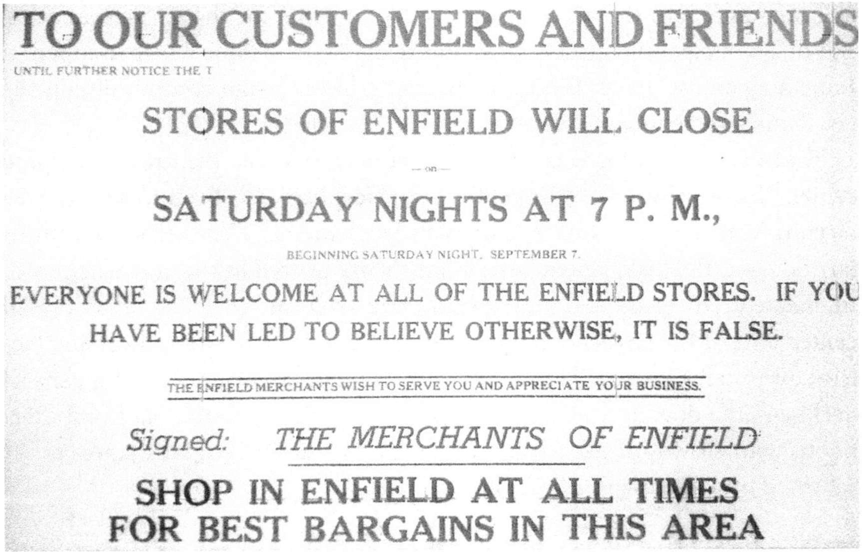

> **TO OUR CUSTOMERS AND FRIENDS**
> UNTIL FURTHER NOTICE THE T
>
> **STORES OF ENFIELD WILL CLOSE**
>
> — on —
>
> **SATURDAY NIGHTS AT 7 P. M.,**
>
> BEGINNING SATURDAY NIGHT, SEPTEMBER 7.
>
> EVERYONE IS WELCOME AT ALL OF THE ENFIELD STORES. IF YOU HAVE BEEN LED TO BELIEVE OTHERWISE, IT IS FALSE.
>
> THE ENFIELD MERCHANTS WISH TO SERVE YOU AND APPRECIATE YOUR BUSINESS.
>
> *Signed:* THE MERCHANTS OF ENFIELD
>
> **SHOP IN ENFIELD AT ALL TIMES
> FOR BEST BARGAINS IN THIS AREA**

Fig. 23.2. Enfield merchants begged Black customers to return. / Advertisement in the *Enfield Progress*, 1963.

They followed this ritual until the fair closed. The firemen, who organized the week, gave different groups a special night; thus there was a night when Black families were admitted free and a different night for white families. Saturday night was the big night, and the crowds that usually filled the downtown streets of Enfield went instead to the fairground.

But in the fall of 1963, the fair was different. The firemen who sponsored the fair had also driven the fire truck down the streets of Enfield to end the demonstration. They had seriously wounded people. The local movement worked hard to convince Black people to boycott this much-anticipated community entertainment. On the opening night of the fair, we picketed along Highway 301 in front of the fairground. We approached Black people who came on foot and tried to convince them that they should not support the firemen's event. Though we were not completely successful, the Firemen's Fair failed to attract the large crowds of Black people who usually filled the fairground. Large numbers of Black people sacrificed this beloved fun week and stayed home in protest.

The boycott of downtown stores continued through November and ended a few weeks before Christmas (Fig. 23.2). Store owners desperate for holiday business appealed to the town leaders to help them find a way to bring Black customers back into their stores. The stores hired a few Black clerks to lure shoppers into the aisles of their stores in time for the Christmas sales. But this strategy was unsuccessful, and many Black people never shopped in Enfield again. We never forgot the brutality of the white community on the last Saturday evening in August 1963.

The boycott, coupled with other social forces, doomed the town's shopping center. Historically, one of Enfield's major purposes had been to supply area farmers with fertilizer, seeds, and farm implements. The mechanization of farming and the disappearance of small farms, as well as the construction of Interstate 95, diverting the tourist trade, negatively affected Enfield as a retail center. One of the largest employers of Black people, a peanut processing factory, eventually closed. The boycott had signaled the beginning of a general decline in the downtown businesses. After August 1963, festive Saturday afternoons with crowds of people lining the streets and filling up the stores never returned to downtown Enfield.

24. Danger Signals at Inborden High School

Early in the fall of 1963, I knew that the school year would differ radically from any other school year that I had experienced. A few days after school opened, I realized that my teaching job was in jeopardy. For twelve years I had taught in the public schools of Halifax County. During the previous school year, Principal L. M. Williams had rated me an excellent teacher, but during the year of 1963–64, Principal Williams appeared to have changed his mind.

In addition to holding the respect of students and parents for my classroom teaching, I loved teaching the youth who lived in Enfield and surrounding communities. I knew many of their families and had taught their older sisters and brothers. When a new student came to my classroom that I did not know, I could describe that student to my mother, and most of the time, she could identify the student.

In addition to doing an excellent job in the classroom, I assisted in preparation of the teachers' handbook during the school year 1961–62 and chaired the school's scholarship committee. I also led the Halifax County English Curriculum Study Group and the Halifax County High School Teachers' Study Group. I represented the school at the annual meeting of the North Carolina Teachers Association in Raleigh in the fall of 1963.

I encountered difficulty early in the school year. When I went in for a scheduled conference with the principal during the fall of 1963, I questioned the old "Silence is Golden" motto on the cover of the Inborden High

Fig. 24.1. Lillie Smith and Willa Cofield (here in 2000) were the only public school teachers involved in the Enfield movement. Fifty years later, they lead freedom songs at a Cofield family gathering. / Willa Cofield personal collection.

School teacher handbook. "Negro people all over the South are standing up and speaking out," I said. "We have been silent too long." The principal and I talked about the civil rights activities that had engulfed our community. During this conversation, the principal predicted the future change in our relationship by saying that he would only "protect any teacher up to a point."

Lillie Cousins Smith and I had been lifelong friends. We both became teachers. Lillie had graduated from Winston-Salem Teachers College and taught fifth grade at Eastman School. She and Reed took the first prospective registrants to the poll after Reed declared his candidacy for the town commission. She and I stood out as the only public school teachers in the Enfield civil rights movement and later the Halifax County Voters Movement (Fig. 24.1). As employees of the Halifax County Board of Education, our jobs were vulnerable and we both knew it.

One day in early September 1963, Superintendent William Henry Overman and his assistant, Fred Young, went to visit Lillie at her school. They first talked to George Young, principal, and then summoned Lillie to the office. First, the superintendent described the role of a teacher, citing among other things that a teacher traditionally must meet certain standards of dress and behavior. He said, "You have participated in picketing during civil rights demonstrations." Lillie answered, "Yes." Then she asked the superintendent what she was accused of, since the meeting seemed to have taken on an accusatory nature and tone. The superintendent told her that her job could be terminated for various reasons under state law and he paraphrased some of the laws.

In response, the feisty teacher and civil rights leader described to the school official a conversation that she had had with Capus Waynick, a representative sent to Enfield by Governor Terry Sanford. She said that she had asked Mr. Waynick if there was a law in North Carolina that prohibited a school teacher from picketing. Mr. Waynick had replied that he knew of no such law. Superintendent Overman appeared displeased by this response.

Fred Young, the assistant superintendent, told Lillie that the county schools had lost a large grant because of her activities, and that this loss was detrimental to all of the county. He provided no details as to how the grant had been lost, what it was to have been used for, or where it might have come from. Lillie responded by saying that she was quite committed to the schools of Halifax County, that she had taught in the system for ten years when she had had attractive offers to teach elsewhere.

Ignoring this comment, the superintendent expressed concern about the violence that had occurred in Enfield the previous Saturday. Lillie responded that she shared his concern, but the violence had been committed by the police. Responding to his comment about appropriate wear for the classroom, Lillie asked him if what she was wearing that day was acceptable. He did not answer her question—she was especially well-dressed that morning—but dismissed her question and told her that the conference was over. Lillie then asked the principal, George Young, to write down the charges against her, and she returned to her classroom.

After the superintendent's visit to Eastman School, I knew that he would visit me at Inborden School. Likely because of Lillie Smith's testy response to his inquiry at Eastman School, Mr. Overman did not call me into the office when he visited Inborden School a few days later. I waited to be called into the office, but Mr. Overman spoke only with Mr. Williams, the principal. In fact, I waited in the outer office for a few minutes where I overheard part of the conversation between the superintendent and the principal. I heard the superintendent say—loudly enough to be heard in the outer office, "I just don't want the school involved!" Beginning the very next day, the principal adopted a radically different posture and our once friendly relationship changed to one of suspicion, derision, and open antipathy.

A unit to bring community speakers to my senior English class became the first battlefield. During the summer vacation, I had conceived of a classroom unit in which I would invite several local people to talk to my senior English class. Our community was rural and isolated, but there were individuals in the community whose stories, I believed, could enrich the lives of my students. Rev. Judson King, United Church of Christ minister and administrator of the Franklinton Center at Bricks, headed the list. I sometimes attended the church Rev. King pastored on the old Brick School grounds, and I found his talks instructive and inspiring. I wanted him to talk to my students about his vision for our community. I was certain that other community people would be willing to speak to my class. I could see students asking questions and learning from people in the community who were not credentialed as teachers but who had traveled to foreign countries, developed businesses, who had lived lives of dignity and courage, and who could teach young people.

When I described my plan to the principal a few days after the superintendent's conference, he immediately objected. He refused to discuss my idea and made it clear that I should go no further in developing this project. In prior years, I had experienced a quite different reception when I asked Mr. Williams for permission to initiate a new project. When I approached him with the idea of starting a school newspaper, he had welcomed the suggestion. When I told him that I would like to establish an Inborden chapter of the National Honor Society, he applauded the idea. When I came up with innovative ideas about the work of the student council, he had shown enthusiasm and appreciation for my energy and resourcefulness.

The principal held midfall conferences with individual teachers with the expressed purpose of "clarifying questions that teachers may have about the entire school program." At my conference I asked questions about free lunches for students ("Why don't we have them?"), about a statement in the teachers' handbook admonishing teachers to "be quiet," and the project for community people to speak to my senior English class. My work in the civil rights movement had emboldened me.

Looking back, I can see that my own level of political consciousness, as well as my world view, was changing because of the movement in our community. My vision of our community and the principal's vision differed sharply. My experience of picketing, telephoning, soliciting participation in our movement, and meeting civil rights leaders like Floyd McKissick had profoundly changed me. I began to see hope for our community, change that would improve the status of Black people, and I began to accept responsibility for my own ability to help bring change about. When my students Evon Anderson, Marshall Harvey,

Fig. 24.2. Mary Hill knew the hardships of sharecropping. Mary (right), her daughter, and Willa participate in a neighborhood clean-up drive, 1978. / *Halifax County This Week*, April 27, 1978.

and others showed the courage to challenge racial segregation in the public library, I felt compelled to support them. They were demonstrating the lessons in courage that we had talked about in my classes. I was learning to respect many poorly educated, downtrodden people. I found that many of them had intellectual gifts that exceeded my own. I had just been more fortunate to have parents who could send me to college. I was learning that people lived in poor circumstances, not because they had inherited some inferior genes, but they and I were at the bottom of a cruel system that limited their chances to live a decent life. Mr. Williams was too closely allied to the existing system to expose himself to changes that threatened the old way.

Later, I was to meet a Black Bottom resident who told me of the cruelties of the life of tenant farm families. Mary Hill told me that she had been raised in a sharecropping family (Fig. 24.2). To meet the demands of the landlord, the girls had been forced to do all kinds of farmwork. In return, they had few comforts and went without basic needs. The landlord family had a little girl the same age as Mary, and in the fall, the mother took the young child and Mary to shop in Rocky Mount to get the white child ready for school—dresses, shoes, underclothing, and so on. Mary, who was taken along, watched, but was never the recipient of anything. Mary said to me,

"Even though I was a young child, I knew it was wrong. We did all the work on the farm, and she never bought anything for me."

I had many children like Mary in my classes. One of my important responsibilities was to keep track of their attendance at school. My attendance register, which was approved early in the year by an inspector from the state and later by a committee of fellow teachers, became a source of harassment. In January, I received an official memo from the principal criticizing a few entries I had made in pencil in the register. This was a harsh reprimand for a minor oversight. I inked in the few words that had been written in pencil, but the principal withdrew his signature.

The principal also began stressing the significance of teacher hall duty, a requirement that teachers stand in the hall between classes. I had always found following this regulation difficult, a practice that the principal had obviously noticed. Often the bell rang before matters in my classes ended. During the brief period before the bell for the next class, I tried to respond to students with questions and complete last-minute preparations before the next class filed in. I found this directive to put everything aside to stand in the doorway of my class grossly inconvenient. I usually complied with the requirement, but not cheerfully.

I felt that I was playing a role in a drama whose ending I already knew. I recognized the pattern, for I had seen other teachers scapegoated and demeaned before they were released. I tried to follow all the rules and change the ending, but sadly, the relationship between the principal and me continued to deteriorate during the 1963–64 school year.

25. BREAKING THE BACK OF RACISM AT THE BALLOT BOX

Fig. 26.1. John Salter (ca. 1970s) sought to break the back of racism in eastern North Carolina. / John Salter Collection.

26. The Halifax County Voters Movement

A sense of prudent restraint and somber watchfulness pervaded our community when, just after Christmas in 1963, a new organizer, John Salter (a.k.a. Hunter Gray), came to town (Fig. 26.1). Raised in Flagstaff, Arizona, in those days John identified as white, but later he declared himself a half-blood Micmac/Penobscot Indian.

John had taught sociology at Tougaloo College in Mississippi and worked with civil rights leader Medgar Evers. In his book, *Jackson, Mississippi*, John recorded his experiences as chief strategist in the Jackson civil rights struggle (Fig. 26.2).

Fig. 26.2. Classic photo of John Salter and Tougaloo College students at lunch counter in Jackson, Mississippi, 1963. / John Salter Collection.

Upon coming to Enfield, where active protests had ceased following the boycott, John met first with Lillie Cousins Smith and Reed Johnson. He told the two Enfield leaders that he was a field organizer for the Southern Conference Educational Fund (SCEF).[18] This civil rights organization was established in 1946 as the educational arm of the Southern Conference for Human Welfare. It became a separate organization in 1947 and directed most of its activities from a New Orleans office. James Dombrowski, staff director for SCEF, was one of the founders of the Highlander School, the renowned center of social justice leadership training and incubator of the civil rights movement. Rosa Parks attended Highlander in the summer of 1955, and Martin Luther King also participated in meetings at Highlander Center. Aubrey Williams, who once directed Franklin Roosevelt's Works Progress Administration (WPA), served as president of SCEF. During the 1950s, Dombrowski and Williams established SCEF as a leading proponent of civil rights and integration in the South. Mary McLeod Bethune once served on SCEF's board, and Ella Baker held a position as field organizer during John Salter's tenure with the organization in the 1960s.

John said that he would do his very best to secure some voter registration specialists for Enfield and Halifax County. He said that he would also endeavor to find out what could be done with respect to getting the registration books opened for much lengthier periods of time than is now the case. After a meeting with leaders of the Enfield movement, John proposed that we work with other communities in the county to mount a strong Halifax County voter registration drive. His proposal was supported by statistics reported in the US Census of 1960. Of the 58,000 people in Halifax County, approximately 26,000 people were white and approximately 32,000 Negro. A total of 15,406 whites (59 percent of the white population) were registered. Only 1,954 Negroes (6 percent of the Negro population) had their names on the voter registration books.[19]

Salter offered to work as an organizer in our community to help register the thousands of unregistered Black people. He was the first European American who offered to help us, and there was some skepticism. After several informal conversations, the local leaders decided to welcome John Salter into the Enfield movement. Salter soon earned our respect and trust.

The intense, thirty-year-old organizer told us of his harrowing experiences in Jackson, Mississippi. Assailants had once fired shots into his home and at a different time, his car had been forced off the road into a terrible accident. His friend, Rev. Edwin King, chaplain at Tougaloo College, had been critically injured in the accident. To protect his wife, Eldri, and their little three-year-old daughter, Maria, John rented living quarters in Raleigh and made the seventy-mile trip to Enfield every day. Often, he returned to his home in Raleigh late at night taking back roads through treacherous Klan country. John was an avid member of the National Rifle Association (NRA), saying that it was imperative that Black people in the South and their advocates own firearms.

In Enfield, where no white person paid a social visit to a Black home, his frequent stops at the home of Lillie Smith and our home on Whitaker Street shocked our neighbors. John frequently sat at our table and ate meals that I prepared for the family. This practice alone blatantly defied local taboos. Enfield white people never ate at the same table with Blacks. I only knew of one white person, a local cop who grew up in the less rigidly segregated town of Beaufort, North Carolina, who dared come into our home and sit down for a friendly chat. In those days, John was a chain smoker and drank numerous half cups of coffee during a two-hour visit while we discussed strategy or planned a new protest.

John's visits to our homes must have rankled the white community. Throughout the months he worked in eastern North Carolina, questions were raised about who he really was and why he was helping Black people. S. H. Conger of Weldon wrote to the *Enfield Progress*:

Why have our Negro citizens never asked why these outsiders are allegedly "helping" them? One of these outsiders who has been in our County is John R. Salter, Jr. Salter is listed on the masthead of "The Southern Patriot" as a Field Organizer of the Southern Conference Educational Fund (SCEF). "The Southern Patriot" is cited in the list of communist and communist front publications on Page 200 of "Guide to Subversive Organizations..."[20]

John owned an old Underwood typewriter which he often used to write letters throughout his eighteen-month stay in Enfield and Halifax County. Sitting at our small dining room table, John often cranked out a single-spaced letter with three copies of onion-skin paper. I never saw him make an erasure, and the letters never had errors. He was smart, focused, fearless.

Many years later in a phone call from Pocatello, Idaho, where he lived his last years, he confided to me that his children told him that in their opinion, there was absolutely nothing that he was afraid of. Certainly, coming into eastern North Carolina to "break the back of racism" in 1963 supported his children's belief. Inevitably, when he left my home, he would extend his hand in a warm handshake and say with great conviction, "Willa, we're going to win!"

In the winter of 1964, in the office of the Enfield Flower Shop, which served as the Enfield movement's headquarters, we organized the Halifax County Voters Movement (HCVM). In an interview many years later, John said that present for that momentous occasion were Reed and Willa Johnson, Tyler Vaughn, himself, and Mrs. Gee, a fine woman who lived in the Daniels Chapel area.[21] I knew Mrs. Gee as mother of the lovely Gee children whom I had taught at Inborden School.

As an early organizational step, John set about finding leaders in various outlying neighborhoods and towns and bringing them into the HCVM. Even though St. Paul Baptist Church had permitted us to hold rallies in its sanctuary, the HCVM held its weekly meetings in the chapel of the Cofield Funeral Home. My father's brother, Augustus C. Cofield, former NAACP president and Weldon funeral home owner, chaired the organization (Fig. 26.3). Troy Lassiter, farmer and veteran activist of Tillery, whom I had met during my work at the Brick Rural Life School, served as cochairman.

Mrs. Doris Cochran, whose husband, Dr. Salter Cochran, had tried for years to win election to the Weldon Board of Education, served as the HCVM secretary. Mrs. Cochran, who had a fine education, was the daughter of Dean Hill, a Howard University chaplain. In meetings with white officials, she could be counted upon to speak with clarity and dignity. My husband, Reed Johnson, pioneer leader of our movement, was treasurer.

Fig. 26.3. Augustus Cofield (ca. 1960), owner of Cofield Mortuary in Weldon, chaired the Halifax County Voters Movement and challenged racism in Halifax County long before the 1960s. / Photo courtesy of Bettie Grace Cofield.

Rev. A. I. Dunlap, pastor of the A.M.E. Church in Weldon, played a leading role in the Halifax County Voters Movement. Once the president of Kittrell College, he had seen active duty in Danville, Virginia, and other sites of the civil rights movement before he took over the ministry of the Methodist Church in Weldon. A tall man with an infectious smile, Rev. Dunlap brought experience and passion as he helped guide and nurture the grassroots organization. The fiery young minister, who when speaking often closed his eyes as if communicating with an inner presence, had the reputation of being able to move a congregation from the pews to the streets swifter than anyone else in the civil rights movement. Rev. Clyde Johnson, pastor of Weldon's First Baptist Church, often raised a strong voice of protest in meetings with white Halifax County officials. Rev. Jeremiah Webb, who was just beginning his ministerial work, brought tremendous heart and humor. The three men, along with Mrs. Cochran, together drove weekly from Weldon to Enfield to the HCVM meetings at the Cofield Funeral Home. Once, in the fall of 1964, the two ministers told us that they had been barred from participation in the regional ministers' conference because of their membership in the HCVM. From Halifax County's largest town, Roanoke Rapids, a town that once boasted that no Negro lived within its borders, John Salter recruited Jettie Purnell. A strong labor union man, Mr. Purnell became a dedicated member of the county organization.

An early list of the neighborhood and community leaders who were members of the Halifax County Voters Movement was compiled by Reed Johnson. The list included my uncle, Augustus Cofield, and my mother, Mrs. Thomas Cofield. Following their names, Reed included the addresses of some of the members.

> Mr. Troy Lassiter, Route 1, Halifax
> Mr. A. Taylor, Route 1, Box 85, Halifax
> Mr. Fred Howell, Tarboro Highway, Scotland Neck
> Rev. Spencer Williams, Scotland Neck
> Mr. Arthur Lee Jones, Scotland Neck
> Mr. Jenkins
> Mrs. Doris Cochran, Chestnut and Fourth Streets, Weldon
> Mr. Augustus Cofield, Weldon
> Rev. A. I. Dunlap, Weldon
> Rev. Clyde Johnson, First Baptist Church, Weldon
> Mr. Jasper Wilkins
> Mr. Jettie Purnell, Roanoke Rapids
> Mrs. Arlene Gee, Route 3, Box A-45, Enfield
> Mrs. Mima Johnson, Star Route, Littleton
> Rev. E. M. Westen, 63B, Enfield
> Mrs. Zelma Johnson, Star Route, Littleton
> Rev. Sinclair
> Mrs. Votie McWilliams, Enfield
> Mr. Billie Simmons, Halifax
> Mrs. Lillie M. Smith, Enfield
> Miss Ethel Beal
> Mrs. Alice Evans, Enfield
> Mrs. Thomas Cofield, Enfield
> Mrs. Reather Cofield
> Mr. P. L. Taylor, 403 West Third, Weldon

Writing in the *Southern Patriot*, John Salter said: "In February, grass-roots leaders from all over the county came together and mapped their campaign.

The representation cut across all class and economic lines—the very poorest farmers working alongside professional people. By summer every community in the county had been touched and many of the rural areas..."[22]

Soon after its organization in February 1964, Salter brought in Black politicians who had won recent offices to provide models for the Halifax County Voters Movement (HCVM). He invited Moses Reddick, who had recently won an election in Southside, Virginia, and John Winters, who had won a seat on Raleigh's city council, to speak at meetings held at St. Paul Church in Enfield. Salter himself maintained a tight speaking schedule, appearing at churches and meetings, wherever Black people gathered all over the county. He brought in two SNCC workers, J. V. Henry, who was white, and Douglass Harris, who was Black. These two young men lived in the community and joined Salter in knocking on doors and button-holing people. The organization held huge Freedom Rallies that filled the churches with people from wall to wall.

Freedom songs rang out in these churches as people poured their enthusiasm and determination into the words accompanied by clapping and many feet keeping time on the floor. Floyd McKissick, Fred Shuttlesworth, and C. T. Vivian assured us that if we kept on, if we held on, we would gain our freedom, and we believed them.

During the last year that I taught, my classroom came fully alive. Many of the students I taught attended the mass rallies and heard the eloquent civil rights orators—Floyd McKissick, Fred Shuttlesworth, Jesse Jackson—as well as many lesser-known speakers of the movement. We had so much to talk about that the bell ending the class rang too quickly.

One unforgettable night, dozens of Inborden students filled the balcony at the First Baptist Church in Weldon to hear Rev. C. T. Vivian of the Southern Christian Leadership Conference. When the audience sang the much-loved freedom song "We Shall Not Be Moved," Inborden High School students literally refused to stop singing. Every time the audience sang the last "We shall not be moved," the students inserted their own introductory, "One more time, sing it over now!" and the audience indulgently followed them. The young people sang until everyone stood and looked up to the balcony to applaud the enthusiasm of Inborden High School students.

27. The Principal Turns Up the Heat

In the spring of 1964, whenever I had fulfilled the requirements of my teaching job, I gave my full support to the countywide voter registration campaign.

My husband, Reed, had filed as a candidate for state senator, and I became a leader in the Enfield precinct, speaking at both local and county meetings. I encouraged registration at freedom schools. I served as a poll watcher at the Enfield precinct. I performed much behind-the-scenes work, making phone calls, and preparing meals for voter-registration canvassers, poll workers, and visiting students who came to help.

Meanwhile, Principal Williams embarked upon a campaign of harassment and ominous threats against me. As the second semester of the school year unfolded in January, the principal began standing beside the sign-in sheet in the school's hall every morning to assure that I entered the correct time on the time-sheet. He said that even though I signed in at the scheduled 8:00 a.m., I was late. He said that to be on time required that I sign in before 8:00, so that I could be in my classroom at 8:00 a.m. I thought this interpretation was incorrect, and I always signed in at 8:00. One morning he erased the time that I had entered and wrote "LATE." Sometimes he made X's with a red pencil beside my time entry. Even if other teachers were signing in at the same time, I was the only one that he ever checked "LATE." It was undeniably clear that he was out to get me.[23]

On January 16, 1964, Mr. Williams asked me to come to his office for a conference. He wanted to discuss my getting to school late. He pulled out the Halifax County handbook and read to me: "Teachers must spend the hours between 8:00 a.m. and 4:00 p.m. at school." Clearly, the handbook did not say that I should be in my classroom at 8:00 a.m. I could see that the principal was building an unfair case against me. I decided to take this criticism away from him, and thereafter, I made sure that I was in my classroom by 8:00 every morning.[24]

I began to feel like a pariah. In other years, I had been asked to perform many out-of-class duties. This year, I was rarely called to serve on a committee or to do anything outside my classroom. In early December 1963, the principal asked me to make up the library book order, a responsibility that I had performed the year before. That was the only out-of-class assignment that I received for the entire year. Since the principal had adopted such a negative attitude toward me, I stayed away from his office as much as possible. If any of the student organizations that I sponsored needed his approval, I sent students to make the request.[25]

At the teachers' meetings, I was tongue-lashed by implication and innuendo. Mr. Williams said that elementary teachers were not perfect, but high school teachers, since they taught older students, tried to act "grown-up." He implied that Inborden High School teachers were inefficient, backward, and irresponsible. Lunchtime was especially bad for high school teachers. Any high school teacher who did not complete lunch by 1:15 was publicly reprimanded by means of the PA system. Finally, he forbade high school teachers from eating in the lunchroom altogether. Most of us began bringing our lunches from home and eating in our classrooms.[26]

At the end of the school day on March 10, 1964, I found an envelope in my box from the principal. When I returned to my classroom and opened it, I quickly glanced through its contents. It upset me so much that I grabbed my coat and rushed home.

March 10, 1964[27]
Mrs. Willa C. Johnson
T. S. Inborden High School
Enfield, North Carolina

Dear Mrs. Johnson:

This is to inform and advise you that you are expected to abide by and adhere to the policies and regulations that govern the operation of the school just as any other teacher is expected to do.

I have reminded you of the following:

1. Being late for game duty on December 2, 1964 [sic].

2. Failing to report to work on time and a conference was held with you January 6, 1964 regarding being late for work.

3. Failing to do ground duty the week of February 3–7, 1964.

4. Failing to give a written explanation as requested for not attending a PTA meeting on February 5, 1964.

5. Failing to do building duty the week of March 2–6, 1964.

6. Failing to stand at your door when students change classes.

7. Failing to see that cabinets in your room were clean and free of fire hazard.

A copy of this information is being submitted to the superintendent for his suggestions or recommendations regarding this matter.

Yours respectfully,
L. M. WILLIAMS, Principal
cc:
W. Henry Overman
R. L. Coppage[28]

I immediately informed my husband, John Salter, Lillie Smith, and other leaders of the movement about the memo. That evening we huddled in our living room and agreed that the other shoe had finally dropped. Although the charges did not appear to be grounds for firing a teacher whom the principal had rated excellent the previous school year, a copy of the charges was being sent to the superintendent and to the district committee. The memo confirmed our worst fears. The movement leaders immediately concluded that the principal was building a paper trail to document my dismissal. We ended the session with the agreement that the next day I would act as if nothing had changed. I would not confront the principal.

They were going to fire me.

The next morning when I entered the school, the principal sat on a table with a direct view of the door through which we teachers made our morning entry. I could see that he was primed for a fight. A large man, he sat on the table swinging his legs and glaring at me as I entered. I simply said, "Good morning," signed in, and walked swiftly to my classroom at the north end of the hall.

To respond to the March 10 memorandum from Principal Williams, John Salter and the leaders of our movement decided to fill the auditorium with parents, friends and members of the HCVM at the next PTA meeting. We asked everyone we knew to come. On the evening of that meeting, parents, students, and community people joined the principal and faculty for the monthly meeting in the Inborden gymtorium. There were about five times more people than usually attended the PTA meeting. In a carefully worded talk delivered in a slow, deliberate manner, Salter promised that if any teacher participating in the movement was fired, the Board of Education and other parties would be sued for hundreds of thousands of dollars in federal court.[29]

The state of North Carolina had adopted a very clever way of keeping its teachers under tight control. North Carolina provided no tenure system for teachers. A few years earlier, its employment practices had changed so that teacher contracts were valid for only one year. If the Board of Education no longer needed a teacher's services, it did not have to fire her; it simply did not issue the teacher a contract to work the next year.

My scheduled spring conference to find if I wished to be nominated for employment for the next year fell soon after the April PTA meeting. The conference differed sharply from any exchange that Mr. Williams and I had had during the previous seven months. The principal smiled, spoke cordially, and asked, "Why would you imagine that I would not recommend you for a teaching job for next year?" Since I had been so perturbed, he had written a memorandum of reassurance.[30]

> Memo of March 31, 1964
> Mrs. Willa C. Johnson
> T. S. Inborden High School
> Enfield, North Carolina
>
> Dear Mrs. Johnson:
>
> I have seen improvement in the areas mentioned in the letter of March 10, 1964. It is hopeful that improvement will continue.
> I am recommending you for re-election for a teacher for the 1964–1965 school term on condition that you continue to show improvement in the areas mentioned in the letter dated March 10, providing that the District School Committee, Board of Education, and the Superintendent approves [sic] of my recommendations.
>
> Sincerely yours,
> L. M. WILLIAMS
> Principal[31]
>
> LMW:hcc
> W. H. Overman
> R. L. Coppage

I no longer believed that I would be fired. I felt greatly relieved that our strategy appeared to have worked. The principal and I resumed our earlier pleasant relationship, and I continued doing my best work in the classroom and immersing myself in the affairs of the voter registration movement.

28. The Voter Registration Campaign

Because appealing to the higher nature of Halifax County whites seemed a slow, laborious, if not futile path, the Halifax County Voters Movement (HCVM) put most of its emphasis upon awakening the Black voter and building political power at the polls. In the early spring of 1964, the HCVM began a strong voter registration campaign with the goal of registering as

Fig. 28.1. Fred Shuttlesworth led a Freedom Rally at Weldon church to get people to register to vote, ca. 1960. / Library of Congress.

many of the thousands of unregistered Halifax County Black people as possible before the May primary election. Fred Shuttlesworth, militant minister from Birmingham, Alabama, and current president of SCEF, spoke at the First Baptist Church in Weldon on May 13, 1964 (Fig. 28.1). Youth and adults from all over Halifax County filled the downstairs sanctuary and overflowed into the balcony. The *Daily Herald*'s report said that Shuttlesworth told the audience: "The suppression of Negroes in this area (Halifax County and eastern North Carolina) mirrors the situation in Birmingham." John Salter urged the resisters to "forge ahead in the battle against segregation." Praising the group's vocal enthusiasm, he said, "This is just the beginning . . . we have other programs planned for the summer and fall. [You must] Use action rather than words . . . it is nice to sing about these things . . . but you have to take action."[32]

The HCVM organized a door-to-door campaign encouraging Black Halifax County citizens to vote in the May 30 primary election (Fig. 28.2). The organization asked its members to canvass their neighborhoods and to speak personally with Black citizens. At that time, the requirement for registration

Fig. 28.2. Freedom Day, Saturday May 2, 1964, was the first day registration books were open. / Willa Cofield personal collection.

to vote as established in North Carolina laws included the following provision: "Every person presenting himself for registration shall be able to read and write any section of the Constitution of North Carolina in the English language. It shall be the duty of such registrar to administer the provisions of this section."[33]

Registrars had broad authority in determining the literacy of the prospective voter. Although the election law stated explicitly that the literacy test consisted of reading and writing a section of the North Carolina Constitution, registrars had been known to test an applicant's knowledge of other matters. While the contents of the test varied, sometimes registrars asked Black people to pass examinations that called for sophisticated knowledge of the structure and function of government. Some determined Blacks seeking to register made numerous unsuccessful efforts to pass the registration test. Dr. Marcellus Barksdale described the experience of Mrs. Maggie Garris in neighboring Northampton County. This sixty-five-year-old woman attempted to register seven times before finally succeeding.[34]

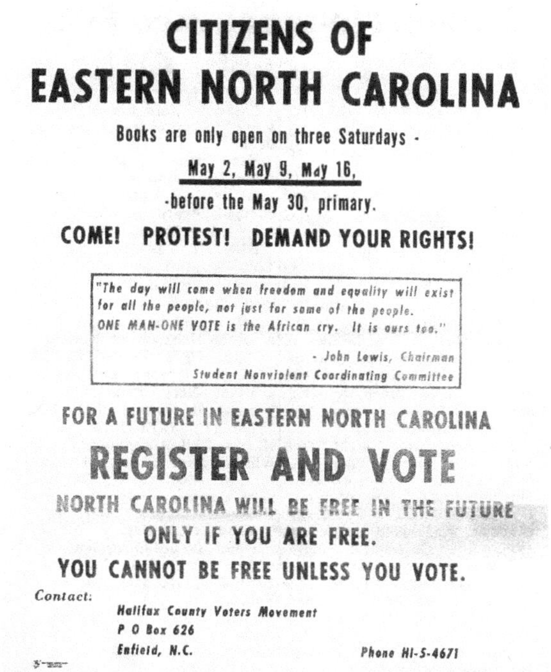

CITIZENS OF EASTERN NORTH CAROLINA

Books are only open on three Saturdays -
May 2, May 9, May 16,
-before the May 30, primary.
COME! PROTEST! DEMAND YOUR RIGHTS!

> "The day will come when freedom and equality will exist for all the people, not just for some of the people. ONE MAN-ONE VOTE is the African cry. It is ours too."
>
> - John Lewis, Chairman
> Student Nonviolent Coordinating Committee

FOR A FUTURE IN EASTERN NORTH CAROLINA

REGISTER AND VOTE

NORTH CAROLINA WILL BE FREE IN THE FUTURE
ONLY IF YOU ARE FREE.
YOU CANNOT BE FREE UNLESS YOU VOTE.

Contact:
Halifax County Voters Movement
P O Box 626
Enfield, N.C.   Phone HI-5-4671

Fig. 28.3. The HCVM called May 2, May 9, and May 16, 1964, Freedom Days and urged people to register to vote. / Willa Cofield personal collection.

The laws, ostensibly designed to assure that voters could read and write, effectively served to keep Black people from voting. Illiterate white people were grandfathered in; that is, if one's grandfather voted before 1867, the individual did not have to take the literacy test. Although the Supreme Court outlawed the grandfather clause in 1915, in the 1960s it was widely believed that white people did not have to pass the literacy test to vote.

As required by North Carolina election law, Halifax County limited registration to a fifteen-day period, and during that period, the registrar was required to maintain open books for at least three days. Limiting the opportunity to register to this short period also operated to discourage wide participation by Black citizens in the voting process. May 2, May 9, and May 16 marked the three important dates in the spring of 1964 when people could register (Fig. 28.3). The Halifax County Voters Movement called these "Freedom Days," reminding people that voting represented a path to freedom. To those who would deter prospective registrants, the message warned, "Anyone who tries to stop a Negro from voting is committing a crime against the United States."

Eleven Negroes Are Filed For Five County Offices

Filing deadline for the May 30th Democratic Primary is only a matter of hours away, arriving at noon tomorrow, for both Halifax and Northampton counties. Registration begins May 2.

In view of this political activity came hot and heavy in Halifax County yesterday — and in a rather dramatic form.

Eleven Negroes, probably the largest slate of candidates of their race to seek political office in a single North Carolina county since Reconstruction days, filed for nearly every major political post.

The candidates, eight men and three women, were put forth by the Halifax Voter Movement, an organization currently conducting a voter registration and political action campaign in the county.

Campaign slogan for the Negroes was reported by the Movement as being, "Food, Freedom and Good Government."

Throwing the Eighth District senate seat into a four-man race was A. Reid Johnson of Enfield.

Thomas Cofield of Enfield will oppose incumbent Halifax state representative Thorne Gregory.

Another Enfield Negro, Tyler Vaughan, boosted the number of candidates running for coroner to five.

Five Negroes filed for positions as Johnson of Littleton and Mrs. Volie B. McWilliams of Enfield.

Mrs. Joyce Shearin of the Davie Community and Jeff Whitehead of Enfield, both incumbent Board members, have not filed.

EIGHTH DISTRICT SENATOR—R. M. Taylor of Roanoke Rapids, L. Taylor Oakes of Roanoke Rapids, Julian R. Allsbrook of Roanoke Rapids and A. Reed Johnson of Enfield.

COUNTY REPRESENTATIVE — Thorne Gregory of Scotland Neck, incumbent and Thomas H Cofield of Enfield,

COUNTY CORONER — W. H. Crawford of Roanoke Rapids, William Pace of Roanoke Rapids, Dr. Roy Creacy of Roanoke Rapids, Victor Burm of Roanoke Rapids and Tyler Vaughan of Enfield.

There is no incumbent, due to the death of the late Rufus Britton of Roanoke Rapids in Febrary.

Over in Northampton County there were no new developments yesterday, according to Elections Board Chairman Russell H. Johnson Jr.

Those who have filed are:
BOARD OF COMMISSIONERS — J. Guy Revelle of Conway, John E. Boone of Jackson, H. C. Bottoms of Margarettsville, John H. Liverman Jr. of Woodland and H. C. Guthrie of Garysburg, incumbents; filing opposition is John

Fig. 28.4. The Halifax County Voters Movement sponsored a slate of eleven candidates who ran on a platform of Food, Freedom, and Good Government. / *Roanoke Rapids Daily Herald*, April 16, 1964.

Then in the spring of 1964, in a stunning move, the Halifax County Voters Movement announced a slate of eleven Black men and women seeking various offices in the county and state government:

- William Alston: Halifax County School Board
- Doris Cochran: Halifax County School Board
- Thomas Cofield: North Carolina State Representative
- Reed Johnson: North Carolina State Senator
- Clyde Johnson: Halifax County Commissioner
- Mima Johnson: Halifax County School Board
- Arthur Lee Jones: Halifax County School Board

Fig. 28.5. Flyer circulated by the Halifax County Voters Movement pushed voter registration, 1964. / Willa Cofield personal collection.

- Votie McWilliams: Halifax County School Board
- Jasper Wilkins: Halifax County Commissioner
- Spencer Williams: Halifax County Commissioner
- Tyler Vaughn: Halifax County Coroner (Fig. 28.4)

A truly historical development, the Black slate represented the largest number of Black candidates to run on a single slate in the South since Reconstruction. Black political involvement in Halifax County had almost vanished at the turn of the century when the Democratic-controlled North Carolina Assembly produced an amendment to the state Constitution, approved by the public in 1900, that disenfranchised Black voters. HCVM's bold strategy surprised many residents of Halifax County. The HCVM candidates ran on a platform of "Food, Freedom, and Good Government," giving the Black community undeniable reasons to register and vote. Getting people to register who for sixty years had been excluded from the political process required a community mind change (Fig. 28.5). HCVM workers engaged in persistent door-to-door canvassing, buttonholing, phone calling, speaking in churches, and passing out flyers.

In addition to making dozens of phone calls to people in Enfield, I used my classroom to teach students the registration process. To this end, we cleared a space at the front of the room and role-played how to register to vote. The students took seriously their roles playing the arrogant registrar and the nervous applicant. After role-playing, they appreciated more the fear that many Black people had of registering to vote. I encouraged them to take this information home and instruct their parents and neighbors on how to register. Many of their parents were sharecroppers and tenants on white farms who faced censure and possible eviction by white landowners who forbade their Black workers to participate in the voters' movement.

To help in the voter registration campaign, Salter also asked Duke University students to help. Young Harry Boyte, at that time a first-year student at Duke University, was among the students who came to Halifax County. Harry's father had been the first representative of SCLC to offer help to the HCVM. Harry Boyte, the son, was an outstanding student at Duke, chairing the Duke chapter of the Congress of Racial Equality (CORE) in 1963. Young Harry graduated from Duke and went on to spend a lifetime engaging in what he described as a different kind of politics—citizen politics of empowerment, which is beyond parties and partisanship. He founded Public Achievement, an international youth political and civic empowerment movement, which operates in twenty-three countries, including the United States, Poland, Gaza and the West Bank, the Ukraine, Northern Ireland, Zimbabwe, and Japan.[35]

A few years ago, I received a letter from another former Duke University student, John Patterson, a lawyer in Sarasota, Florida. Patterson helped the HCVM with voter registration in the spring of 1964. John wrote:

Dr. Cofield,

Many years ago, I was one of the Duke students that did voter registration work in Enfield. My girlfriend at the time, and now my wife of 47 years, Nora, accompanied me several times. You and your husband were gracious hosts for several spaghetti dinners, in your home as well as being leaders of the movement . . .

We lost track after that but we have never forgotten you and all that you and your husband and many others who lived there did for the cause of justice ... My wife Nora has been in local politics now for over 20 years as an elected official and I've had a good life practicing law and supporting access to justice causes.

Best wishes for everything you have done over many years.

John Patterson, Esq.

29. County Registrars Stage Voter Registration Slowdown

Early on the morning of May 2, many prospective registrants arrived at the Enfield registrar's office, strategically located in a room across from the city jail in Enfield's municipal building. On election days, when I was a child, the sidewalk in front of the building was roped off, denying even the use of the sidewalk to disenfranchised Black people. I did not understand my father's anger when we passed the polls on an election day. On the morning of May 2, 1964, however, a long line of Blacks waiting to register filled the sidewalk and snaked through the municipal building to the door of the registrar's office.

After the registrar kept the first prospective registrants in the office for long periods of time, we realized that people would wait hours before their turn came. Telephone calls to polling places in other precincts confirmed that lines were moving slowly all over the county. Salter contacted civil rights attorneys whom he had met in Jackson, Mississippi. In the meantime, we poll watchers urged people not to leave. We told them, "You are providing important evidence of the violation of your right to register to vote by standing here. The registrars are willfully slowing down because they don't want you to register." We kept careful records of the time that people joined the line and the time they either went into the registrar's office or left the line. Despite the delaying efforts of the registrars, over five hundred Black people in Halifax County registered on that day. The leaders of the HCVM estimated that twice that number had been turned away.

On May 2, Augustus Cofield, chairman of the Halifax County Voters Movement, wired the Justice Department:

We want to formally protest with the greatest emphasis the slow-up initiated by registrars in registration of prospective Negro voters that is right now occurring in several precincts in Halifax County. Very excessive periods of time are being taken to register each person. Prime examples are in the Enfield Precinct, Weldon One and Two, among others. We hold this slow-up to be deliberately initiated in order to continue the disenfranchisement of the Negro people in the county. We call upon the state and federal governments to see to it that registration is expedited within the context of both state and federal laws.[36]

Alston v. Butts

At the beginning of the next week, several civil rights lawyers came to Enfield. In the chapel of the Cofield Funeral Home, they conferred with witnesses to the slowdown far into the night. On May 8, these lawyers, who included Samuel Mitchell, Earl Whitted, Jr., William Warner, Morton Stavis, and Arthur Kinoy, filed a complaint with Judge John D. Larkins in the US District Court for the Eastern District of North Carolina. In the complaint, known as *Alston v. Butts*, they charged:

> [S]hortly after it became known that a substantial number of Negro residents of Halifax County will seek to register to be able to vote in the primary election on May 30, 1964, the Defendant Rom Parker (attorney for the Halifax County Board of Elections and owner of the Levon Theatre) and the defendant precinct registrars, and other persons to the plaintiffs unknown, entered into a plan, agreement, and conspiracy willfully and with intent, under the color of state law, statutes, constitution, custom, policy, and authority to deprive the plaintiffs and the Negro citizens of Halifax County of rights, privileges, and immunities granted to them as citizens of the United States and in particular, the 14th and 15th amendments...[37]

They charged that precinct registrars had undertaken a general slowdown of the registration process, taking an average of fifteen to twenty minutes, and sometimes twenty-five or thirty minutes, to register individual Negro applicants, thereby keeping long lines of Negroes waiting for registration, and closing the office at sundown, with large numbers of Negroes unregistered and turned away. They said that arrangements had been made to register white applicants at a location away from the polling place at a more convenient time and place unknown to the plaintiffs.

The complaint also alleged that registrars had required that Black applicants write out entire sections and read long, complicated parts of the

Constitution while white applicants were either not required to read at all or given simple sections of the Constitution to read and write. Regardless of the number of prospective registrants, the registrars had refused to permit more than one person to register at the same time and insisted that only one applicant could enter the registration room.

Deloris English was one of the persons whom the lawyers interviewed. She said that when she arrived at the Registrar's Office, she found the hallway filled with Black people.

> I waited in line until closing time because it [the line] moved so slowly, but I still did not get a chance to register. Many people left the line because it moved so slowly. Many people came to register but didn't even get in the line because it was so slow. I went back to the police station at 7:45 p.m. Tuesday, May 5. I stood in the line until the office closed at 9:45 p.m., but I still did not get to the registrar. Most of the people became very tired while waiting. Nearly all of the people trying to register were Negro. There were hardly any white people.[38]

Mrs. Barbara Eatmon, who resided in Enfield, said that when she arrived at the polling place at the Enfield Police Station at 11:00 a.m. on the morning of May 2, 1964, twenty-five people had already lined up. She stayed in line until 2:30 p.m., when she had to leave. She returned on the night of May 7, when she successfully registered. Mrs. Eatmon said she saw no white people applying for registration while she was there.[39]

Elderly Mrs. Lottie Pittman, grandmother of student protester Eldon Pittman, also attempted to register on May 2, at the Enfield polling place. She said,

> The line was moving so slow and there were so many people ahead of me that I left about 2:30 PM when it was obvious that I would not be reached. I went back Tuesday night, May 5, about 7:45 PM. I waited until 9:30 PM, and still I was not reached. I went back Thursday, May 7th, and this time I was finally registered. When I registered, Mr. Dickens was permitting two people to register at the same time.[40]

Reed Johnson reported that 113 people had come to the Enfield polling place, but only forty-one persons, all but one of them Negro, had successfully registered. He said that large numbers of Negroes had come to the police station to register but, seeing the long line, had turned away. He said that the long delays had nothing to do with whether the applicant was qualified.

During the three sessions, the books had been opened, only one Negro had been turned away because of literacy. He charged that white applicants were not subjected to the literacy test and that precinct registrars arranged for white applicants to register in the registrar's home.[41]

Black applicants in other Halifax County towns faced similar discouraging tactics when they attempted to register on May 2. Ernest Leach, Jr., a resident of Roanoke Rapids's precinct seven, said that when he went to Butt's (old) Store, which was being used as the place of registration, he was third in line, excluding the person who was being registered. He waited in line for an hour after which the registrar gave him a fairly long section of the North Carolina State Constitution to write. After Mr. Leach was successfully registered, he went to pick up three other people, and, returning, he found the person who had entered the office after him, still in the registrar's office. Shortly thereafter, the registrar left, and the office remained closed for ninety minutes. His wife, who was third in line, waited another ninety minutes before she could enter the office.[42]

At 9:15 a.m. on May 2, Vivian Mima Johnson found no one at the Aurelian Springs polling place to register anyone. She found the registrar in the back of a store across the street. She said that the registrar, Mr. Reed Warren, set himself up in the back of the store to register people. Mrs. Johnson recorded the names of all the applicants and the time each person spent in the registration process. Of the sixteen applicants, registration times ranged from six to sixty minutes. She said that when white applicants approached the registrar, he spoke quietly to them and they left.[43]

Dr. Salter Cochran, a practicing physician in Weldon and husband of Mrs. Doris Cochran, HCVM secretary, served as a poll watcher at Weldon Precinct #2 Poll from 3:30 p.m. to 6:45 p.m. on May 2. When he arrived, he found fifteen people waiting to register, and he brought two prospective registrants. During his stay, he said, "It took from twenty-five to forty minutes for each [applicant] to be registered." When the office closed, he said there were a "number of people who were not reached."[44]

In response to the complaint, on May 8, Judge Larkins issued the following order:

> It is therefore ordered that the defendants, precinct registrar, their agents, servants, and employees and persons acting in concert with them are hereby temporarily restrained from directly or indirectly adopting and pursuing a course of conduct by which more time qualifying Negro applicants for registration is spent than is the case with White applicants,

Halifax Registration Speed-Up Is Ordered

TRENTON — An order to speed up registration of Negro voters in Halifax County was signed here Friday night by U. S. District Judge John D. Larkins Jr.

He took the action on the basis of a complaint filed under the Civil Rights Act.

The temporary restraining order is returnable before Judge Larkins in the Wilson Division of Eastern District Court at 4 p m. on May 13.

He decreed that Halifax registration officials "are hereby temporarily restrained from directly or indirectly pursuing a course of conduct by which more time qualifying Negro applications for registration is spent than is the case of white applicants."

A time limit of five minutes was directed for qualifying any applicant for registration.

The order further directed: "Whenever it appears that applicants to register are in line, to permit three applicants to be processed for registration at the same time.

"To give immediate notice of a public nature of the places where applicants may register on week days other than Saturday and Sunday up to and including May 16, 1964, such places to be a place other than the residence of the registrar, to be fixed with the approval of the County Board of Elections and to be at a place convenient to the electorate in such precinct.

"That whenever it shall appear that waiting time to register is more than 30 minutes, that one or more assistant registrars be designated to register applicants to vote.

In signing the order, Judge Larkins, referring to supporting affidavits, said it appeared to the court that "defendants have been engaging and continue to engage in a course of conduct which discriminately deprives Negroes in Halifax County to register to vote causing immediate and irreparable injury, loss and damage to the plaintiffs."

Judge Larkins declared it further appeared that "a temporary restraining order restraining such acts would be granted without notice or hearing in view of the shortness of time in which registration is permissible under North Carolina law."

The complaint noted a 1960 Halifax County population of 58,000, including 26,000 whites and 32,000 Negroes, with 15,406 white registered voters and 1,954 Negroes.

The complaint alleged that Negro candidates will be deprived of being voted for by large segments of the community.

See HALIFAX, Page Two

Fig. 29.1. Judge John D. Larkins issues injunction against Halifax County registration officials, ordering them not to take more time with Negro voters than with whites. Report in the Raleigh *News and Observer*, May 9, 1964.

and in any event barring any defendant precinct registrar from spending more than 5 minutes qualifying any applicant for registration, and it is further ordered that the said defendant precinct registrars, their agents, servants and employees and persons acting in concert with them are temporarily ordered:

(a) Whenever it appears that applicants to register are in line, to permit three applicants to be processed for registration at the same time.

(b) To give immediate notice of a public place where applicants may register on weekdays other than Saturday and Sunday.[45] (Fig. 29.1)

On May 9, large numbers of applicants, poll watchers and HCVM workers gathered at the polls. Lillie Cousins Smith[46] reported that at 11:40 a.m., Robert Shields, chairman of the Halifax County Board of Elections, came into the Enfield Police Station and read aloud the following statement that he had written out:

> Judge Larkins has ordered, as of today, the Applicant be given 5 minutes to complete his registration. If not completed in 5 minutes, he or she will be entitled to try again at a later date or appeal to the Halifax County Board of Elections. The polling place will be open from 9 a.m. to sunset each day next week.

From this point onward, the HCVM leader said, the registrar began rejecting people if they could not complete the application in five minutes. Poll watchers in other precincts reported a similar visit from the chairman of the Halifax Board of Elections and a similar speedup in the registration process.

Harry Boyte, a first-year student at Duke University, served as poll watcher at the Halifax County Court House, the polling place in the town of Halifax, from 11:10 a.m. to 7:00 p.m. on May 9. He said forty-eight Negro citizens had attempted to register during that period. Of that number, twenty-six emerged from the registration office and told Harry that they had successfully registered. Those rejected had been guilty of a technical flaw, such as failure to form one letter in a signature to the satisfaction of the registrar, writing an "a" to resemble an "o," submitting a "messy" application, or messy writing.[47]

Thomas J. Andrews, a third-year student at Duke University, was poll watcher at Precinct #2 in Weldon from 2:00 to 6:00 p.m. on May 9. He said that the registrar told applicants that they must complete the registration process in five minutes and that no one who was able to complete the form in five minutes was denied registration. He estimated that at least twenty-five people, however, were turned away because they failed to meet the time deadline.[48]

In response to the registrars' misguided interpretation of the court order, lawyers representing the plaintiffs filed a show cause motion with Judge Larkins, requesting that the registration period be extended seven days, that five additional registrars be appointed, and that the Court appoint a registrar for the Enfield precinct (Fig. 29.2).[49] Robert Dickens, former Enfield registrar, had resigned and the Halifax County Election Board appointed Bert Ricks, whom leaders of the HCVM deemed unacceptable because of his known racist attitude.[50]

At the second hearing, Morton Stavis told the court:

> Robert Shields, Halifax election boards chairman, turned the time limit provision upside down and had registrars to cut off applicants when the five minutes were up, even when they had finished all but a few words of the reading and writing requirements for literacy testing.[51]

Judge Larkins concluded the hearing by saying he thought that the respondents had shown cause, except for the time limit, and that a permanent injunction would not be issued.[52]

Halifax Registrars Are Charged Again

ENFIELD (UPI)—The Halifax voter movement charged Saturday that county registration officials continued a "slowdown" in the registration of Negro voters despite a federal restraining order.

Halifax County Elections Board Chairman Robert Shields said the order was not served on him until about 4 p.m.

The voter movement spokesman said his organization had protested the action by telephone to various U.S. Government officials, including the Justice Department and were "awaiting action on their part."

U.S. Eastern District Judge John Larkins signed the order Friday restraining precinct registrars from using alleged "slowdown" tactics to discourage Negro voter applicants.

He said that no longer than five minutes would be allowed for the qualifying of each applicants and that registrars should arrange for assistants when it appeared that applicants would have to wait 30 minutes or more to register.

John R. Salter, a member of the Halifax movement, said registrars were still taking 10 to 15 minutes to register persons Saturday.

Shields said county registrars and election board members also got copies of the order, but that he did not know at what time.

Fig. 29.2. Federal Judge John Larkins issues new order after registrars twist meaning of earlier injunction, 1964. / John Salter Collection.

The case was widely reported in newspapers around the state, as in the following excerpt from the *Statesville Record and Landmark* quoting Judge Larkins's comments:

We did not think, when we issued the order, that it would mean someone would be standing at the applicant's shoulder with a stop watch.... We are dealing with people's rights and liberties and nothing is more precious. We're not dealing with statistics, we're dealing with people.[53]

In response to HCVM Chairman A. C. Cofield's telegram, the US Justice Department sent several FBI agents to the county. The agents met with the Halifax County Board of Elections and its attorney, Rom Parker, and interviewed several leaders of the Halifax County Voters Movement.

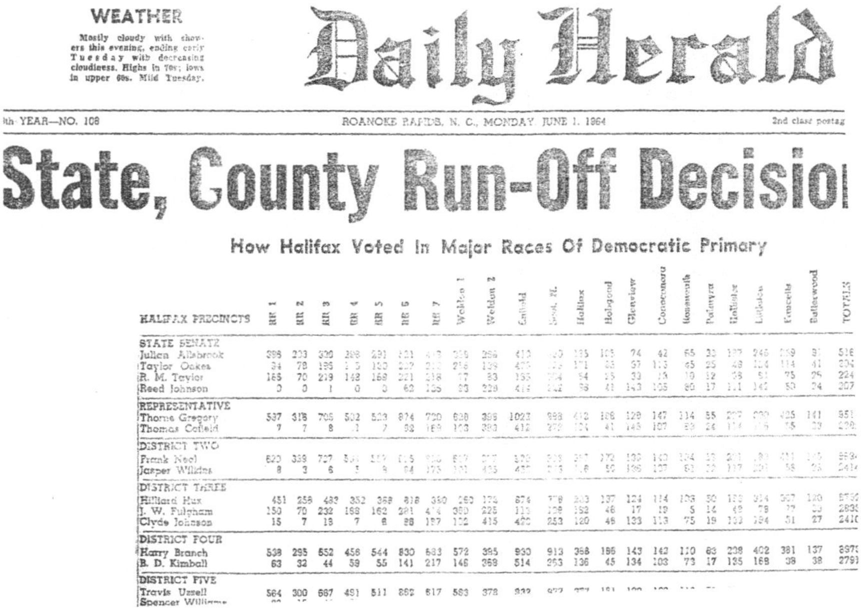

Fig. 30.1. *Roanoke Rapids Daily Herald* reports historic election results.

30. The May 30 Primary

The *Daily Herald* reported that the May 30 primary saw the "largest vote in the county's history" with 12,627 votes cast (Fig. 30.1). The Halifax County Voters Movement estimated that three thousand Negroes had voted. No candidate on the HCVM slate won, but they all reflected the support of the newly registered Black voters, making a solid promise of a winning potential in the future. John Salter wrote in his report to the SCEF Board:[54]

> As had been our practice, Doug Harris of SNCC and myself traveled the county, during the May 30th primary—from one precinct to another. We were both mighty impressed by the hundreds of Negro people who turned out—despite the large numbers of police and white people standing around and despite the high tension in the air ... The defeat of our eleven candidates has in no way dampened the spirits of the people. They are ready to be up and at it again.

The *Daily Herald* published the following report[55] on the number of votes won by the Negro candidates:

1. William Alston: Halifax County School Board. 2,237
2. Doris Cochran: Halifax County School Board 2,604
3. Thomas Cofield: NC State Representative 2,383
4. A. Reed Johnson: NC State Senator 2,075
5. Clyde Johnson: Halifax County Commissioner 2,410
6. Mima Johnson: Halifax County School Board 2,095
7. Arthur Lee Jones: Halifax County School Board. 2,084
8. Votie McWilliams: Halifax County School Board 2,104
9. Jasper Wilkins: Halifax County Commissioner 2,414
10. Spencer Williams: Halifax County Commissioner*
11. Tyler Vaughn: County Coroner 2,112
    *Unreported

Before the registration drive, only 1,600 Blacks in Halifax County were registered to vote. After the HCVM's spring drive, 3,600 Blacks were registered. The legal battle that the organization waged in the court had broad significance for the state. Salter commented, "Observers said that this ruling probably means that no county in this state will ever again try a massive effort to block Negro attempts to register and vote."[56]

The HCVM workers put forth a massive effort to get the newly registered voters to the polls on May 30. They organized car pools, telephone campaigns, and door-to-door canvassing throughout the county. John Salter said: "The large Negro turnout happened despite great tension in the air, large numbers of hostile police and segregationists in evidence, and the increased Ku Klux Klan activity in the area."[57]

Several years later, when Thomas Hardaway was elected to the North Carolina Legislature, I remembered those harrowing days in the spring of 1964. I remembered the dogged, all-out effort that so many of us, believing in the promise of the future, exerted to convince Black people in Halifax County to vote. Years later, I wrote a letter of support for John Salter, who at that time was fighting another battle at a university in the northwest. I wrote:

With John Salter's help, we initiated a countywide voter registration drive, and when local officials set up obstacles, John convinced a battery of top-notch lawyers to challenge the county board of elections in court. Our side won. For the first time since the disenfranchisement of Blacks in the late 19th century, thousands of eastern North Carolina Blacks registered. In the 1980s, those voters helped send two Black men to the North Carolina Legislature. In 1992, they sent Eva Clayton, a Black woman, to Congress where she served for many years. John Salter was not present for the victory celebration or the happy bus ride to Raleigh for the inauguration of Thomas C. Hardaway as Representative from our District, but many of the bus riders recalled Salter's courageous work during the 1960s. He helped break the fierce wall of resistance, thereby setting the stage for the Voting Rights Act and the election of Black people to local, state, and federal legislative bodies.

Many others deserve praise for their courageous, selfless participation in the Halifax County Voters Movement. Augustus Cofield, who had a long record of community activism, chaired the Halifax County Voters Movement. Reed Johnson invested his heart and soul in the freedom movement. Lillie Cousins Smith remained fearless in the face of white resistance. All the men and women who volunteered to run on the largest slate of Black political candidates since the days of Reconstruction deserve recognition for the courage they displayed in the spring of 1964. In addition, recognition goes to the organizers and leaders of the Halifax County Voters Movement, the men and women who served as coordinators in their neighborhoods, the Inborden High School students who helped, the Duke University students who came to the community numerous times, the brave tenants and sharecroppers who provoked the ire of their employers and risked their livelihoods, and the men and women who stood in line for hours waiting to register and vote.

31. THE POLITICAL BECOMES PERSONAL

32. No Contract for You

At the beginning of June, soon after school closed, I went to Mr. Williams's office to pick up my teaching contract for the next school year (Fig. 32.1). Mr. Williams told me that when he had picked up the contracts for Inborden teachers, he was surprised to find that there was no contract for me. He said that was when he learned that I had been terminated. I asked why, and he answered: "Insubordination." I asked, "To whom?" He answered, "To me."[58] Thirty days after Mr. Williams informed me that I was fired and did not have a contract, my lawyers filed a class action lawsuit in the Eastern District Court of the United States.

This swift action was possible because after I received the March 10 memo, John Salter appealed for help to the New York attorney William Kunstler. John had met Kunstler during the Jackson, Mississippi, civil rights campaign. When John called, Kunstler immediately agreed to help. This early start made it possible for the lawyers to do legal research and file a complaint against the Halifax County School Board and other defendants: *Willa Johnson v. Joseph Branch*. Kunstler asked Philip Hirschkop, a recent graduate of Georgetown University Law School, to join him in preparing the case. Samuel Mitchell, a well-known NAACP lawyer based in Raleigh, and Professor Chester Antieau of Georgetown University Law School also joined the legal team. In the later stages of the suit, Richard Morgan, National Education Association lawyer, assisted in the legal work. All the attorneys were white except Samuel Mitchell.

The young Jewish lawyer Philip Hirschkop did the research and groundwork for the case (Fig. 32.2). Later, Hirschkop gained fame as attorney for the Lovings, who successfully challenged the law against interracial marriages in a benchmark case in the United States Supreme Court. Within the same week in which I learned of my dismissal, Hirschkop came with his wife to my home in Enfield. The young attorney interviewed me while his wife kept my five-year-old daughter entertained.

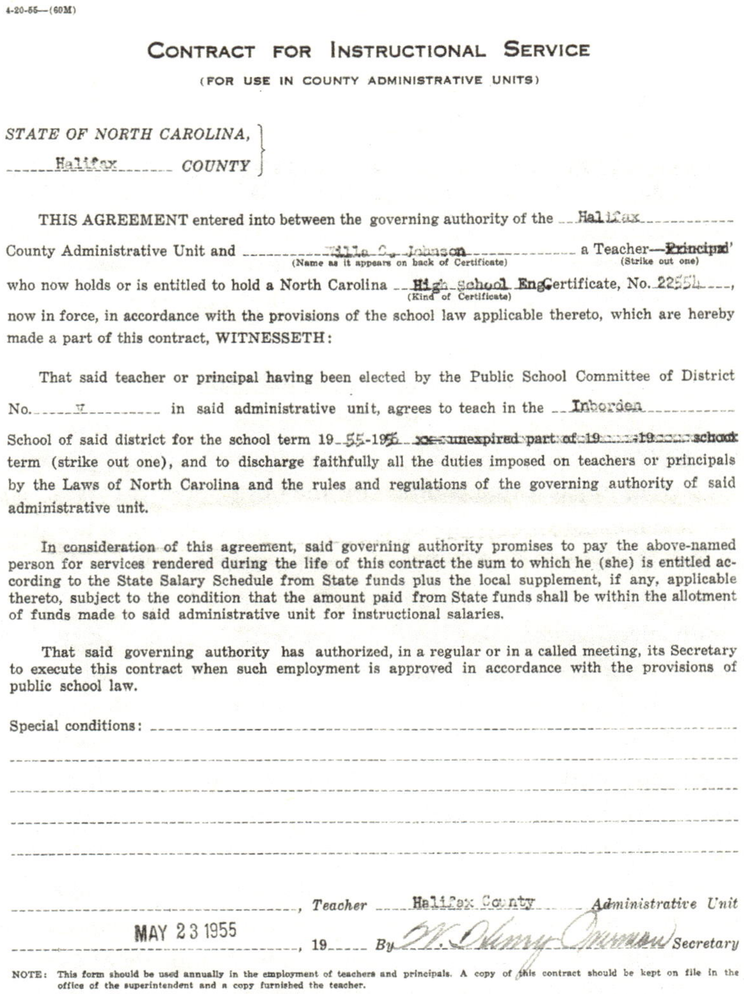

Contract for Instructional Service

(For use in County Administrative Units)

STATE OF NORTH CAROLINA,
Halifax COUNTY

THIS AGREEMENT entered into between the governing authority of the Halifax County Administrative Unit and Willa C. Johnson a Teacher—Principal' (Name as it appears on back of Certificate) (Strike out one) who now holds or is entitled to hold a North Carolina High School Eng. Certificate, No. 22554, (Kind of Certificate) now in force, in accordance with the provisions of the school law applicable thereto, which are hereby made a part of this contract, WITNESSETH:

That said teacher or principal having been elected by the Public School Committee of District No. 1 in said administrative unit, agrees to teach in the Inborden School of said district for the school term 19 55-1956 or unexpired part of 19....19 school term (strike one out), and to discharge faithfully all the duties imposed on teachers or principals by the Laws of North Carolina and the rules and regulations of the governing authority of said administrative unit.

In consideration of this agreement, said governing authority promises to pay the above-named person for services rendered during the life of this contract the sum to which he (she) is entitled according to the State Salary Schedule from State funds plus the local supplement, if any, applicable thereto, subject to the condition that the amount paid from State funds shall be within the allotment of funds made to said administrative unit for instructional salaries.

That said governing authority has authorized, in a regular or in a called meeting, its Secretary to execute this contract when such employment is approved in accordance with the provisions of public school law.

Special conditions: _____

_____, Teacher   Halifax County Administrative Unit
MAY 23 1955 , 19____ By _____ Secretary

NOTE: This form should be used annually in the employment of teachers and principals. A copy of this contract should be kept on file in the office of the superintendent and a copy furnished the teacher.

Fig. 32.1. Sample teacher's contract from 1955. / Willa Cofield personal collection.

After introducing himself to me and hearing my story, Phil assured me that he would give my case his best effort. The young lawyer then gave me a yellow legal pad on which to write my account of what had happened at Inborden School during the past school year. I sat at our kitchen table and put down the facts as I remembered them. When the attorney read my account, he said, "I will use this statement as your affidavit." With some less-than-major changes, he did.

Phil made several trips to Enfield, taking affidavits from people who supported me. On one occasion, Professor Chester Antieau, who had been Phil's mentor at Georgetown University Law School, and a Georgetown University

Fig. 32.2. Philip Hirschkop led the legal team that represented Willa in her battle against Halifax County's school and public officials (ca. 1968). / Courtesy of Philip Hirschkop.

law student accompanied him. I remember that the Georgetown professor explained the presence of the student by saying that inexperienced students sometimes come up with ideas that senior attorneys miss. I also remember that I was baking candied sweet potatoes for our dinner later that evening, and the Georgetown professor leaned into my kitchen door as he sniffed the sweet, spicy aroma and asked, "What on earth are you baking?"

Later, Philip made other trips to Enfield to take depositions from the defendants who were listed on the complaint as follows:

Joseph Branch, attorney for the Halifax County Board of Education, Enfield, NC
W. Henry Overman, superintendent of Halifax County Schools, Halifax, NC
Rom Parker, county attorney for the County of Halifax, Enfield, NC
L. M. Williams, principal of Inborden High School, Enfield, NC
C. M. Moore Jr., Halifax County Board of Education, Littleton, NC
Mrs. J. C. Shearin, Halifax County Board of Education
Henry Harrison, Halifax County Board of Education
Mrs. V. I. Mohorn Sr., Halifax County Board of Education, Halifax, NC
C. H. Leggett, Halifax County Board of Education, Scotland Neck, NC
Mrs. Robert Robinson, Halifax County Board of Education, RFD, Littleton, NC
J. D. Whitehead, Halifax County Board of Education, Enfield, NC
R. L. Coppage, District V School Committee, Enfield, NC
Frank Thorne (replacing John McGwigan), District V School Committee, Enfield, NC

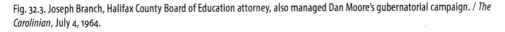

Fig. 32.3. Joseph Branch, Halifax County Board of Education attorney, also managed Dan Moore's gubernatorial campaign. / *The Carolinian*, July 4, 1964.

Mrs. Willis M. Morrisette, District School Committee, Enfield, NC
Mrs. Frances Arnold, District School Committee, Enfield, NC
E. W. Copeland, District V School Committee, Enfield, NC[59]

The principal defendant, Joseph Branch, practiced law in Enfield and handled legal matters for the Halifax County School Board of Education. Branch was a member of a wealthy and politically well-connected Halifax County family. Joe's brother, Harry, was chairman of the Halifax County Board of Commissioners.

Another brother, Edwin, operated a funeral home in Enfield and actively competed with the Cofield Funeral Home in serving the Black community. From 1947 to 1953, Joseph Branch represented Halifax County in four sessions of the North Carolina House of Representatives. During the 1957 session of the General Assembly, he served as legislative counsel for Governor Luther Hodges. Branch's obituary states that he was a close and valuable advisor to Governor Hodges. The Branch family was generally regarded as among the most powerful people in Halifax County.

In 1963 Daniel Moore hired Joseph Branch to manage his gubernatorial campaign, and Moore won in the 1964 election (Fig. 32.3). After his election, Governor Moore appointed Branch to the North Carolina Supreme Court, and in 1979, Governor James B. Hunt appointed him chief justice, a position Joseph Branch held until his death in 1991.

When my attorneys filed the suit, *Johnson v. Branch*, Joseph Branch was managing Dan Moore's campaign. He attended the first hearing in New Bern but got himself excused from attending future hearings.

33. The Community Shows Support

As soon as news of my suit became known in the community, former colleagues, parents, and students rallied to my support. While teachers had generally refrained from joining the local civil rights movement, after my firing a few brave teachers put themselves in jeopardy by signing affidavits. My former student Margie Ford and her sister, Ethel Speight, submitted affidavits attesting to my effectiveness as a teacher. Some parents, including Mrs. Votie McWilliams, and June and Rebecca Scott, signed affidavits. Associating themselves with my case required a great sense of independence and courage.

Ina Alexander Mitchell, a teacher of French and English at Inborden High School, heard of my firing while attending summer classes at the University

Fig. 33.1. Courageous Ina Mitchell, English and French teacher at Inborden High School, supported Willa (ca. 1964). / Grassroots Media Productions.

of North Carolina in Chapel Hill (Fig. 33.1). She immediately wrote to me expressing dismay and offering her help. With great courage and selflessness, she submitted an affidavit that became a part of the legal brief presented to the Court. In the sworn statement, Mrs. Mitchell said that she had worked at Inborden High School for eight years and had worked with me on both school and county projects. She also stated that students she taught who previously took my classes said that I was a good teacher.[60]

Attesting to her status at Inborden School, she later told me that she received no recriminations or criticism from the principal because of her courageous action.

Erie Barton had taught at Inborden Elementary School for eleven years. When I asked her to draft and sign an affidavit for my complaint, she said that she was happy to support me. Mrs. Barton had served as chairman of the publicity committee for the school, and in her affidavit, she spoke of my help in readying Inborden School news articles for release. She also pointed to my work with the National Honor Society and the school newspaper, *The Reflector*, as valuable programs that enriched the education of Inborden High School students.[61]

In her affidavit, Mrs. Ethel Speight, teacher and librarian, spoke of my work with her on the library committee and my consistent efforts to see "that the job might be completed successfully." Her sister, Margie Ford, who had been one of my students, also submitted an affidavit. Margie said that I had inspired her to become an English teacher.[62]

One of the most amazing affidavits came from Mildred Bobbitt (now Dr. Mildred Sexton, one of the coauthors of this book). She was seventeen years old at the time and an active participant in the Enfield civil rights movement. Mildred had been president of her junior class at Inborden High School and was serving as senior class president when she signed the affidavit. In her sworn statement, Mildred described her experience as a member of the Inborden Chapter of the National Honor Society. She said that becoming a member of the Honor Society, which I had helped found, had become a popular goal among Inborden students.

Affidavit of Mildred Bobbitt

I, Mildred Bobbitt, being duly sworn and put under oath, do hereby depose and state as follows:

That I am of the age of 17 years and am a resident of Enfield, North Carolina.

That I was a student at Inborden High School from 1961 to 1964 when I graduated. That during the past three years, I have been a student of Mrs. Willa Johnson in her English classes. That I am now an entering freshman at North Carolina College Durham.

That I believe Mrs. Willa Johnson to be an excellent teacher. I found her teaching technique indicated ability to present material in an interesting and varied manner. I found the reading skills of speed and analysis which she taught have been helpful in taking the Scholastic Aptitude Tests for admission into college.

That Mrs. Johnson was the faculty sponsor of the Honor Society and I was a member thereof during the past two years. That during the 1963–1964 school year the Honor Society has had a very active program to which Mrs. Johnson freely gave her time and efforts. For example, the Society made a weekend trip to Williamsburg, Virginia, and Hampton Institute, Hampton, Virginia. With Mrs. Johnson's encouragement, we had an Honor Society breakfast one morning before the start of school. These activities were in addition to the more standard and usual program of recognition at student assemblies and "special days." That Mrs. Johnson spent many extra hours in the preparation and execution of these activities and showed a continuing concern for the scholastic achievements of Inborden students.

That membership in the Honor Society seemed to be a general goal among students at Inborden. That, as for myself, it was a central motivation for my scholastic achievements and the most valuable, interesting, and rewarding of my high school activities.

That Mrs. Johnson was the sponsor of the advanced English class in its preparation of the student newspaper, "The Inborden Reflector." This was a very good and useful student paper which provided us with information on a variety of student activities and school projects. When it was not published this past year, I heard several expressions from students to the effect that they missed it and felt that it should have been continued.

That I was President of the Junior and Senior classes at Inborden High School. In these offices, I worked with Mrs. Johnson in the preparation of a proposed student year book—the first publication that Inborden would have ever had. Despite the students' efforts in raising money and preparing the copy for this book and despite Mrs. Johnson's aid and advice in its preparation, permission to publish it was ultimately refused by Principal L. H. Williams.

That Mrs. Johnson never approached me during school time with regard to my participation in any civil rights demonstrations or voter registration projects.

That Mrs. Johnson exerted many efforts in my behalf as a student and was instrumental in providing me with a scholarship which will assist me in my college education.

I consider my contact with Mrs. Willa Johnson as one of the most enriching and rewarding aspects of my time at Inborden High School.[63]

M.C.B.

In addition to the help that I received from my students, many parents and "pillars of the community" rallied to my cause. Mrs. Votie McWilliams, vice-president of the Inborden Parents and Teachers Association, said in her affidavit that she had heard students describe me as one of the best teachers in the school.[64]

June and Rebecca Scott, well-established farm owners, readily agreed to submit an affidavit in my behalf. I had taught all their six children: Clementine, Bertha, Fred, Donald, Clintus, and John, as well as their grandson, Gerald. The Scotts owned a farm in the Daniel Chapels community of Dalmyra, a well-known area of independent Black farmers and landowners. During the time that their children attended Inborden, the Scotts stood out as hard-working members of the PTA. They always helped get the school year off to a pleasant and entertaining start at the first PTA meeting of the year by naming each of their six children who attended Inborden School and the name of each child's teacher. On the affidavit which June Scott, treasurer of the PTA, submitted, he said that he never knew of my missing a PTA meeting.[65]

During the hectic preparation of my suit against the school and town authorities, Morton Bradley, an attorney from Buffalo, New York, was one of the many volunteer workers who came to Enfield and slept overnight in our guest bedroom. The next morning as I cooked breakfast, he expressed his concern that Halifax County school authorities had fired me from my teaching job. Looking at my nicely furnished home, he said, "I think that I can get your job back. If you say so, I'll drive to Halifax and talk to those people. I think that I can get them to change their minds." Without stopping to consider his offer, I answered, "No, I'm in this fight for the community, not for my individual gain. I think that the community will benefit from this suit. I don't want you to go." My voice was so strong and sincere that the attorney just shook his head and silently continued sipping his coffee.

Something had happened to my community in the year since Reed had filed for a seat on the Enfield Board of Commissioners. Invisible walls that once existed had fallen. In the small circle of our movement, the stiffness had dissolved between the town people and the country people, the residents of Black Bottom and New Town, youngsters and the elderly, not so well-off people and those better off, the professional and nonprofessional. There was a closeness that I had yearned for all my life. When I needed help, these people had generously risked their safety and well-being to help me. I felt a kinship and a loyalty and a fierce faith that what we were doing was important. We were making our community and other communities like ours better. I could not let these people down.

34. The Literacy Class

In the middle of June, the Southern Christian Leadership Conference sponsored a citizenship education training in the Franklinton Center at Bricks. The staff included Septima Clark, Dorothy Cotton, Bernice Robinson, and Fred

Bennett. They came to prepare teachers of literacy classes to assist potential voters in registering. Freedom fighters from Monroe, North Carolina, joined us for the weeklong session. They had fought along with Robert Williams, a militant Black leader of the Monroe NAACP who challenged white supremacy with armed resistance and later escaped to China.

Eleven Inborden students could not attend the SCLC workshop at Bricks, and I was asked to accompany them to the SCLC training in Georgia. While we were making our final preparations for the trip, on June 21, 1964, the news media reported that three young men did not return after a civil rights meeting with people at a rural church in Mississippi. James Chaney was a Black Mississippian. Andrew Goodman and Michael Schwerner were Jews from New York. Their disappearance put fear in the hearts of civil rights workers throughout the South. The whole nation waited for news of Chaney, Goodman, and Schwerner.

At midnight on the following Sunday, while the search for the missing workers intensified and fears for their well-being escalated, I boarded a Carolina Trailways bus, along with the Inborden students, heading to the SCLC training center in Dorchester, Georgia. For years, I was reminded of that trip when I heard Gladys Knight sing, "I'm Leaving on a Midnight Train for Georgia." As I remember, we were the only passengers, and we didn't have to sit in the back of the bus, for interstate buses had been desegregated. We rode all night and arrived in Charleston, South Carolina, the next morning.

While we waited for hours in the bus station, we were the object of many curious stares. Because one of my Black students looked white, we appeared to be an integrated group, and I was very concerned for our safety. I was greatly relieved when our connecting Trailways bus to McIntosh, Georgia, pulled up late in the day and we boarded it without incident. By the time we arrived in McIntosh, it was early evening. After a short wait, we boarded a school bus and rode through miles of moss-draped trees until we arrived at the campus of Dorchester Training School just before dark.

My heart sank as I walked into the dormitory room in which I was to sleep for the next five nights. There was only a small cot with a very thin mattress, no sheets on the bed, or anything at all covering the window. A single electric cord with a dim bulb hung from the ceiling. Later, I did get sheets for the bed, but the window remained bare for the whole week. I wondered how the young people who came with me would react when they saw their rooms. None of them had ever been to Georgia before. When we met later that evening for dinner, I found that they were quite upset by the bareness of their rooms.

Despite our poor sleeping accommodations, we spent the next five days attending well-organized classes, engaging in highly energized conversations, and hearing about freedom struggles in towns all over the South. Septima Clark, Dorothy Cotton, and the other SCLC staff demystified government and politics in our classes. We learned the difference between a strong and weak mayor, how to stage a protest, the meaning of direct nonviolent action, how to use passive resistance, how to respond to an arrest, and how to file a complaint. We learned new words and concepts: *incorporation, amicus curiae, habeas corpus,* power structure.

Septima Clark directed the training session that week. Septima had been a schoolteacher in Charleston, South Carolina who organized Black Charleston teachers in the 1920s. After she taught for forty years, school authorities fired her because she would not drop her membership in the NAACP. She was fifty-eight years old. Instead of retiring, she went to the Highlander Folk School, in Tennessee, directed by Miles Horton, and instructed students in citizenship education, a model that she, Esau Jenkins, and Bernice Robinson had developed in the Sea Islands of South Carolina.

The Highlander School adopted Septima's ideas and included them in the curriculum. Three weeks after Septima Clark taught Rosa Parks at the Highlander School, Rosa refused to give up her seat on the Montgomery, Alabama bus. In 1962 the SCLC, in association with the American Missionary Association, took over the Highlander Folk School experiment in basic adult education. They hired Septima to direct the program and spread literacy throughout the South.

The Citizenship School played a basic role in building the civil rights movement by helping those African Americans who were functionally illiterate in the eight states that participated in the program. The schools helped southern Blacks pass arduous literacy tests that authorities used to disenfranchise them.

Dorothy Cotton, an activist from Petersburg, Virginia, taught workshops at the Citizenship Schools from 1962 to 1967. She said that in all the areas of the Deep South where there was intense protest—Birmingham, the Mississippi Delta, Southwest Georgia—the people who provided leadership had come through the Citizenship School program.

Dorothy Cotton said that, as the movement progressed, she could feel the energy in the Citizenship Schools rise. People came from communities where they had waged fierce battles with the police and the Klan. They were all fired up and eager to share their stories. As participants related their experiences, they strengthened and encouraged each other.

The Dorchester Training School hummed with excitement. The movement was transforming our lives! Newly empowered leaders had come from Mississippi, Alabama, and Georgia, as well as North and South Carolina. We heard stories of Klan attacks on churches and homes. We told students from other communities about our fight in Enfield, how the Klan had burned a cross in my family's backyard, picketing downtown businesses, and how I had been fired from my teaching job in Halifax County.

Spirits soared and enthusiasm bubbled over. Every session began with the question, "Who is our leader?" We all responded, "Dr. Martin Luther King!" Freedom songs erupted spontaneously, everywhere—at meals in the expansive dining hall, during a class on passive resistance, in the large first-floor lounge, in evening meetings, on the aging veranda, on the grounds while people were enjoying a break between classes. We, the North Carolina group, shared our songs and learned new songs from other flashpoints of struggle around the South. We renewed our determination to keep on fighting for freedom, regardless of the consequences.

When I returned to Enfield, I immediately set about recruiting members for my SCLC literacy class and ultimately succeeded in enrolling ten elderly persons, nine women and one man. We met in the flower shop, next door to the Cofield Funeral Home. The flower shop served as the movement headquarters. The oldest student was seventy-nine. These elderly learners had had little, if any, formal schooling. They had grown up on farms where children as well as adults were expected to work, and school attendance was a luxury that struggling tenant and sharecropping families could not afford. We met weekly for six weeks. I faithfully followed the SCLC Citizenship Education curriculum. At the end of the training, I sent the names of all the students and a report to the SCLC office in Atlanta. That office sent certificates from the program signed by Dr. Martin Luther King. We all dressed up in our Sunday best, and I presented each student with a certificate during morning worship services at the New Bethel Baptist Church.

35. The KKK Burns Crosses

In the beginning of July, after the lawyers filed *Johnson v. Branch*, headlines of newspapers across the state informed their readers of the lawsuit (Fig. 35.1). Late in the evening of July 4, 1964, the Ku Klux Klan burned a seventeen-by-eight-foot cross wrapped in tobacco cloth on a lot across from our Whitaker

Fig. 35.1. The *Carolina Times*, edited by Enfield native Louis Alston, covered the Enfield story. / *Carolina Times*, July 11, 1964.

Fig. 35.2 Tanya was only five years old in 1964 when she witnessed her second cross burning. / Willa Cofield personal collection.

Street home. While the Klan had burned many crosses in our community since our movement began, it was the biggest cross of them all.

The lot on which it stood had once been the site of the white Enfield Graded School, but at the time of the burning, the aging building was empty and in a state of total disrepair. I was home with five-year-old Tanya when Paul James, my next-door neighbor and former colleague at Inborden School, rang my doorbell and asked, "Have you seen that shit across the street?" I looked across Whitaker Street and saw a huge cross with flames licking toward the black sky.

From the front door with my five-year-old in my arms, I watched the burning cross (Fig. 35.2). It stood a few feet from the street and its flames leaped toward a nearby pine tree in a scraggly patch of dog fennels. It could set the tree and underbrush afire. I went back into the house and called the Enfield Fire Department. I picked up my little five-year-old and walked to the porch between the garage and the house that we called the breezeway. From this position, I had a clear, straight-line view of the burning cross.

I watched it burn as I waited for the fire truck to arrive, all the time holding Tanya, who was witnessing her second cross burning. The fire truck pulled

Fig. 35.3. Charred remains of the seventeen-foot cross burned on July 4, 1964, in front of the Johnson home. / Willa Cofield personal collection.

up. One of the white firemen jumped from the truck and ran to a nearby fire hydrant. The other man followed and the two attached a hose, which they soon trained on the burning cross. In a few swift minutes, they doused the flames. It didn't take long and soon the fiery, hateful cross became a mess of charred and blackened wood (Fig. 35.3). Following that incident, armed neighbors and friends stood watch in our garage for the next several nights, just in case.

I read the burning of this seventeen-foot cross as a clear response to the suit that I had filed against sixteen white Halifax County educational and political leaders. I expected both sides to be heard in court, and I hoped that a fair decision would be reached in my favor. I did not think that the Ku Klux Klan would be called to testify, so I was not intimidated by this second cross burning at my home.

Since the spring of 1963, the Klan had become increasingly active in the community. People reported numerous mass rallies and cross burnings around the town. In the fall of 1964, a group of excited young men came to our home to report a huge Klan meeting in a field on the Scotland Neck Road. People who lived on the west side of the town had described

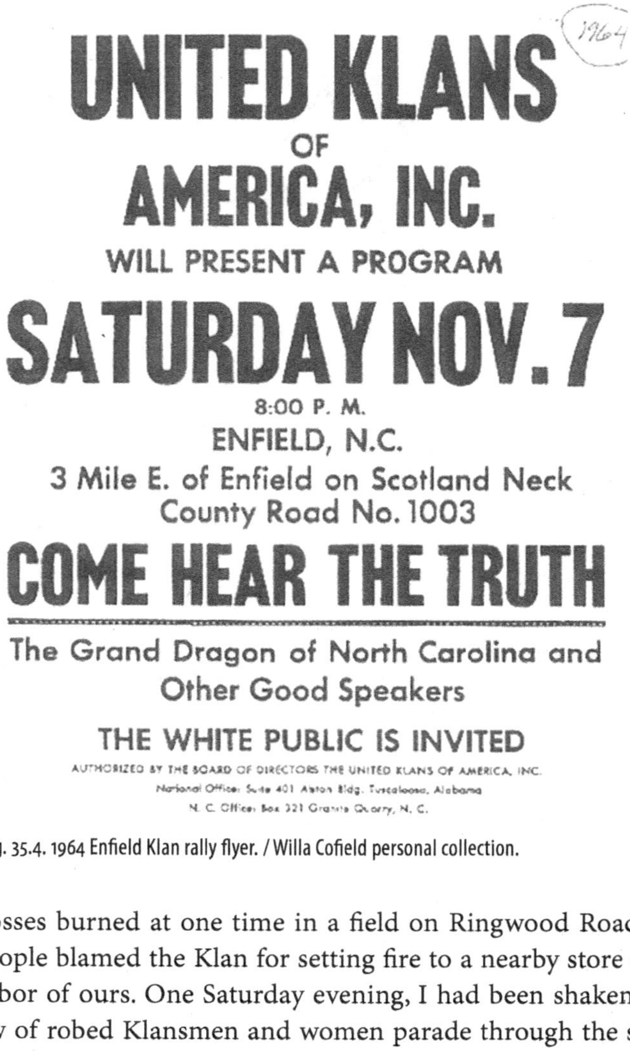

UNITED KLANS OF AMERICA, INC.

WILL PRESENT A PROGRAM

SATURDAY NOV. 7

8:00 P. M.
ENFIELD, N.C.
3 Mile E. of Enfield on Scotland Neck
County Road No. 1003

COME HEAR THE TRUTH

The Grand Dragon of North Carolina and Other Good Speakers

THE WHITE PUBLIC IS INVITED

AUTHORIZED BY THE BOARD OF DIRECTORS THE UNITED KLANS OF AMERICA, INC.
National Office: Suite 401 Alston Bldg. Tuscaloosa, Alabama
N. C. Office: Box 321 Granite Quarry, N. C.

Fig. 35.4. 1964 Enfield Klan rally flyer. / Willa Cofield personal collection.

several crosses burned at one time in a field on Ringwood Road. Earlier in 1964, people blamed the Klan for setting fire to a nearby store operated by a neighbor of ours. One Saturday evening, I had been shaken to see a double row of robed Klansmen and women parade through the streets in the nearby city of Rocky Mount. People said that the Klan met regularly at the Enfield fairgrounds in a small, cinderblock building on South Railroad Street. Meetings of the Klan were posted regularly at the Enfield police station (Fig. 35.4).

Later that same summer, the Ku Klux Klan attempted to burn yet another cross in Enfield. One night Mrs. Alice Evans looked out her window and saw a group of white men unloading a cross from a pick-up truck parked near her home. Mrs. Alice Evans was an outspoken leader in the Enfield and Halifax County Voters Movement. Her daughters and granddaughter had picketed and participated in many of the protests. She knew how to respond to the

The Ku Klux Klan Takes Over in Enfield

It probably provides a convenient source for the intimidation of the Negro citizens of Enfield, and a feeling of superiority for its white citizens and others of Halifax County, to have the Ku Klux Klan burn crosses in front of Negro homes, parade the streets in robes and hoods while armed with rifles, shotguns and other weapons. Sometimes human beings can sink so low morally that only the most despicable conduct of others can give comfort to their consciences. Thus, we find in Enfield and other sections of Halifax County; the law is glad to take a holiday while the Ku Klux Klan or any other group of white persons who wishes to do so, exercises the liberty of heaping insults and abuses on Negroes.

In line with the activities of the Klan in Enfield is the discharging of one of its Negro teachers for no apparent reason other than she had been active in the recent registration and vote campaign conducted by its Negro citizens. Thus, instead of the Board of Education and principal of the school, in which the teacher worked, encouraging all of the teachers to take an active part in the community life, it appears that the Board and the principal have entered into an unholy conspiracy to discharge any teacher who encourages such.

its nefarious acts, is having a field day in Enfield in its endeavors to create fear and trembling in the breasts of the Negro citizens. All the while the town, instead of showing signs of industrial growth, is reaping the harvest of the law's neglect and the Klan's freedom, while other nearby towns are constantly being selected as sites for new industries. Add to this the fact that more and more Negro motorists, who once stopped for gasoline, food and other commodities, so essential when traveling, are by-passing or driving through as the information continues to spread that Enfield is reeking with race hatred, interracial illwill and Ku Klux Klanism.

Now and again the fact that Negro citizens of the town are beginning to quietly but assuredly put on the squeeze by driving on over to nearby towns when in need of food, clothing, shoes, home appliances, automobiles and other necessities, and you will understand why economic stagnation is slowly but surely beginning to take over in Enfield. So we declare here and now the town of Enfield to be on the BLACK LIST. Until further notice, we would urge Negro motorists to buy what they need, while traveling, before they get to Enfield or after they have passed through it.

Fig. 35.4a. Editor Louis Alston condemns the Ku Klux Klan. / *Carolina Times*, July 11, 1964.

imminent cross burning. She called her husband to bring his gun. As the men started to plant the cross on the grounds of the old peanut mill across the street, Mr. Evans fired into the small circle of men, who hastily abandoned the cross, jumped into the truck, and sped away. To my knowledge, that carefully constructed cross—complete with a strong metal prong for hasty thrusting into the soil—was the last cross that the Ku Klux Klan attempted to burn in Enfield (Fig. 35.4a).

36. The Hearing in Eastern District Court

I had never walked inside a courtroom before. I felt a bit anxious, but I looked forward to the opportunity to clear my name. I believed that the school authorities had deeply wronged me and that the district court hearing would give me a chance to set the record straight. In preparation for the hearing, I had submitted a second affidavit, responding to each of the charges of Principal Williams's March 10 memo (Fig. 36.1).

Affidavit of Willa Johnson

I, Willa Johnson, after first being sworn and put under oath do hereby depose and state as follows:

1. That I am above the age of twenty-one years and a resident of Enfield, North Carolina.
2. That I am the plaintiff in this action.
3. That I received a letter from Mr. L. M. Williams, the Principal of Inborden High School, dated March 10, 1964. That this letter appeared to be an enumeration of criticisms of my work as a teacher for the school year 1963–1964 to the date of this letter.
4. That I offer this affidavit as my answer to the Statements made in the above mentioned letter.
5. That the letter states that "I have reminded you of the following:" and goes on to enumerate seven statements. Whereas, I had never previously been told of any of the matters save those numbered 2, 3, and 7; the nature of the discussion of these points will more fully appear hereinafter.
6. [point] That I was notified of the "game duty" which I was to serve that evening at 7:00 o'clock about 3:00 o'clock p.m. and that I was about fifteen minutes late. This was occasioned by the fact that since I had not known previously of the obligation, I could not plan to avoid my regular evening obligation to prepare dinner for my husband and child and perform my regular chores as a parent and a housewife. That when I arrived at the gymnasium there were five teachers on duty who were having no difficulty supervising the students in attendance at the game.
7. (Point 2) That while I was occasionally a few minutes late during the time preceding this letter, this was an unusual occurrence and Principal Williams' claim that I was late was based partially on his demand that I arrive before the 8:00 a.m. sign-in time required by the school rules. That after the conference on this matter I was not late again with the possible exception of one occasion when I had an important houseguest.

T. S. Inborden High School

ENFIELD, NORTH CAROLINA

L. M. WILLIAMS
Principal

March 10, 1964

P. O. BOX 457
Telephone HI 5-4001

Mrs. Willa C. Johnson
T. S. Inborden High School
Enfield, North Carolina

Dear Mrs. Johnson:

This is to inform and advise you that you are expected to abide by and adhere to the policies and regulations that govern the operation of the school just as any other teacher is expected to do.

I have reminded you of the following:

1. Being late for game duty December 2, 1964.

2. Failing to report to work on time and a conference was held with you January 6, 1964 regarding being late for work.

3. Failing to do ground duty the week of February 3-7, 1964.

4. Failing to give a written explanation as requested for not attending a P.T.A. meeting on February 5, 1964.

5. Failing to do building duty the week of March 2-6, 1964.

6. Failing to stand at your door to supervise pupils as they change classes.

7. Failing to see that the cabinets in your room were clean and free of fire hazard.

A copy of this information is being submitted to the superintendent for his suggestions or recommendations regarding this matter.

Yours respectfully,

L. M. Williams

L. M. Williams,
Principal

LMW
cc: W. Henry Overman
    R. L. Coppage

Fig. 36.1. Defense lawyers based their case on the ill-conceived March 10 Memo. / Willa Cofield personal collection.

8. (Point 3) That I did not fail to do ground duty for the week of February 3–7; I organized student patrols which were on the playground at the appropriate times and which immediately reported any incidents to me. I investigated the two incidents which occurred during this time. When I was approached by Principal Williams about this matter, I described the system that I had used and he stated that it was all right, which I took as a ratification and approval of my method.
9. (Point 4) I was not able to attend the P. T. A. meeting of February 5, 1964. The next day a memo was circulated to all teachers asking them to check whether or not they had attended. I checked "no." We were then asked to fill in a reason for failing to attend, which I did not do. I had been at the beauty parlor and had my hair lightened, a fact which Mr. Williams commented upon the following day. I felt the reason for my absence was obvious and so, out of a sense of embarrassment, failed to write in my explanation. This was the only time in the eleven years I have taught at Inborden that any such procedure was ever used.
10. (Point 5) That I did not fail to do building duty during the week of March 2–6, but on the contrary, I brought my lunch with me the entire week and ate in my classroom. I would leave the room to inspect the hall area every few minutes, interrupting my lunch to meet my obligation. That this matter was never called to my attention as being an improper or otherwise unacceptable method of performing this duty.
11. (Point 6) That I have been irregular in standing in the door to supervise class changes. I have found that the necessities of last minute preparations for the next class and of having a moment to meet the demands of my students for individual attention required my presence in the classroom. I was, however, near enough to help should any occasion arise and no incident has ever occurred due to my absence from my doorway during class changes.
12. (Point 7) That upon one occasion without warning or explanation, Principal Williams entered my classroom and opened some old cupboards which had been placed in my room and which I used for the storage of construction paper. Since the cupboard was often gone through by students looking for materials and also used by them to store their lunches, it was not as neat as it might have been had it not been open to student use. When I went through the cupboard

Fig. 36.2. William Kunstler (1919–1995), the renowned civil rights attorney, represented Willa. He is pictured here with Rev. Martin Luther King (left), and attorney Mrs. Constance Motley. Credit: Stocktrek Images, Inc. / Alamy Stock Photo.

after the principal's inspection, I found no refuse or anything which might be considered a fire hazard except the paper which was regularly stored there for use in the classroom.[66]

I had looked forward to the hearing as a day of vindication. My lawyers spoke optimistically of my chances of winning. They reminded me that Judge Larkins, who would hear the case, had ruled favorably in the *Alston v. Butts* case against the Halifax County Board of Elections a few months before. The attorneys assured me that the judge would give me a fair and favorable ruling. I had never heard of William Kunstler before John Salter came to town, but John said that Kunstler was an outstanding lawyer, that other lawyers would probably attend the hearing just because Kunstler would be trying the case (Fig. 36.2).

Because there were no hotels in our town, on the evening before the trial, Philip Hirschkop brought William Kunstler to our home to sleep in our guest bedroom. Before Kunstler retired for the night, Phil wanted him to meet our daughter, Tanya, who had just turned six years old earlier that month. Kunstler warmly greeted the little girl and gave her a big hug. I felt reassured to see this tender side to the attorney who would represent me in court.

Very early in the morning of July 31, 1964, my colleague and friend, Lillie Smith, and her daughter, Cynthia, joined Reed and me for the one-hundred-mile trip to New Bern for the hearing in the Craven County Courthouse.

Cynthia (now Cynthia Samuelson, one of the coauthors of this book) had completed her freshman year at Hampton the previous spring. She had just received her driver's license, and she was excited to be our driver. Roberta Nicholson Cherry had agreed to look after our six-year-old daughter, Tanya. She had spent the night with us so that we could make an early start. Berta, as we called her, had been Tanya's caretaker for several years, and I felt very comfortable leaving my little girl in her care.

When I was telling wise little six-year-old Tanya that I was going to court, I hesitated as I sought a way to explain the process that would take me away from home for the day. While I searched for words, little Tanya chimed, "Aw, Mama, I know what court is. I watch Perry Mason!" *Perry Mason* was a popular television courtroom drama of that time. It was a show that Berta liked to watch, and Tanya had seen many of its daily screenings.

When I walked through our breezeway and garage into the bright, July morning, I saw our white Impala shining in the sun. My husband had parked it in the circular drive on the side of our brick home on Whitaker Street. I wore a light blue cotton suit with a crisp white blouse. I selected my medium heel pumps with care, for I did not want to stumble as I walked to the witness stand. After giving my little girl a last hug, I climbed into the back seat beside Lillie.

Cynthia had taken the seat behind the wheel, and Reed sat on the front passenger side. Lillie and I chatted as Cynthia whizzed us down NC Highway 121. I remember that as Cynthia steered the car, she described the different ways to place her hands on the steering wheel, the three o'clock, the nine o'clock, or the eleven o'clock position, evidence of her newly licensed skills.

It was the second time that I had traveled to New Bern. When I was eight years old, my father had taken his family along when he attended a convention for funeral directors at a colored funeral home in the Craven County town. I had never forgotten the visit because before we left, Dad had driven a few miles beyond the town, and for the first time, I got a thrilling glimpse of the Atlantic Ocean.

On this somber morning as we entered the interior of the courtroom, even though I, too, had watched *Perry Mason*, I found the dark-paneled room impressive. We sat on the left side of the room. Friends and family, who joined us later, also sat on the left side of the formal, imposing courtroom. Not too long after we claimed our seats, sober-faced members of the Halifax County School Board, the local district committee, the other defendants, and the two defense lawyers filed in and took seats on the right side of the courtroom.

I had sued for $250,000, which seemed like a huge mountain of cash in those days. I was representing other Negro teachers similarly situated, and I sought injunctive relief, as well as damages and attorney fees. As I waited to be called to the witness stand, I reviewed the advice of my attorneys. I would answer the questions as truthfully and clearly as I could. I was not unduly nervous. I believed that I had excellent lawyers, a well-prepared and timely case, and that, ultimately, the truth would prevail.

Mr. Kunstler, the tall, long-haired, New York lawyer, was coolly confident as he presented my side of the argument. He boldly called the decision of the school district not to renew my employment "unconstitutionally arbitrary, capricious, malicious and without legal cause." He said that it was designed to intimidate, deter, and harass me and other Negro teachers. He told Judge Larkins that I did not claim that I had a right to teach any more than a lawyer has a right to be a member of a state or federal bar, but I did contend that I as a teacher could not be denied my teaching position on the basis of "arbitrary criteria or capricious state action."[67]

Kunstler said that there were only two plausible views concerning the defendants' actions toward me.

1. I was released because of my and my husband's activities on behalf of our race or
2. that the reasons the defendants offered for releasing me were completely arbitrary and capricious.

He said that either reason was indefensible and neither offered a reasonable or legal basis for my dismissal. None of the reasons offered related to my teaching accomplishments or teaching competence. He pointed out that such actions have been time and again condemned and rejected by our courts.

Rather than focus on the actions of the principal, Kunstler told the court that the action of the School District Committee at its meetings of April 23 and May 27 held the key to understanding my dismissal. He said that the record is clear that the principal signed my contract, which is all the law required him to do.[68] He charged that the decision to deprive me of employment was the result of a plan, agreement, and conspiracy entered into by the defendants and that these actions violated the Constitution of the United States.

The defendants said that the memorandum of March 10, 1963, with its seven charges, represented their sole reason for dismissing me. Eddie Copeland, a wholesale grocer and Texaco distributor, told the Court that he had introduced the motion to hire all of the teachers except Willa Johnson "based on that letter that the Board received suggesting that she was not doing what she should do in school." When Hirschkop asked if the March 10 letter was the "sole and exclusive" reason that he voted against her, the school district committeeman, answered, "That is right."[69]

Robert Coppage, chairman of the District Committee, presided at the May 27 meeting and did not vote. In court, Coppage said, when asked if Johnson had continued to show improvement after the March 10 memorandum, "To my knowledge she apparently continued to show improvement, because we didn't hear anything to the contrary."[70]

Percy Thorne said that he had questioned Principal Williams about the March 10 memo at the April 23 meeting, but when asked what question he had asked, he did not recall his question. He said that he had voted against renewal of my contract "on the basis of the seven things in the letter [March 10 memo] we had."[71]

Frances Arnold was present for the April 23 meeting but did not attend the May 27 meeting. She said that she knew nothing at all about my participation in the civil rights movement. Frances Arnold said that she believed that the committee should take the word of the principal that Willa Johnson improved after receiving the March 10 memo.[72]

Mrs. Natalia J. Morrisette, who was present at the March 27, 1964, meeting of the district committee, voted to renew my contract. That made the final vote of the committee two to one against me. Since both of the two votes against me were based on the March 10 memo, when Mr. Williams took the stand he was asked about the memo.

Mr. Williams said that in the ten years that he had served as principal of Inborden, he had written a similar letter [as the March 10 letter] to one other teacher, but in that case,[73] he did not send a copy to the district committee and to the superintendent. Clearly, in my case, he wanted to inform individuals beyond our school of his actions.

Under cross-examination by Phil Hirschkop, the principal said that he did not know of my activity in the civil rights movement. This statement could not have been true because he and I had discussed my participation in the civil rights movement, as my affidavit alleged. In a town the size of Enfield where nothing like the events of the spring and summer of 1963 had ever happened before, it is highly unlikely that anyone did not know who the leaders were.

During his cross-examination, Mr. Williams attempted to modify his earlier deposition with his statement in the March 31, 1964, letter. In that letter, the principal said that I had shown improvement in all the areas he had addressed [in his March 10 memo] and that he was recommending me for employment for the school year of 1964–65. Upon examination by Phil Hirschkop, Principal Williams said that the memorandum was not the only basis for his discontent, but he just selected some of the things about me that he found unsatisfactory for the letter.

The first hearing at New Bern on July 31, 1964, ended with a consent order continuing the case until August 31, 1964, when a final hearing would be held at Washington, North Carolina. The Court directed that the defendants "not fill the plaintiff's former position except on a temporary basis, until after the final hearing is concluded."[74]

At the end of the long day in court, we walked from the Craven County building to see a parked bus filled with ministers from the North on their way to Atlanta for a meeting with Dr. Martin Luther King Jr. and the Southern Christian Leadership Conference staff. They had heard about my case and the civil rights attorneys who were representing me and had altered their route to Georgia to come further east in North Carolina to make a surprise stop in New Bern.

37. Six Black Children Integrate the "White" Enfield School

Early in the summer of 1964, before the lawyers filed the suit *Johnson v. Branch*, a small group of Black citizens had met with Joseph Branch. They had raised the question, "What would happen if we sent our children to the white school?" Without hesitation, the Enfield lawyer had answered, "It would be a disaster." His comment was repeated many times in the Black community. It was not just the statement, but the powerful position held by the person who made the statement that gave such ominous meaning to the words.

Despite his dire warning, the Halifax County Voters Movement pressed to find parents willing to send their children to white schools. At our community meeting in late July, someone announced that two children were signed up to go to the white Enfield School in September: Lillie Smith's high school–age son, Ira Dale Sanders, and a first grader, Tanya Johnson. When I heard my daughter's name read, I sat shocked and speechless. My husband had submitted her name without my knowledge or consent. As a leader of the movement, I could not ask other parents to send their children to the white school if I was not willing to do the same. I did not ask to withdraw her name although I was afraid for her to go.

In great distress, I talked to John Salter. John explained that white people in Enfield relied upon Joseph Branch for leadership. He said, "Joseph Branch has his eyes on something bigger than anything in this town. As the manager

Fig. 37.1. White children attended this school on the west side of Enfield. / Courtesy of the North Carolina Office of Historic Preservation.

of Dan Moore's campaign for governor of North Carolina, Joseph Branch will never let a violent incident occur in the integration of Enfield's white school. If he tells this community not to engage in violence, there will be no violence." At the time, I did not understand exactly what John meant, for I had little idea about how the white community functioned. With great trepidation, I finally accepted what appeared to be inevitable: my six-year-old daughter, Tanya, would go to the white school in September.

The school building itself was located in a large open area in Sherrod Heights. Built after the end of World War II, Enfield Graded School stood behind a row of pristine homes in which resided the Branches, Sherrods, and other leading white citizens of the town (Fig. 37.1). The school not only boasted a large auditorium and separate gymnasium but even had an outside swimming pool.

The new white school had been constructed during a time when Enfield's Black youngsters of high school age had no school to attend within the town limits. Showing little concern for this group of children, the Board of Education had relocated the white Enfield Graded School, leaving the old building on Whitaker Street empty, and constructed a beautiful new school building in Sherrod Heights. That Black students could use the former building that had been abandoned by the whites was never a consideration.

After my father and other Black Enfield parents pleaded with the board to provide a school for their high school children, the Board built a nondescript, minimal school for Blacks on the grounds of the Inborden Elementary School. The Inborden High School was opened in 1952 just two years before *Brown v. Topeka* declared that separate was not equal and ordered the desegregation of public schools. Ten years later, in 1964 Halifax County schools were not racially integrated, and the school board had no plans to do so.

The town had seen many unprecedented events in the twelve months since Reed Johnson ran for the town commission, but nothing more shocked Enfield Black people that summer than to hear that Black kids would go to the white Enfield School in the fall of 1964. Wherever we went during the hot, humid August days, someone would inevitably say to my daughter, "I hear that you will be going to school with white people." And often she asked me, "Mama, what are white people?" I pointed to the white people who were helping us and said, "Buddy Tieger (a Duke student) and J. V. Henry (a SNCC worker) are white."

While we tried to prepare our children for their entry into the white school in the fall, local white citizens organized an alternative school for children whose parents did not want them to attend school with Black children. They founded a Christian Academy, occupying an old, un-used elementary school about four miles from town. Later, the sponsors moved the school to Whitakers, a small town six miles south of Enfield. Parents who did not want their children to attend the integrated Enfield School could send them to the Enfield Academy. Later, we learned that the local bank offered low-interest loans to white parents who could not afford the tuition.

Earlier in the summer, we had reached out to the white Christian community in Enfield by attending two white church services in the town. On the first Sunday, Reed and Lillie Smith went to Enfield's white First Baptist Church. No one stopped the two civil rights leaders from entering the church and they stayed for the service, although church officials did call the police, who blocked Dennis Street to vehicular traffic. On the next Sunday, Reed and I attended the Episcopal Church not far from the closed Levon Theatre. We sat near the back of the church and no one said anything to us. They did not call the police.

In the hot days of late summer, tempers flared and the strained relations between the races reached the breaking point. One day in late August, Reed, while standing in the cashier's line at Davis' Grocery Store, casually asked the young white boy in front of him if he was ready for school to open. The boy's father walked up to Reed when he left the grocery store, and, without any warning, knocked him to the ground.

Tanya remembers the day. She had just turned six, but she knew that something was unusual because her father rang our front doorbell. He never used that entrance. Always, he drove his car into the garage, walked through the breezeway, and entered our home through a side door. I opened the door

Fig. 37.2. Tanya Johnson (Watson), who had just turned six, helped integrate the all-white Enfield Graded School, 1964. / Willa Cofield personal collection.

and cried out when I saw the anguish on Reed's face, the dirty stains on his usually neat clothes, and the ugly, bleeding abrasions on the back of his right arm. Tanya had been exposed to two burning crosses and several nights of fearful watching for attacks upon our home. I did not want her to hear her father describe whatever had happened to him, so I sent her off to her room, where she confided many years later, she decided that someone had chased her father to the front door and had stabbed him. After applying first aid to the abrasions on Reed's arm and some comfort to his hurt feelings, I called a Black doctor in Rocky Mount and asked if we could come to his office. Later, Reed went to the Enfield police station and pressed charges. The unprovoked assaulter, a local white man, claimed in municipal court that he attacked Reed because the Black man was harassing his son when he asked about his feelings toward school opening. The court fined the assailant thirty dollars.

By the end of the summer, six Black students had signed up to integrate the former all-white Enfield Graded School. The three elementary students were Pamela Ward, Tanya Johnson, and Victor Marrow, who were all six years old (Figs. 37.2 and 37.3). The three high school students were Ira Dale Sanders, Beverly Bailey, and Cornelius Tillery.

I remained apprehensive, for I had no idea what would happen on the first day of school. The night before the school opened, I laid out the clothes that

Fig. 37.3. Six-year-old Victor Marrow, one of the Enfield Six who integrated the Enfield Graded School, 1964. / Grassroots Media Productions.

Tanya would wear: a blue cotton dress with a white sailor collar, little white panties, a white crinoline slip, and hair ribbons.

The next morning, Reed, Tanya, and I met the other parents and their children in the parking lot beside Cofield Funeral Home. Victor Marrow did not join us because he lived with his parents on Ringwood Road within walking distance of Enfield School. His mother, Geraldine Marrow, said that while she was very fearful, Jeremiah Marrow, his father, had no fear because he was strong and had served in the war in Vietnam. Those who gathered in the parking lot decided that the five children would ride in two cars to the white school in Sherrod Heights. In our little blue Mustang, Reed and I led the way with three children in our car: my daughter Tanya, Pamela Ward, and Cornelius Tillery. The other two children, Ira Dale Sanders and Beverly Bailey, rode in the car with John Salter and his minister friend, Rev. Ed King from Jackson, Mississippi. A Tougaloo College chaplain and civil rights worker, Rev. Ed King had been a white victim of Klan violence in Mississippi.

We drove down Burnette Street, turned onto Sherrod Drive and before I knew it, we were in sight of the school. Two Enfield police cars were parked at curbside. Lined in front of the large two-story, brick structure were dozens of white adults, not yelling or cat-calling, but standing stony-faced and silent. They stood as witnesses to the desecration of this beloved citadel of

Fig. 37.4. Quiet and friendly, Ira Dale Sanders (ca. 1960) often went unnoticed as he integrated the formerly white school. / Courtesy of Cynthia Samuelson.

the white community. Scores of curious, younger white faces peered from the upstairs windows of their classrooms to gape at this historic event. As we parked in front of the school, six-year-old Tanya looked at the crowd and soberly remarked, "Now I know what white people are."

John and Reed walked with the six kids to the edge of the long cement walk that led to the front door of the school. Mr. Brooks, the principal, had promised that he would meet them there. He emerged from the building, briskly walked to meet the Black students, said "Good morning" to the adults, and escorted the six integrationists down the walk and through the front doors of the school. The three little kids followed the high school students, with Tanya's blue dress bouncing on her crinoline slip and Pam's ribbons flying in the wind as they walked past the cold eyes of the hostile crowd into the Enfield School.

Once inside, the children were sent to assigned classrooms. Six-year-old Victor Marrow and Pamela Ward were taken to one classroom, and that left Tanya alone as the only Black student in the other first-grade classroom. Victor, like the other two first graders, had just turned six. He remembers that on his birthday, the week before, the Marrow family had witnessed a Ku Klux Klan cross burning on Ringwood Road as they returned from an evening church meeting. To help prepare the little boy for his first day of school, Victor's parents, Jeremiah and Geraldine Marrow, actually took him

Fig. 37.5. Cornelius Tillery (ca. 1965) bravely participated in integrating the Enfield High School. / Grassroots Media Productions.

to Enfield School the day before school opened. Victor met his teacher, Ms. Harris, and the teacher showed him his desk by the window.

Little Victor knew exactly where he would sit. Victor remembers that things went smoothly in Ms. Harris's classroom except for Price Harrison Jr. who sat next to him. And every time Victor looked his way, this little six-year-old white boy stuck his tongue out at him. This rude behavior continued through a third day. Without any word of disapproval or correction from the teacher, Price became more aggressive. Finally, when he leaned far out from his chair to get almost in Victor's face, little Victor punched Price solidly in the nose. Ms. Harris assumed her role as teacher and sent both little boys to Mr. Brook's office. After listening to their stories, the principal told them if there were any more fights he would spank both of them. Victor remembers that as the two little boys left the principal's office and the door closed, they both burst out laughing.

As the lone Black student in her class, Tanya suffered slights and snubs, much of which she did not understand. One question that she asked me during that first year was, "Mama, why won't Tammy hold my hand when we are playing Red Rover?" Miss Fisher, the teacher, seemed kind and supportive, but on the playground, beyond the teacher's view, the children practiced their own version of segregation, often leaving Tanya ostracized and alone.

Fig. 37.6. Beverly Bailey Herbert integrated Enfield High School when she was a tenth grader. She is pictured here (ca. 2020) in Groton, Connecticut, where she served one term on the city council. / Herbert personal collection.

In appearance, Ira Dale looked so white that for several weeks many of the Enfield students thought that he was just a new student. He overheard a white Enfield High School student say, "They say that there is a Negro in our class, but where is he?" (Fig. 37.4). Years later, Ira Dale said that he could never figure out why he was chosen to integrate Enfield High School.

Cornelius Tillery was a ninth grader (Fig. 37.5). He remembers his experience at Enfield Graded School as "real tough." Cornelius says, "They really didn't want us over there. They wanted to make us give up, but I was determined to stick it out." He also heard that some Black and white preachers got together and said that there should be no violence when the Black children went over to the white school. Cornelius says that he could really see that the Black school he came from did not provide the same level of education that the white school offered its students.

Beverly Bailey remembered that in 1954, when she was in elementary school, her father had announced to the family with a look of satisfaction, the Supreme Court's decision to desegregate the schools (Fig. 37.6). At that time, Beverly never imagined that she would be one of six students to implement the decision in the local white school. During the days before the school opened in the fall of 1964, Jeff Whitehead, local druggist and a member of the Halifax County School Board, went to the Bailey farm, a few miles from the town of Enfield, to persuade Mr. Bailey to withdraw Beverly's application to attend Enfield School. The white man pointed out the danger of sending Beverly, a young girl, into such a contentious situation.

Mr. Bailey ignored the white man's warning, but he and his wife did go to the school to speak to Mr. Brooks, the principal. They wanted to check out in person the man who headed the Enfield School. Mr. Brooks assured them that their daughter would be safe, that no one would harm her. He would see to that. Beverly says that the principal was correct. "Nobody touched me. Nobody harmed me. Nobody said anything to me." Being ostracized in the white school deeply hurt Beverly. She did not attend the prom either her junior or senior year. In addition, her education was disrupted and she was late going to college. Beverly said that integrating the Enfield School was tough and depressing and it colored the rest of her life. These stories of courage are only representative of the sacrifices that many Black children made to racially integrate public schools in the 1960s.

38. The Second Hearing of Johnson v. Branch

While Enfield held its breath during the integration of the white school, the lawsuit, *Johnson v. Branch*, moved slowly through the courts. The second hearing took place on September 28, 1964, in the Wilson Division of the Eastern District of North Carolina's United States Federal Court. At stake in this hearing was whether my old job at Inborden High School could be filled permanently by someone else.

Ralph Moody, North Carolina attorney general, joined the defendants' counsel in the role of *amicus curiae*, having said earlier that the case could "drastically affect" North Carolina's system of hiring teachers.[75] Shortly after the Supreme Court decision in *Brown v. Topeka*, North Carolina, like other Southern states, had put teachers on a year-to-year contract, so that they could be easily terminated. It was this practice that the attorney general thought *Johnson v. Branch* threatened. On the list of defendants, school district member Percy F. Thorne replaced John McGwigan, whose name had been incorrectly submitted.[76]

I did not attend the hearing because my attorneys assured me that my presence was not required. Court records show that the defense attorney, Richard Allsbrook, spent much of the morning attacking the argument and testimony that we presented at the first hearing in New Bern. Allsbrook "totally denied" that I had been fired because of my civil rights activities. He asserted that I had lost my job because of personal difficulties with the principal. He said that I had become a victim of paranoia, developing "a persecution complex."[77]

Reviewing each of the charges that the principal made in his memorandum of March 10, Allsbrook claimed that each one was a significant neglect of duty, ridiculing Kunstler's description of the charges as "picayunish."[78] Commenting on the disagreement that the principal and I had about getting to school on time, Allsbrook charged that I was telling the school principal what the regulation meant. Clearly, he stated, the teacher's job was simply to obey the regulation. "You can't run a school with the teachers telling the principal what the regulations mean."[79] The truth was that after it became clear early in the fall that the principal was building a case to fire me, I took great pains to respect and follow all school regulations.

Although the principal and each of the members of the School District Committee all agreed that the March 10 memo was the only basis for their decision not to give me a contract, Allsbrook said that the deficiencies listed in the March 10 letter were not all-inclusive.[80] He said that the principal could have picked out any day and I would have been deficient in it because "she was just bucking him all of the way."[81] Allsbrook said that one thing stood out in the entire record: "... there was a conflict between the plaintiff and the principal during the entire year."[82] He said that returning me to my former position at Inborden School would be "intolerable."[83]

Allsbrook pointed to another teacher who was just as active, perhaps more, than I. He said that this teacher is still employed.[84] If the school board had opposed a teacher's participation in civil rights activities, surely it would have terminated this teacher. Here, he undoubtedly referred to Lillie Cousins Smith, whose affidavit appears below.

Affidavit of Lillie M. Smith[85]

I, Lillie M. Smith, being duly sworn and put under oath do hereby depose and state as follows:

1. That I am over the age of twenty-one years and a resident of Enfield, North Carolina, Halifax County.
2. That I am a teacher at Eastman High School, Halifax County, and was so employed at all times mentioned herein. That the principal of the school is George T. Young. That the superintendent is W. Henry

Fig. 38.1. Bold and daring, Lillie Smith (here in 2007) held the spirit of the Enfield Movement. / Willa Cofield personal collection.

Overman and the assistant superintendent of schools was at all times mentioned herein, Fred Young.

3. That on or about September 7, 1963, I was summoned from one of my morning classes to come to the office of the principal. That upon arriving there I found Mr. Overman and Mr. Young waiting to talk with me along with Principal Young.

4. That Mr. Overman first described the role of a teacher, citing among other things that a teacher traditionally must meet certain standards of dress and behavior. Mr. Overman stated that I had participated in picketing during recent civil rights demonstrations; to this statement I agreed. I asked what I was accused of, since the meeting seemed of an accusatory nature and tone, and being completely unexpected and unknown in my prior experience.

5. Superintendent Overman then pointed out that my job could be terminated for various reasons under state law, which he paraphrased.

6. In response to the above statements, which I felt were threatening in tone and intent, I described a conversation that I had had with Mr. Capus Waynick, a representative from Governor Sanford's office, in which he stated that there was no law in North Carolina, so far as he knew against a teacher's picketing. Superintendent Overman appeared disturbed and discomfited by this response.

7. Assistant Superintendent Young then claimed that my activities had resulted in the loss of a large grant to the county schools and that this loss was detrimental to all educational efforts in the county. He gave no details as to how the grant had been lost, what it was to have been for, or where it might have come from.
8. I answered Mr. Young's claim by expressing my concern for our local school system. I offered as evidence the fact that I had taught in this county for ten years, when much more attractive conditions and salary were available elsewhere.
9. Superintendent Overman and I then discussed the violence which had occurred at recent demonstrations, and I expressed the opinion that the violence was committed by the police and public officials against unarmed and nonviolent demonstrators.

Lillie Smith's spirited response to the superintendent and assistant superintendent's visit, as well as her apparent support from the principal of Eastman School, may have influenced the decision not to dismiss her (Fig. 38.1).

Allsbrook continued the argument for the defendants by reminding the judge that North Carolina Statute 115-72 required that a principal recommend a teacher, and the District Committee elect the teacher, "if they see fit to do so."[86]

He said that the four members of the district school committee who were there that night when her contract was not approved each testified that none of them had ever heard of her at all, didn't even know who she was except they knew by name that a Willa Johnson taught school at Inborden School. And their sole basis for not seeing fit to reemploy the plaintiff was these items set out in this March 10, 1964, letter, which they considered serious.[87]

In conclusion, Allsbrook told the court: "There is more at stake here than just the plaintiff and the defendant, Your Honor, there is the whole public school system throughout the State of North Carolina. There is the welfare of these students of all ages and all groups there at Inborden High School."[88]

Attorney Kunstler responded to the defendants' attorney by agreeing:

Your Honor, may it please the court. I agree with Mr. Allsbrook, there is more at stake here than the plaintiff or the defendants.... We have a very serious case before Your Honor. It is not a question of one school teacher. First of all, it is a class action. It is brought on behalf of all the teachers in the district and in the county. I don't think that we are here to try before

Your Honor a case involving a dispute between a teacher and principal, while I don't think the dispute really existed.[89]

Kunstler stated that the principal had a right to criticize me for the items in the March 10 memo. But after calling them to my attention, Principal Williams had written to me on March 31, informing me that he had seen improvement and that he had recommended me for employment for the upcoming school year. Kunstler reminded the judge that I was an exemplary teacher. He said, "When your Honor reads the depositions, he will find that she is characterized by almost every one of the adverse witnesses as an above average teacher." Kunstler asked, "Why was his recommendation not accepted?"[90]

When Judge Larkins asked why the district committee did not follow the principal's recommendation in the March 31 letter, Allsbrook said that the district committee sensed a "reluctant recommendation."[91] The attorney said that they were "exercising under the statute, their discretion."[92]

School district committee members claimed that they did not know me and they certainly did not know of my civil rights activities.[93] Mr. Coppage and Mr. Thorne—both of whom voted against my reemployment—admitted that they knew Reed Johnson, my husband. In his statement to the Court, Kunstler pointedly said:

Now they make a big to-do that they did not know exactly who Mrs. Johnson was.[94] But I submit to your Honor that there is certainly a reasonable belief that if they knew who Reed Johnson was, they knew who Mrs. Johnson was. A twelve-year teacher does not suddenly become something different from what she was, and the only reason that she suddenly became something different than what she was, was her civil rights activities which ran from April of one year to April of another year and which encompasses the entire period that we are concerned with here.

Kunstler admitted that I had no right to a contract. I had no right to public employment. Yet, the civil rights lawyer averred, I did have constitutional rights under the First Amendment, and I had been working to secure rights under the Fourteenth Amendment.[95] Kunstler called the judge's attention to a case in Arkansas, *Sheldon v. Tucker*, where a teacher had been dismissed because he refused to admit that he had contributed to certain organizations within a five-year period. The teacher was dismissed, but the United States Supreme Court had upheld his right to his job. The Court said that the statute deprived Sheldon of certain First Amendment rights, certain Fifth Amendment rights, and certain Fourteenth Amendment rights. At the risk of losing public employment, Kunstler said, "A teacher should not have to give up her rights to the constitution."[96]

Minutes of the District Committee meeting, recorded by Mrs. Morrisette, showed that the meeting had been held on May 27 with all members present. Jeff Whitehead of the Halifax County Board of Education was also present. The motion was made and seconded that contracts for teachers at Inborden High School be renewed with the exception of Mrs. Willa C. Johnson. Failure to renew the contract was on the grounds of a letter from principal L. M. Williams written to Mrs. Johnson, with copies going to Superintendent Overman and Chairman R. L. Coppage. The vote was two to one.

Kunstler said:

I think that you can take notice from the very testimony before you that there is not a single credible affirmative reason why her contract was not approved. Everyone admits she was improving. The principal recommended her. The Board members said he said she was improving. The only serious thing you have for explanation is an inference that because he said she was improving in some areas, she was not improving in others. You cannot acknowledge that he was there at that meeting [on April 23, 1964].[97]

Despite Allsbrook's motion that the defendants be allowed to fill my old job permanently, Judge Larkins decided to continue holding the position open. He said that it would provide time for the respondents to get the rest of their case before him and for the judge to consider the memorandum of law that Kunstler promised to submit.

39. NEA to the Rescue

As the school year began in the fall of 1964, a temporary English teacher filled my former position at Inborden High School. I was without a job. We turned to the National Education Association for help. In 1949, the NEA had founded the DuShane Legal Defense Fund to ensure the fair and equitable treatment of all educators. The NEA offered assistance in any of the following circumstances:

1. A serious violation of the teacher's professional or legal rights, indigenous to his [sic] professional assignment
2. The establishment of a legal precedent affecting other members of the educational profession
3. A serious welfare need of a teacher, a group of teachers, or an association.[98]

Working with officers of the North Carolina Teachers Association, we were able to meet the requirements established by the DuShane Defense Fund. It was a very fortunate development, as I was unemployed and my husband's salary could not support us. The DuShane Defense Fund provided modest support throughout the school year of 1964–65 when no school would employ me. The NEA made it possible for me to continue living in Enfield.

On December 14, I sent the NEA DuShane Defense Fund the following letter:

P.O. Box 626
Enfield, North Carolina

December 14, 1964
Mr. Oscar E. Thompson, Chairman
DuShane Defense Fund Committee
1201 Sixteenth Street, Northwest
Washington, D.C.

Dear Mr. Thompson:

Without doubt, the decision of the National Education Association to support my suit has been the most encouraging development in my legal fight against the school authorities in this county.

As the period of litigation has lengthened, the question of my family's economic survival has become of paramount importance. It had seemed likely that even before the court ruled, we would be forced to leave this area to seek work in a less hostile climate.

I am, therefore, deeply grateful for the check for $1200, which greatly aids in defraying living expenses incurred since September.

The next court hearing, already postponed twice, has been rescheduled for January 11. In the meantime, I expect to be quite busy with the activities of the Halifax County Voters Movement and the organization of a literacy class, which I hope to begin teaching next year.

Yours sincerely,
Willa Johnson

A week later on December 22, I received a letter from Mr. E. B. Palmer, Executive Secretary of the North Carolina Teachers Association. He said that he had recently assumed the office of executive secretary and the board of directors had directed him to offer me the assistance of the NCTA in whatever way they could be of help. He requested that I meet with him and Mr. F. D. McNeill Jr., field representative of the NCTA, in early January because my case had become of paramount importance.

The North Carolina Teachers Association was the segregated African American division of the National Education Association in North Carolina, headquartered in Raleigh. The letterhead on E. B. Palmer's letter includes all the names of the North Carolina Teachers Association's State Board of Directors as listed below:

NCTA-NEA Officers
4. S. E. Duncan, '66, President, Salisbury
5. M. M. Daniel, '66, Vice President, Wilson
6. Mrs. Geneva J. Bowe, '66, Recording Secretary, Murfreesboro
7. N. H. Harris, '66, Treasurer, Raleigh
8. Lafayette Parker, '66, Immediate Past President, Winston-Salem
9. Mrs. Juanita Corin, '65, President, Classroom Teachers, Bolton
10. John H. Lucas, '66, State NEA Director, Durham
11. Mrs. Elizabeth D. Koontz, '67, President-Elect, NEA, Dept. of Classroom Teachers, Salisbury

DISTRICT PRESIDENTS
James R. Barnes, East Piedmont—Henderson
A. R. Bowe, Northeastern—Murfreesboro
J. A. Brown, Southeastern—Lillington
A. D. Smith, Coastal Plains—Dover
James A. Clarke, Southwest—Charlotte
Charles H. Coleman, Piedmont—Reidsville
L. H. Moseley, North Central—Gumberry
L. R. Campbell, Western—Statesville

MEMBERS-AT-LARGE
G. A. Page, '65, Raeford
Mrs. Jettie D. Morrison, '65, Statesville
Edna S. Smallwood, '65, Trenton
O. N. Freeman, '66, Charlotte
J. H. Twitty, '66, Saint Pauls
King A. Williams, '66, Winfall
Mrs. L. P. Burton, '67, Asheville
Mrs. L. B. Daniel, '67, Raleigh
S. O. Jones, '67, Greensboro

40. Halifax County Board of Commissioners

With the financial support of the NEA, I was able to devote my time and give my full support to the Halifax County Voters Movement. The determined members of the HCVM took on the daunting task of appealing to the Halifax County Board of Commissioners.

In the fall of 1964, Halifax County still largely maintained the attitudes expressed by Judge R. Hunt Parker of Roanoke Rapids, Superior Court judge of Halifax County. Responding to proposed civil rights legislation before Congress in 1948, he wrote: "Large numbers of people within this nation seem determined to do all within their power to destroy segregation laws between the races, and to tear down our traditions and manner of life in the South.... they propose measures ... that can achieve no practical good and can only lead to trouble and tragedy between the races."[99] Despite the widespread conditions of poverty among Black Halifax County residents, the gross differences in educational facilities, and the political domination of the white community, the judge said: "We of the white race can be justly proud of what we have done for the Negro race in this county. We are living together in peace and harmony and progress and prosperity."[100]

Writing two years later in 1950, Louis Austin, editor of the Black weekly the *Carolina Times* and a native of Enfield, provided a stark contrast:

> It is in eastern North Carolina that the vicious sharecropper system still flourishes; it is in eastern North Carolina that the worst schools for Negroes exist. Here, justice for Negroes in the courts is a disgrace to our entire legal system, and here, police brutality abounds. It is in eastern North Carolina that Negroes receive the lowest wages for their labor

and a Negro who happens to own a few acres of land or a few pieces of real estate is looked upon with contempt by a majority of white people. It is in this section of the state that Negroes are kept from voting and intimidated if they even try to register to vote.[101]

Halifax County is located in the heart of eastern North Carolina. The Halifax County Voters Movement had sponsored its own efforts to deal with widespread poverty in the county. On Saturdays in the summer, the organization distributed clothing sent by donors from all over the nation. The donations had come in response to urgent requests for help sent out by SCEF and SNCC. Carloads of individuals who came for free clothing filled the parking lot and nearby street. A meeting regarding food stamps held in Halifax, the county seat, that brought hundreds of people to the small town. Many had misunderstood the purpose of the meeting and thought that free food would be distributed. John Salter, Reed, and I drove to Halifax together and arrived late. We could not find a parking space within blocks of the First Baptist Church where the meeting was held. The packed church could offer no standing room to latecomers, but John Salter, who was scheduled to speak, went through a back door and with great difficulty made his way to the podium. Reed and I never did get in, and we remained outside with the crowd of other latecomers.

In view of the widespread need and pervasive racism, the HCVM also sought to become an affiliate of the Southern Christian Leadership Conference. Not long after we became an affiliate, Harry Boyte Sr., who worked as a special assistant to Dr. Martin Luther King and headed SCLC's Operation Dialogue, came to Enfield and spoke at the St. Paul Baptist Church. Boyte, who was a Southern white man, told us that mayors of Southern towns, eager to have Northern industries relocate within their borders, initially welcomed him when he told them that his organization wanted to come to their town. When he stated that his organization was the SCLC, however, they became hostile and threatening. Mr. Boyte also told us that we should become more assertive in dealing with local white people.

Following his advice, the leaders of the Halifax County Voters Movement appealed to the all-white Halifax County Board of Commissioners with demands for change. A delegation of HCVM members appeared before the Board of Commissioners in early December 1964. More than fifty persons attended the meeting of the commissioners to call for an end to racial discrimination in the schools, hospitals, law enforcement agencies, and municipal and county governments. The petition began with the statement: "... [W]e insist that Negro citizens, who constitute a majority of the people in this county, are entitled to equal opportunity in the economic and civic life of Halifax County without resort to legal measures, which cause commotion, enmity, and division." We cited statistics to show the wide economic disparity in Black and white citizens in the county. The median income for white Halifax County residents was $4,600 and for Blacks, $1,300.[102]

Rev. Dunlap pointed to the total absence of Blacks in county and municipal governments, the almost complete segregation of the public schools, the squalor and poverty in which many Blacks were forced to live, and the repeated attempts by the Ku Klux Klan to intimidate Blacks. He said:

> We are puzzled and chagrined by your indifference to these injustices which constitute a blot on Halifax County our state and our nation. . . . [W]e respectively petition the Board of Commissioners to direct all mayors, school board members, town commissioners and hospital boards to lift the barriers of segregation wherever they may be found in this county.[103]

The ten-point program from the Halifax County Voters Movement demanded:

1. That qualified Negroes be employed in municipal and county jobs as police officers, deputies, sheriffs, tax collectors, clerks, stenographers, meter readers, social workers, engineers, etc.
2. That jails and rest homes be integrated.
3. That the present system of jury selection be altered so that Negroes are not systematically excluded from jury duty.
4. That Ku Klux Klansmen and other terrorists be deterred from burning crosses and riding through Negro communities.
5. That a Fair Employment Practice law prohibiting employers from discriminating against applicants or employees because of race, color, or national origin be enacted in Halifax County.
6. That surplus food and food stamps be made available to needy families in this county.
7. That a county bi-racial committee be formed to find solutions to many of these problems.
8. That the Community Hospital, Scotland Neck, and Roanoke Rapids Hospital be directed to integrate all facilities.
9. That racial labels be removed from all public buildings.
10. That an investigation be made of the practice of segregation existing in the schools of Halifax County and that the County Board

of Education be directed to present a plan of desegregation of the system forthwith.[104]

Though the chairman of the County Board of Commissioners called for the inclusion of the ten-point program in the official minutes, no comments came from other commissioners. The chairman told the delegation that they would take the petition under "advisement" and the petitioners would be "informed" of any action that the commissioners took on their proposal. Rev. Dunlap responded, "We've been taken under advisement for 340 years. We want some action." Rev. Johnson added, "We are appealing to your honesty and integrity for an answer, not all this evasiveness."[105]

Finally, Chairman Harry Branch said: "This Board is fully aware of the great need to improve relations [but] this kind of strife is only a hinder to growth. We want to improve [sic] the Negro race in Halifax County. It is a necessity that this be done. If you can take this as a belief we can get along fine."[106]

Recently, in my files, I found a draft of a letter that I wrote to Mr. Boyte shortly after the HCVM made this appeal to the Halifax County commissioners. In that letter I said that we had followed his advice and had become more assertive in confronting the white community. My letter stated that the meeting of the Halifax County Board of Commissioners lasted from 2:00 until 3:30 p.m. while the Black delegates "pelleted [sic] the tight-lipped commissioners with questions." I said that though the board failed to make concessions, we believed that we had made some progress when the commissioners "grudgingly admitted a need for a bi-racial committee." Reverends Dunlap and Johnson and Mrs. Cochran returned the following week and succeeded in extracting from the board an agreement that they would place the ten-point program on the agenda for the January meeting.

The *Roanoke Rapids Daily Herald* published the response to the petition the day before the January meeting. The commissioners prefaced their answer to the petition by saying that they would not tolerate any violence or unlawful act by members of groups of any race. In response to the request that a fair employment practice law be enacted in Halifax County, they stated that the commissioners did not have the power to enact such a law. They said that the requested food stamp program would be put into effect within the near future. Responding to the request for a biracial committee, the statement pointed to the existence of three races [Native American, Caucasian, Black] in the county and promised that they would have representation from all the races residing in the county on any committees that they should appoint. They said that the commissioners had no control over hospitals and no legal authority to direct any phase of their operation. In response to the request for removal of racial labels from public buildings, they responded that they had already ordered that racial labels be removed from county buildings and that they had no authority to remove labels from buildings not owned by the county. They said that they had no control over the operation of the schools, and other than providing the money for schools' operation, they had no connection with the public schools.[107] The commissioners had noted openings in the county's Welfare Department, and a few weeks later, Margaret Dunlap became the first Black professional to work in the county government. The HCVM considered it a major breakthrough. If the commissioners thought that the employment of Rev. Dunlap's wife would silence his voice, they were mistaken, as the voice of the fiery leader remained as strident as ever.

41. My Interrogation by NEA Panel

While I was focused on the struggle of the HCVM with the county board of commissioners, my lawyers appealed to the National Education Association for further help with my suit. The NEA responded by convening a panel to investigate my case on March 8, 1965. The panel met in Washington, DC, and I was asked to attend. I remember being fearful of this interrogation, but John Salter reassured me that the panelists were not adversaries; they were people who wanted me to win. On the Monday before the hearing, Reed and I drove to Washington and checked into the Mayflower Hotel, which I had read about as the site of many important government-sponsored activities. I still remember my awe when I saw the white balloon chandeliers that hung in a block-long row from the entrance of the huge lobby to the distant exit.

Five active educators sat on the panel that had been assembled by the NEA Commission on Professional Rights and Responsibilities (CPRR): a state college president and past chairman of the NEA Citizenship Committee: Dr. Thomas Robinson, president of Glassboro State Teachers College in New Jersey; a university department chairman and past chairman of the NEA Commission on Tenure and Academic Freedom: Dr. Theodore Jensen, Dean of Education at Ohio State University; two NEA directors, one a classroom teacher: Mrs. Carrie Brown from Newport News, Virginia, and one a principal: Dr. H. Phillip Constans Jr., principal of Cocoa Beach High School in Cocoa Beach, Florida; and a current member of the CPRR, who was also a classroom teacher: Mrs. Edna Griffin, past president of the Philadelphia Teachers Association.

The members of the panel formed by the large, influential teachers' association listened with empathy to my story. Mrs. Edna Griffin, a member of the panel, later reported the outcome of the panel's interrogation at the annual NEA Convention held in New York City, June 27–July 3, 1965. She said that the panel had used a full day to look at the details surrounding my dismissal.

In her report, Mrs. Griffin described the work of the panel.[108] During the interview, I had responded to scored of questions regarding the charges brought against me. She reported that the selected CPRR Panel gave careful scrutiny to the charges. She said that the committee questioned me about my philosophy, attitudes, standards, practices, plans, and performance to determine my professional competence. The committee also examined judicial records and other data as a part of their investigation. These items were weighted, and the committee made an overall evaluation of my performance. There had been an exemplary twelve-year record, an immediate correction of the seven points contained in the principal's letter, an unqualified recommendation by the principal that I be rehired, a signed contract, and an absence of any other derogatory information beyond the seven listed points.

She said that the panel also took into consideration the political and civil rights activities in which I, my husband, and my father had been engaged. Considering the factors noted above, the committee concluded that there was sufficient evidence to warrant a conclusion that something other than my record as a teacher had prompted the termination of employment.

Mrs. Griffin said that it was the unanimous opinion of the expert panel that in the total background, in intelligence and interest in knowledge and production, "Mrs. Johnson portrayed not only an outstandingly desirable teacher, but also presented herself as a person of highly desirable traits. It seemed to the panel that the issues of professional competency would not have been cause for nonrenewal of contract but rather her direct activities on behalf of a Negro voter registration drive."[109]

Mrs. Griffin stated that the committee chose Dr. Constans to represent the panel of experts and to testify in a federal district court on behalf of Mrs. Johnson as she sought reinstatement in her job. Mrs. Griffin added that this was the first time that a federal court had recognized a representative of the organized teaching profession as qualified to give expert opinion on a matter involving teacher competency and fair dismissal procedures.

42. The Third Hearing of Johnson v. Branch

At the third hearing, held in Wilson on March 15, 1965, Dr. Constans represented the NEA Commission on Professional Rights and Responsibilities as an expert witness in the field of education, teacher qualifications, and teacher dismissals.

During his long testimony, Dr. Constans said that the Commission "considered" Mrs. Johnson's credentials to teach in North Carolina, her college background, the principal's evaluation, and information relevant to her competency in the principal's deposition. He said that they looked at whether she was keeping abreast of developments in her subject matter, her knowledge of her subject matter, and her general attitude toward teaching.

Phil Hirschkop asked the witness to consider each of the accusations on the March 10 Memo. The Florida principal said that none of them merited her dismissal, singly or collectively.[110]

Mr. Hirschkop then asked Dr. Constans about the fair dismissal standard set forth by the NEA. Dr. Constans said that the standards were supported by the Congress of Parents and Teachers, the American Association of School Administrators, and various departments of the National Education Association. He explained that the principles had been in published form since 1950 and the profession believed that they should be followed whether there are legal requirements that must be met, or whether the teacher had tenure, or, regardless of the length of the teacher's employment. He outlined the following five steps:

1. The complaint should be brought promptly to the attention of the teacher.
2. Every effort should be made to help the teacher correct the condition.
3. Except for extremely serious cases, time should be given for the teacher's improvement.
4. The charges should be bona fide and verifiable and clearly stated to the employee in writing.
5. An employee should be given the opportunity to explain or otherwise defend himself.[111]

Dr. Constans said it was the opinion of the panel that these procedures should apply in all cases where a teacher is not to be reemployed, or is to be dismissed, whichever the case may be. He said, "From the information we had, the committee did not follow any of these systems."[112]

Hirschkop: Mr. [sic] Constans, in arriving at a final opinion concerning the failure to rehire Willa Johnson, in view of all her academic background, the principal's rating of her and in view of the depositions which you read, is it your opinion that the reasons given by the school committee, and by the principal for the failure to rehire Mrs. Johnson are reasonable reasons over which to fail to rehire this teacher?

Mr. Constans: I do not think that they were sufficient reasons.[113]

At the final hearing, over the objection of plaintiff's counsel, the Court permitted Mr. Williams to file an affidavit saying that he had "rather reluctantly" recommended me for rehiring. Hirschkop went over each charge on the March 10 letter to have the principal answer whether or not I had shown improvement in each area.

Hirschkop: And she had done everything, had she not, that you had pointed out in those seven areas?
Williams: She had improved.[114]
Hirschkop: Well, were there any areas—was she late for game duty after March 31st?
Williams: I do not recall her being late.
Hirschkop: Was she late for work?
Williams: No, I do not recall any.
Hirschkop: Did she refuse to do ground duty?
Williams: After March 31st, I do not recall.
Hirschkop: Did Mrs. Johnson fail to attend any further PTA meetings after March 31st?
Williams: I do not recall she [sic] not attending any.
Hirschkop: Did she fail to do building duty after March 31st that you know of?
Williams: I do not recall.
Hirschkop: Did she fail to stand at [the] door to supervise pupils as they changed classes?
Williams: I do not recall.
Hirschkop: Were her cabinets free and clear?
Williams: Well, she cleaned it up after the first time we had this.
Hirschkop: Did she refuse to do ground duty?
Williams: After March 31st, I do not recall.[115]

District committee members Percy Thorne, Frances Arnold, and Robert Coppage also testified at the final hearing. All three repeated that they had no knowledge of my civil rights activities before the suit was made public. They had relied upon the March 10 memorandum as adequate reasons for not renewing my contract.[116]

43. Judge Larkins Rules on Johnson v. Branch

Four months later, in June 1965, Judge Larkins of the Eastern District of the United States Federal Court issued a ruling in the *Johnson v. Branch* case. His conclusion: the plaintiffs failed to present sufficient facts that the defendants were depriving her of her constitutionally protected rights.

> The Court has serious doubts about whether a Federal jurisdictional issue has been raised. The North Carolina General Statutes (G. S. 115-72 and 115-42) have given the various school committees, superintendents of county and city schools, boards of education of county and city administrative units the power to employ or not employ public school teachers. There are no conditions or vested rights in regard to employment or re-employment of school teachers, and the methods and reasons for employing a teacher would seem to be a local matter.[117]

He said that to hold these local officials liable when they are exercising their discretionary duties would be to place such a burden on them that it would make it hazardous for them to exercise that discretion with which they have been endowed by statute. The Judge said that he had examined the plaintiff's allegations, in light of the record, pleadings, testimony, depositions, affidavits, and exhibits to weigh the evidence according to its credibility and conclude the matter on its merits.

The Court concluded: "There has been a failure by plaintiff to show a conspiracy on the part of the defendants when they failed to re-employ plaintiff for the school year 1964–1965. The Court specifically finds that there was good cause for not re-employing the plaintiff as established by the evidence." He continued, "Plaintiff failed to observe the school rules as interpreted by her immediate supervisor and published in the Teacher's Handbook."[118]

The judge said that it was reasonable to infer that the plaintiff's civil rights activities did have a bearing on her ability to perform her work, but not in the

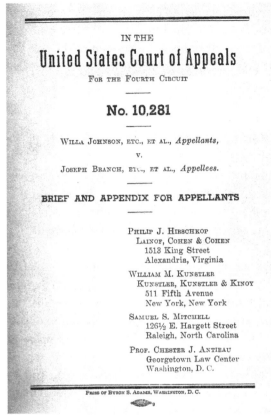

Fig. 43.1. Cover of the appeal brief that Willa's lawyers filed in the Fourth Circuit Court of Appeals. / Willa Cofield personal collection.

way that the complaint alleges. Judge Larkins said that the civil rights activities prohibited the plaintiff from performing her teaching job satisfactorily, but he said that those activities were not the reason for her dismissal.

The additional demands made on her time by the civil rights activities of 1963–1964 prevented her from devoting the usual amount of time which plaintiff normally devoted to her teaching profession, and in that respect one might conclude that she was not rehired because of her civil rights activities.

Therefore, it is ordered that upon a determination of the factual issues before the Court, this action being determined on its merits, defendants' motion to dismiss be, and the same is hereby granted. It is further ordered that plaintiff's prayer for injunctive relief be, and the same is hereby denied.[119]

This decision, needless to say, created grave disappointment in our community. Based upon Judge Larkins's earlier decisions in the *Austin v. Butts* case, we had hoped for a similarly fair and even application of justice in *Johnson v. Branch*. Salter and my attorneys informed me of the ruling, and in the next breath, told me of their desire to appeal Judge Larkins's decision. I strongly supported an appeal, but we had no funds to pay the expenses that would inevitably accompany an appeal to the Fourth Circuit Appellate Court.

Salter and my attorneys worked assiduously to find funds to support an appeal. Here again the primary source was the National Education Association's DuShane Defense Fund. In addition, the NEA filed an *amicus curiae* and Richard Morgan, NEA attorney, collaborated with my attorneys in filing our appeal to the Fourth Circuit Appellate Court (Fig. 43.1).

44. Building a New Life

Because I had lost the case in the Eastern District Court against the Halifax County officials, I found it impossible to find a teaching job in Halifax County. I heard of a vacancy in Nash County, but when that school system did not even offer me an opportunity for an interview, I realized that I was no longer able to work as a teacher in northeastern North Carolina.

In midsummer of 1965, Chauncey Stokes II, a funeral director and friend who lived in the nearby city of Rocky Mount, drove my husband and me to Durham and introduced us to his friend, Dr. William Darity. Dr. Darity, who was the first Black person to receive a PhD from the University of North Carolina, was also the husband of a friend of my teenage years, Ann Royall Darity of Wilson. Dr. Darity was program development director at the North Carolina Fund, a new state agency that sought to address poverty in eleven North Carolina communities. He had heard of my case and after we met, he asked me to send him a curriculum vitae. I was not sure what a curriculum vitae was, but I wrote a narrative describing the salient events in my life. At a second meeting, Dr. Darity offered me a job as a technical assistant with the responsibility of coordinating one of three seminars that the Fund planned to sponsor that summer. I was assigned the seminar that explored the maximum feasible participation of poor people in community antipoverty programs. The job required that I work in Durham, eighty-five miles from Enfield. I would live in Durham during the week and drive to Enfield for weekends.

I left home late on a Sunday afternoon toward the end of June. Tanya's and my clothes filled the back seat of our white Chevrolet. We drove over to South

Dixie Street and picked up Deborah Jones, who had been one of our youngest participants in the civil rights protests. Deborah had agreed to watch Tanya while I worked at my new job at the North Carolina Fund.

I took Highway 561, which wound through Louisburg and Franklinton and finally intersected Interstate 85. Once I reached the interstate, I was soon in the Piedmont city of Durham.

Through a realtor, I had made arrangements to share an apartment with a woman named Lettie, who leased a two-bedroom apartment near North Carolina Central College. She worked outside the city and only needed the apartment during the weekends. A few weeks into the deal, I walked into the apartment on Cecil Street and found that she had moved out and taken all the furniture. Tanya and I literally had an empty apartment.

Through the help of my parents, Reed, and friends, I was able to acquire a sofa and beds for the three of us. Lettie had left a picnic table with attached benches, so that we could sit and eat our meals. Over the next few weeks, I worked hard to make the apartment a habitable place for Tanya, Debbie, and me. I found an old-fashioned chest in a used furniture store in Chapel Hill. I bought two yellow canvas director's chairs, and I found a used round table that reminded me of our dining room table in Enfield. I refinished the chest and felt very satisfied with the outcome. In a Durham fabric shop, I found a soft flannel-like fabric printed with sprightly turquoise daisies. I made a floor-length tablecloth from the cotton material and covered the small, round table. The beautiful blue tablecloth and the yellow canvas chairs lent a bright, cheerful look to the living room. A few years earlier when the interior decorator had suggested accessories or fabrics for my Enfield home, I had been hesitant and full of doubt that my choice would not represent "good taste." In the apartment, I felt free to exercise my own judgment.

The North Carolina Fund had been a brainchild of Governor Terry Sanford and preceded the Office of Economic Opportunity, for which it became a model. Operating from 1963 to 1968, the Fund received and spent over $13 million to stimulate growth and to alleviate poverty in the state. The Ford Foundation supplied an initial grant for a demonstrative program to be dissolved after five years. Additional money came from other North Carolina foundations and the federal government.

The many programs that the Fund sponsored included Manpower Improvement through Community Effort, which established field offices in eastern North Carolina to assist unemployed workers and their families, and Mobility, which recruited unemployed workers in eastern North Carolina and helped them and their families move to jobs in industrial areas in the central and western part of the state. Other Fund programs included a summer volunteer project for college students, training for community leaders and workers, training for the federal program VISTA (Volunteers in Service to America), Outward Bound (a survival training program for youth), and internships and curriculum development programs in colleges.

When the Fund closed in 1968, several organizations continued its work. They included the Low Income Housing Development Corporation (where I worked from 1968 to 1969), the Foundation for Community Development, and the Learning Institute of North Carolina.

At the Fund I found myself surrounded by white people. Beyond my work with the activists who had volunteered their help in Enfield, I had never worked with white people before. I had had several white teachers at Hampton, and I think there were two white students in my graduating class, but interacting with white people on a daily basis in a workplace was a novel and somewhat unnerving experience.

I joined a three-person staff composed of myself and two young white men: Terry was a Duke University law student and Gary was a very confident, brash student from the University of North Carolina. We occupied an office together and were supported by a lovely young Black secretary who lived in Carrboro, a less well-known community near Chapel Hill. A white student intern, whose first name was Dotty, also helped with the office work.

Dr. Darity accepted a position at the University of Massachusetts and left the Fund a few weeks after I began working there. There was literally no experienced senior staff member to guide our work, and we carried out our assignments as best we could. My major responsibility was to identify and recruit participants for the seminar on the maximum feasible participation of poor people in community antipoverty programs. I learned that senior staff feared that the seminar, which would involve leaders from civil rights movement, might be explosive.

Much of the work took place on the telephone, a mode of communication at which I did not excel. Someone suggested that I write down the major points that I wanted to cover before I made calls, a practice that helped but hardly supplied me with the self-assurance and confidence that my colleagues obviously displayed. Gary had been editor of the *Daily Tar Heel*, the student newspaper at UNC, and highly valued his own opinions, so much so that after the Watts uprising in August, he called the White House with suggestions about how to prevent future urban outbreaks.

John Ehle, the novelist friend of the Fund's director, George Esser, sent word to me that he had met a bright young lawyer in Atlanta that he thought would make a good moderator for the seminar. Following this suggestion, I invited Vernon Jordan, a young Black lawyer raised in the Atlanta projects, to chair the seminar. While working in Enfield, I had met Floyd McKissick and Goldie Frinks, so I found it easy to invite them. Goldie Frinks came and brought Sarah Smalls, who had led the struggle for freedom in Williamston, a Martin County town less than fifty miles from Enfield. I thought someone who taught political science on the college level would have ideas about the subject and somehow came upon the name of John Strange, professor of political science at Duke University. Professor Strange agreed to attend if I promised to invite the president of the Duke University Custodial Workers' Union. I was happy to comply with this request and they both attended. Another participant came from the mountains of West Virginia and informed us that he had never seen a commercial airliner before he made the flight to Durham. I also invited a Black woman who organized her Los Angeles neighborhood from the laundromat but, because of budget constraints, I had to rescind the invitation, which deeply distressed her and me. The daylong meeting was taped on less-than-proficient equipment, and I spent months transcribing the dialogue and then writing a report of the day's discussion.

Later in the fall, at the request of Floyd McKissick, I coordinated a statewide conference at which he proposed that the Black community establish trading posts, or cooperative stores, across the state of North Carolina. The conference, which was held in Raleigh, attracted a full house. Jerry Voorhis, director of the Cooperative League of the United States, came to deliver the address. Mr. Voorhis had served five terms as a California representative in the US Congress before being defeated by Richard Nixon. The trading post idea never went anywhere, but it may have helped Mr. McKissick develop the concept of Soul City, which he announced while serving as national director of the Congress of Racial Equality. Soul City was to be a planned Black city located on 1,800 acres on Interstate 85. Soul City never became a town, but after McKissick supported Nixon in the election of 1968, federal grants permitted the developers to pave streets and install water lines. A few people built homes in full faith that the dream of developing a city would one day become a reality.

For a short period, I had no assignment at the North Carolina Fund, but then James (Kwame) McDonald, Black director of the Department of Community Support, asked me to join his staff as a technical assistant. The Department of Community Support had as its mission supporting people in the eleven communities that the Fund assisted. I was happy to join what seemed the most vibrant and active part of the agency. Jim McDonald had come to North Carolina from St. Paul, Minnesota, and was full of energy and ideas about

Fig. 44.1. Jim (Kwame) McDonald (here in 1965) led the Department of Community Support at the North Carolina Fund. / Willa Cofield personal collection.

empowering Black people (Fig. 44.1). He had a half-burned Confederate flag on the wall over his desk, a defiant statement of his antiracist, pro-Black politics. People who worked in Community Support supported groups like the one I had worked with in Enfield and Halifax County. In addition, the staff included an impressive number of Black workers. I felt that I was on familiar ground and hoped that I could upgrade my community organizing skills.

The community action program in Rocky Mount had chosen to attack poverty by using its grant from the North Carolina Fund to recruit new businesses into the community. The Community Support staff found this use of program funds questionable. Our staff wanted to make our opposition to the Nash/Edgecombe Economic Development program clear to other people at the Fund who controlled the purse strings. At a meeting scheduled for the next day, Jim wanted to make the charge that poor people were not participating in the Rocky Mount program. So he sent me on a trip to Washington to get background documentation at the Office of Economic Opportunity (OEO). To prepare for his presentation, I took the early morning flight to Washington, caught a taxi, and went directly to the OEO, where it took me only an hour or so to find the information Jim needed. Emerging from the Washington building, I hailed a taxi that drove me swiftly to the airport where I boarded a flight for Raleigh-Durham and walked into Jim's office before three o'clock that afternoon. Jim incorporated the evidence I had found in Washington into his searing censure of the Rocky Mount antipoverty program.

In addition to the insecurities I faced at work, the first year away from my home challenged my role as a parent. Tanya had been one of six Black students to integrate the Enfield Graded School. I wanted her to take advantage of our efforts to provide new opportunities for our children, so I enrolled her in Durham Academy, considered by the Black parents I spoke to the best elementary school in Durham. Only a few Black children attended the independent school, but I wanted the best for Tanya. The only Black adults at Durham Academy were maintenance workers, but Tanya was a plucky little girl and maintained her own in the second-grade class. I wanted to expose this little child to things I never had growing up in the little town of Enfield. I enrolled her in both the YWCA and Durham Ballet, where she took dance lessons.

I struggled to live in two worlds. I faithfully went home every weekend to maintain a presence in Enfield and to keep that household operating. Though our car had been outfitted with new tires, I had seven flat tires that first year, many of them on the country roads that I traveled between Enfield and Durham. I had to give up most of my work with the Halifax County Voters Movement because there simply was no time or energy left over. My boss saw my dilemma, telling me that I experienced reentry problems when I returned from Enfield on Sunday evenings. I was emotionally destabilized and made an appointment with a therapist at Duke Medical Center, who listened to my story and assured me that given the upheaval in my life during the past three years, I was functioning pretty well. I embraced my new life with courage, holding close my memories of living in my small community and teaching at Inborden High School.

45. The Fourth Circuit Court of Appeals Reverses Ruling of District Court

After a year of waiting, we heard from the United States Court of Appeals for the Fourth Circuit. The Court receives appeals from five states: Maryland, Virginia, West Virginia, North Carolina, and South Carolina. Finally on June 6, 1966, the appellate court reversed and remanded the decision of the United

States District Court for the Eastern District of North Carolina. The appellate court directed the Halifax County Board of Education to "renew the teacher's contract and to determine her damages." Sitting on the court bench and supporting the decision were Chief Judge Haynesworth and Judges Sobeloff, Boreman, Bryan, and J. Spencer Bell, who wrote the opinion. Judge Albert V. Bryan dissented.

In reviewing the case, Judge Bell wrote:

> The record discloses, the defendants concede, and the court found that the plaintiff, a Negro, was a well-qualified, conscientious and competent teacher of English at the T. S. Inborden High School in the town of Enfield, North Carolina, for a period of twelve years preceding the incidents involved here. In addition to her teaching duties, she had done a great deal of "extracurricular" work for the school and for student activities which indicated her devotion to her professional task. During the year 1962–1963 the Principal graded her in all fields as excellent and above average, the two highest possible ratings used in the system of grading teachers by the Halifax school system. Her superintendent, a defendant, testified that she had been an above average teacher and was doing very satisfactory work.[120]

The appeals court explicated the principles of law involved, saying that the law of North Carolina is clear on the procedure for hiring teachers.

> All contracts are for one year only, renewable at the discretion of the school authorities. A contract must be signed by the Principal as an indication of his recommendation and then transmitted to the District School Committee, whose business it is either to approve or disapprove in their discretion. There is no vested right to public employment. The plaintiff had no constitutional right to have her contract renewed, but these questions were not involved in this case. It was the plaintiff's contention that her contract was not renewed because of reasons which were either arbitrary and capricious or in order to retaliate against her for exercising her constitutional right to protest racial discrimination.[121]

Citing recent consideration of the law in this area, the Fourth Circuit Court noted that the Supreme Court "... has pointed out on numerous occasions the importance of the teaching profession in our democratic society and the necessity of protecting its personal, associational and academic liberty. . . . Scholarship cannot flourish in an atmosphere of suspicion and distrust. Teachers and students must always be free to inquire, to study and to evaluate."[122]

The appeals court stated that this principle is supported by *Sweezy v. State of New Hampshire*, *Wieman v. Updegraff*, and *Adler v. Board of Education*. The Court cited the historical case *Alston v. School Board of City of Norfolk*, which struck down the widespread practice of paying lesser salaries to Negro teachers. In that case, Chief Judge John Parker said:

It is no answer to this to say that hiring of any teacher is a matter resting in the discretion of the school authorities. Plaintiffs, as teachers qualified and subject to employment by the state, are entitled to apply for the positions and to have the discretion of authorities exercised lawfully and without unconstitutional discrimination as to the rate of pay to be awarded them, if their applications are accepted.

Among other relevant cases, the court cited *Franklin v. County School Board of Giles County*, *Zimmerman v. Board of Education*, *Garner v. Public Works*, *Torcaso v. Watkins*, *Konigsberg v. State Bar of California*, and the Supreme Court of North Carolina in cases involving schoolteachers. Having related the body of law in which the case fell, the court turned to the facts in the case. The Fourth Circuit found some ambiguity in the lower court's findings and conclusions, but set forth as a key finding of the District Court: "The plaintiff's civil rights activities consumed so much of her time and interest that they interfered with her 'extracurricular' activities at school; created some dissension between her and the Principal, and caused the Board's refusal to renew her contract." [123]

The Fourth Circuit appellate court found this finding to be irrelevant because it was not the reason advanced by the board members for refusing to renew her contract. The appeals court stated:

The statute gives discretion to the school board in deciding whether or not to continue the employment of a teacher. Discretion means the exercise of judgment, not bias or capriciousness. Thus it must be based upon fact and supported by reasoned analysis. In testing the decision of the school board the district court must consider only the facts and logic relied upon by the board itself.[124]

The appeals court held that a simple but fundamental rule of administrative law requires a reviewing court, in dealing with a determination or judgment that an administrative agency alone is authorized to make, must judge the propriety of such action solely on the grounds invoked by the agency. If those grounds are inadequate or improper, the court is powerless to affirm the administrative action by substituting what it considers to be a more adequate or proper basis.[125]

The court stated that similarly, the district court "may not usurp the discretionary power of the school board but must judge the constitutionality of the action on the basis of the facts which were before the Board and on its logic."[126]

The testimony of all the members of the school board was that they did not know of the plaintiff's civil rights activities, or at least the extent thereof, and that their action was based solely upon the letters of March 10 and March 31.

> We accept the defendants' statements that they were not aware of the extent of the plaintiff's personal participation in this activity because the district court credited them. Thus the record offers no objectively substantiated facts known to the Board with regard to the plaintiff's civil rights activity which would justify the Board's action as found by the court. Additionally the finding of the district court as to cause for cessation of employment is clearly in error because it is not supported by the record.[127]

The appeals court said that both the record and the principal's testimony supported the fact that the disagreements between the principal and plaintiff had been satisfactorily settled by March 31 in such manner as not to interfere with the plaintiff's school work. The members of the board had testified that they acted solely on the basis of the March 10 and March 31 letters and their personal opinion that the principal did not want the plaintiff's contract renewed.

The Court affirmed:

> Thus there was no support for the court's finding that the extent of the plaintiff's activities interfered with her school work or that the Principal and the plaintiff had not reached a satisfactory understanding of their differences. We take it to be self-evident that the objections held either by the Board or by the Principal to the Plaintiff's exercise of her personal and associational liberty to express her feelings about segregation would not justify refusal to renew her contract so long as these activities did not interfere with her performance of her school work.[128]

Expressing support for a key contention of my attorneys and the expert witness, Phil Constans, the appeals court said:

We feel that the infractions enumerated in the March 10th letter were neither individually nor collectively such as to justify failure to renew the contract of a teacher with the plaintiff's record of twelve years. The district court did not seek to rely on these infractions to support the dismissal. These being the only basis for the school board's decision, we find that the action of the school board was arbitrary and capricious.[129]

In an eloquent and memorable statement, the court concluded:

In the factual context we think that the court committed error in separately weighing the facts with respect to the plaintiff's two contentions: first, that the Board either acted arbitrarily or capriciously or second, that it acted to penalize her for her civil rights activity. In weighing the contention of the Board that it did not act arbitrarily, we cannot ignore the highly charged emotional background of a small eastern North Carolina community caught in the throes of the civil rights campaign where more than 51% of the population was Negro and where the two members of the Board who voted against the plaintiff confessed to knowledge of her husband's activity and their opposition to school desegregation. To accept such an analysis is to pretend not to know as judges what we know as men.[130]

Lawyers for the defendants unsuccessfully appealed the Fourth Circuit Court's decision to the US Supreme Court, which upheld the decision made by the Fourth Circuit Court.

46. *The Settlement*

Sometime after I received the happy news of the Fourth Circuit Court's decision in my favor, Phil Hirschkop called to tell me that he would be coming to Enfield to see me. We agreed on a date and the white Virginia attorney came to my home to tell me that the Halifax County Board of Education had offered the paltry sum of $20,000 to settle the suit. I had sued for $250,000. The $20,000 represented 8 percent of the amount of the suit. Hirschkop explained that the attorneys had encountered many expenses for their work on the case and up to that point they had received no compensation. They would take half of the $20,000 and I would receive the other half. In addition, to complete the settlement, the Board would require that I sign a statement saying that I would never again seek employment in Halifax County public schools.

The attorney advised that I take the offer. He pointed out that used wisely, my $10,000 could go a long way. He said that he had spent less than that, $6,000, to set up his law office. John Salter informed me that I didn't have to take this settlement. Later, Salter said that I could fight for more and he would be on my side. In the end, I decided to take the $10,000 check. Money had never been the reason that I sued. I had won the case. I had been vindicated. The truth of my unjust firing had been affirmed. The seven bogus reasons stated by the principal in the March 10 memo had been disproven, revealing the conspiracy to punish me for challenging the racist system that kept our community in economic dependence and political chains. The conspirators would live forever in ignominy and shame.

A year after the settlement, the National Education Association invited me to Minneapolis to its annual conference on July 5, 1967. My mother and father accompanied me, and we flew first class. It was my mother's first flight, and my father teased my mother saying that on their next flight they would go to London. At the conference, I told my story to the morning assembly of 12,000 conference participants. That evening, the NEA presented Abraham Lincoln Awards to eight people for their outstanding service in defense of democracy through education. I was honored to be one of the recipients.

In the early 1980s, my youngest sister, Claudette Hardaway, said that while attending law school at North Carolina Central University, she came upon the brief of *Willa Johnson v. Joseph Branch* in a volume of benchmark cases in the school's law library. She said that the worn pages suggested that *Johnson v. Branch* had been read more than any of the other cases included in the volume. After receiving her doctorate in jurisprudence, Claudette achieved eminence by becoming the first African American woman to be appointed to the post of assistant attorney general for the state of North Carolina (Fig. 46.1).

In 2009 I told my story at a luncheon for teachers at the NCAA Basketball Tournament in Charlotte, North Carolina. Dr. Al-Tony Gilmore, historian of the National Education Association, was in the audience. He came up to me after the presentation and said that he was familiar with my case because he had seen so many references to it in files at the NEA. Later, he called me at home and asked to interview me. On the agreed-upon date, Dr. Gilmore rang my doorbell around nightfall, apologizing that he had experienced many

Fig. 46.1. Willa's youngest sister, Claudette Hardaway, North Carolina Associate Assistant Attorney General, seated in her parents' family room, ca. 1973. / Willa Cofield personal collection.

difficulties trying to find my home in Plainfield, New Jersey. We sat at my kitchen table and he taped my story. Later in his book, *All the People: NEA's Legacy of Inclusion and Its Minority Presidents*, the NEA official stated that Black teachers suffered after the *Brown v. Topeka* decision and during the civil rights movement. He said that by the mid-1960s, Black teacher dismissals resulted from desegregating schools and teacher involvement in the civil rights movement had reached epic proportions. "Biased school administrators, local school boards, and politicians conspired to terminate over 30,000 Black teachers, mostly in the southern and border states."[131] In a handwritten note on the title page of my copy of his book, Dr. Gilmore said that the NEA credited my suit with saving these jobs.

On February 23, 2009, Dr. Gilmore wrote to me: "Thank you for the 'historic' courage you demonstrated when you brought the NEA into the vortex of the civil rights movement. All who have followed you—3.2 million members—owe you a deep debt of gratitude."[132]

47. ENDING NOTES

48. My Legacy of Struggle

Over the years I have reflected on the decision that Judge Larkins made when he ruled against me. I have concluded that he denied as a judge what he knew as a man. In his final opinion he stated, "Plaintiff is a member of a negro [*sic*] family of Enfield which has actively and vigorously championed the cause of negro [*sic*] rights." This statement confirmed my belief that his support of my dismissal from the teaching job at Inborden School was not because of any inadequacy in my teaching. Judge Larkins's decision was a continuation of the racist tradition of discouraging and attacking Black people who defied white supremacy in Halifax County in any way.

This fierce resistance to white domination was deeply rooted in my family history in Enfield, which began in 1768. My maternal grandparents, George and Mary McWilliams, raised fifteen children. Born into servitude, my grandfather worked to leave each of his children land, so that they could be independent. He said, "My mother put me out to work when I was twelve years old. I had to work for white people." He did not want his children forced into dependency upon members of the dominant community. When two of his sons visited New York City and came home raving about the tall skyscrapers that they had seen, my grandfather was unimpressed, and commented, "You will never own one."

My paternal grandfather, whom I called Grandpapa Cofield, set up a business after his eight sons and one daughter grew up. He named it H. C. Cofield and Sons. This business sold wood and coal, rented houses, and operated a grocery store. My father, Thomas Cofield, left school when he was in fifth grade. Toward the end of his life, I asked him why he left so early. His answer: "I thought I was wasting my time." So as a young teenager, he took over the management of his father's grocery store. This fierce entrepreneurship in my family was strong resistance to white domination and was deeply rooted in my

Fig. 48.1. Mae and Thomas Cofield washing turnip greens from their garden, ca. 1987. / Willa Cofield personal collection.

family history in Enfield. Our leadership in the civil rights movement was possible because of our economic independence based in the Black community.

My father, his seven brothers, and one sister inherited Grandpapa's entrepreneurial talent. They all sought to find ways of making a living by serving the needs of the Black community. When I was growing up, my father's sister and four of his brothers operated their own businesses. The generation of my father and mother had made independent entrepreneurship a keystone in their lifelong struggle for dignity and economic survival. They managed their money carefully and raised vegetables to keep food on the table (Fig. 48.1). The civil rights movement in my town became possible because there was an economic base in the Black community apart from the dominant white community.

In 1910, Grandpapa Cofield joined with Jacob Johnson and Frank Bullock to establish the Cofield, Bullock, and Johnson Funeral Home, which later became Cofield Funeral Home, where Reed Johnson worked. Reed's candidacy for a seat on the town commission could not be thwarted by the threat of losing his job. When local churches denied us access to their meeting space, the same Cofield Funeral Home opened its chapel to meetings of the protesters. When picketers were arrested and jailed, Thomas and Curtis Cofield supplied the money for their bail.

My husband, Reed Johnson; my father, Thomas Cofield; and my uncle, Augustus Cofield were plaintiffs in *William Alston, et. al., v. L. M. Butts, et al.* They

Fig. 48.2. Willa's daughter, Tanya, speaks at the Black Women's History Conference Reunion Breakfast in Plainfield, New Jersey, ca. 2016. / Willa Cofield personal collection.

were among the plaintiffs who were granted an injunction against various precinct registrars and members of the Board of Elections of Halifax County. All three men ran for public office in the spring of 1964, on the slate of eight Black men and three Black women supported by the Halifax County Voters Movement.

When Judge Larkins wrote in his opinion, "Plaintiff is member of a Negro family that is actively and vigorously championing the cause of Negro rights," he was correct. I continued the legacy by walking on picket lines in front of Plantation Grill, buttonholing Black people on the sidewalks of Enfield during the registration campaign, serving as poll watcher, speaking at public programs, and teaching my students how to register and encouraging them to go home and teach their parents. I continued the Cofield legacy of struggle against white supremacy, and I wear the badge with honor. I pass on this concern for community and the fight for justice to the next and succeeding generations (Fig. 48.2).

49. Epilogue

The gains of our community are not always easily documented. But in the case of the Enfield struggle for freedom and the Halifax County Voters Movement, one can look at the direct political impact of the bitter struggle by counting the Black politicians who have been elected to office since 1965.

Fig. 49.1. Thomas Hardaway (ca. 1987), the son of Willa's youngest sister, Claudette, served five terms in the North Carolina House of Representatives. / Willa Cofield personal collection.

It took twenty-eight years of voter registration to gain a Black majority in the First Congressional District, but on November 3, 1992, Eva Clayton became the first woman to represent the district at the federal level. She was the first Black Congressional representative of the district since George H. White left the national body in 1901. Ten years later, she was succeeded by Frank Balance, who served from January 3, 2003, to June 11, 2004. Congressman G. K. Butterfield, who took office on July 20, 2004, served in the US House of Representatives until 2022 when he was succeeded by Don Davis. In addition, dozens of Black officials have been elected to municipal, county, and state offices. They include my nephews, Kai Hardaway, who served as mayor of Enfield for twelve years, and Thomas Hardaway, who served five terms in the North Carolina House of Representatives (Fig. 49.1).

My aunt, Elizabeth Bias Cofield, wife of James Cofield, my father's youngest brother, brought fame to the Cofield family. She worked at Shaw University, first as a professor of Education and later as an administrator, for a total of forty

Fig. 49.2. Willa talks to construction workers about repairs to her father's rental house on Cofield Street, 1977. / Willa Cofield personal collection.

years. She was the first Black citizen elected to the Raleigh Board of Education. She was the first woman and the first Black elected to the Wake County Board of Commissioners. For her exemplary contributions to young people and the community, she was inducted into the Raleigh Hall of Fame in 2008.

In March 1977, after being away from Enfield for twelve years, I returned and lived there until 1980. Reed and I divorced after living apart for seven years, and I had married Warren Blackshear of Plainfield, New Jersey. Warren and I turned the old headquarters of the Enfield and Halifax County Voters Movement into modest living quarters while we worked to upgrade housing in the Black community. We began by gutting one of the double shotgun houses that months before had suffered serious damage from a fire (Figs. 49.2, 49.3, and 49.4) We wanted to show that if houses were brought up to standard, they could offer much better living conditions, and if the tenant qualified, much of the rent could be paid through the use of government-assisted rental housing programs.

We made grand plans to develop a five-acre tract with fifty subsidized units of one-, two-, and three-bedroom units. We were able to secure the

Fig. 49.3. Neighborhood children gather to watch renovation work on the burned-out house, 1977. / Willa Cofield personal collection.

Fig. 49.4. Adults gathered on the porch next door to the burned-out house, keeping an eye on the progress of the renovations, 1977. / Willa Cofield personal collection.

land but unable to get guarantees for the rent, and without assistance, the people who needed housing could not pay the rent. We built a foundation for a three-bedroom, factory-built house with central heat and air that we were able to offer for $28,000, but no one interested could afford the monthly mortgage payment of $150 per month. We learned that a contractor in the neighboring town of Tarboro was offering the same house and selling houses as fast as he could build them. His buyers were all receiving Farmers Home Administration (FmHA) loans. The Halifax County Office, on the other hand, rejected all the applicants who wanted to buy the house in Enfield.

The situation only changed after Warren described the housing crisis in Enfield at a hearing on housing in Raleigh. We declared a housing crisis in Enfield, prompting a visit from Howard Lee, Secretary of the North Carolina Department of Natural Resources and Community Development (Fig. 49.5). Enfield residents mounted street protests in each neighborhood that Mr. Lee visited. The protests got full coverage in area newspapers and finally succeeded in forcing the Farmers Home Administration in Halifax to approve an Enfield applicant. It became clear during the push for decent housing that Black people in Enfield lacked real representation in government. The work of the sixties had not yet produced a Black voting bloc powerful enough to elect Black officials.

Part I: The Nine O'Clock Whistle

Fig. 49.5. Howard Lee, Secretary of NC Department of Natural Resources and Community Development, visited Enfield during housing crisis, ca. 1978. / Willa Cofield personal collection.

We called a meeting of a few people at our home. After some discussion, the group agreed that three Black candidates should run for the town board of commissioners in the next election scheduled for early November. The group settled upon Charles Swindell, principal of Pittman School; Leroy Brantley, former head chef at Plantation Restaurant and preparation technician at Abbott Laboratories; and Coreen Gardner, parent, former school patrolwoman, and also an employee at Abbott Laboratories. A few days later, we held a community meeting and presented the slate of potential candidates. The body unanimously endorsed all three. To support their campaigns, we organized an intensive voter registration effort, going door to door and buttonholing shoppers on the downtown streets. In the 1980 election, only Charles Swindell won, taking a seat on the Enfield Board of Commissioners as Enfield's first Black commissioner. In 1986, he began serving a tenure as mayor, becoming Enfield's first Black mayor, first as pro tem and then as official mayor (Fig. 49.6). Mr. Swindell was followed by a long line of Black commissioners and mayors. Kai Hardaway served as Enfield's second Black mayor for twelve years from December 1990 to September 2002 (Fig. 49.7).

Records in the office of the Clerk of Enfield show the full list of Black mayors and commissioners who have served the town of Enfield since 1980:

Fig. 49.6. Charles Swindell is sworn in as mayor, becoming Enfield's first Black mayor, 1986. / Grassroots Media Productions.

Fig. 49.7. E. Kai Hardaway III (right), second Black mayor of Enfield, with Bud Albert Whitaker, who served thirty-two years as Enfield commissioner, from 1991 until 2023, ca. 1998. / Willa Cofield personal collection.

ENFIELD BLACK MAYORS

Figures 49.8–49.12A courtesy of Grassroots Media Productions unless otherwise noted.

Fig. 49.8. Charles Swindell 1986–1987. / Grassroots Media Productions.

Fig. 49.9. E. Kai Hardaway III 1990–2002. / Grassroots Media Productions.

Fig. 49.10. Edward Jones 2002–2005. / Grassroots Media Productions.

Fig. 49.11. Warnie Bishop 2005–2009. / Grassroots Media Productions.

Part I: The Nine O'Clock Whistle   211

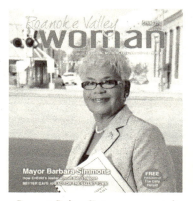

Fig. 49.12. Barbara Simmons 2009–2017. / Grassroots Media Productions.

Fig. 49.12A. Mondale Robinson 2022–present. / Courtesy of Mondale Robinson.

ENFIELD BLACK COMMISSIONERS

Figures 49.13–49.27 courtesy of Grassroots Media Productions.

Fig. 49.13. Charles Swindell 1980–1986.

Fig. 49.14. James Whitaker 1987–1993.

Fig. 49.15. E. Kai Hardaway III 1987–1990.

Fig. 49.16. Bud Whitaker 1991–2023.

Fig. 49.17. Earl Sledge 1993–1999.

Fig. 49.18. Freeman Reynolds 1999–2007

Fig. 49.19. Warnie Bishop 1999–2005.

Fig. 49.20. Sandra Wheaten 2002.

Fig. 49.21. Gloria Caudle
2002–2012

Fig. 49.22. Wilbert Bishop
2007–2010.

Fig. 49.23. Earl Harvey
2009–2018.

Fig. 49.24. Tracey Joiner
2011–present.

Fig. 49.25. Therman Hunter
2013–2018.

Fig. 49.26. Bobby Whitaker
2017–present.

Fig. 49.27. Kenny Ward
2017–present.

The work of the Halifax County Voters Movement extended beyond the limits of the town of Enfield and included the whole of Halifax County. The impact of the work that the Halifax County Voters Movement started in 1964 is reflected boldly in the present political leadership of the county. Today, Halifax County has a Black majority board of county commissioners, a Black sheriff, a Black woman district attorney, four Black judges who are women, an all-Black county school board, a Black county superintendent of schools, and a Black chairman of the election board.

50. The Whistle Today

After that bitter night in 1963, Enfield's nine o'clock whistle never blew again. Indeed, the need to get Blacks off the streets on Saturday night disappeared altogether. No crowds of jostling, laughing Negroes filled Enfield's downtown streets and sidewalks ever again. The town, however, continues to alert its residents of the weekday noon hour by blowing the whistle. The town acquired a new post office, but all three drugstores—Harrison, Whitehead's, and Beavans—finally closed, succumbing to competition from drugs by mail. One by one, the bustling department stores that had been the focus of picketing in the summer of 1963 became outlets for cut-rate school supplies, Halloween masks, and household bleach. The Rives Hardware Store with its many shelves and counters overflowing with fertilizer, flower seeds, cookware, straw hats, garden hoses and rakes, house paint, and thousands of other commodities closed its doors. The owners of Rose's Five and Ten Cent Store recognized the end of an era and moved on. For several years, the town used the store's large windows to display interesting artifacts of the area and its copious interior to host weekly bingo games. An enterprising developer converted the once proud Enfield High School into apartments for the elderly, and Halifax County Schools abandoned Inborden High School after reducing it to an elementary school and then allowing it to quietly decay in ignominy over the years. Most of the leaders and participants of the 1963 movement lie in graveyards. Cofield Funeral Home hosts a spirit-filled church, and New Town has only a few houses standing to remind old timers of the past. Many of the homes in the former white area have been purchased and updated by well-placed Black people, who having made their fortunes in more prosperous areas, retired to the home of their youth. New white families have come to live in Enfield, and they are not as closely tied to the old ways as the earlier generation, opening the possibility for a different conversation across race. There are reasons for hope.

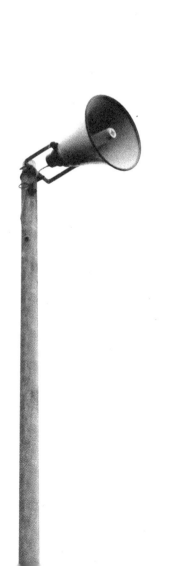

PART II

NEXT IN LINE

Cynthia Samuelson

Fig. 0.2. Cynthia Samuelson, Inborden High School graduation photo, 1963. / Cynthia Samuelson personal collection.

51. PREFACE TO PART II

Memories of my childhood in Enfield, North Carolina, are primarily about family, about other people who made lasting impressions, and about a variety of seemingly unrelated things. Until the sixties, I was a happy, carefree child and a happy teenager growing up in Enfield, a small southern town in North Carolina. That is when I became acutely aware of discrimination and became very angry at "the system." The system in my mind comprised local, state, and federal governments and their leaders. The president, governors, and mayors should have ensured protection and fair treatment of all people. I found it unacceptable that these leaders mistreated Black people or permitted White people in their jurisdictions to mistreat Black people as well.

But I believed we could force a change in the system and that it was time to confront the injustices and indignities that were imposed on Black people. I did not think about the impact that the subsequent events would have on the courageous people who would participate in the protests in Enfield nor did I consider the impact those events would have on my life. However, Enfield was changing for everyone, and a new reality was settling in my seventeen-year-old bones, too. Life as we knew it would never be the same again.

52. Growing Up in Enfield

Enfield is located in the northeastern section of North Carolina in Halifax County. It is about forty miles south of the Virginia state line and about one hundred miles inland from the Atlantic Ocean. The town of just 1.2 square miles is surrounded by over one hundred square miles of houses, businesses, and farmland, and the Atlantic Coast Line Railroad runs right through the center of town.

US Highway 301 runs through town about two blocks east of the railroad. Until the seventies, the highway was the main road for motor vehicle travel between Delaware and Florida. It narrowed from four lanes in Virginia to two lanes when it crossed into North Carolina. This caused drivers to slow down as they passed through the small towns such as Weldon, Halifax, and Enfield along the route. In addition, the two traffic lights on Highway 301 in Enfield created several miles of traffic jams on holidays when the traffic load increased.

The businesses located along the two-mile stretch of Highway 301 that ran through Enfield thrived as travelers passed through on their journeys north and south. There were three restaurants, three motels, and at least seven places to buy gasoline along that Enfield route. And although Blacks worked at a few of the White-owned businesses and could purchase gasoline at the service stations, neither they or the Black travelers could get their cars repaired, use the bathrooms, dine at any of the White-owned restaurants, or sleep at any of the motels.

Fortunately, there were a few Black-owned businesses along that same two-mile stretch of Highway 301 that provided places for Blacks to dine, sleep, or get their cars repaired. Powell's Garage was one of those businesses. It was owned by Mr. Robert Powell and was one of the largest Black-owned businesses in Enfield. Mr. Robert, as we called him, also owned a successful taxi service that was run from the same location. Black businessmen in the community and in the surrounding area also came to Powell's Garage to discuss business opportunities and to socialize.

Mr. George Dancy owned Dancy's Café, which was directly across the street from Powell's Garage, and Mr. Harry Cofield owned the Little Palace Restaurant that was just a few yards down the street. Mrs. Catherine Pittman used part of her house, advertised as Pittman's Tourist Home, as a place for travelers to dine and sleep. These Black-owned businesses were open to anyone, but Blacks were the primary customers. Occasionally a White person ate at the Little Palace. It is also interesting to note that travelers rarely ventured away from the businesses along Highway 301 to buy goods or services from businesses in the other sections of town.

The section of town where the local residents shopped, called downtown, was about two blocks west of Highway 301. The businesses there were concentrated along a one-block section of Whitfield Street on the west side of the railroad and along a one-block section parallel to the railroad on North Railroad Street. Rose's 5¢ 10¢ 25¢ Store and People's Bank were located on the corners of Whitfield and North Railroad streets. Other businesses downtown included the Enfield Savings and Loan Association;[1] Mears Jewelry; Cuthrell's, McPhail's, and Meyer's department stores; Harrison, Whitfield, and Beavans drug stores; and at least two hardware stores—Reeves and Company

Fig. 52.1. I was about eight years old when this photo was taken. / Cynthia Samuelson personal collection.

and Western Auto. Meyer's Grocery, the Levon Movie Theater, and the post office also were located on Whitfield Street. The police station, fire station, railroad station, and Reeve's hardware store were across the railroad from the shopping area on South Railroad Street. Most of the stores downtown were open from about 9 a.m. to 5 p.m. Monday through Friday, 9 a.m. to 9 p.m. on Saturday, and closed on Sunday. The Levon Movie Theater had different hours. It was open on Wednesday and Friday from about 6 p.m. to 9 p.m., 12 noon to 9 p.m. on Saturday, and 1 or 2 p.m. to 7 p.m. on Sunday.

There were very few places for entertainment nearby other than the Levon Movie Theater and a few Black-owned juke joints. Clyde's was located on Highway 301 across from Dancy's Cafe. George's Café was on Pope Street not far from Highway 301. The White Swan Inn was located two miles east of town, and Tempsey's was about six miles south on Highway 301 in Whitakers. Other than the traffic backups and an occasional sound of a juke box, there was not much excitement or noise in or around Enfield.

Fig. 53.1. My maternal grandfather, Robert Mason, was a US Army World War I veteran. He died when he was in his early sixties; however, his legacy lasted for several generations after his death. / Cynthia Samuelson personal collection.

Enfield was a quiet town that had very little crime. Most people in the Black community left their doors unlocked. I knew the doors were open because I frequently visited houses unannounced and the doors were always open. I recall hearing about two murders when I was growing up in Enfield. One man was shot as a result of a domestic dispute less than a block from our house. And my cousin Sam Mason was stabbed to death during a fight in the pool room about a half mile from our house. When I was a teenager, a teenage Black boy was accused of raping a teenage White girl and sentenced to ten years in prison. There was also an occasional fight in the community on Saturday night and once in a while someone was cut during a fight. Because the community was safe during the day, I was permitted to walk or ride my bicycle around the neighborhood from one end of Dixie Street to the other (Fig. 52.1).

53. Dixie Street

My maternal grandfather, Robert Mason (Fig. 53.1), and some of his friends built our house on Dixie Street in 1927. It seems as if he wanted it to be a place where

Fig. 53.2. My maternal grandmother, Lillie Saunders Mason, was a small, soft-spoken, hard-working woman of great strength and influence. She instilled values when I was a child that guided me for a lifetime. / Cynthia Samuelson personal collection.

many adults and children would visit and enjoy, because he surrounded the house with trees, shrubs, and a large, pretty lawn where children could play. He also planted a pecan tree and several fruit trees, and cleared a large space across from the fig bush to plant a garden for my grandmother in back of the house.

Years after our house was built, my family opened it to travelers and offered them a comfortable place to rest. They did this because places for Black travelers to stay or dine were limited in many sections of the South prior to the late sixties, and were not safe. Some areas did not permit Blacks to be on the streets after sundown, and that was considered legal until the passage of the Civil Rights Act of 1964.[2] Until then, the sign that read Mason's Tourist Home stood in our front yard near the street. And although the only two forms of advertising were the sign and word-of-mouth, cars and station wagons filled the backyard and the driveway during the summer and throughout the hunting season. Teachers who accepted positions at Inborden School and Eastman School also stayed at our house during the school season. My maternal grandmother, Lillie Saunders Mason (Fig. 53.2), prepared meals for the guests, and enjoyed their company and conversation around the kitchen table. During the conversations, she often told stories about my grandfather.

I was well into adulthood when I realized the significance of what my grandfather had done. He had completed the house in 1927, at a time when racism affected almost every aspect of public life, when the Klan was active, and when Blacks were still being lynched. Further, creation and enforcement of the Civil Rights Act of 1964 was still thirty-seven years away, yet he managed to secure the finances to purchase the land and to buy the materials needed to build our house. Not only was it rare for a Black man to build such a nice house for his family in 1927, he was a thirty-five-year-old Black man with a wife and three children to support. He was also a World War I veteran who had not finished high school, yet he had acquired sufficient skills to work as a carpenter and a bricklayer and to build several houses for White families in addition to our house.

And even though my grandfather was able to overcome major obstacles to build the family house, there was still a major difference between the section of town where we lived and the section of Enfield where White people lived. There were paved streets and sidewalks in the predominantly White sections of town, which began just two blocks west of our house. Some of the streets that ran through the White sections also ran into the Black neighborhoods. However, the pavement ended on the sections of the same streets where Black families lived. That meant that the part of Dixie Street that ran in front of our house was frequently dry and dusty during the summer. To combat the dust, my grandmother would close the doors and windows to keep some of the dust out of the house. At other times, Dixie Street was muddy and had large holes filled with standing water after a rainstorm. Occasionally, someone who worked for the Town of Enfield would drag a large plow over the street to make it smooth again. Eventually, during my teenage years, town officials decided to pave Dixie Street and add sidewalks. And although several feet of our front yard was replaced with a sidewalk, the neighborhood looked much better and my grandmother no longer needed to close the doors and windows to keep the dust out. And, of course, it was also much safer to walk along Dixie Street than it had been.

My childhood memories of living on Dixie Street are pleasant ones. When I moved away, I remembered the smell of the magnolia that grew outside my bedroom window, the smell of Johnson's paste wax on the hardwood floors, and the sound of rain on the tin roof. I also remember the large family gatherings during the summer and on holidays, playing in the yard, and relatives sitting on the front porch laughing and talking, and people from the community stopping by.

Our neighbors on Dixie Street were more than just friends. They were part of our extended family and they looked out for each other. The families in the area knew everyone and the environment was a safe one where, since I was about five years old, I could go to any of my friends' houses and visit with any of our neighbors.

I remember Miss Florence and Mr. Arthur who lived directly across the street in front of our house. Miss Effie and Mr. Solomon lived on their left. Miss Veenie lived on their right and Miss Mattie and her daughter Pauline lived next door to us. I ate biscuits at all of those houses except Miss Veenie's; I do not know if she made biscuits. When I was about seven years old, my grandmother asked Miss Veenie to help do something more important than allowing me to eat biscuits in her house. She asked Miss Veenie to help break my fever. I had a high fever and my grandmother had called Dr. Winston Bryant, who was our family physician and the only Black physician in town. Dr. Bryant could not bring the fever down. So Miss Veenie dipped grape leaves in vinegar and repeatedly placed the leaves on my forehead until my temperature dropped. I can still remember the feel of something cool and damp on my forehead.

I also remember when the pear tree that my grandfather planted fell onto the house during Hurricane Hazel in 1954, and when one of the two apple trees blew over during the storm but continued to produce fruit long after its having fallen. However, when I was growing up, the fig bush and grapevine that he had planted in back of the house were my favorite places when the grapes and figs were ripe. My second favorite place was the space across from the fig bush where we played ball after my grandfather passed and my grandmother was no longer able to take care of the garden. I remember the clothesline that ran between the fig bush and the garden. The wire for the clothesline was wrapped around two poles that were stuck in the ground at each end of the line. The poles were anchored by wires, attached at about forty-five-degree angles, to wooden stakes that were hammered into the ground. I tripped over one of those wires when I was about nine years old and got wire burns on my arm and leg. It happened when I ran to second base during a baseball game my friends and I were playing in the backyard. My grandfather would have laughed if had seen this incident. He often told my grandmother that the chemicals she put on the plants in her garden were going to kill me because I would sit in the garden and eat the raw vegetables right off the vines and stalks.

Robert Mason died in 1953 when I was only seven years old. Therefore, I do not actually remember much about him other than that he had been paralyzed on one side of his body as a result of a stroke and that I enjoyed being around him. I did remember my grandmother telling the family that during the time my grandfather was confined to bed, she would give me a cup of coffee to take to him each morning. And although he could not talk and would become annoyed with the adults sometimes, he would always give me a few sips of his coffee. The family story is that, thanks to my grandfather, I have been drinking coffee since I was four years old.

Stories about my grandfather continued to be told until the people of his generation in the family and in the neighborhood who knew him passed away. Among the stories that I heard, I do not recall anyone indicating why he selected the location on Dixie Street to build our house. Did he deliberately choose the land that was near the church or was it a coincidence?

54. St. Paul Baptist Church

St. Paul Baptist Church was an important part of our community. That was the place where church leaders reinforced values we had learned at home: be kind to everyone, treat others the way you would like to be treated, and you will receive help if you help yourself. In addition, we knew the church leaders because most of them worked in our schools during the week and volunteered to work at the church after school and on weekends. We also knew the church members because they lived in the community.

The white wooden church, which was located on Highway 301 near the back of our house, had been there all of my life and was an integral part of our family life. In addition to attending St. Paul services and events, my family was frequently involved in the fund-raising efforts for the church. I remember my grandmother and Miss Bertha Lewis making Brunswick stew in a large three-legged iron pot that was placed over a fire in our backyard. They would begin with beef and chicken purchased from Mr. Thorne's grocery store and put in vegetables they had canned during the summer. When the Brunswick stew was ready, they sold the stew to raise funds for the church. When my grandmother was not making Brunswick stew to sell for the church, she was making chicken salad, fried chicken, or barbequed chicken for special church events. I liked it when my grandmother prepared food for church activities because she would let me sample the food as it was prepared. As I reflect on the church activities I remember when I was a child, church activities were a lot of fun, with the exception of funerals and sitting in church for long hours on fourth Sundays.

I enjoyed going to Bible school, and to Sunday school, and helping with the collection, and singing in the junior choir. Hearing Mr. Julian "Buster" Lyons play the piano during church services was an added treat. That is probably

Fig. 54.1. St. Paul Baptist Church, built during the 1960s to replace the church that was destroyed by fire. / St. Paul Baptist Church collection.

where I learned to love Gospel music. I remember when Mr. Lyons asked me to lead the singing of "Ring Dem Bells" at one of the Sunday church services. I started out singing softly. Both my confidence and voice grew stronger when the congregation began clapping their hands and smiling. The congregation applauded when we finished singing.

Church activities ended abruptly when St. Paul burned on Christmas morning in 1959 before sunrise and before the congregation could hear the new sound system that had been installed the previous day. Church leaders had chosen a remodeling plan that enclosed the existing wooden structure with a cinder-block facade. When firemen got the fire under control, the entire wooden church had burned down and left most of the cinder blocks that surrounded the wood frame standing. Church leaders reported that the fire was caused by the wiring and encouraged church members to attend services at the other churches in town.

There were two other Black Baptist churches within a mile of St. Paul and several churches outside of town for members to attend while St. Paul was being rebuilt. As such, some church members attended First Baptist Church on the first Sundays of each month and New Bethel Baptist Church on the second Sundays until St. Paul was finished and services resumed on the fourth Sundays of each month. The church was rebuilt on the same site a year later (Fig. 54.1). The remodeled church had larger rooms in the back of the church, a raised roof and two balconies for seating on the left and right sides above the pulpit. It also had a larger baptizing pool under the pulpit. And although St. Paul has had several renovations since the sixties, the church remains at the same location on Highway 301 today.

Because St. Paul had been such a prominent and influential part of the community and our family, it remained a special part of my life long after I had moved away. One Sunday in June 1992 when I was living in Virginia, my mother called to tell me that the members of St. Paul had posted my biography and a photograph on the church bulletin board as part of their Black history program. The members had also inserted my photograph and summary of my biography in the program for their annual Youth Day Service and acknowledged my accomplishments during the service. This made my mother very proud. When she mailed a copy of the church program to me, she wrote in her note, "See what hard work and perseverance can do!" The recognition by the church leaders and the members of St. Paul was one of my most memorable achievements. It was the recognition by my hometown community that made it special.

55. Grocery Stores

The grocery stores near our house were also an integral part of the community. Just about everyone walked to these stores. And the families in the community knew the store owners and their families because the grocery store owners and their families not only worked in the stores, they also lived only a couple of blocks away from St. Paul. The small grocery stores and the service station that also sold groceries were owned by Mr. Thorne, Mr. Horton, and Mr. Barnhill, who were all White. There was also one grocery store that was owned by Mr. Exum, who was a Black man.

Since I was about five years old, I was permitted to go alone to the stores that were closest to our house. I could count the change for my purchases, so going to the grocery stores was not a problem. The store owners knew me and I knew them. And although these store owners were White, as a five-year-old child who had not heard any discussions about race in my house, I was completely unaware of their race. I also had no indication that their ethnic backgrounds were supposed to make them different from the people in my family or anyone else. The primary trait that I was aware of was that they were kind, and I never felt that I or my family was treated any differently from any other customer. In fact, I was sad when I learned that sometime during the late sixties or early seventies, two young Black men, who had not grown up in our community, had beaten and robbed Mr. Thorne.

My family had purchased our groceries from Mr. Thorne for as long as I could remember. His grocery store was the closest one to our house. Frequently, we called the store to order our weekly groceries, and Mr. Thorne would send someone to our house to deliver them. Sometimes, Mr. Thorne would deliver the groceries himself. Mr. Barnhill owned the service station next to Thorne's Grocery. My grandmother loved to tell the story of my going into the service station when I was about six years old or so and asking Mr. Barnhill to zip up my jacket. He zipped my jacket and I was on my way. I do not recall when I became aware that Mr. Thorne, Mr. Barnhill, and Mr. Horton were White. It did not become an issue until Blacks were asked to patronize Black businesses during the sixties. That is when my family stopped buying groceries from Mr. Thorne and began purchasing them from Mr. Exum even though Mr. Exum's store was not as close as Mr. Thorne's. This was one of the many changes that would occur in our community, our house, and my ongoing education.

56. Inborden School

My introduction to public education, which was another vital part of our community, began just before I turned six years old when my mother enrolled me in Inborden School. I attended classes there until I graduated from high school twelve years later. The school was located about a half mile from our house and I walked to and from school each day. When I entered first grade, the elementary school was the only building on the property. The high school was added in 1954, the gymnasium a few years later, and the agriculture building was completed during my junior year in high school. There was also a large area behind the elementary school for children to play games including softball. Overall, the school was kept clean, but it was not as attractive as the segregated White school.

Inborden School was segregated during my entire time there. In fact, all public schools in North Carolina were segregated at that time. And although I was aware that there was a White school in Enfield called the Enfield Graded School, it was not an issue or a concern. It was just a fact that the principal and teachers in the Black school were all Black and the principal and teachers in the White school were all White. My teachers seemed to enjoy their work and their students. However, I had no way to compare the quality of the education we were receiving in relation to what the White students were receiving.

I was a young adult when I learned that the educational materials provided to Black students in Halifax County were of inferior quality when compared to the supplies provided for White students. The White schools in Halifax County, I learned, regularly received new books and the Black students were given used books from the White schools that were frequently in poor condition. It was 2011 when I read the Duke University study[3] that documented the redistricting procedures the Halifax County School Board had used to keep the Black and White students segregated. I also learned that Black school facilities were inferior to White school facilities and that the student-teacher ratio was much higher in Black schools than in White schools. That made it far more difficult for Black students to receive the appropriate level of academic attention. The rationale of separate but equal schools used by the Halifax County School Board to maintain segregated schools was a callous deception, and it was consistent with racist practices throughout the South. In spite of this, I do not know if my education was limited because I attended the Black school in Enfield instead of the White one.

However, I do know there were major inequalities between the White school and Inborden. For example, there were not enough classrooms or teachers at Inborden for the number of Black students. I now know that the White school had fewer students and had a sufficient number of teachers for their students. In addition, there were not enough classrooms at Inborden to house all of the students. Because of this, my seventh-grade class was held in the gymnasium. Our desks were set up just inside the front doors on the left side of the basketball court facing the stage. Mr. Richardson, who was our seventh-grade teacher, was also the coach for the girls' basketball team. Some of the male students played basketball when Mr. Richardson was called out of the class to assist the principal in another building. After he left the gymnasium, one student would stand by the door to alert those playing basketball when he was returning. Although he never said anything, surely he noticed the dust in the air when he returned to the gymnasium.

Fortunately, this was the only class I attended in the gymnasium and all of my other classes at Inborden were held in the classrooms. I am sure my seventh-grade learning would have improved if we had been in a classroom where class was not stopped because the gymnasium was being set up for an event or because the teacher was frequently called away to assist the principal. And although my other classes were held in classrooms, the White school probably had better teaching materials.

To teach multiplication in third or fourth grades, Mrs. Bullock used chalk, a trash can, and a chalkboard. Each day we held a trash can against the chalk board and used the top of the can as a guide to draw a circle. We wrote the numbers two through twelve in a column in the center of the circle. We also wrote the numbers two through twelve in a somewhat random array on the outside of the circle. Each student would go to the board, begin with the twos and state the results of multiplying two times each of the numbers on the outer ring of the circle. That student would complete the twos, continue sequentially down the column and repeat the exercise for each multiplier the teacher had selected for that day. When that student sat down, the next student took a turn. I struggled with learning multiplication and dreaded standing in front of the class not knowing correct answers.

Each student was given a small card that contained tables with the results of multiplying each number from two to twelve by the numbers two through twelve, but we were not permitted to take the card when we were called to the front of the class. I studied the tables on that card over and over again after school and on weekends, but nothing seemed to help. Finally, with help from my Aunt Olive Mason, I learned how to multiply and looked forward to standing before the class when it was my turn. Little did I know at nine years old that my teachers might have had inferior teaching materials, but I did know that I learned how to multiply in Mrs. Bullock's class and that I had no difficulties with multiplication after leaving her class.

During that same period of time, there were other activities at school that would help me prepare for college. For example, I joined the 4-H Club and attended its summer camp when I was nine years old. The 4-H Club is a nationwide youth development program where the H's represent areas for growth: Head, Heart, Hands, and Health. Mr. D. J. Knight and Miss Ruth Whitworth, who were Halifax County extension agents, were our chaperones. They picked up children from Enfield, Tillery, and Scotland Neck and drove us to Swansboro, North Carolina, for the weeklong camp. I received my first swimming lesson during this camp when I was nine years old. I returned to the camp each year until I was twelve. My swimming skills continued to improve each year, and I enjoyed being in the water. By the time I was sixteen, I was teaching other children how to swim. As a result of this exposure, I knew how to swim when I arrived at Hampton Institute.[4] This was especially beneficial because learning how to swim and the completion of a swim class were mandatory unless a student was exempt for a medical reason. I was also able to join the Hampton water ballet team at the end of my freshman year.

That is just one example of the many benefits I received from teachers and others at Inborden School and in Halifax County.

My biology teacher, Mr. James Perry, gave us a series of standardized tests during my sophomore year in high school. The test results showed that I had above average analytical and reasoning abilities; in fact, my abilities were deemed to be at the college sophomore level. We were tested again when I entered Hampton to determine where we would be placed in English, literature, and mathematics. My scores permitted me to skip several freshman-level math courses. These test results also helped me select mathematics as my college major and pursue a career in mathematics and science. They also established a foundation to make decisions based on facts and logic. I used analytical techniques and reasoning abilities when I began my career as a mathematician in private industry and as a computer programmer in the federal government. These techniques also helped when I moved into senior leadership positions in federal agencies and in private industry. We were lucky to have had instructors at Inborden who focused both on the scientific side of our education and on literature and literacy.

Mrs. Willa Cofield Johnson introduced us to literature classics in high school. We recited Shakespeare, read poetry by e. e. cummings and Robert Frost, and learned about the *Canterbury Tales* in her class. This exposure reinforced the appreciation for literature and poetry that my mother provided at home. What Mrs. Johnson and my mother provided most likely contributed to my being selected as one of sixteen students to register for an advanced literature class at Hampton. However, the lessons I learned in Mrs. Johnson's classes lasted well beyond college.

On one occasion, I misspelled *separate* three times in a paper I had written for Mrs. Johnson's class and received a B grade on the paper. I was so disappointed because I had worked diligently on my research and writing and was sure I would get an A. However, I have never misspelled *separate* again. I also recall the vocabulary lessons in Mrs. Johnson's class. She used exercises that incorporated words into stories to help us learn and retain their meanings. And although I did not use the words in my conversations at that time, I understood their meaning whether they were used in verbal or written communications. My test results indicated my grasp of these words and helped me maintain top grades in the class. These results also contributed to my status as an honor student.

When Mrs. Johnson established the first chapter of the National Honor Society during my junior year in high school, I was among the first students at Inborden to be inducted. This selection and graduating as valedictorian were two of my most memorable academic achievements in high school. My family was so proud.

The education provided by my high school teachers established a good knowledge base for college. Mrs. Willa Cofield Johnson taught English and literature. Mr. James Perry taught biology and Mr. Augustus Witherspoon taught mathematics and physics. Mr. Guion Davis came to Inborden after Mr. Perry and Mr. Witherspoon left, and he taught biology, mathematics, and chemistry. These three teachers also coached the basketball teams. My mother, Mrs. Lillie Cousins Smith, taught us English, social graces, and acrobatics and read poetry to us. Together with my father, she taught us sports and games that included tennis, ping pong, badminton, and croquet during the summer. She also taught us how to play bid whist and pinochle, and we loved that. When our schools were closed because of snow, we sat around the dining room table and played cards most of the day. We were lucky to have so many people in our community to teach and to serve as mentors. They were people I admired and I still enjoy talking to and learning from those who are still alive today. But in spite of our teachers' best efforts to provide a good education in that segregated environment, there were still very limited job opportunities in Enfield for any of us when we graduated from high school or college.

And because there were so few options for employment, many Black students left Enfield when they graduated from high school and moved to cities in the North, where there were more job choices for them. Others found jobs at companies in Rocky Mount and other locations near Enfield. Some students completed college first and then moved away. A few stayed in North Carolina after college and accepted positions teaching in Black schools. I left Enfield in the fall of 1963 to attend college at Hampton Institute in Hampton, Virginia. For the next four years after entering Hampton, I spent holidays, a few summers, and some spring breaks in Enfield. However, I knew I could not live in Enfield after college. There were no job opportunities for me to pursue a career in mathematics if I did not want to teach. I accepted that fact and was not concerned about it. It was simply a reality that I needed to deal with effectively to succeed. Besides, I had confronted challenges long before I reached high school.

57. Introduction to the Arts

My first exposure to the performing arts occurred when I was about seven years old. My mother played the role of Cinderella in a performance at

Eastman High School, where she was teaching. She reserved a front-row seat for me and all was going well until the next-to-last act. I had sat on that front row and held back my tears for as long as I could. At some point, I could no longer stand it. The stepmother and stepsisters were being so mean to my mother. And my mother was dressed in such ragged clothes. I got up, rushed up the stairs and headed for the stage while the performance was still in progress. I was going to help my mother! Miss Notie Howell was backstage. She also taught at Eastman and was someone I knew. She saw me and stopped me before I could rush onto the stage. She explained that the ladies were acting, and that, if I waited until the next act, I would see that my mother would be just fine. I was too upset to wait until the next act. When the curtain lowered, I headed onto the stage to see my mother with Cousin Notie—that's what we called Miss Notie Howell—right behind me. My mother assured me that everyone was acting and that she was all right. When my mother came back on stage, she had changed into nice clothes, and she looked so much better. However, I stood backstage where I had a good view of all the people on stage. I remained there for the duration of the performance and watched closely. After that performance, it took many years before I could warm up to Mrs. Hannah Boga, who was the teacher who played the role of Cinderella's mean stepmother in the play. I do not remember who played the role of the stepsisters, but I learned later that I had delayed the start of the final act.

My introduction to music also began when I was a child. My mother played jazz on the stereo, and I knew the music of artists such as Dinah Washington, Joe Williams, and Jimmy Smith before I was a teenager. My mother also attempted to generate some interest in my playing the piano when I was about ten years old. She arranged piano lessons with Mrs. Lana Joyner. She also scheduled dance lessons that I requested with Mrs. Elnora Jarrett. Neither of these efforts revealed any real talent for playing piano or dancing on my part. And although I preferred to play softball or build model airplanes, I did advance out of the beginners' green book for piano lessons to the red book and participated in my first and last dance recital dressed in a tutu and ballet shoes. But those less-than-successful efforts did not stop me. I went on to join the Inborden School band and play the clarinet. In spite of Mr. Quantella Knight's best attempts at teaching me how to play the instrument, I was not good at it. As a result, this adventure met with the same results as my piano lessons and dance lessons. However, I did learn that I was not good playing a musical instrument and did not attempt to do that again. I was also fortunate that none of these early experiences with musical instruments had any impact on my willingness to try a new learning venture.

My introduction to music, literature, and the performing arts had begun in our home. Mrs. Willa Johnson taught me classical literature at Inborden and my arts teacher at Hampton introduced me to the visual arts. The arts class at Hampton was mandatory, but I questioned the rationale for the arts class especially because I was going to major in mathematics. My counselor explained that the class was a component of a well-rounded education. And he was right. My arts teacher and the overall arts environment at Hampton expanded my appreciation of various art forms. Having that background made my future job at the National Endowment for the Arts (NEA) more enjoyable than it would have been without the prior exposure. It also exposed me to different ways of learning.

There was usually one right answer to solve a problem in my mathematics classes. In the arts environment, however, I learned that there can be many right answers to solve a problem. For example, while at the NEA I visited an elementary school in Salmon, Idaho, to see the results of a grant awarded to teach children how to write poetry and how to tell stories. I saw children who had learned to express themselves through writing and listened to children who had gained confidence and self-esteem through storytelling. I observed a quiet student's demeanor change when he began to tell his story. I also encountered one of the most memorable expressions of anguish and resolution that was written by an elementary school student in Salmon. And although I do not remember the name of the student who wrote the poem, I cannot forget the words that this child wrote:

Heaven must be a pretty place.
I will go there someday.
My mother is there.

58. Confidence and Optimism

Growing up in my environment also helped establish a sense of confidence and optimism. I do not recall hearing any conversations about failure. Everyone was treated with respect in our small Black community. People in the community appeared to be happy about another person's success, and they showed compassion and understanding when someone had problems. When my family was faced with the darkness of alcoholism and the cruelty of Alzheimer's, people in the community were supportive and encouraging throughout both ordeals. They were there to help without being judgmental.

And I am eternally grateful to a community that gave us hope and support during those extremely sad times.

There were no rich people in the community, yet people helped each other. If someone was ill, the pastor would announce it at the church, and people would stop by to check on the person who was ill, and someone would bring that person food. Usually, the food included homemade soup. I observed this behavior when I was quite young and took it to heart.

A family of four moved into a house that was three doors down from our house. There were three children who lived with their grandmother and they did not have much. I was about eight or nine years old at the time. One of the children was my age and the other two were younger. On the first Christmas that they lived there, we were playing with our toys in the yard, and they came over to play with us. They did not receive toys or new clothing as we had and it made me sad. I gave them some of my toys and asked my mother and father to give them food for Christmas. My family shared fruit, nuts, candy, and cooked food with the family. Each Christmas after that one, my family purchased food for the family and clothing and toys for the children until the family moved away.

My family instilled values such as helping others that would have a continuing influence on our behavior as children and as adults. We were to treat others with respect, use good manners, tell the truth, get a good education, and be yourself. My grandmother also told us that we could learn from anyone. We were also to respond to adults with "Yes ma'am" or "No ma'am" and "Yes sir" or "No sir." Sometime around seventh grade our responses were shorten to "Yes" and "No" responses to younger adults. However, under no circumstances were we to "talk back" to adults. And unless you were told otherwise, adults were addressed as Miss, Mrs., Mr., or Dr. followed by their first or last names, and occasionally by both names. Sometimes we included a middle name, as was the case with Miss Mamie Lee. That was a fairly straightforward process because the adults would tell you what to call them. This courteous process became somewhat awkward for me when some of the teachers asked me to call them by their first names after I graduated from college. That was very difficult to do. However, there were some adults who were called by their first names by everyone other than their own children.

Cockie and his wife Snootie were examples of that practice. Their names were Willie and Olivia Wills, but I doubt that there were many people who knew their real names. They were friends of the family and lived about two miles from our house when I was a child. They moved into their new house on Dixie Street, a couple of blocks from our house, sometime after I graduated from high school. But Cockie stopped by our house whenever he could. My grandmother treated him the same as she did her sons and prepared food for Cockie whenever he stopped by our house. Cockie was a large man with a great sense of humor, who also loved to eat. He often told the story of his ordering a pound of pork barbeque, some hush puppies, and coleslaw for his meal at a restaurant, and then asking if he could have some low-calorie peaches for dessert. When I was a child, Cockie gave me a dollar each time he came to our house whenever he had an extra one. When I became an adult and returned to Enfield, I gave Cockie twenty dollars each time I saw him. After a year or so of my doing this, whenever Cockie saw our car in the driveway, he would walk in the front or back door and say to me, "Where is my twenty?" When Cockie became ill and could no longer drive, Sam and I would go to his house to see him and give him twenty dollars. When we knocked on the door, Snootie would say, "Cockie, your daughter is here." Cockie and Snootie were more than just friends of our family and we had called them by their first names since we were children. They were among the individuals in the community who made us feel special when we were children and continued to do so long after we became adults. They were also people who also worked hard to get ahead.

Getting a job so you could take care of yourself as an adult was understood as a necessity in our house, and graduating from college was expected. Young people were also encouraged to always do our best. We were taught to work hard, earn our way, and not expect anything to be given to us. We were also taught that we were not better than anyone else nor were we less than anyone. With these principles in mind, I began to formulate my plan for the future during my sophomore year in high school. Following high school graduation, I would study college-level courses that included mathematics and science and then complete graduate-level studies in a physical science specialty. I would work hard and be successful. It was inconceivable to me that some people would believe they were superior to other human beings just because of the color of their skin. I needed to learn much more about racism and would have to confront its many shapes and disguises throughout my life.

59. SOUTHERN RACISM EXPOSED

Black activists began to confront White segregationists in the South during the fifties and early sixties. They challenged White elected officials who accepted or tolerated racism, and set out on a course to expose the nation to the horrors that were inflicted on Black people. Concurrently, Black leaders demanded that Southern and nationally elected officials protect the rights of Black Americans. Sometime these confrontations and the associated outrage that erupted across the nation put enough political pressure on elected officials to make them protect Black children and adults. Nonetheless, the events, the victims, and the people who resisted racial segregation initiated and sustained a civil rights movement throughout the South that could not be ignored.

60. Brown v. Board of Education

The 1954 US Supreme Court decision in *Brown v. Board of Education* struck down the separate but equal 1896 US Supreme Court determination of *Plessy v. Ferguson*, which permitted separate but equal, that is, segregated schools for Blacks and Whites. The fifty-year-old *Plessy* decision had provided the legal basis for racial segregation until the Brown decision in 1954. This time, the justices ruled that racial segregation of children in public schools violated the equal protection clause of the Fourteenth Amendment which states that "no state shall make or enforce any law which shall ... deny to any person within its jurisdiction the equal protection of the laws."

This landmark court decision that paved the way for school desegregation throughout the nation happened because a Black family in Topeka, Kansas, and the National Association for the Advancement of Colored People (NAACP) were brave enough to confront the White-controlled justice system. Nine-year-old Linda Brown walked several blocks through questionable areas to reach the bus that carried her almost two miles across town to the all-Black school in Topeka, Kansas. Linda's family lived in an integrated neighborhood where Black and White children played together near a White elementary school. Linda's family attempted to enroll Linda in that White elementary school, but the Topeka, Kansas, school board denied their request. The Browns then joined a NAACP class action suit to protest the segregated elementary school systems. When the US District Court ruled in favor of the board of education, the NAACP appealed the case to the US Supreme Court and finally won. The Supreme Court ruling issued in May 1954 required desegregation of schools throughout the United States.

Linda's obituary in the March 26, 2018, *Washington Post* read, "Ms. Brown, a third-grader who simply wanted to avoid a long walk and bus ride and join her White friends in class, went on to become the symbolic center of Brown v. Board of Education, the transformational 1954 Supreme Court decision that bore her father's name and helped dismantle racial segregation in the United States."

The Brown ruling did not address segregation in any other public areas such as public transportation and restaurants, and did not set a timeline for desegregation in public schools nationwide. The Supreme Court ruling required integration "with all deliberate speed" but omitted detail. It also left implementation decisions to the lower courts. As a result, the desegregation of schools simmered in some areas in the South and met with strong resistance and violence in other jurisdictions. And no court decision could address the contempt some Whites felt toward Blacks, nor could it change their resolve to maintain a privileged-class status, to control Blacks economically, and to keep Blacks in subservient roles.

The Supreme Court decisions were widely publicized in both the Black and White presses. Some Blacks hailed the court's action because it was dismantling the separate but equal decision of *Plessy*. Others in the Black community were disappointed that the court did not set a deadline for states to integrate schools. They believed opponents of the decision would delay the implementation indefinitely. However, the Supreme Court justices were vigilant in their plan to end segregation in public schools, as evidenced by their ruling on subsequent cases brought to the Court. Southern White leaders and politicians were equally determined to maintain segregated public schools in their states, towns, and districts. For example, White education leaders and politicians in North Carolina implemented various methods to circumvent the integration ruling while giving the appearance of compliance. In some counties in North Carolina, the school boards drew district lines to place schools in all-Black or all-White districts to avoid integration. Some school districts permitted parents to apply to the school they wanted to send their children to and permitted the school to approve or disapprove the application. Other jurisdictions permitted parents to simply select the school they wanted to send their children to. The result was a very slow and often litigious integration process, but proponents of school integration had the Supreme Court ruling to back up their arguments. There were other cases of racial injustice across the nation that would draw the attention of the Supreme Court; however, the tragic death of Emmett Till in 1955 was not one of them.

61. Emmett Till

In August of 1955, Emmett Till, a fourteen-year-old Black young man from Chicago, was kidnapped, beaten, lynched—shot in the head—and then put into the Tallahatchie River in Mississippi. This happened because a twenty-one-year-old White woman accused him of whistling at her while he was visiting with relatives in Mississippi. The murder gained national attention when Emmett's mother decided to draw widespread attention to her son's horrible death. Mrs. Till held an open-casket funeral for the public in Chicago where thousands of people saw the mutilated body during the viewing at the funeral, and in photos published by *Jet* magazine and the *Public Defender*, a Black-owned Chicago newspaper. The horrific photos and the story created an outcry in the Black community and got the attention of the White media. Blacks had been killed in Mississippi before Emmett Till, but there was little, if any, media coverage prior to Till's death. And there was more exposure to come.

The husband and brother-in-law of the woman who accused Emmett of whistling at her were indicted for the kidnapping and murder of Emmett, but a jury of all-White males acquitted them. The national media covered the trial and published articles that criticized Mississippi lawmakers. The international press also wrote articles about racism in the state of Mississippi and in the United States generally. The news articles informed both Black and White readers across the country about the horrific crime and the injustice in the southern court system. The resulting protests in Black communities and the outrage expressed by Black politicians and activists were met with rebuttals by White southern politicians. Sadly, neither President Eisenhower nor FBI Director J. Edgar Hoover took any action and left the entire case to local officials. In addition, the two men who killed Emmett Till sold their story to *Look* magazine and admitted their guilt. They knew they could not be prosecuted twice for the murder after being acquitted. Their story that was published in 1956 did not bring about any further charges against the two men. Other than White rejection in the community that caused them to move away, they suffered no other obvious consequences and both died years later of natural causes.

Emmett Till's murder in 1955 did not impact racism in this country at that time. The two White men who killed an innocent Black boy were set free. Black people protested, but local White politicians defended the decision and attempted to discredit the Black leaders who expressed their opinions publicly. National politicians took no action either, and the killings of innocent Black men continued. It appeared at the time that Mrs. Till's efforts to get justice for her son's murder had failed. However, some historians believe that the killing of Emmett Till was the beginning of the civil rights movement in this country. Other historians believe that it was Rosa Parks's actions just a few months later that initiated the civil rights movement.

62. Rosa Parks

Rosa Parks was a Black seamstress and NAACP organizer who lived in Montgomery, Alabama. One day while on her way home from work, she refused to give up her seat to a White man on a Montgomery City public bus. She said she was thinking about Emmett Till on that day[5] in December 1955. But unlike Emmett, her decision was voluntary. She made the choice to defy the city ordinance. The Montgomery City ordinance required Blacks to sit in the back of buses and give their seats to Whites if the front and middle sections of buses were full. As the bus Mrs. Parks was riding filled with White riders, the White bus driver asked her give up her seat. Mrs. Parks refused and was arrested and jailed.

63. Montgomery Bus Boycott

In response to the arrest of Rosa Parks, Black leaders in Montgomery asked Black people not to ride Montgomery city buses on the day of Mrs. Parks's trial which was December 5, 1955. Because that boycott was so successful, community leaders decided to extend the boycott and demand an end to segregation on Montgomery city buses. The group selected the twenty-six-year-old Dr. Marin Luther King to lead the effort and he established a peaceful and nonviolent strategy for the huge protest. The event was widely publicized. Black ministers announced the planned boycott in their churches and local newspapers carried articles about the event. Local television and radio stations also broadcast information about the boycott. The publicity helped inform people throughout Montgomery's Black community about the boycott and aided in increasing the number of people who participated. The boycott that was initially intended to be a one-day event lasted over a year. It ended in December 1956 after the Supreme Court upheld a lower court ruling that racial segregation on city buses was unconstitutional.

The court further ruled that the Alabama and Montgomery segregation policy violated the equal protection clause of the Fourteenth Amendment of the Constitution that requires state governments to protect and treat all people the same. That ruling was a major accomplishment for the Black people in Montgomery, Alabama, and it established a precedent for others to use in their struggles to integrate public transportation systems in other parts of the South. However, it was just the beginning. There were still many segregation battles to fight in cities and towns throughout the South. In fact, the next major battle would occur in a city that was about a seven-hour drive from Montgomery.

64. Little Rock, Arkansas

Three years after the 1954 Supreme Court ruling that segregation in public schools was unconstitutional, the NAACP registered the first nine Black students to attend the all-White Central High School in Little Rock, Arkansas. These students, later called the Little Rock Nine, would be the first Black students to integrate Little Rock schools.

The NAACP organizers, the students, and their parents had anticipated some resistance to the school integration, but none of them expected the level of violence that occurred. The night before the students were to attend Central High School, the Arkansas governor had called in the Arkansas National Guard and ordered them to prevent the nine students from entering the school. When the nine teenagers arrived at Central High School, they were met by an angry White mob that threw stones at them, shouted racial slurs, and threatened to kill them. The students, who had been coached to remain calm, continued to walk through the crowd toward the school. As they approached the school entrance, they encountered National Guard soldiers armed with rifles and bayonets who permitted White students to enter the school but not them. After several attempts to get past the soldiers, the nine students turned around and quietly left the school grounds. They did not come back until the school board requested their return two weeks later.

When they returned to school, the governor had withdrawn the National Guard, leaving just the Little Rock police to manage the angry White mob that had grown much larger than it had been on their first day at Central High School. The Little Rock police force was too small to handle the mob, so a few of the policemen slipped the students through a side door of the school to avoid the crowd. When the White protesters found out that the students had entered the school, they assaulted the Black reporters who were on the school grounds and broke through police barriers to get inside the school. As the violence outside escalated, the mayor ordered the city police to get the students out of the school. After that incident, the mayor of Little Rock requested federal assistance to protect the nine Black students from the White mob that threatened them. In response to the mayor's request, President Eisenhower sent the US Army 101st Airborne Division to Little Rock to maintain order and to make sure the students were admitted to the school safely. He also placed the Arkansas National Guard under federal control.

Those soldiers escorted the students to and from the school in a convoy armed with machine guns and rifles for the entire school year. The armed soldiers also guided the nine students into the school past the large angry White mob with the media capturing the racial slurs and other insults that were directed at the teenagers. One soldier was also assigned to escort each student from one class to another throughout the day. However, since the escorts did not enter the classrooms, gym classes, or restrooms, the nine students were exposed to verbal and physical abuse at various times throughout the school day.

While the children were bullied, insulted, and assaulted by some students, they were treated kindly by others. Outside of the school, Blacks and Whites who were involved in desegregating the Little Rock school received threats on their lives and threats that their houses would be bombed. Others lost their jobs, a few lost their businesses, and some survived gunshots into their houses. In spite of that hostile environment, the nine students completed the first year of the 1957–58 Central High School term and the one senior in the group graduated.

The television coverage of the 1957 attack on the nine students in Little Rock exposed the cruelty of racism in real time. The visuals brought actual footage of the injustices against Blacks to the attention of a national audience. Americans throughout the country saw the vicious behavior of White segregationists in Little Rock and the courage of the Little Rock Nine. These nine Black children set an example that other young people would follow.

65. Greensboro Sit-Ins

Four Black students from North Carolina Agricultural and Technical College sat down at a Whites-only Woolworth lunch counter in Greensboro, North Carolina, in February 1960. At that time, Blacks could purchase items in the Woolworth dining area but were not permitted to sit at the Whites-only lunch counter. The students refused to leave when they were denied service and taunted by Whites, but they remained at the counter until the store closed. They returned the next day where they were joined by other protesters who continued the nonviolent sit-in and spread it to other businesses in the downtown area. The students continued the sit-ins through the end of July 1960, when the Greensboro Woolworth Department Store integrated its lunch counter. As small integration progress was being made in some states such as Kansas, Arkansas, and North Carolina, other states such as Alabama and Mississippi would be among the last to comply with Supreme Court rulings that abolished segregation in public facilities. The next major protest would bring national and international attention to the bigotry in those two states.

66. Freedom Riders

The Congress of Racial Equality (CORE) leaders wanted to get President Kennedy's attention for the South's blatant violation of federal laws that prohibited segregation on interstate buses, trains, and in public transportation facilities, and they succeeded. The group of Black and White Freedom Riders began their journey through the South in the spring of 1961. They had planned to confront segregation on interstate buses and in the facilities along the bus routes.[6] The riders were trained to maintain nonviolent behavior throughout the trip regardless of insults or physical attacks. The initial group of thirteen riders and a couple of journalists boarded the Greyhound and Trailways buses in Washington, DC, for a trip through the South to New Orleans. A Black Freedom Rider sat in the front of the bus and pairs of Black and White Freedom Riders and individual riders sat throughout the bus. At bus stops, Black Freedom Riders would use the restrooms and restaurants that were reserved for Whites. White Freedom Riders would use the facilities identified for "colored." The riders had no problems at stops in Virginia and Georgia, but a few riders were beaten in North Carolina and the worse attacks were yet to come. Angry White mobs firebombed the Greyhound bus in Anniston, Mississippi, and attacked the Freedom Riders when they got off of the burning bus. Riders on the Trailways bus were also attacked and beaten severely. The Trailways bus proceeded on to Birmingham, Alabama, where the Commissioner of Public Safety for the City of Birmingham, Eugene "Bull" O'Connor, permitted a White mob to beat the riders again. The riders were beaten so severely that many of them needed to be taken to a hospital for treatment. A photographer from Anniston took photographs of the bus after the bombing and circulated them to the media. These photographs were published across the country, and CBS did a broadcast on the events in Birmingham. This brought national attention to the Freedom Riders.

When the riders were released from the hospital, they decided to continue their ride on to the next stop, which was in Montgomery, Alabama. However, the two bus drivers quit because they were afraid of being killed. The riders were eventually flown to New Orleans after President Kennedy sent a representative from the administration to intervene. Soon after the original riders arrived in New Orleans, ten new Freedom Riders from Fisk University made preparations to travel from Nashville to Birmingham. These new Freedom Riders planned to continue the last leg of the trip to New Orleans through Montgomery, Alabama, and Jackson, Mississippi. When the riders reached Jackson and attempted to use the restrooms, they were arrested and sent to the state penitentiary. CORE responded to the arrest by sending more riders to Jackson. As each group of Freedom Riders was arrested, another group arrived. The riders continued to come to Jackson. The total number of Freedom Riders reached over three hundred before the Kennedy administration pressured the Interstate Commerce Commission to prohibit segregation in transportation facilities in the fall of 1961. However, the governor of Mississippi, the mayor of Jackson, and other Jackson segregationists would continue their efforts for another two years to maintain segregation in the capital of Mississippi.

67. Jackson, Mississippi Sit-In

The Jackson sit-in, which was patterned after the Greensboro sit-ins, was an integral part of the Jackson movement. It was organized by John Salter, a former labor organizer and recently hired professor at Tougaloo College in Indianola, Mississippi. John was also an advisor for one the NAACP's Jackson Youth Councils. He worked closely with Medgar Evers, who was head of the NAACP Mississippi office that was located in Jackson. The two of them worked together and developed a plan to fight racial segregation in Jackson. Their strategy included sit ins, an economic boycott of White-owned businesses in Jackson, and four demands for White Jackson officials and businessmen:[7]

- Use courtesy titles Mister, Miss, Mrs., when addressing Black people.
- Provide service on a first-come, first-serve basis.
- Use equal hiring practices.
- End segregated facilities in the stores.

The mayor of Jackson and members of the White business community were defiant and refused to respond to any of the demands. They also brought in policemen from across the state and increased their capacity to incarcerate protesters. John recalled that some of the White businessmen in Jackson wanted to negotiate but were afraid to take a position against the Jackson Citizens' Council[8] that threatened to shut down any businessman who tried to negotiate.

To increase the pressure on Jackson's White businessmen, John Salter and three of his students organized a sit-in at the Whites-only lunch counter at Woolworth's on May 28, 1963. This nonviolent protest was a planned event to bring attention to racial segregation in Jackson, the Mississippi state capital. The response from the White mob that gathered turned out to be the most violent reaction of all the sit-ins. In addition to yelling insults at the protesters, the mob beat, kicked, poured condiments onto the protesters, and burned them with cigarettes. They dragged one protester off of the stool at the counter and beat him until he was unconscious while FBI agents and the Jackson police did nothing to stop the violence. After several hours of abuse, John and the students left Woolworth's and were immediately arrested and jailed. William "Bill" Kunstler, a lawyer from New York and a civil rights activist, served as one of the lawyers for the Jackson movement. Kunstler, who had alerted the media prior to the sit-in, also brought the money to bail John and his students out of jail. The media published photos of them sitting at the Woolworth counter with the angry White mob around them.

The Woolworth sit-in was followed by protest marches and other demonstrations in the streets of Jackson. City officials responded by issuing an injunction in early June 1963 that restrained all protest activities. John recalled, during an interview, that the restraint was issued against him, and against Tougaloo College, the NAACP, CORE, and Medgar Evers. John, Medgar, and other NAACP leaders ignored the injunction and continued the protests.

On June 12, 1963, a klansman shot and killed Medgar Evers. Following the death of Medgar, the protest marches in Jackson grew larger. After intervention by President Kennedy and Robert Kennedy, the mayor initiated negotiations with protest leaders and began implementing changes. These actions ended the Jackson movement and John accepted an offer to continue his work in eastern North Carolina, where the Ku Klux Klan had a major presence. As he was leaving Mississippi in the fall of 1963, members of the Klan in Birmingham would use the same method they had used in the failed attempt to kill Freedom Riders on the bus in Birmingham. This time they would bomb a well-known meeting place for civil rights leaders. This time they would kill Black children.

68. Sixteenth Street Church Bombing

Members of the Ku Klux Klan placed a bomb at the Sixteenth Street Baptist Church in Birmingham, Alabama. They ignited it shortly before the Sunday services began on September 14, 1963. It was Youth Day at the church. The explosion killed four Black teenage girls: Addie Mae Collins, fourteen; Denise McNair, eleven; Carole Robertson, fourteen; and Cynthia Wesley, fourteen.[9] It also injured twenty or so other people, including Sarah Collins, who lost her right eye. Sara was the twelve-year-old sister of Addie Mae Collins. Reports and photos of the Sixteenth Street bombing were carried on the front pages of newspapers across the country. The headline on the September 16, 1963, front page of the White Plains, New York *Journal News* read, "Birmingham Seethes: Hate-Triggered Church Blast Kills 4 Little Girls."

Dr. Martin Luther King attributed the bombings to Alabama Governor George Wallace. He wrote to Governor Wallace and stated that, "the blood of our four little children is on your hands. Your irresponsible and misguided actions have created in Birmingham and Alabama the atmosphere that has induced continued violence and now murder."[10] In June of the same year, the governor was seen on national television standing at a University of Alabama entrance to block Black students from entering the school. The governor had told reporters nine days before the bombing that Alabama needed a few first-class funerals to stop integration.[11]

The FBI identified four members of the Ku Klux Klan who were responsible for the bombings. However, the case was closed in 1968 without any arrests. The state of Alabama reopened the investigation three years later. Three of the klansmen were convicted and sentenced to life in prison. One was sentenced in 1977, the second was sentenced in 2000, and the third in 2001. The fourth klansman had died.

69. RACISM IN ENFIELD

Although racial tensions were slowly heating up across the South during the fifties, I do not recall any mention of Ku Klux Klan activity or protests near Enfield until the sixties. Until then, racial discrimination appeared to be the accepted reality in Enfield. Public facilities including restaurants, hospitals, and public schools in North Carolina were segregated. Black children who lived on the west side of Enfield rode the bus past the White Enfield Graded School to get to Inborden School. There were no Blacks serving in any elected or official positions in the town, county or state governments or in any administrative positions. The mayor, city commissioners and police chief were all White. There were no Black policemen or firemen. There were a few Black laborers who worked for the Town of Enfield, but there were no Blacks working as salespeople in any of the retail stores or in either of the two financial organizations in Enfield. Whites owned all of the businesses in the main section of downtown, which was on the west side of the railroad. The only Black business I can remember was a taxi stand that was located east of the railroad near Highway 301 and about a block from the main business section of town. The town had one newspaper, the *Enfield Progress*, which was also owned by Whites. At the state level, Jesse Helms was a news editorialist on one of the major North Carolina television networks throughout the sixties. He was eventually elected to the United States Senate from North Carolina in 1972 and was reelected four times to the Senate. Living in this segregated environment was simply the way of life for Black people. Blacks and Whites coexisted in the segregated, White-controlled state and in the White-controlled town. And racism was apparent in Enfield from the doctor's office to the playground.

70. The Doctor's Office

Dr. William K. Craig was one of the three White physicians in Enfield. Both Black and White patients walked through Harrison Drug past the soda fountain to get to Dr. Craig's office in the back. Our family began seeing Dr. Craig after Dr. Bryant, the only Black physician in town, died. Although Dr. Craig was always pleasant and effective, the thing I remember most is the separate seating rooms for "Whites" and "Colored" when I went to Dr. Craig's office. The room for Whites was large and decorated with comfortable chairs. The room for Colored people was smaller and had hard wooden chairs. It was austere and depressing.

Regardless of how depressing Dr. Craig's waiting room for Blacks was, Park View Hospital in Rocky Mount, North Carolina, was worse. I hoped that I would never have to be taken there for medical care. There were no hospitals in Enfield. The segregated Park View Hospital was the largest and closest hospital to Enfield. It was about eighteen miles away. There were two other hospitals in the area: the Roanoke Rapids Hospital in Roanoke Rapids, North Carolina, and the Black-owned Quigless Clinic-Hospital[12] in Tarboro, North Carolina. These hospitals were about twenty and twenty-four miles respectively from home. When I was about eight years old, my family went to Park View Hospital to visit my grandfather's brother, Willie Mason, who had had a stroke. I remember the strong odor of Lysol disinfectant and the dimly lit hallways with single bare bulbs in the ceilings as we walked through the hospital basement to Uncle Willie's ward. Park View was the first hospital that I had seen. As a result of that unpleasant experience, I did not like hospitals or the smell of Lysol.

Sure enough, when I developed bronchial problems, my mother and father took me to Black-owned Quigless Clinic-Hospital in Tarboro. That hospital was much better looking than Park View. It had bright lighting and no Lysol smell, but I was having no part of any hospital. Dr. Quigless, however, advised my mother that I should remain in the hospital. I cried continuously and so loudly that Dr. Quigless finally told my mom to take me home and call him at any time if my condition worsened. To this day, I do not like the smell of Lysol, and I am still not fond of hospitals.

The Park View Hospital that I saw and smelled as a child differed vastly from the descriptions I found in news articles and on various websites. A June 2014 article in the *Rocky Mount Telegram* described the hospital from a very different perspective:

Before Nash General Hospital became the staple medical facility in Rocky Mount, Park View Hospital was the place people would go to take care of their medical needs in the community.... This year marks the 100th commemorative anniversary of Park View Hospital.... Park View Hospital stood on the vacant lot that is beside Braswell Memorial Library. Park View opened its doors in 1914 and closed in 1971. The hospital opened with a 25-bed capacity and increased to 145 beds by the time it closed. Park View maintained modern facilities and medical equipment during the hospital's 57 years of existence as the largest hospital in Rocky Mount....

The information in the news article was partially accurate. However, none of it captured the dark, segregated place I saw as a child, nor did any of the photographs or articles I found about the hospital. Hopefully, this document will add another perspective about the hospital as well as about other segregated places and racist practices in Enfield.

71. Harrison Drug

Harrison Drug was a bright place with large glass windows in the front of the store. There were small round tables with chairs in the soda fountain area inside. However, the tables and chairs were for White people to sit and eat ice cream and drink beverages purchased at the counter. Blacks could purchase items from the soda fountain, but they were not allowed to sit. There were no signs for Whites or Colored, and I am not sure how I learned that I was not supposed to sit. Both Whites and Blacks picked up their prescriptions from the same pharmacist, at the same counter, and paid for the prescriptions at the same register. The staff was friendly and everyone entered and exited through the same front door to get to their cars or to walk to other businesses.

72. The Friendly Grill

The Friendly Grill was a few doors down the street from Harrison Drug. It was the only restaurant located in the downtown shopping area. However, it was quite clear where customers were to enter the building and where to sit. The owner placed signs that read WHITE above one door and COLORED above the adjacent entrance into the restaurant. I did not go there; however, I found it interesting that the food served to Whites was the same as the food served to Blacks.

The doors for the separate entrances were beside each other at the front of the Friendly Grill. Blacks and Whites would enter through the separate doors and sit at counters inside the restaurant that were divided by a wall with an opening in it. The people serving the food would bring the food out of the same kitchen and take it to one side of the wall to serve White customers at their counter and go on the other side of the wall to serve Black customers who were seated at their counter.

Segregation in the Friendly Grill was obvious. The signs eliminated all doubt about where you were supposed to enter the restaurant or where to sit based on race. The rules for Blacks and Whites were more subtle in other Enfield businesses such as Rose's Five and Dime.

73. Rose's Five and Dime

When I went to Rose's 5¢ 10¢ 25¢ Store—we called it Rose's Five and Dime—I had to wait for White people to be served before anyone would acknowledge my presence. It made no difference that I had arrived at the counter ahead of a White person. This practice annoyed me then and annoys me now whenever I think about it. On one occasion, when I was about ten years old, the salesperson started to wait on a White person instead of me when I was the next person in line at the counter. I told her politely that I was next. She did not appear to be annoyed by my interruption. She simply dismissed my statement as though I was just a child who did not understand the privileges that gave White people the right to be served ahead of me. She said she would be with me in just a minute. I knew that serving someone ahead of me was inappropriate when I was there before the other person was. Yet, there seemed to be nothing I could do but wait or leave. So I waited to purchase the corn candy at the only place in Enfield that sold it.

When she completed the sale to the White person, she turned to me and asked if she could help me. Those incidents of White people being served ahead of me had a lasting impact. Nowadays, if an employee attempts to serve someone ahead of me when I am next in line, I manage my resentment and say, "Excuse me. I am next in line." Thankfully, most people ask who is next.

My childhood memories of Rose's Five and Dime are also quite clear over sixty years later. The candy counter at Rose's was in the front of the store. It was also taller than the other counters in the store and the top section was made of glass so that customers could see the items available for purchase. There were dividers to separate each of the items: salted peanuts, Spanish peanuts, chocolate covered raisins, chocolate covered peanuts, orange slices, corn candy, and many other selections. This display was higher and also seemed to be longer than other displays in the store. Most of the clothing and household items were placed on shelves or neatly arranged on tables throughout the store. I could see all the other items, but I was not tall enough to see over the counter where the candy was sold.

74. The 9 O'Clock Whistle

The Enfield Fire Department was located downtown just across the railroad tracks from Rose's Five and Dime and next door to the Enfield Police Station. There was a large siren installed on top of the Enfield Fire Department. It was blown at noon each day and when there was a fire in the town. Town officials used this extremely loud alarm to alert the volunteer firemen that their services were needed immediately. This alarm also sounded on Saturday nights at 9 p.m. to notify Blacks that they had to be off the downtown streets of Enfield. The 9 p.m. whistle and the curfew for Blacks was eventually eliminated during the 1970s. The whistle still sounds today in Enfield at noon and when there is a fire. It is the sound that some midwestern municipalities use to warn people of a tornado in the area. That sound is still quite vivid in my memory: I heard it each day of my life until I left Enfield. Just as the harsh sound of the whistle is still clear to me, the day that I learned that I could not use the Enfield Public Library is another vivid and unpleasant memory.

75. The Public Library

I began my eighth-grade class in August 1958 and completed the class in May 1959. I was thirteen years old. Our eighth-grade teacher, Miss Smith, gave us an assignment that required research. Until that time, whenever I needed to conduct research, I could find information in the Inborden school library, encyclopedias at home, or in books from the Eastman school library where my mother taught. This time none of those sources provided the information I needed, so I decided to look for books in the Enfield Public Library.

I walked to the library that was located downtown on Market Street behind the old Masonic building about five blocks from home. Although I did not know it at the time, the library was located in the building that was previously the Enfield town office and jail. I recall that the lighting was poor in comparison to the school libraries and that there were bars on the windows. It was also the polling place where Enfield residents went to register and vote. When I went inside and asked the librarian for assistance, she said I could not use the books because the library was for use by Whites only. That made no sense. The facility was supposed to be a public library. When my mother came home from work, I told her what had happened. That was when I learned the reason she kept a set of encyclopedias at home. I became angry because Blacks could not use the public library. She agreed that that was an unacceptable situation and assured me that that would change. She had tolerated inequitable treatment for herself that she would not accept for her children, especially when it affected their learning. She was also determined that the town should have a safe place for Black children's recreation.

76. The Park

There was a swimming pool on the west side of Enfield for Whites only. Black children played in yards, in the streets, and on the school grounds. However, my mother loved children and decided that Black children needed a playground. She approached the all-White group of Enfield officials with the idea of creating a park for Black children. She did not receive a favorable response. However, she refused to give up and collaborated with Mr. Reed Johnson, a civil rights activist in Enfield, to find solutions for each obstacle Enfield officials put before her. She eventually convinced town leaders to allocate funds and make land available to establish the first playground for Blacks in Enfield. They also selected her to manage the park.

The town workers cleared the land and created an extension of Bell Street to permit access to the park. The park opened in the summer of 1957 or 1958 with picnic tables, a ping pong table, horseshoes, badminton, and croquet equipment, and a few other games. Although the park grounds were open all the time, there was no equipment to play ping pong, horseshoes, or any of the games after five o'clock. The games and equipment were available from nine to five, Monday through Friday during the summer months only and were not available once North Carolina public schools opened in August.

When the park activities ended each day, we brought the ping pong net, balls and paddles, horseshoes, and badminton and croquet equipment to our house, and many of the children left the park and came to our house to play. They played in our yard until it was dark. They also played there on Saturdays when the park was closed. Initially, we were awakened on Saturday mornings by children eager to play until Mother made a rule that children could come over to play starting at noon. My grandmother also made a rule that we children in the household could only play after we completed our work in the house.

During the first or second year after the park opened, my mother organized a Wednesday night dance at the park. I remember chopping onions for hot dogs and bringing our record player and records from our house. She eventually borrowed a sound system from the school, and we hung the speakers in the trees at the park. The Wednesday night dances were quite popular even though the ground served as the dance floor. Initially, a few of the neighbors who lived near the park complained about the loud music on Wednesday nights, but after we lowered the volume on the sound system, there were no more complaints.

My mother later requested and received funding to add a tennis court, a basketball court, and the equipment needed for those sports. As a result, the park for Black children was a success and as good as the play areas set aside for White children with the exception of the swimming pool and lighting. The success of the park project is attributable to two significant factors: Lillie Smith's refusal to accept a negative response from the all-White town leaders, and her determination along with that of Mr. Johnson to confront racist leaders in Enfield to get a safe place for Black children to play.

77. FIGHTING RACISM

During the fifties and early sixties, Black individuals and Black organizations began to fight racism in the South. In 1963 a few Black people decided to confront racism in Enfield. I do not think that any single incident caused the change. It was probably brought on by a combination of factors: awareness of the growing resistance to racism throughout the South, knowing that the same discrimination existed in Enfield, and the actions of a few courageous people deciding it was time to make a change.

Mr. Reed Johnson was one of those individuals. In 1963, he decided to run for one of the Enfield town commissioner positions. He and his wife, Mrs. Willa Johnson, organized a voter registration campaign to get more Black people registered to vote, and they reached out to adults and students in the community for help. They asked the volunteers to knock on doors, encourage people to vote, and offer transportation to the polling place for those who needed it. Reed and Willa were successful in getting the attention of Black people in the community, but they also attracted unwanted attention.

78. The Klan

Reed and Willa's activism obviously drew the attention of the Ku Klux Klan. That was when the Ku Klux Klan became real for me. One night Willa and Reed called my mother to tell her the Klan had burned a cross near a window in their house. I experienced a growing sense of anger when we saw the large cross that had been burned so close to them. The Klan could have killed Reed and Willa that night had they chosen to do so. That was the first and last time I had seen a cross burned other than in a movie or on a television show. There were also rumors that klansmen were planning to kill Reed. I think it was about that time that Reed began carrying a handgun.

A few months later, I experienced my own terror one evening when I noticed a car following me when I was driving home. The driver made the same turns as I did. I could see White men in the car and they had rifles that were visible. At seventeen, my instincts told me not to lead them to our house where they would likely harm my family. I decided to drive through the Black neighborhood so someone else would see what was happening. I repeated my route through the neighborhood several times. Eventually, Blacks lined the streets. The men stopped following me as the crowd grew larger on each street. I had not seen or heard of any Klan activity in Enfield until Reed announced his candidacy for Enfield town commissioner. After his announcement, the Klan became a visible and constant threat to all Black people in Enfield. Their presence also triggered a response from the Black community that had not been anticipated.

19. The Boycott, Picketing, and Jail

During Reed's run for town commissioner, several of us—students working on his voter registration campaign—met at Reed and Willa's house to discuss the next steps to get more Black people out to vote. It was during one of those meetings that we, the students, expressed a desire to do more to fight racism in Enfield. That is when we began talks about boycotting and picketing the segregated movie theater and White-owned businesses that did not hire Blacks.

Blacks comprised about half of the Enfield population in the 1960s, yet Blacks were employed in only three of the stores downtown: Meyer's Grocery, Meyer's Department Store, and the Fish Market. To protest the discrimination in hiring practices, Blacks in Enfield and the surrounding areas were encouraged to boycott the businesses that did not hire them. This included the grocery stores, department stores, service stations, and the movies. Blacks who owned cars drove twenty to thirty miles to shop and to support the boycott, and they took relatives and friends who did not have transportation with them. They travelled to Rocky Mount and Roanoke Rapids to conduct all of the activities that they had undertaken in Enfield and were also encouraged to support Black businesses. That is when my family began purchasing our groceries from the Black-owned Exum's grocery store instead of buying them from Mr. Thorne, who was White. They did this even though they had shopped with Mr. Thorne for as long as I can remember. The boycott was our first organized effort that involved the Black population in Enfield and the surrounding area. The level of participation by Blacks was exceptional. It

Fig. 79.1. Derrick Green, Bernard Mason, Joyce Mills, and others were Willa's students when they joined the first picket line in Enfield during the summer of 1967. / Cynthia Samuelson personal collection.

gave us a sense of accomplishment. It made us feel we were taking action in a nonviolent way to protest discrimination in our town.

The Levon Movie Theater was the only movie theater in Enfield, and it was, of course, segregated. Blacks sat upstairs and Whites sat downstairs. It was very hot upstairs during the summer, but the next closest place to see a movie was twenty miles away in Rocky Mount. Several of the students who worked on Reed's voter registration campaign, including me, decided that the segregated seating at Levon Movie Theater was unacceptable and that a change was needed. We held our initial planning meetings at Reed and Willa Johnson's house where we decided to picket on Saturdays and place the first picket line in front of the theater. We made picket signs and practiced how we would march in front of the theater. Reed, Willa, and my mother coached us on how to handle insults and other incidents that might arise (Fig. 79.1).

Picketing occurred without major incidents most of the time, although occasionally there were verbal insults and few eggs thrown at the picket line. We gradually increased the number of picket lines and placed them in front of several stores including Rose's Five and Dime, Cuthrell's Department Store, and McPhail's Department Store. We also needed a larger place to meet and moved our meetings to Cofield's Flower Shop.

The local White businesses were hit hard by the boycott and picket lines. Many White people stayed away to avoid the picket lines and no Black people crossed the picket lines to enter the stores. One Saturday, the police decided to end the picketing. They began by arresting the people who were picketing in front of Rose's Five and Dime. They dragged my cousin, Doris Johnson, from the picket line to take her to jail when she refused to walk there. I, among the others who were picketing in front of Rose's, walked to the jail.

My mother drove the students to and from the picket lines throughout the day as we changed shifts so I knew she would be outside and would get us out of jail. After being held in jail for several hours, I recall yelling that I wanted my mother. Much to my surprise she responded. She was locked in another jail cell and so was my brother Ira.

Willa's father, Mr. Thomas Cofield, and her uncle, Mr. Curtis Cofield, posted bail, and we were released that Saturday night. However, Blacks gathered on the downtown streets and refused to leave when town leaders turned on the 9 o'clock whistle. When the Black crowd refused to leave, the volunteer firemen brought out the fire trucks and turned the firehoses on. They directed the water from the firehoses onto the Black adults and children who were on the downtown streets. Several people were injured. My younger brother, Bill, was one of the individuals hit by the water from the firehoses that evening. The force of the water caused damage to his inner ear. The arrests and use of firehoses were some of the initial tactics White segregationists in Enfield used to discourage further protests. They did not, however, expect their actions to attract outside attention to the racial unrest in Enfield.

80. People Who Joined the Fight

During that turbulent time, several people who were experienced in organizing community efforts to fight racism came to Enfield to help. Three of them had been jailed and beaten and had received threats on their lives, but they were not intimidated by their opponents. White segregationists called them outsiders and agitators because they had not grown up in the towns where they went to help. And although they were outsiders in Enfield, their commitment to participate in our fight was unwavering, and we needed the help.

Civic leaders in Halifax County recognized the need for additional help as tensions grew between Blacks and Whites in Enfield. One of those leaders was Reverend Alexander "A.I." Dunlap. He was well aware of the politics in Halifax County as well as the civil rights struggles in Enfield and brought in John Salter to help us. It is notable that Salter, whose mother was White, changed his name to John Hunter Gray in 1994 to reflect the Native American name of his father, Frank Gray.

81. John Salter

John was a quiet, determined Native American (Fig. 81.1). He came to North Carolina in the fall of 1963 after working with Medgar Evers to organize the Jackson, Mississippi, movement and had served as the NAACP Youth Council's adult advisor. He had organized the Woolworth sit-in and led several protest marches in Jackson. Because of his active role in the Jackson protests, he had been beaten and jailed on numerous occasions. He had also survived several attempts by Mississippi segregationists to kill him, including the throwing of a firebomb into his house while his wife and daughter were there. And although he described his time in Jackson as a "bloody epic," none of the violence stopped him. He did move his wife and daughter out of Jackson after his house was firebombed, but he stayed.

He was determined to continue the fight against racism in Jackson. However, the White city leaders were equally determined to keep their positions of power and control and to maintain their segregated businesses. Eventually, city officials and businessmen made some concessions by hiring a few Blacks and promoting a few sanitation workers, but there were no significant changes in Jackson until after passage of the Civil Rights Act of 1964 and the Voting Rights Act of 1965.

John left Mississippi when he was asked to help with civil rights movement in eastern North Carolina. After a short assessment of the contentious areas within the eastern part of North Carolina, he came to Halifax County. Reed and Willa Johnson were part of his initial interviews because of their active voter registration campaign. He began work immediately and spoke at over a hundred voter registration rallies throughout Halifax County and negotiated with Governor Terry Sanford to bring state troopers into Halifax County when a Klan rally was held near Enfield.

John was also a key component of the brain trust behind many of the successful strategies that advanced civil rights and voter registration in Halifax County and Enfield. For example, he was key strategist in the suit Willa filed against the Halifax County School Board and the State of North Carolina. He also brought in attorneys from New York and Virginia to provide legal support to fight Willa's case until the courts ruled in her favor. He was resilient in

Fig. 81.1. John Salter during my interview with him in Pocatello, Idaho. Although his health was failing, we spent several hours with him, listening and learning about his fight against racism. Much to my surprise, he recalled how much he enjoyed sitting at the kitchen table in my childhood home where my grandmother prepared food for him. / Willa Cofield personal collection.

spite of threats on his life by klansmen. At one point during the movement, he was falsely accused of being a Communist, as were other civil rights activists including Martin Luther King. John eventually left Enfield but continued his work in other parts of the country.

When Willa decided to make a documentary film about the Enfield civil rights movement, she wanted to include John in the film. However, Willa was in New Jersey and John lived over two thousand miles away in Idaho. Plus, his health was not the best. So when my husband Sam and I were on vacation in Nevada in March 2018, Sam drove the two of us to Pocatello to see John. Willa had arranged for a videographer from the University of Idaho to film the interview and sent us a list of questions she wanted us to ask John during the interview. We spent several hours in John's house talking about his life, and reminiscing about his work in Enfield. I had not seen him since he left Enfield in 1963, fifty-five years prior to that visit. Yet his recall of details was exceptional. He gave us details of his civil rights work in Jackson and in Enfield, including the fact that he carried a .38 Smith and Wesson revolver and occasionally a Winchester rifle when he worked in both places. And although he did not fire his weapon at anyone, he told us that just by showing that he was armed had dissuaded several Klansmen attempts to intimidate him.

We all listened attentively as John gave us a history lesson we would not forget. Sam, the cameraman, John's daughter Maria, and I sat and listened with amazement as John recounted several life-threatening incidents, the people he had worked with, and the strategies he had used to fight racism. As such, the time we spent with John was worth every mile we had travelled. Sam and I talked about John and his life as we travelled across Utah and Wyoming and off and on until we returned to Florida. This remarkable man had devoted his life to the fight for racial equality and had not asked for anything in return. Thanks to Willa, Sam and I were able to spend several special hours with John ten months before he died on January 7, 2019.

82. JV Henry

John brought a young man from SNCC, the Student Nonviolent Coordinating Committee, to Enfield to help. One of the young men that I remember was JV Henry. He was a tall, thin, soft-spoken White man who came from Asheville, North Carolina. JV was older than I and called me Miss Cindy. He did this to reverse the tradition of Whites calling Blacks by their first names and Blacks addressing Whites as Mister or Miss regardless of their ages. John helped JV gain acceptance into the Howard University Law School after JV left Enfield. We lost track of JV after the civil rights movement subsided, but I learned during an interview with John that JV had completed Howard law school and moved to California, where he died in 2005.

83. Robert Blow

Robert Blow was a civil rights activist for the NAACP. He was just the opposite of JV. Blow was a large, assertive Black man who had a beautiful voice that was frequently heard over the singing crowd during our meetings and rallies. He often confronted White business owners in Enfield who operated segregated facilities. On one occasion, he and Ellen Davis, another NAACP activist who came to Enfield to help, attempted to enter the Plantation Grill in Enfield in August 1963. Both were arrested and convicted of trespassing. The US Supreme Court overruled the North Carolina Supreme Court's decision to uphold their trespassing conviction in 1965.

Fig. 84.1. Civil Rights activists TT Clayton (center), my mother, Lillie Smith (right), and Willa Cofield Johnson (left) together for the last time at my mother's seventy-ninth birthday celebration, October 2007 in Rocky Mount, North Carolina. / Photo courtesy of Demond McKenzie.

Blow, however, had a great sense of humor. On one occasion, when the Enfield police arrested and frisked him, Blow pretended he was gay and told the policeman he was touching him inappropriately. Blow laughed as he told us about the red-faced police officer who abruptly ended the frisk. I do not know where Blow went after he left Enfield.

84. TT Clayton

Theaoseus T. Clayton, TT Clayton (Fig. 84.1), was a Black attorney from Warrenton, North Carolina, who provided legal advice and support to Enfield civil rights participants. Clayton led the team of attorneys—W. O. Warner from Rocky Mount, Samuel S. Mitchell from Raleigh, and Floyd B. McKissick from Durham—who represented Robert Blow in *State v. Robert Blow* and represented Ellen Davis in *State v. Ellen Marie Davis*. Blow and Ellen had been convicted of trespassing when they tried to enter the Plantation Grill. I remember how calm Clayton was during one of his presentations at the Enfield Police Department. The room was crowded with angry White people around him, yet he remained composed. He held his notes with a steady hand and presented his argument in a calm, confident voice. I have emulated this technique on several contentious occasions.

Each activist who came to Enfield had his own style, expertise, and experience, but they all were fearless and determined to fight racism wherever it existed. They also brought with them a civil rights network that connected Enfield activists to sources that no one knew would be needed. Their network connected Enfield activists to a protest that extended beyond the town boundaries. In fact, we were about to participate in the most memorable civil rights protest that was ever held in the country.

85. The March on Washington

Several of us from Enfield boarded a chartered bus for the trip to Washington, DC, on the morning of August 28, 1963. We were the last group to be picked up, and we filled the bus to its capacity. None of us knew what to expect because the March on Washington was the first of its kind. However, we were excited about the event, and it seems as if we sang freedom songs all the way to DC. Robert Blow was one of the young men on the bus. His beautiful tenor voice could be easily heard as we sang a medley of freedom songs: "Keep Your Eyes on the Prize," "Oh Freedom," "We Shall Not Be Moved," and "Ain't Gonna Let Nobody Turn Me Around."

As we approached Fredericksburg, Virginia, we joined a long line of buses with police escorts for the remaining fifty-mile trip into Washington, DC. I have not seen that many buses traveling together since that day. It was an impressive sight. When we got off the buses, we marched toward the Lincoln Memorial. We arrived on the Mall ahead of schedule and continued to sing. Reports show that there were over 200,000 people there that day. I remember how quiet the city became when Dr. Martin Luther King gave his famous "I Have a Dream" speech at the Lincoln Memorial. You could hear Dr. King's voice clearly anywhere on the Mall. It sounded as if there were huge speakers mounted on the federal buildings that surrounded the Mall in addition to those placed at the Lincoln Memorial itself. The march and the speech renewed our energy and determination. On that day, we became acutely aware that we were part of a much larger effort to fight segregation and discrimination wherever it existed in the country. However, that evening during the return trip to Enfield, we wondered what level of retaliation would occur next.

86. Retaliation

Soon after the picketing began in Enfield, the all-White volunteer firemen stopped responding to fires at houses where Black people lived. After one house burned, Black people managed to control some of the fires by using hoses and buckets of water. Occasionally, a fire was so large that it required large quantities of water to contain it. When this happened, the only thing Black people could do was watch these houses burn.

As the boycotting and the picketing continued, some of the White businessmen refused to approve credit for Black people, and others threatened to cancel existing credit accounts and loans. One of the threats to our family came from the superintendent of Halifax County Schools. He tried putting pressure on my mother, who was a teacher in the county. The White superintendent came to Eastman School where my mother taught and asked the principal to call my mother into the office. When she arrived, the superintendent told her that she was not dressed properly when she was seen in Enfield on weekends. He further insinuated that her conduct was inappropriate for a teacher in the Halifax County school system. After receiving that notification, she wore dresses and high heels to the picket lines regardless of the weather. A subsequent threat from the superintendent indicating that she could lose her job was the last time he tried to intimidate her because of the suit Willa filed against the superintendent, the county, and the state.

One of the most severe forms of retaliation occurred when the all-White Halifax school board did not renew Willa's teaching contract for the 1964–65 school year. That was their sly way of firing her because she was an active organizer in the civil rights movement, although that was not the official reason given for her dismissal. She had helped organize picket lines in Enfield, had been instrumental in getting Blacks to register to vote, and had also held planning meetings in her house. Willa and my mother were the only teachers who were active in the fight against racism in Enfield.

Willa sued the Halifax County School Board and the State of North Carolina in June 1964. She charged that she had been fired because of her civil rights activities and her work on voter registration, and that the firing violated her constitutional rights that were protected under the First, Fifth,

Thirteenth, Fourteenth, and Fifteenth Amendments.[13] Her team of attorneys was led by William "Bill" Kunstler of Kunstler, Kunstler & Kanoy, New York City, who was the same attorney who represented John Salter and the participants of the civil rights activities in the Jackson, Mississippi, movement. I returned to Enfield to testify on Willa's behalf at her first hearing and drove Willa and my mother to the US District Court for the Eastern District of North Carolina that was located in New Bern. Although the judge did not rule in Willa's favor at that first hearing, she finally won her case in July 1967 after a series of appeals and the US Supreme Court refusing to hear the final appeal by Halifax County school officials. The final ruling on her suit established a precedent that helped others who publicly expressed their views on civil rights and cases where, like Willa's, the defendants' First or Fourteenth Amendment rights had been violated.

When Willa's teaching contract was not renewed, we knew my mother would be the next teacher to lose her job in the Halifax County school system. However, that was not to happen. Willa's suit, in fact, helped save my mother's job, but it could not save her summer job working for the town. Enfield officials fired her from the job at the park in 1964. And although there were no warnings prior to her firing, she was not surprised. She had decided early on that the people who joined the fight for civil rights would have to make sacrifices. She also believed that some hardships were necessary to bring about change.

87. ENFIELD AFTER THE SIXTIES

There were changes in the town of Enfield after the protests ended in the sixties. However, most of the changes were made slowly and reluctantly. The agitators, as they were called by the segregationists, were gone. John Salter, JV Henry, Robert Blow, and Ellen Davis had moved on to other areas. Signs reading WHITE and COLORED were removed. The two town cemeteries were integrated, but the churches remained segregated. Eventually, the schools were desegregated, consistent with the legal requirements of the Civil Rights Act, although inconsistent with the intent of the legislation.

88. School Integration

The first six Black students transferred from Inborden to the White Enfield Graded School in 1964; however, it was not until the 1970s that the two schools in Enfield were fully integrated. Inborden became Inborden Elementary School, and the Enfield Graded School became Enfield High School. As integration in the schools progressed, many White families moved their children to the private, all-White Enfield Academy.[14] But in spite of the continued resistance to integrate the school system by some White families, Blacks were elected to fill positions on the Halifax County Schools Board of Education and town officials finally took action to desegregate the library.

89. The Public Library

The library was opened for everyone's use and became a part of the Halifax County Library System. It was moved to its new location in the 1970s and is now next door to the Town Administration office on South Railroad Street. The library is bright, cheerful, and without bars on the windows—quite a contrast from the previous library building. I went to the public library in Enfield to do research for this document. That was the first time I had been to the Enfield library since I was turned away in the 1950s. The all-Black staff was very pleasant and helpful to each person who came in for assistance. The library is an example of a sincere desegregation effort in Enfield, while other attempts reflect creativity on the part of the individuals who were responsible for making the changes.

90. Downtown

Town officials eliminated the curfew that required Blacks to leave the downtown streets of Enfield by 9 p.m. on Saturdays. They also stopped sounding the 9 o'clock alarm on Saturday nights. On the business side, Dr. Craig desegregated his waiting rooms so that Black and White patients could sit in either area. The owner of Harrison's Drug avoided the desegregation issue entirely. Instead of permitting Black and White customers to sit together, he removed the tables. In contrast, the Friendly Grill removed the COLORED and WHITE signs and permitted Blacks and White customers to sit together on both sides of the restaurant. Enfield Bank owners, who had previously employed no Black cashiers, eventually filled some of those positions with Black employees. Cuthrell's and McPhail's Department Store owners and Rose's Five and Dime hired Blacks to work as salespeople, which gave the appearance of desegregation, but these owners did not permit Black employees to use the cash registers. So once again, the Black employees were subjected to a more subtle form of discrimination. These changes in employment practices were indications of progress, but other changes were occurring in Enfield that were not anticipated.

Fewer Blacks shopped downtown after the protests ended in the sixties. Blacks who had crowded the downtown streets of Enfield on Saturdays did not return in the same numbers as there were prior to the demonstrations. They continued to shop in Rocky Mount, Roanoke Rapids, and elsewhere as they had done during the boycott of businesses in downtown Enfield. Tarrytown Mall, built in Rocky Mount in 1962, provided a major shopping facility that was about twenty miles from Enfield, and shoppers could remain inside as they walked from one store to another. Several shops from the old downtown Rocky Mount shopping area also moved to Tarrytown Mall.

Most of the businesses in downtown Enfield that were open during the sixties closed. For example, the owner closed the Levon Movie Theater in the summer of 1963 rather than integrate it. The property was renovated and converted to a grocery store where everyone could shop. Meyer's, Cuthrell's, and McPhail's department stores eventually closed. Harrison and Whitfield's drug stores closed. Beavans Drug Store became Drums Pharmacy and remained open. The Friendly Grill and Rose's Five and Dime closed. The latest business to occupy the Rose's space was an antique store. Reeves's hardware store closed, leaving just one hardware store open downtown. Branch Banking and Trust remained open, but the Enfield branch of the Southern Bank and Trust Company closed in 2015. The police station remained in the same location. The fire station was relocated to a new facility on the west side of town. The railroad station is still there but is now used for office space. It is still owned by the Atlantic Coast Line Railroad; however, trains no longer stop in Enfield. Meyer's Grocery is still open. The post office was moved to a new building and a new location down the street from the side of Meyer's Grocery on Dennis Street. And although Whites still own most of the businesses downtown, there are a few Black-owned businesses there as well.

The reduction in Enfield housing discrimination permitted Blacks to purchase and rent residential properties throughout the town also. As a result, Blacks purchased and rented many of the houses surrounding the downtown shopping area that were previously owned and occupied by White families only. Concurrently, the Black population within the town boundaries increased.

91. Population and Demographics

The population of Enfield within the 1.2 square miles of the town's boundaries reached its peak of 3,272 in 1970. That was about a 10 percent increase over the 1960 population of 2,978. Since the seventies, the population has experienced a downward trend with the exception of two periods of growth during the 1980s and between 2000 and 2005. The projections for 2018 continued the downward trend, offering a population estimate of 2,379 for 2018. The town's racial composition has also changed since the sixties. The mix of Black and White residents of Enfield was close to 50 percent each during the sixties. The census data show a continuing growth in the Black population with a corresponding decrease in the White population. The Black population continued to grow from 79 percent in 2000 to 87 percent in 2010, with a projection of 91 percent by 2017. The White population was 19 percent in 2000 with a projection of 8 percent by 2017. As the Black population increased, Blacks became more active in town politics.

92. Black Officials

Blacks in Enfield gradually gained political influence and power as they registered and voted in increasing numbers after the sixties. They elected their first Black town commissioner, Charles Swindell, in 1979. Mr. Swindell was also appointed as the first Black mayor in the late 1980s to complete the term of the mayor who had died while in office. The town swore in its first elected Black mayor, Kai Hardaway, in March 1991 and the first of its Black police chiefs, Ed Jones, soon after that. Hardaway was the second of the five Black mayors to hold that office in Enfield. He was followed by Ed Jones, Warnie Bishop, and then Barbara Simmons, who was elected as mayor in 2009 and served consecutive terms until 2017. With the election of the Black leaders, Blacks were hired to fill various positions throughout the town government and its police department.

Thomas Hardaway was the first Black from Enfield to be elected to the North Carolina House of Representatives. He was elected in 1987 and, with the exception of the 1993 and 1995 terms, he served in that role until 2000. When he was selected for the Board of Elections in the 1980s, Representative Hardaway moved the polling location for Enfield Precinct #2. He moved it from the Enfield Public Library, which was located downtown, to Inborden School on Hannon Street. Precinct #2 comprised the largest Black population in Enfield, and the move made the polling location more accessible to Blacks.

The second Black from Enfield to serve in the North Carolina House of Representative was Ed Jones. Ed, a retired North Carolina state trooper, was appointed to that position in 2005 when the representative holding that position died. He campaigned for that position and was subsequently elected in 2006. In 2007 he was appointed to the North Carolina Senate and was the first Black from Enfield to serve in the North Carolina Senate. Ed was reelected to the state Senate three times and served in that capacity until his death in 2012. A portion of US Highway 301 that runs through Enfield was named the Senator Edward W. Jones Highway in 2018.

93. Highway 301 and Interstate 95

The completion of Interstate 95 just a few miles outside of Enfield in 1969 had a major impact on businesses in Enfield.[15] Interstate 95 ran almost parallel to Highway 301 through the state of North Carolina. When the section that ran about six miles west of Enfield was completed in 1969, service stations, restaurants and motels were gradually built along the interstate. As a result, the interstate traffic bypassed the town completely. Patrons who had once stopped at the service stations to purchase gasoline and snacks and to rest at motels on Highway 301 were gone.

I remember seeing the long lines of traffic on Highway 301 during holidays when I was a child. Those traffic jams were eliminated when traffic was rerouted west of town onto Interstate 95. The motel on the south end of town closed and two motels located a few miles outside of town on the north end closed after the owner converted one of them to a rental property for several years. The small motel buildings next to the Plantation Grill were also converted to rental units and a few are still in use. Mr. Dancy's café is now an antique store, but the Little Palace is still open. Exum's Grocery store, Thorne's Grocery, Barnhill's, and Horton's stores are closed. The Big Top Grocery was sold after the original owner, Mr. Henry Pittman, died. It remains open under new ownership and a new name, Big Jim's.

94. Dixie Street

The changes on Dixie Street were different from those on Highway 301. For example, the name of Dixie Street was changed to Dr. Martin Luther King Jr. Avenue. However, the other changes were more personal to me. Most of the older people in the community who I admired and respected were no longer there. All of the people who lived near our house when I was growing up are dead. Miss Effie and Mr. Solomon's house was torn down and the lot remains empty.

Miss Mattie's house was torn down and is now part of the parking lot for St. Paul Baptist Church. Miss Florence and Mr. Arthur's house is still standing, but it is not occupied. Miss Veenie's granddaughter and her family moved into Miss Veenie's house and established a close relationship with my mother. We also replaced the house that my grandfather built with a smaller, newer house for my mother. The new house was much easier to maintain and my mother loved it. And as soon as the house was ready, she invited her Brick Club[16] members to hold a meeting and have dinner there.

One of my mother's favorite stories about her new house was the day one of her former Eastman High School students, Raymond Williams, had difficulty finding her. Raymond had stopped by to visit my mother many times at the old house when he returned to his parents' house for holidays or other special occasions. On one such occasion, Sam and I walked out onto the front porch and saw Raymond driving past the house. He went down the street, turned around, and was about to drive by again when he saw us. Raymond parked his car in front of the new house and walked toward the porch shaking his head. At the same time, my mother saw him and came out of the house. He said he was so glad to see us on the porch. He told us he had driven by the new house several times looking for Miss Cousins's old house and did not understand why he could not find it. This made her laugh, as he usually did when they were together. Raymond was one of my mother's students who had grown up in one of the farming communities just a few miles west of downtown Enfield and moved away to pursue a career in teaching after graduating from my mother's alma mater, Winston-Salem State University.

95. Farming

There were significant changes in farming practices in Enfield after the sixties that were not caused by the civil rights movement. One that had a major impact on the town economy was the ongoing change in farming practices that was occurring throughout the county and the state. It had a major impact on Enfield because of the town's continued reliance on farmers for a significant part of its economy.

Historical accounts about the farm-based economy in Enfield date back to the late 1890s. These reports describe tobacco and then peanuts as the dominant markets. The North Carolina Regional Economic Development Council documented a decrease in the number of farms and the amount of farm employment in the state of North Carolina between 1938 and 2002, even though the state's farm income ranked sixth in the country. The trend was attributed to changes in farming practices that were making the farms more efficient. These changes were occurring in Enfield and throughout the state. As farms became more industrialized and more efficient, production increased. However, there was a corresponding reduction in the amount of manual labor needed. As such, owners reduced the number of people working on their farms.

This change was also documented in various accounts of North Carolina and Enfield history.[17] In the tenth edition of *Our Account: A History of Branch Bank and Trust*, the author summarized the concerns of the bank's president that were expressed in the 1950s about the reduction in farm labor in Eastern North Carolina (where Enfield is located). The bank's president believed that one way to offset the economic change was to "... encourage industry, especially food processing plants, to build in the East [in Eastern North Carolina]."

He further described the reasons for the change and stated: "Farms produced more tobacco poundage per acre because of higher yielding varieties and better farming practices, and fewer laborers were required because of such things as improved farm machinery. The trend turned away from tenant farming, with the surplus labor force gradually drifting away from the area, taking its purchasing power with it."

In 1950, the *Rocky Mount Evening Telegram* published an interview with an Enfield businessman who was also a farmer. During the interview, the businessman expressed his concern about Enfield becoming too reliant on farmers for the town's economic health. He shared the same vision as the president of Branch Bank and Trust that the town needed an industry, or some industries, to offset the dependence on farming for its economic well-being. He warned: "As is the case with most eastern Carolina towns, the farmers provide the economic lifeblood. It's all agriculture: that's not good . . . because there's no steady payroll in town, no firm on which merchants can rely to pump weekly dollars into the economy."

I observed the exodus of people leaving the farms during the sixties. These families lived in the areas that surrounded the formal 1.2 square miles of the town boundaries. Many of my friends and classmates whose parents had been farmers did not themselves continue to work on the farms when they graduated from high school or college during the sixties. They moved to other towns or cities to live where there were jobs for them. The young men chose careers in private industry, law enforcement, and education. Some of them chose careers in the military even though there was a high probability that they would be sent to fight the war in Vietnam. None of the young women that I knew considered anything related to farming as career options.

96. IMPACT OF THE SIXTIES ON MY LIFE

I worked and studied diligently to grasp the subjects taught in my high school classes to get good grades. The teachers and the subjects that were covered established a foundation for college learning. However, there were no courses that covered racial issues or power and politics. Those lessons and experiences began outside the classroom during the sixties and had a profound impact on the way I approached life and solved problems as an adult.

97. Mentors May Not Support You

I was angry at elected and appointed officials who took no action against racism. I was also angry at the Black preachers and teachers in Enfield who would not support the civil rights movement in any way. They would not permit us to hold meetings in their facilities nor would they get involved in voter registration or any aspect of the civil rights movement. Those same people, ironically, in Sunday school, church, and classroom had talked to young people about the importance of standing up for what was right.

We young people had gone door-to-door in the Black community asking people to register and vote. We also offered transportation for anyone who needed it. The voter registration desk was located in the Enfield Police Station, and we knew that some Black people would not want to go there. We, in fact, encountered multiple surprises. Some Black professionals would not register to vote; however, many nonprofessionals did not hesitate to register and to vote. Miss Mattie, who lived next door to us, was about eighty years old and had never voted. We knocked on her door and told her why we were there. She came outside and asked us to sit with her on her front porch. Miss Mattie was a domestic worker who cooked and cleaned for the White Pope family that lived at the southern end of Dixie Street. She also took care of their children. We had expected her to turn us down. She did not. Miss Mattie registered and proudly voted for the first time in her life. Miss Mattie told us that Mr. Pope, her employer, had driven her downtown to register and to vote.

The behavior of the professionals who would not support us had taught me as a teenager that the people who activists try to help and who would benefit from the efforts might not support those efforts and might, in fact, discourage them. That was a rude awakening. It was a long time before I could understand their perspectives. I learned that not everyone is willing to risk losing their jobs, endure financial hardships, or make sacrifices for a cause regardless of how just the cause is. People like Willa, Reed, Miss Mattie, and my mother were the exceptions. They believed that you must confront difficult problems to resolve them.

98. You Must Overcome Obstacles

I received the foundation for the college-level courses such as algebra, trigonometry, biology, English, and literature in high school. However, there were no calculus courses offered at Inborden when I was there. My academic life changed abruptly when I enrolled in my first calculus class at Hampton. The concepts of calculus were completely new to me and I struggled. Students who had attended large high schools had taken calculus courses already and did not have the challenges that I encountered.

Mr. Urquhart, the calculus instructor, was an eccentric man who always used green ink when he wrote on our papers. He rarely smiled. Yet he seemed to be a kind person. He walked into the classroom each Monday, Wednesday, and Friday, at 7:30 a.m., immediately turned his back to the class, and began writing on the chalkboard without saying anything. His behavior was the same whether it was a lecture session or a quiz day. When he finished writing on the board, he would turn around, face the class, and talk to us, occasionally with a slight smile under his large beard when he saw our blank stares.

Mr. Urquhart gave quizzes each Friday morning. During one of my calculus quizzes, he looked over my shoulder, observed my struggle, and said softly, "Miss Cousins, why don't you just give up?" I was not about to. I was a mathematics major and knew I could learn calculus. That course was nothing compared to being followed by Klansmen with rifles, picketing in front of an angry White crowd, or seeing a burnt cross on Willa's lawn. Giving up never crossed my mind. Learning calculus was just another obstacle I would have to overcome. Besides, I had not run into any other subjects at Hampton that I could not master.

I finally went to Mr. Urquhart's office one day after class and asked what I should do to learn calculus. He was very gracious and suggested I get a tutor to help me. I asked a few of my classmates who were not having problems with calculus if they would be my tutor. Some of them were already tutoring other students, but others were not interested in tutoring at all. So Mr. Urquhart agreed to be my tutor. During my tutoring sessions, he explained the concepts of calculus and how it was used to solve practical problems. He taught me how to look at a problem and create a formula to solve it. Once I understood concepts, I was able to recover from my previous failing scores on his quizzes and pass his course with a C. After completing that first calculus course, I received an A in the next course and two Bs in subsequent advanced calculus courses. And although he never acknowledged my improvements, he did ask me to be his assistant to help him grade papers and to monitor his exams in classes other than my own. I accepted his offer and my experiences with Mr. Urquhart turned into very pleasant and rewarding ones. Unfortunately, another encounter with one of my instructors at Hampton did not turn out as well.

99. Do Not Hate Anyone

I enrolled in a mathematics class that was designed primarily for education majors. I took that class because it covered imaginary numbers, which was an area of mathematics that I knew nothing about. I had not been taught that concept in any of my high school or college classes. I was the only senior student and the only mathematics major in that class. The other three ladies were sophomore and junior education majors and the class was much more of a challenge for them than it was for me. They engaged in the teacher's conversations about her cats, problems with her car, and the faulty plumbing in her house during the beginning of each class. I was quiet during these exchanges, but asked an occasional question related to mathematics and responded to all questions the instructor asked me. I also studied and received As on all of my homework assignments, and As on all of the quizzes and tests given during the semester.

During that same semester, Hampton issued a new policy that gave instructors the option to waive final exams if a senior maintained an A average in a class. I did not know it was an option for the instructor. I had an A average in the class and did not go to take the exam. However, the teacher sent a message to me on the day of the exam to tell me that I had to take the exam if I wanted

Fig. 99.1. Dr. Jerome Holland (left), former president of Hampton Institute assisted by Dr. Hugh M. Gloster (center), administrator, presenting the diploma to me for a Bachelor of Arts degree in mathematics, May 1967. / Cynthia Samuelson personal collection (Reuben V. Burrell photographer).

to receive a passing grade in her class. I went to see her and we scheduled a date for the exam. When I returned to take the final exam, it contained problems to solve and complex concepts that I had not seen before in any class. Most of them were well beyond the concepts that were taught in her class or any other class I had taken. I have no doubt that all of the other three ladies who were in the same class would have failed that exam.

I received a C on the final exam and a B in her class. When I complained to the head of the mathematics department about the teacher requiring me to take a final exam and a different, more difficult exam than the one she had given to the other students in the same class, that is when I learned that waiving the final exam was, in fact, at the instructor's discretion. My behavior probably cost me the A in this course and lowered my overall average grade slightly.

After graduating from Hampton in 1967 (Fig. 99.1), I told Mr. Peyton, the chemistry teacher at Eastman High School, about the White teacher at Hampton who gave me a different and far more difficult mathematics final exam than she had given to the other students. I recounted how much I hated her. It was during this conversation that I learned a valuable lesson that stays with me to this day. Mr. Peyton said I should not hate anyone. He explained that my hating someone had no impact on the other person. In fact, my hatred only disturbed and distracted me. It took about a year to accept that reality. However, I am glad that I finally understood he was right. That lesson has served me well. I do not hate anyone today. I also decided not to ever become as angry again as I had been during the sixties. The lesson I learned from Mr. Payton has been more valuable to me throughout my life than the grade I received in that mathematics class—and I still had so much more to learn.

Many years later, I realized that I might have avoided the teacher's seeming dislike for me had I engaged in the conversations about her personal issues during the class. And although I studied diligently, listened attentively, and responded to her questions during the class, these actions were not enough. I could have also explained my reasons for taking that class during the first session and should have asked her if she planned to exercise her option to waive my final exam because I had maintained an A average in her class instead of not showing up for the final exam without talking to her. I also believe that this White instructor, who had only taught high school students prior to this job, held prejudices about Black people and preferred subservient behavior from her students. I also believe she resented my behavior in class and wanted to show me that she was in control of the grades students received in her classes.

100. Life Isn't Fair

I complained about the same Hampton teacher to Mr. Williamson (Fig. 100.1), a teacher and a basketball coach at Eastman High School. I told Mr. Williamson that I was extremely disappointed that nothing had happened to her after I told the head of the mathematics department at Hampton what the teacher had done. I went on to say it was not fair for a teacher to do what she had done to me and get away with it. I will never, however, forget his response. He said, "CC, life isn't fair." His statement was difficult to accept. No one had ever told me that life was fair. It was an assumption on my part. I remained silent for a while as I absorbed that shocking reality. It was just another disappointment that this naïve twenty-one-year-old would have to live with. And so I did. It was a valuable lesson and I have since passed this wisdom on to other young adults who struggled with the same misconception that life is fair.

Fig. 100.1. Clemon "Clem" Williamson, Korean War veteran and Purple Heart recipient, and former Halifax County Schools teacher and administrator, speaking at my mother's seventy-ninth birthday celebration, October 2007. / Cynthia Samuelson personal collection.

101. Perception Can Become the Reality

My history teacher at Hampton was a White man who told us he was teaching in a Black school for the first time. He taught the students in our class about both the strengths and weaknesses of our founding fathers. I had only heard the positive side of American history in my elementary and high school history classes. He also dispelled myths that I had learned in elementary school such as George Washington cutting down a cherry tree and saying, "I cannot tell a lie."

I was quiet in his class unless called upon. I also studied, worked hard on my assignments, and received As on his assignments. Near the end of the semester, I told him how much I had learned in his class and that I enjoyed the class. He said he felt that I stared at him during class and wondered why. I told him that I was not staring at him. I had been taught to look people in the eye when they were talking to me or when I was talking to them. I further explained that I was listening attentively to what he was saying. He seemed to recognize my sincerity and was pleased to hear the candid explanation from an eighteen-year-old student. The mathematics teacher at Hampton, who had given me a more difficult final exam than the other students, could have thought that

I was staring at her also. Fortunately, my habit of looking teachers in the eye when they were talking did not cause problems in any other classes.

102. Change the System

I recounted my anger about the unjust federal government to Mr. Williamson. I wanted to tear down the government that ignored the civil rights of Black people. Mr. Williamson told me that I needed to understand a system before I could change it and that I could not learn it from the outside. He added that I had to get into the system to change it.

That conversation with Mr. Williamson influenced my decision to select a career in federal service. I entered the federal service with the determination to treat everyone fairly. I recruited, hired, and recommended people for positions, promotions, and recognition based on their qualifications and achievements. I served as a mentor for men and women in several federal agencies. I also met with individuals and spoke at conferences to help large, small, woman-owned, and minority companies learn how to compete for federal contracts. Mr. Williamson's advice not only influenced my decision to pursue a career in the federal government, it also led me to a rewarding and enjoyable career as a civil servant.

103. Get a Good Education

About a year after I began working in the federal government in a marine research laboratory in New Jersey, I looked for universities near me that offered a master of science degree in computer science. This was in 1970 and there were not a lot of universities offering advanced degrees in computer science because it was a relatively new discipline. Fairleigh Dickinson University met the criteria that I wanted. The computer science degree would be issued by the school of engineering, which had a good reputation, and I could take most of the courses in the evenings at Fort Monmouth, New Jersey. That permitted me to work full-time and attend classes in evenings after work.

That was the first time I had attended a White school. I was the only Black person in all of my classes at Fairleigh Dickinson and the only female in all but one of my classes. I had no social interaction with any of my classmates. I experienced the same isolation that my brother encountered when he transferred to the first integrated high school in Enfield. One White female student talked to me briefly in one class, but she dropped out. I studied and worked alone. When I realized my classmates were not going to talk to me, I would enter each class and take a seat on the front row where I could look the professor in the eye and learn.

When I moved from New Jersey to the Washington, DC, area, my Fairleigh Dickinson advisors permitted me to take courses at George Washington University and return to the Fairleigh Dickinson campus during the summer to complete my course work. That plan worked out well until I arrived on the Fairleigh Dickinson campus a year later to attend summer school and to live on campus. First, I was assigned to a two-bedroom apartment that was to be shared with a young White student. When she came to the room and saw me, she left immediately. I was reassigned to another two-bedroom room apartment with a Black roommate within a few hours. Then the Black roommate, who arrived a few days later, was not overly excited about sharing the apartment either, but I was not moved again. It helped that my classes were held in the evenings and her classes were held during the day so we rarely saw each other. Besides, I was there to learn and to complete my studies for a master's degree. It would take more than the lack of conversation or an unhappy roommate to stop me.

I met a few Black female students who were in other departments but saw no Black professors or teachers. I became accustomed to the absence of social interaction and recognized that I would need to work harder. My workload was very demanding and I frequently studied late at night and into the early morning hours. If I had questions, the professors were available to help. I already knew that my life would not be easy and that I would run into obstacles, but I was not about to give up.

104. Overcome Adversity

My family taught my brothers and me that we had to learn how to respond to adverse situations with positive action. That helped me redirect my anger into constructive behavior during the sixties and later to deal with prejudice and resentment in the workplace. My mother read "Mother to Son" by Langston Hughes (Fig. 104.1) to us when we were young children. It is one of my favorite poems. She read it with a marked Black dialect. She never needed to explain its meaning. As I grew older, I realized that my mother was telling us that, although our lives seemed easy and carefree as children, she had encountered many difficulties but did not let that stop her from achieving her goals, and

> **Mother to Son**
>
> *By Langston Hughes*
>
> Well, son, I'll tell you:
> Life for me ain't been no crystal stair.
> It's had tacks in it,
> And splinters,
> And boards torn up,
> And places with no carpet on the floor—
> Bare.
> But all the time
> I'se been a-climbin' on,
> And reachin' landin's,
> And turnin' corners,
> And sometimes goin' in the dark
> Where there ain't been no light.
> So boy, don't you turn back.
> Don't you set down on the steps
> 'Cause you finds it's kinder hard.
> Don't you fall now—
> For I'se still goin', honey,
> I'se still climbin',
> And life for me ain't been no crystal stair.

Fig. 104.1. Langston Hughes, "Mother to Son." 1922.

she had continued to face obstacles and had continued to overcome them throughout her life. She was also alerting us that we would face difficulties throughout our lives as well and that we had to overcome them, and under no circumstances were we to give up. That lesson has helped me throughout my life and my career.

When I transferred from New Jersey to a Department of Commerce job in Washington, DC, in 1973, I was the first female and first Black to hold a professional position in that federal office. The White secretaries, with one exception, refused to treat me as a professional. They provided administrative support for the men in the office but no support for my projects. The Black secretaries, however, were very supportive. I was angry about the actions of the White secretaries but did not let that deter me. I began work on a master's degree in computer science at night and continued to work full-time on my job. I also worked diligently to excel in whatever task I was assigned on the job. Concurrently, my computer skills were becoming more visible.

One of the division directors asked if I could develop an electronic system to help Department of Commerce law enforcement agents manage the large volume of data reported about foreign vessels that were fishing off the coasts of the United States. The electronic system was needed to help the agency comply with a Congressional mandate. I worked with the law enforcement agents who were responsible for collecting the data and preparing the report to Congress. After gaining an understanding of their requirements, I developed the electronic system and trained them how to use it. The law enforcement officials and the head of the agency were pleased with the results. I received an award for designing and writing the code for the electronic system and completing it in sufficient time for the agency to meet its Congressional reporting requirements.

My supervisor and mentor invited me to join a group of analysts who were forming a new Information Systems Division within the Department of Commerce. I would also receive a promotion if I moved to the new division. I accepted the offer and moved to the new division reporting to a new director. There were three White men in the new office, a Black secretary, and me. The three men were fifteen to twenty years older than I. The secretary was about five years younger. Ironically, the secretary had grown up in Enfield. The director was an economist, the other two men were systems analysts, and I was a computer systems analyst.

All was going well for about a year. Then one of the men decided to take over the lead for the electronic law enforcement system I had designed. He convinced the director that the design needed upgrades that he could provide. He also convinced the director that I should work with a team of contractors that he led. When the director told me of this plan, I did not agree that the other analyst should take the lead or that I should report to the analyst. However, the director added that he did not feel comfortable with me, but did not give me the reasons for his discomfort. It made no sense: he had rated my performance during the previous year as outstanding, the highest evaluation an employee could receive. And while this situation was hurtful, I fortunately had learned in Enfield that life isn't fair, and so used that unpleasant situation as opportunity for advancement. I applied for a position at the Federal Trade Commission that offered a promotion. I was selected for the new position, received a promotion, and continued to advance in my career.

In hindsight, I had experienced my first power grab. The analyst who made the power move was determined to take control of the law enforcement system. That was a business decision for him. He later left the government as a federal employee, formed his own company and returned to the same office, worked for the same office director as a contractor, and worked on updates to the same system he had taken over. I continued to advance in my federal career and learned to recognize and deal with power moves regardless of how they were presented.

105. Let No One Intimidate You

My introduction to the real working world began as soon as I left Hampton. I was recruited by Westinghouse in 1967 to be a mathematician and sent to Pittsburgh, Pennsylvania, for orientation and training. I attended my first training session where there were about five hundred males and about four or five females. One of the speakers told jokes that degraded women. One of the women was so disturbed by the speaker's jokes that she decided not to attend the second session the next day. At the end of the session, I approached him and asked if he would have told those same jokes if his mother-in-law was in the audience. He responded that he would have, although he appeared to be surprised by my question. However, there were no more inappropriate jokes when he spoke to the group the following day.

I left Westinghouse and took a job in the federal government, where jokes about women eventually would be considered sexual harassment. However, I was faced with attempts to intimidate me instead. One day in 1980, I returned from a vacation and learned that my supervisor had blamed me for a decision she had made that had upset a customer. She had decided to make changes to a computer system design while I was away. The customer was a powerful person in the agency and was very displeased with the change. He was also concerned that no one had discussed the changes with him. Instead of accepting responsibility for her mistake, my supervisor advised me to take the blame and insinuated that my career could be in jeopardy if I told the customer the truth. I wrote a letter to the customer telling him that I had no knowledge of the design change until I returned from vacation. I explained further that I had no part in the decision to make the change. I sent a copy of the letter to my office director. He called me into his office and asked me to retract the letter. I refused. I called my mother when I left the director's office to tell her that I was probably going to be fired. When I described the situation to her, she said, "I would not expect you to do anything differently." She was reiterating one of the lessons she had taught me as a child: "Life ... ain't been no crystal stair." I was not fired and received no repercussions from the incident.

I do not recall anyone saying, "This is how to handle intimidation." I had learned to do so by watching the adults who had worked with us during the sixties. My perception was validated when I interviewed John Hunter Gray in the winter of 2018 about his civil rights work in Enfield during the sixties. He had no fear of the Klan, the police, or anyone else, nor had Reed, Willa, or my mother. We had been focused on our purposes, our determination to fight the injustices that were inflicted on Black people, and we were determined to succeed. I grew into an adult who would not be intimidated by anyone or be fearful of losing a job or a position: simply, I told the truth and stood up for what I believed was right.

106. Be Yourself

When I was a child and my grandmother said, "Be yourself," and I thought she was telling me to behave, but when I was growing up during the sixties, I learned that the phrase meant more than that I should behave. It also meant that I should be a genuine person and not engage in deception. Those same values were reiterated in our community and in the church. As a result, I was guided by those values throughout my career. If I was asked to do something that would compromise my integrity, I politely refused the request. This sometimes made my job more challenging. It certainly did not help me make friends. However, in most instances, it earned respect.

One day my mentor suggested that I apply for a Senior Executive Service (SES) position working for a President George H. W. Bush appointee. SES positions are key positions in the federal government that are just below top leaders that are appointed by the president of the United States.[18] I was flattered by the suggestion, but decided not to apply for the job. First of all, the newly appointed chairman for the National Endowment for the Arts (NEA) did not know me, and he was not going to select someone he did not know to become one of his deputies. Besides that, I was taking graduate courses in the evenings and had recently submitted my application for a doctoral program. I did not want to waste my time completing the onerous application for a job that I would be selected for. However, Antoinette Handy, who was a friend as well as the deputy director of the NEA Music Program, challenged me to apply for the position. My mentor, Jack Basso, had also suggested that I apply for the position. He and Antoinette were two people I admired and respected. So I finally applied for the position. When I was asked to come for an interview with the chairman, that meant that, based on the information I had provided on my application, I, among other applicants, had met the basic criteria for a federal senior executive service position. However, I was still convinced that the chairman would select someone that he knew. Besides that, in my position as the NEA information technology director, my staff and I would provide technology support for him and report to his deputy instead of reporting directly to him. So I decided to use the interview as an opportunity for the chairman to get to know me and made no special preparations for the interview. I would "be myself" and answer his questions with frank responses, which is exactly what I did. Because of that, I was very relaxed. The chairman was kind and gracious, and I enjoyed meeting him and answering his questions. After the interview, I went back to work.

About two weeks later, on October 30, 1989, I was notified that John Frohnmayer, the newly appointed chairman for the NEA, had selected me to become one of his deputies. He had selected me for what turned out to be the most rewarding job I have ever held in either the federal government or in private industry. The NEA artists and members of the National Council on the Arts were genuine, kind, gracious and talented. I am eternally grateful to John Frohnmayer for giving me the opportunity to serve as his deputy; to Jack Basso, who was my mentor; and to D. Antoinette Handy, who encouraged me to apply for the position. These individuals helped with my career advancement without my asking, but I learned that there were other people in influential positions who would not help me even though I asked for their advice.

107. You Can Learn from Anyone

I expected to advance into increasingly demanding federal leadership positions and wanted to learn more about how to be an effective leader. While I was working as the information technology director at the National Endowment for the Arts, I began taking one graduate-level course each semester at the University of Southern California's (USC) Washington Public Affairs Center (WPAC). Public administration was the only curriculum taught at WPAC, and the school was conveniently located in Washington, DC, just a few blocks from the Old Post Office where I worked. I continued taking classes after I was selected as the deputy chairman for management at the NEA.

One of the USC class assignments was to identify a position we wanted to hold in the federal government and select people we would like to interview who were in those positions. The purpose of the interviews was to gain insight into the skills and abilities of the individuals who held those positions. I chose the assistant secretary for administration position and requested separate interviews with Jon Seymour, who was the assistant secretary for administration at the Department of Transportation, and John Frankie, who was the assistant secretary for administration at the Department of Agriculture. Although I did not know either of these gentlemen personally, they were highly regarded in the federal government for their effectiveness and accomplishments in those positions. Both men agreed to the interviews. They spent over an hour with me, provided invaluable insight into their jobs, and offered to help if I needed to talk to them again.

I also wanted to interview a female who held a leadership position in the federal government and selected Lynne Cheney. She was chairman of the National Endowment for the Humanities (NEH) and I was deputy chairman for management at the National Endowment for the Arts. I was also the first Black and the first female to hold that position and the selection was well-publicized in the local media, including in the *Washington Post* and the *Washington Times*. I include this information because it was highly unlikely that Mrs. Cheney was not aware of my selection for that position. She and the chairman of the National Endowment for the Arts were both appointed to their positions by President George H. W. Bush. Both organizations had related missions and were located in the Old Post Office in Washington, DC. Although I had seen her only once and spoken to her in the elevator, my office was just down the hallway from hers. I went to her office, talked to her secretary, and explained the reason I was requesting an interview. The secretary said she would get back to me, and she did. We selected a date and time for the interview. When I returned for the interview, the secretary informed me that my interview had been set as an interview with Mrs. Cheney's deputy. I offered to come back at another time to interview Mrs. Cheney and was informed that she would not be meeting with me. I declined the offer to interview Mrs. Cheney's deputy. I was hoping to gain insight from one of the few females who had been selected to lead a federal agency. I was surprised and extremely disappointed that Mrs. Cheney would not meet with me. I do not know why she did not consent to the interview. However, that incident made a lasting impression that was far different from my initial thoughts about the lady I read about in *Washingtonian* magazine when she was selected to head the NEH.

The incident with Mrs. Cheney reminded me of a valuable lesson that my grandmother had taught me. She said I could learn from anyone and I did.

I learned to make time for anyone who asked for my help to improve themselves or their careers. I did not ever want to make anyone feel the disappointment that I experienced in dealing with Mrs. Cheney. Besides that, I had had role models who helped others and they put themselves at risk to do it.

108. THEY WALKED THE WALK

There are several people who worked on the Enfield civil rights movement that made a lasting impression on me. I admire them and am indebted to them for their courage, tenacity, and sacrifice. They did not receive awards for their bravery or their sacrifice. Most people today do not know that these individuals were the early responders in the civil rights movement and paved the way for much of the progress that we enjoy today. Recounting my growing up has given me the opportunity to tell a small part of their story and to say, "Thank you."

I was frequently asked to be a guest speaker or to serve on a panel after I was selected to the Federal Senior Executive Service in 1989, and the audiences and topics I spoke about were usually related to the position that I held. When I worked in civilian agencies, I talked about career strategies for working in the federal government or departmental plans for information technology. When I worked in the Department of Defense (Fig. 108.1), the topics ranged from software engineering to contracting opportunities for command, control, and communications systems. The first time I spoke to an audience about the civil rights movement in Enfield was in the 1990s. I was invited to serve on a Congressional Black Caucus panel that was chaired by Congressman John Conyers from Detroit, Michigan. During that panel, I talked about my experiences in dealing with discrimination in Enfield for the first time since I left there over twenty-five years earlier.

On another occasion, a young Black man that I mentored was selected to serve as the eastern area director for the Bureau of Land Management. He asked if I would be the guest speaker for the agency's February 2004 black history program. He also asked that I talk about *Brown v. Board of Education*. I agreed to do that and decided to talk about *Brown v. Board* from a national perspective and from the perspective of some Enfield teachers and students.

Desegregation of the Enfield public schools had begun in 1964. I was already in college and had not experienced the transition challenges in

Fig. 108.1. I am firing a 5.56mm Special Operation Forces Modified M4A1 Carbine during a Department of Defense training session for senior executives. Although a stark contrast to the arts environment, this too, was an unforgettable experience. / Cynthia Samuelson personal collection.

Enfield firsthand. Yet I wanted the audience to remember the importance of the *Brown* decision and the impact it had on Black people. I began my talk with a brief history of events leading to the US Supreme Court decision that abolished segregation in public schools. I also informed the audience that I had interviewed several people who were directly involved in school desegregation in my hometown and that I would describe the effects of *Brown v. Board of Education* from the perspectives of those individuals. However, I did not say anything about my relationship with the people I had interviewed and proceeded to talk to the audience about Willa Cofield Johnson.

109. Willa Cofield Johnson

First, I summarized Willa's background by telling the audience that she was a retired Rutgers University professor and former high school English and literature teacher at Inborden High School in Enfield, North Carolina. Then I added that Willa was fired from the North Carolina school system in 1964 because of her active role in the civil rights movement, that she had sued the Halifax County Board of Education and the State of North Carolina, and that she had won the suit after three years of depositions, hearings, and appeals to higher courts. The last thing I told the audience about Willa was that she was seventy-five years old and was making a documentary film on Black history in North Carolina.

Next, I reminded the audience that I had interviewed Willa for this event and then I read Willa's comments about the *Brown* decision:

> We all thought the *Brown* decision represented such progress. We felt that we did not want a second-class experience for our children. We could see vast differences between the White school and the Black school. Although we could only see the outside of the facility, we felt there were differences, and we wanted the same quality of education.
>
> In terms of value, we did not know what to expect. In terms of losses, we lost the sense of community in the Black school. There were no Parent Teacher Association (PTA) meetings. We gave that up. What did we gain? We gained courage to go out into the world. Once we got into the [desegregated] classroom with people who were not from our community, there was no longer this mystique.
>
> The *Brown v. Board of Education* was an outstanding decision that brought about changes that occurred over the next fifteen years. It seemed so radical and we saw that we could make a difference.

When I completed Willa's comments, I looked around room at the audience and their eyes were on me. They appeared to be listening closely as I continued.

110. Lillie Cousins Smith

The next person I described for the audience was Lillie Cousins Smith (Fig. 110.1). I informed them that Lillie was a retired English and special education teacher who had taught at Eastman High School, which was located about twenty miles west of downtown Enfield. I added that the assistant superintendent of the Halifax school system had threatened to fire Lillie from her teaching position when she was active in the Enfield civil rights movement, but when the assistant superintendent of Halifax County schools had instructed Mr. George Young, the principal of Eastman, to fire Lillie, he had refused. Mr. Young had stated that he did not have the authority to fire teachers. I explained that Willa's suit had stopped the further firing of teachers for their involvement in civil rights. I made the audience aware that Lillie had been arrested and jailed for helping the people who were picketing in Enfield. I added that Lillie was seventy-five years old and that she had stated the following about the impact of *Brown v. Board of Education*:

Fig. 110.1. Lillie Cousins Smith shortly after she accepted a teaching position at Eastman School in Halifax County, North Carolina. / Cynthia Samuelson personal collection.

Before the *Brown v. Board of Education* decision, Black children did not have the same facilities as White children. Black children received used books from the White schools. They had little beyond the used books and the paper that parents contributed in the Black school. The children got better materials, heating, and meals in the White school. Teachers received better salaries after desegregation, and teachers were also able to receive more training.

When I finished reading Lillie's comments, I moved on to give them the perspective of one the students who had transferred from the Black school to the White school in Enfield.

111. Ira D. Saunders

To emphasize the age difference between the student and the teacher, I described Ira as a fifty-five-year-old man who had a graduated from Winston-Salem State University and said that he had retired from the US Army after completing college. I added that Ira (Fig. 111.1) had walked the picket lines in Enfield during the sixties. I explained that, after the decision to end segregation in public schools, parents in Halifax County where Ira lived were given

Fig. 111.1. US Army veteran Ira Saunders transitioning to civilian life in Enfield, North Carolina, October 1994. / Cynthia Samuelson personal collection.

the option of sending their children to the White school or keeping them in the Black school where they were currently enrolled. Ira was the first of six Black students to attend the White Enfield Graded School in 1964 when he was in the eleventh grade. The other students were in lower grades.

After giving the audience some background information about Ira, I read his comments where he described his transfer to the White school as follows:

> Attending the White school was different from Inborden. I had to study a lot more and it was harder. The Black students did not have anyone to talk to so they had nothing to do but study. I did not want to go to the White school because I was giving up all of my friends at Inborden, but I stayed at the new school because I felt that I would have let Lillie down if I did not stay.
>
> Attending the White school helped me become a better person. I had to earn everything at the White school. Black students did not have anyone to go to. We had to do everything on our own. We had no classmates to help us. It would have been better to have had the mix of students more evenly balanced among the grades so everyone would have [had] friends.

I followed Ira's comments with those of Ira's brother Bill, who had transferred to the White school six years later at the beginning of his junior year.

Fig. 112.1. US Navy Vietnam War veteran William "Bill" Jones and I still teasing each other as we did when we were children in Enfield. This time we are spending time on the beach in Destin, Florida, July 2022. / Cynthia Samuelson personal collection.

112. William "Bill" Jones

I told them that Bill (Fig. 112.1) was forty-nine years old, that he worked in construction restoring historical houses, and that he had a high school diploma. I added that his eardrums had been damaged by the force of the water when the Enfield firemen turned firehoses on the adults and children in the summer of 1963. I also made the audience aware that Bill's entire class was the first full class to be integrated in Enfield. His junior class of about seventy or eighty students was transferred to the White Enfield High School in the fall of 1970 and he, unlike Ira, had no choice about which school to attend. I told the audience that when I asked Bill about his experiences with the school desegregation, here is what he said:

> I wished I could have stayed at my old school. I felt as if I was part of an experiment and the White teachers took no time with the Black students. People were left behind. And although it was worse for people like me who transferred first, it improved over time, and my children received a better education than they would have received at the segregated school.

I ended the speech by telling the audience that Willa was my high school English teacher, that Lillie was my mother, and that Ira and Bill were my brothers. And to my surprise, almost everyone in the predominantly White audience cried. I had been so focused on giving the audience information to help them remember the importance of the *Brown* decision and the impact it had on Black people that I had given no thought to how the audience would respond. It did not occur to me that anyone would shed tears. However, as people in the audience talked to me after the speech, I realized that for a brief moment on that day in 2004, that that audience understood the intent of the *Brown v. Board* decision. They had also gained insight into the positive impact and the anguish it caused on a few very strong people in Enfield, North Carolina.

113. GOING HOME

My husband Sam and I were in Enfield during one of our many trips to spend time with my mother. We made this trip from Springfield, Virginia, frequently to take her out to dinner, to doctors' appointments, run errands, or just to spend time with her. Eventually, we increased the frequency of our trips because we had noticed that she needed more help around the house. And on one of our trips, her neurologist told us that my mother should no longer live alone. He said she was suffering with dementia of the Alzheimer's type. I remember the shock that we experienced and recall saying to Sam, "What are we going to do?" He replied very quickly: "We are going to move to Enfield to take care of Mom." And we did.

When we moved back to Enfield in 2008, I had not lived there full time since I had graduated from high school in 1963. And although most of the people who lived on Dixie Street when I was a child had died or moved away, there were still many kind people in that community where I had grown up. I was surprised to find that the kindness and support that I experienced as a child was still there. One Sunday, for example, Rosa Lee Daniels, who was in her eighties and recovering from a major illness, walked down the street to see how Mother was doing. Another lady who lived on Dixie Street, Evelyn McCullough, we called her Mae West, checked on my mother regularly, helped her get to and from the senior citizens center each week, and made sure that she ate a good meal while she was there. On other days, Mae would walk down Dixie Street to check on her or stop by after church if my mother was not able to attend services. Other neighbors, Albert Salmond and Gladys Joseph, we called them Rat and Sis, checked on Mother regularly whether Sam and I were there or not. Sometimes Rat, Sis, and their grandson, Kamazi Joseph, would come over and sit on the front porch with Mother, Sam, and me. At other times, Rat cheerfully helped Mother with tasks in the yard. In fact, there was an article in the *Enfield Progress* with a photo of Mother and Rat picking up trash along the street in front of Mother's house. Other help came from people Sam and I did not know. One example was Officer White. He was a White policeman from the Enfield Police Department who frequently completed his paperwork sitting in the marked police car at night in front of Mother's house before and after we moved there. He did this regularly until Mother's health changed again.

As the disease progressed, Mother needed around-the-clock help and we decided that it was best for her to remain as close to her house as possible. We moved her into The Fountains at the Albemarle in Tarboro, North Carolina, a retirement community that provided assisted living, independent living, skilled nursing, and memory care services. She lived there until she died in 2010. It was ironic that Dr. Craig, the White doctor from Enfield that we waited in segregated rooms to see when I was a child, was also in the same facility. I would take my mother to visit with Dr. Craig and listened as they laughed and exchanged stories about their lives in Enfield. It was great to see them laughing even though they both were experiencing deteriorating health. But I found comfort in knowing that they both had a team of experienced professionals there to help them.

We were fortunate to have such a large and caring support system comprising healthcare professionals, family, friends, and my mother's former students. We would take her to St. Paul on Sunday for church service, and, after church Sam or my brother Bill would cook one of her favorite meals. Sometimes we would spend the afternoon at Bill's house. Other times when the weather was nice, Mother and I would sit on the front porch of her house after dinner. Neighbors, friends, and many of her former students from both Inborden and Eastman continued to stop by to see her. And she enjoyed these visits and conversations immensely. The visits always brought a smile to her face regardless of how her day was progressing.

We wanted to give Mother an eightieth birthday party. But the Alzheimer's disease was on another schedule—an accelerated schedule that neither physicians nor medication could control. We decided to hold the party for her seventy-ninth birthday in October 2007, so she could enjoy it. And she did. Her family, friends, and former students came from near and far, over two hundred and fifty of them. She told us that was one of the happiest days of her life.

Demond "Dee" and J'Vette McKenzie had decorated the Gateway ballroom for Mother's birthday party. And then Dee knelt beside her during the program and sang to her. This made her so happy. Mother was having a great time and later took over the program when Willa and former students began speaking. Her students had selected representatives from their classes to speak, but Mom asked all of her students to come forward. I think she hugged each one of them! That was her day and her show.

We were blessed that she knew the immediate family and maintained her pleasant and caring personality until the last day of her life. We slowly lost the small, strong, caring, civil rights activist to the disease on October 27, 2010. Her funeral was held at St. Paul Baptist Church on November 5, 2010. A few months after my mother's funeral, Sam and I left Enfield and returned to our house in Springfield, Virginia, bringing both sad and pleasant memories with us.

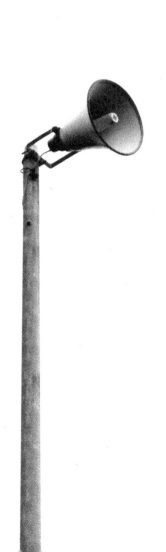

PART III

THE IMPACT

Mildred Bobbitt Sexton, EdD

Fig. 0.3. Mildred Sexton, Inborden High School graduation photo, 1964. / Mildred Sexton personal collection.

114. PREFACE TO PART III

Fig. 114.1. Mildred Bobbitt Sexton, EdD. / Mildred Sexton personal collection.

It is the year 2019. I am retired and residing in Yorktown, Virginia, after a very successful forty-three-year career in education at the elementary, middle, high school, and higher education levels. Until I reunited in December 2017 with Dr. Willa Cofield, my high school English teacher (and one of the coauthors of this book), I never gave too much thought to the impact that my role as a youth involved in the civil rights movement in Enfield, North Carolina, had had on me. I now realize that the years from 1960 to 1972 had a tremendous influence on the rest of my life.

I was only fourteen years old when the movement began. The isolation of the segregated world I knew as a child was about to undergo a metamorphosis that would change the course of both Black and White people's lives. The signs and symbols of racism and segregation became targets for demonstrations as this new world exploded. The nationwide civil rights movement of the 1960s changed the life of every single person in the United States. It transformed me from living in the vacuum of segregation to living in a whole new world of integration. The looming question now is how my life's experiences from birth through the 1960s and early 1970s specifically made me who I am today.

115. MY FAMILY

My parents, James and Addie Bobbitt (1960s). / Mildred Sexton personal collection.

As I think back over the years of my youth, I now understand that the adults that surrounded me were super role models and protectors. With coaching from sincere adults and my momma and daddy, I learned that I was the only one who could determine my future destiny. I have shared this thought throughout my forty-three-year career in education.

116. My Paternal Grandparents

My fathers' parents, Erastus and Minnie Bobbitt, purchased land in the New Deal Resettlement Community near Dawson Crossroads prior to 1940. The Franklin D. Roosevelt New Deal program provided low-interest rates so poor farmers and Black sharecroppers could buy their own farms. In the Dawson

Fig. 116.1. Grandpa Erastus Bobbitt. / Mildred Sexton personal collection.

Fig. 116.2. Grandma Minnie Bobbitt. / Mildred Sexton personal collection.

area, Negro and White farmers were segregated. Negro farmers were given the opportunity to purchase land in the flood zone of Halifax County. The White farmers' land was on higher ground. My grandparents' acres were designated Lot 140 and a small house was built on the property as a part of the New Deal package. I grew up knowing many of the farmers who were part of the Dawson Resettlement community because they were my dad's and grandparents' friends. Unfortunately, my grandparents' land and house were destroyed in the 1940 flood. Farming was what my grandfather did all his life. After the flood, my grandparents' only choice was to become sharecroppers.[1]

Sharecropping is a form of agriculture in which a landowner allows tenants to use the land in return for a share of the crops produced on the sharecropper's portion of the farm. Throughout the year, sharecroppers made purchases for the items they needed with advances kept on a running tab by the owner. At the end of the year, the sharecroppers had to "settle up" with the White farm owner. I heard my grandfather use the words "settle up" around Christmas time. Usually, the amount of money he earned was barely enough to take care of the family's needs for a few months. This economic situation was really challenging for my fathers' parents and their fourteen surviving children.[2]

My grandfather was very resourceful. He grew his own vegetables, including sweet potatoes, for the family. He raised farm animals for meat

Fig. 117.1. Sgt. James S. Bobbitt, US Army. / Mildred Sexton personal collection.

that was cured to feed the family throughout the year. The cured ham and bacon were the best. My favorite food from my grandpa's farm was the chopped pork barbecue that was served outside from great big iron pots. The chopped vinegar barbecue was like no other. Dairy products were right at hand from the cows, and eggs came from the chickens. My grandfather was very smart because he knew how to have food for his family year-round. He and my grandmother were survivors.

117. My Father's Military Service

My dad left the farm on the outskirts of Enfield, North Carolina, in 1943, when he was drafted into the United States Army during World War II. His segregated civilian life continued into his military life. He was stationed in St. Louis, Missouri, in a segregated army. As a sergeant first class, he was given an assignment that was not in the war zone. With his rank, he cooked for the White officers and served his two mandatory years. He passed the marksmanship-training course and earned an Army marksmanship badge. He was honorably discharged as Sergeant James S. Bobbitt, Master Sergeant, from the Army in 1945.

Fig. 118.1. James Bobbitt. / Mildred Sexton personal collection.

Fig. 118.2. Addie Clark Bobbitt. / Mildred Sexton personal collection.

118. My Parents' Wedding

Prior to his discharge, Daddy and my mom were married on February 19, 1944, at the home of my Mom's parents. Her father, Rev. William Henry Clark, married them on his front porch that was decorated with flowers grown in my grandmother's flower garden. Because my dad was still in the army, my mom lived with her parents when Daddy was away in Missouri. After Daddy was discharged, he and Mom moved in with his parents, Erasmus and Minnie Bobbitt.

119. My Birth and Birthplace

I was born in the home of my father's parents on Luther "Bud" Marshall's farm, where my grandparents were sharecroppers. Bud Marshall was the White landowner and a lifelong friend to my dad. The farm was located approximately three miles outside of Enfield near the intersection of Highway 1001 and Thirteen Bridges Road. The two-story farmhouse sat off the road at the end of a long path. It was a very hot Sunday afternoon in early September 1946 when the first daughter of James Sylvester Bobbitt and Addie Bobbitt came into the world at the beginning of the Baby Boomer generation following World War II.

The Black midwife, Mrs. Anna English, was a very tiny lady who probably did not weigh anywhere close to a hundred pounds. Mom said that she was too little to deliver me and that was probably the reason Dad rounded up all three White doctors in Enfield, Dr. Craig, Dr. Joyner, and Dr. Smith, to help with my delivery.

My mother and Uncle Will, my dad's brother, tell the story that my dad was so nervous and distraught while mom was giving birth to me that he promised he would never do that to my mom again and then he fainted. My mother declared that I took my own good time arriving.

Mrs. English said sarcastically, "It's a girl. She is up there taking her time primping before she is born."

The doctors stated that they had never seen a baby born with a double birth caul or veil on her face. A caul is a thin filmy remnant of the amniotic sac, often called a head helmet that covers the baby's face.[3] The doctors asked my Black midwife what meaning or superstition was associated with the double caul. She explained that it meant that I would be very smart, perceptive, and could see visions.[4]

Later, Daddy named me Mildred Carole Bobbitt, giving me his youngest sister's middle name. The name Mildred means gentle and quiet spirit.

120. Places Lived and the Births of My Brothers and Sisters

As a family, we lived in several places the first eight years of my life. My brother, Linwood, my father's son, was born in 1944. About a year after I was born in 1946, we moved down the road from Daddy's parents. This is where my brother, James Sylvester Junior, was born in July 1948. He was a beautiful baby who my daddy was so happy to have. In fact, Daddy was hoping that I was going to be a little boy. My parents eventually moved to Scotland Neck and lived with my mom's parents, Rev. William Henry Clark and Minerva Moore Clark. My brother, Edward, was born on the Clarks' farm in April 1950 at Dawson's Crossroads, Scotland Neck, North Carolina.

Although Daddy had served his country, when he returned home, the segregated treatment of Black soldiers greeted him even after being honorably discharged. Seeking employment was a challenge that caused him to move our family from place to place. When he got a job working on roads with the North Carolina State Department of Transportation, he found it more convenient to move our family to Enfield on Pope Street. Working on roads throughout the state was hard work with little pay. Daddy realized that he had to decide on a career that would give him an income to take care of his family. If a Black man was not self-employed during that time, he farmed, worked for the White man, or sought an education or vocation that opened up opportunities in the Black community. Segregation was the way of life. Daddy decided to go to barber school in Raleigh, North Carolina.

While Daddy attended Harris Barber College, we moved to a duplex on Hannon Street in Enfield where my brother, Larry, was born in November 1952. Once Daddy completed barber school, he began to barber at a shop in Scotland Neck, approximately fifteen miles from Enfield. We moved to Scotland Neck into an area called Moonlight and that is where I finally received a much-wanted sister. Joyce (Cookie) was born at home in 1953. When I heard her cry, I said, "I have a sister!" I was so happy. My cousins were there with me and asked me how I knew the baby was a girl. My reply was, "I know because she cries like a girl."

Because of circumstances related to the family farm where my mother's parents lived, my grandparents, William and Minerva Clark, moved to the Moonlight community with us. Grandma Minerva passed away there. Shortly after my grandmother's death, my brother James Sylvester Jr. passed away at the age of six in the hospital for Blacks in Tarboro, North Carolina, from cerebral palsy complications. My grandfather, Rev. William Henry Clark, continued to live with us until he moved to Enfield with my aunt, Beatrice Horton, and her family.

Having lost two family members, my Daddy worked toward stability for my grief-stricken mother, my sister, my brothers, and me. He sought an ideal place for us to live, and he soon rented his own barber shop on Whitaker Street in downtown Enfield. We moved back to Enfield to a location on Whitaker Street approximately three blocks from the barber shop. The one thing I remember the most about our Whitaker Street home was the treehouse that Daddy built for us in the huge persimmon tree in the woods at the edge of our backyard. Because I was the oldest girl at age eight, I felt like the treehouse belonged to me.

In the same month that I turned twelve years old, my parents' youngest child, Dalphne, was born in 1958. She is the only one of us born in a hospital. Quigless's Clinic and Hospital in Tarboro is approximately twenty miles southeast of Enfield. It was owned and operated by a Black doctor, Dr. Milton W. Quigless. After he graduated from Meharry Medical College, Dr. Quigless opened up his medical practice in Tarboro in 1936. For the next

Fig. 120.1. James S. Bobbitt, Jr. 1948–1954. / Mildred Sexton personal collection.

Fig. 120.2. Minerva Moore Clark. / Mildred Sexton personal collection.

Fig. 120.3. James Bobbitt cutting a child's hair. / Mildred Sexton personal collection.

ten years as a Black physician, he tried to obtain hospital privileges at the Edgecombe General Hospital, but segregation laws prevented him from performing surgery and admitting ill patients to this local facility. Finally, after years of frustration, Dr. Quigless decided to establish the first hospital for Blacks in Tarboro. Quigless Hospital-Clinic opened its doors to patients in 1946, and twelve years later my youngest sister was born at that historic site.[5]

121. MY GRADE SCHOOL DAYS

122. Inborden School: Segregated Beginnings

I began first grade at segregated Inborden School in 1952 when I was five years old. The elementary school was built in 1946 and given the name T. S. Inborden, honoring the prominent Black educator, Mr. Thomas Sewell Inborden, who was the founder of Brick School. Inborden School was located at the end of Hannon Street, where my family lived when we first moved to the town of Enfield. Black children from all over the town had to walk to school, and the children from the rural areas rode the yellow school buses that were driven by high school students.

Mrs. Joyner, my first-grade teacher, was very kind and soft-spoken. I admired her so much that I looked forward to going to school every day. My favorite times in her class were when she read to us and we read to her about Jane and Spot. I looked forward to putting on my painting apron and painting huge and colorful pictures of trees and flowers. During music time, Mrs. Joyner would play the piano and we would sing the songs she taught us. While sitting in my classroom, I could smell the cafeteria-made yeast rolls baking. I loved going to the cafeteria where lunch was only twenty-five cents. My favorite meal was vegetable soup with a peanut butter or grilled cheese sandwich. Near the end of the school year, my dad moved us to Scotland Neck, North Carolina, in order to be closer to the barber shop where he worked. The teacher whom I loved so much was sad when she learned that I was moving away. I cried and cried because I had to leave her and my friends.

123. Dawson Elementary School: A Family Legacy

Segregated Dawson Elementary School was a very small three-room school that housed grades first through fifth. It had a pot-bellied stove that heated the small gray, cinder-block building. Restrooms were outdoor toilets with two holes in each privy. There was no cafeteria. The school was located at Dawson Crossroads, Scotland Neck, North Carolina.

Mom was born on a farm near the school. My mother, her sisters, and her brothers attended segregated Dawson Elementary School. When I was growing up, my mom telling stories about her school days was a part of our Thursday night drama time that consisted of storytelling, poetry, and dramatizations. My mom loved her elementary school and the memories of her "good old days" there. She was excited that I was enrolled in her alma mater.

Needless to say, I was not excited at all. I had to ride the yellow school bus to that strange place in the middle of "the country." It was not as convenient as walking out of my house on Hannon Street when I lived in Enfield and in minutes arriving at school. My family had moved to the rural area where the closest neighbor was a mile or more away and I had no friends my age nearby. I had to get out of bed very early in the morning, stand on the porch or near the road, and wait for the bus to arrive.

My new first-grade teacher, Mrs. Thompson, was tall, pretty, and brown-skinned with long black hair. My time in her class was not as much fun as being in Mrs. Joyner's class. I missed all my friends who lived on Hannon Street and those in my class at Inborden Elementary. I should have been happy and very comfortable at Dawson because most of the students in my class were related to me or their parents were friends of my parents. I knew them all because every third Sunday of each month, I saw them all at my parents' church.

Cedar Creek African Baptist Church was next door to Dawson Elementary School. My mom grew up in that church where her dad was an assistant pastor. I soon made friends at school and when I attended Cedar Creek Baptist Church, I sat together with my cousins and new friends.

My second-grade teacher at Dawson was Mrs. House. She taught a combined class of second and third graders. Although the classes were combined, they were very small. I am sure that I learned much of the third-grade lessons. I loved my teacher. She was like a mother to all of us and we did creative things in her class. I made my first doll dress as an assignment she gave us. I still have my report card from Mrs. House's class. My grades were great, but she wrote on my report card that I always complained about my stomach hurting. If my tummy was aching, it was probably because I missed my old Inborden School.

124. Back to Enfield and Inborden Elementary School

I was so happy when school closed for the summer because we moved back to Enfield on Whitaker Street. Our home was located right across the street from Red Harrell's store and First Baptist Church. Red Harrell was White and a very friendly man. He lived in the back of the little store with his wife, son, and daughter. Red Harrell was always cordial to the Blacks in the neighborhood because we were his major customers.

Although I was in a new community, the surroundings were familiar and I had friends and relatives who lived closer to me. In the fall of the year, I was super excited because I was returning to the school I loved and reuniting with many of my classmates from first grade. I was assigned to Mrs. Ashley's third-grade class. She was a very strict teacher. She was very clear as to what her expectations were regarding student behavior and academic achievement. I was always on my best behavior and continued to make good grades. I was very happy to be back at Inborden with indoor toilets, radiator heat throughout the building, great cafeteria food, and my friends. At the end of third grade, I was really pleased with all that had happened that school year, and I was ready to move on to fourth grade.

One door down from Mrs. Ashley's third-grade classroom was Mrs. Bertha Bullock's orderly fourth-grade classroom. She was the wife of Rev. Frank L. Bullock, the pastor of St. Paul Baptist Church. I was a member there and attended Sunday School, church, and Baptist Youth Union (BYU). I also sang in the junior choir. Mrs. Bullock was very fair-complexioned with dark, curly hair and could easily be mistaken as White. Her class was very orderly and very, very quiet all of the time. I do not remember anyone ever making a sound. She was a very smart lady. I adored her as a teacher. Sometimes she would have sessions with just the girls in the class about the importance of young ladies exhibiting good character and presenting themselves in a respectable manner.

In my opinion, there was no one who did a better job of teaching about the importance of having good character, showing respect, and developing one's talents than my fifth-grade teacher, Mrs. Lossie Lee Whitaker. She was a very creative and spiritual teacher who shared her strong faith and belief in God. From September to around November, I was usually the only student in her class. The majority of the students lived on farms and had to help with the harvesting: "shaking and stacking" peanuts, picking cotton, and working in tobacco. Many of the students who lived in town would work on the farms to make money. My parents would not allow me to miss school to work on the farm, so I was able to attend school every day.

Mrs. Lossie Lee Whitaker started the beginning of every school day with devotion. We would sing "God Bless America" or "The Star-Spangled Banner," recite the Pledge of Allegiance to the flag, and read scripture from the little red Bible that was passed to every student every morning. After we recited a Bible verse of our choice, we were ready for the day. Mrs. Whitaker taught us much more than reading and writing and arithmetic. There were assigned days for storytelling, reciting poetry, and sharing our talents. We had to learn and recite poetry or major speeches from different historical events. When the peanuts were ready on the farms, she taught us how to make peanut brittle candy. I loved the hands-on activities.

I vaguely remember grade six. Mr. Woodson was my first male teacher, and he was responsible for the presentations and performances during the weekly assemblies. I participated many times in these assemblies. As a member of Mr. Woodson's sixth-grade class, I learned to appreciate the arts and drama.

125. My Neighborhood

When I was ten years old, Dad became established and really successful in his own barber shop, and he built our house. We moved from Whitaker Street to Hannon Street, where we spent the rest of our childhood and teen years.

"It takes a village to raise a child" is an African proverb. It expresses that a whole community of people must interact with children for them to grow up in a safe and healthy environment. I grew up in such a community. Hannon Street was a loving and nurturing village.

126. Protection of Children

The Negro adults protected and sheltered the children from the cruelties of racism. Being in a segregated world was the norm for me and I am sure for all the children during that time. I knew no other world except the world created by my parents, my sisters and brothers, family, teachers, church, community, and friends. All these people looked like me. They were people of color: dark-skinned, light-skinned, and all shades in between.

We children were community children. We were part of a village where adults were respected. Our parents taught us well, and we knew our boundaries. Children were taught good manners in order to survive in a segregated world. Saying "Yes, sir" and "No, sir" to adults when I was growing up was just plain old good manners.

Fig. 125.1. Bobbitt's Hannon Street home, built in 1958. / Mildred Sexton personal collection.

Fig. 125.2. Mildred's childhood home, photo taken 2023. / Mildred Sexton personal collection.

The three most important rules were always respect adults, do not leave the yard without permission, and make sure that you are in the house before the streetlight comes on. These rules, for the most part, were enforced by the entire village.

All of the adults in the neighborhood looked after everyone's children. We were taught to respect our elders and to obey all adults when they corrected us. Negro children were taught to honor their mother and father and their days would be long on this earth.

Every family had rules and curfews. There was a streetlight right in front of our house. When the streetlight came on, we had to go inside unless an adult was with us. Our parents had to know where we were at all times.

To keep us safe, Dad fenced in our back yard. My brothers, sisters, and I could not leave the yard, but our friends were welcome, and they spent lots of time visiting us. We were creative and made up our own games. My brothers and the boys shot marbles and played backyard basketball and baseball. The girls would pretend to bake mud pies and to cook meals with weeds using leaves for fried fish. When we played school, somehow, I was always the teacher. The girls would also play jack rocks, jump rope, hopscotch, and a card game called Old Maid.

Sometimes the boys and girls would make a seesaw by placing a long plank of wood horizontally on a stack of bricks. We would have tire races with old tires Dad had discarded and play tag, dodge ball, and hide-and-seek. We always enjoyed it when the neighborhood children gathered at our house.

There were places that were off-limits to Negroes in Enfield. Our parents taught us about safety zones as a means of protecting us. We had our own park where we mingled only with other Negro children and adults. Lillie Smith, the mother of my friend, Cynthia Cousins Samuelson, was the recreation director at segregated Oak View Park, which was open during the summer months. There were mainly swings, basketball hoops, seesaws, and a sliding board. I learned to play croquet and badminton there.

Because our hometown was segregated, all of the activities outside of our homes and backyards took place in the Black communities and neighborhoods. There were churches, schools, the park, visiting friends, and the 4-H Club. The church offered a place to assemble not only to worship and serve the Lord, but also to participate in the choir, Sunday school, BYTU (Baptist Youth Training Union), Vacation Bible School, and other organized activities. There was a tremendous amount of community service even though it was not called that. We helped the elderly by going to the store for them, cutting their grass, sweeping their yards, and taking them food. In return, we were taken care of in our community by the adults who kept us busy in our neighborhood in order to keep us out of trouble and away from the White folks.

We were greatly protected and did not realize the magnitude of the protection until we ventured outside of our Hannon Street village. Hannon Street was the last street on the southeast end of Enfield at the intersection of Highway 30l which was the main route for travel from the New England states to Florida. There was a service station at the corner of Hannon Street and Highway 301 where White travelers would stop to get gas, buy food, and stay at the motel beside the corner store. Whenever my brothers, Edward and Larry, and I went to the corner store, the White travelers would buy us candy, sodas, and cookies. My parents instructed us not to go near their cars or eat any of the things they bought us until we brought the items home for them to examine. I always felt some fear and anxiety in the presence of the White travelers. My parents gave us instructions not to allow them to take pictures of us. If they attempted to take our pictures, we were to run home. We did lots of running. I am sure there are many pictures across the United States of our backs as we obeyed our parents' instructions and fled.

127. Hannon Street

We lived in a neighborhood where even the White town commissioners made decisions to make improvements on our street. Prior to my going to first grade, Hannon Street was paved during the 1950s. Because it was paved, we did not have to worry about cars and school buses getting stuck in a muddy road during rainstorms. Eventually, the town placed a paved sidewalk on the side of the street across from our house. The sidewalk ran from Highway 301 the entire length of Hannon Street to Inborden School. I speculated that the street was paved and the sidewalk was placed there because Inborden School was at the end of the street and because Black students walked from all over Enfield to Inborden School. In my mind and sheltered world, the sidewalk gave our community a prosperous appearance. Streetlights were placed along the street, and a fire hydrant was installed right in front of our house. There was a very small church, Mt. Olive Holiness Church, that enhanced the character of the street. I felt good about living on Hannon Street.

My parents built a safe and secure home for us with three bedrooms. The boys had their bedroom, the girls had a bedroom, and my parents had the third bedroom. The kitchen and living room were large. The most wonderful thing about our house was the indoor bathroom. There were very few indoor bathrooms in the houses on our street when we moved into our home.

There was no sewerage line, so we had to have a septic tank. We could never drive into our backyard on the side where the septic tank was located for fear that the weight of the car would cause the tank to cave in. The fence around our backyard had tall white gates on each side of the house so we could enter the backyard on either side. The fence and gates added character to the house. There was a large garden at the far end of our backyard. It had all types of vegetables such as tomatoes, cabbage, carrots, cucumbers, collards, kale, corn, okra, squash, watermelon, and cantaloupe. In addition, my mom always planted long rows of her favorite flowers. A grapevine was at the entrance to the garden. There were apple, pear, peach, and pecan trees in the garden area as well. There were plenty of trees to climb and during the fall, pecans to bag and share with the neighbors.

Hannon Street was our village consisting of twenty-two single homes and three duplexes that made up the New Town neighborhood. All Hannon Street adults who were not sick, old, or disabled worked, but many owned very little wealth. Some families worked on farms or did domestic work. The peanut mill employed many Blacks. Many people worked very hard for three dollars a day. The majority of the houses on Hannon Street were rented. Some of the landlords, Black and White, contributed little to the upkeep of their properties. The renters took pride in where they lived, and Hannon Street was well taken care of by them. Many of the yards had beautiful lawns and shrubbery. There was a magnolia tree on the north side of Hannon Street near Highway 301, as well as a huge oak tree at the corner of Hannon and Dixie Streets.

For our family and a few others, there was indoor plumbing and indoor running water. Others still had outdoor toilets in their backyards and outdoor pumps for water. Because I was so young, I did not feel that my family was poor. I seriously doubt that I knew what poverty looked like or if I ever thought about the Blacks in my community being poor. My brothers, sisters, and I had no idea whether or not we were poor because not only did my parents provide shelter for us, but they also provided plenty of food, security, and clothing for our family. I remember being told by someone who did not live on my street that I thought I was something. I thought Hannon Street was a great place to live and I considered all who lived there "Something."

128. Caring Community

People on Hannon Street cared about each other. There were very few fences or walls separating property. Their porches served as places for relaxation and entertainment. People loved to sit on their porches and wave to the cars that passed by even if they did not know whom they were greeting.

Our house was located in the middle of the neighborhood. I could easily observe the happenings in the community from my front porch or living room and kitchen windows. It felt like the place where I belonged because the residents of Hannon Street cared about one another, especially the children. If there was anger among the adults, I was not mature enough to understand that the root of the anger for some of those who lived on Hannon Street was because of the poverty and racial disparity. In spite of the infrequent show of anger, I never felt intimidated or insecure because there were adults in the community who expressed their love for me and others who cared for me through their acts of kindness and their giving hearts. If someone was sick or in need, families would prepare food, take them to the doctor, shop for them, or simply spend time with them. If there was a death in the family, the community would provide food for them and gather at the sit-ups in the home of the deceased. I felt loved because my family and neighbors were very loving and nurturing.

In the village, there was always someone who became a second parent to the children. Mr. George and Mrs. Vernon Thornton lived next door to my family and mentored me in many ways. Because they did not have children, I guess I became their daughter. Mr. Thornton always called me Julia. Julia was a nurse played by Diahann Carroll, who was the first Black female to have a leading role in a television series. I never thought I could be as beautiful as

Diahann Carroll, but I liked it when he called me Julia. Mr. Thornton was a very successful businessman in Enfield and very respected by his Black clientele. He dressed in a suit and tie every day of the week. We thought Mr. Thornton was rich. He always had the newest cars and appeared to go about his business in such a professional manner. He owned a taxi service and was a bail bondsman. My dad and he were very good friends and worked together in their businesses. Mr. Thornton helped my dad start his taxi and bail bondsman businesses. He was also instrumental in helping my dad attain the property next door to them where my dad built our house.

The Thorntons lived in the only brick house on Hannon Street. Their house was just like the White homes in Enfield. I always equated walking into their house to walking into a mansion. It was filled with the most beautiful furniture. Mrs. Thornton had each room decorated in such a classy, sophisticated way that the décor reminded me of the homes in magazines. Mrs. Thornton was an elementary school teacher and she was always interested in how I was doing in school.

She gave me piano lessons and tried to teach me how to sew. I would help her with things around the house. I learned so much from Mr. and Mrs. Thornton. They were true role models for me. The Thorntons were like parents to me and contributed greatly to my upbringing.

Our house was across the street from Mr. Jesse and Mrs. Lula Arp. Mrs. Lula was a housewife. She took very good care of her mother-in-law, Mrs. Ellen Arp, and her three grandchildren, who lived with them, Robert, Dianne, and George. Mrs. Lula was up early in the morning making sure that their yard was swept clean all of the time without a sprig of grass to be seen anywhere. She was always friendly and loved to talk.

Mr. Jesse was a carpenter, and his specialty was making screen doors. He would set up his work area under the great big, beautiful magnolia tree in their front yard. Then he would begin to saw and hammer and nail and sing to his heart's content. He had a beautiful baritone voice that could be heard from one end of Hannon Street to the other. He could have been the star in any Broadway or Hollywood performance. The richness of his voice demanded attention. He was our Hannon Street Paul Robeson. Whenever I heard him sing Negro spirituals, it was as if I was lost in my very own space and time. Silence would fall over the village. Dogs stopped barking and birds stopped singing. All one could hear was the perfect pitch and raw emotions that Mr. Arp expressed in every note he sang. When he finished singing, he would begin to whistle with such clarity and volume that one would think that his whistling was amplified. Mr. Arp's serenade was soothing to me as a child. His melodious voice brought about peace and calm throughout the neighborhood.

Next door to the Arps lived Mr. Raymond Johnson. His wife was Mrs. Beulah and their children were Doreatha, Rosetta, Raymond Junior, and Cornelius. Mr. Raymond's major strength was perseverance. He could have been a master chef in any restaurant and who knows, even the White House. He worked as a cook at the White-only Southland Restaurant on Highway 301 on the north end of Enfield just inside the city limits that is called McDaniel Street. How amazing was it that Mr. Raymond could cook for the White clientele in what was considered an upscale restaurant in Enfield, but Negroes could not be seated and have a meal on the premises. I witnessed Mr. Raymond Johnson, who was a big man and not in the best of health, come out of his house dressed in a white uniform and slowly and painfully walk the long distance to his work at the Southland Restaurant in order to support his family. Mr. Raymond's perseverance impressed on me that one had to work hard to survive in the most difficult of times. I saw him as a kind man with a gentle spirit who was truly a man of determination.

As one turned onto Hannon Street from Highway 301, the first house on the left belonged to Mr. and Mrs. Eatmon. Their house was always clean, immaculate, and beautifully decorated. They had three sons, George, Charles, and Percy. They were older than I was, but I thought they were the most handsome guys on our street and, as a matter of fact, in the whole town. I was in awe of them because they were cool and drove their own car. They were always dressed impeccably. The thing I remember most about Mrs. Eatmon is that she was a classy dresser. Her make-up was beautifully done and much more than what most women were doing at that time. On Sundays she wore large, pretty, colorful, and extraordinary hats. She had her own unique and flamboyant style of dressing. She should have been modeling in New York or even Paris. She cooked the best food ever. The aroma of the breads and whatever she was cooking made its way down Hannon Street. She was inspirational and one of my favorite role models.

Mr. Eatmon was always working at Georgia-Pacific, a lumber company located approximately two miles south of Enfield on Highway 301. Mr. Eatmon was highly respected. He was a very quiet gentleman who enjoyed one-on-one conversations. Although Mrs. Eatmon loved entertaining and talking with people in group settings, Mr. Eatmon could take it or leave it. He spent much of his spare time making improvements on their home. As a little girl, my sister Dalphne found refuge by going to the Eatmons' house and sitting on their front doorsteps. If she was missing from our yard, Mom always knew where to find her. We could count on love and protection from the Eatmons. They were an extension of our family.

Miss Mary Battle lived next door to the Eatmons. She never said very much but her demeanor let us know that she meant business and she would not accept any nonsense from either the children or adults. She was a small-framed lady with attractively chiseled facial features and a beautiful light tan complexion. As a longtime member of the Hannon Street village, she welcomed our family and built a lifelong friendship with my mom. Miss Mary's mother, Mrs. Nin, and her nephew, Ronald, lived with her.

Miss Mary worked at the motel next door to the 301 Filling Station store on the corner of Highway 301 and Hannon Street. The busy motel with travelers from up and down the Atlantic coastline and beyond was for Whites only. I helped her clean the motel rooms by placing the sheets and towels in the rooms, making the beds, and dusting. Miss Mary did the cleaning. She taught me how to make up a perfect bed. Sometimes tips were left in the rooms and Miss Mary would share them with me. One day she could not work and asked my parents if I could fill in for her. They consented and sent my brother, Larry, with me. All went well until one of the White guests at the hotel began to harass my brother and me. He tried to lure my brother into his room by coaxing, "Come here, little boy!" I reported the guest to the owner and was told to go back to work. I felt threatened and unsafe. I left the laundry cart and all the cleaning items right on the sidewalk and the two of us ran home. Miss Mary never mentioned that day or the incident to me. She probably talked with my mom about the situation. I do know she didn't want anything to happen to us. She was a true friend to our family. Miss Mary was a positive force in the village and an excellent example of how the adults loved, protected, and nurtured the children in the community.

129. My Intermediate Years

Because my mother was a beautician and my dad was a barber, as children, we all had little jobs in their shops. My brothers shined shoes and helped keep the shops swept and clean. I worked the cash register, sold popcorn, and swept up more hair than I can remember. We took care of our two younger sisters who had no real assignments. We were paid on Sunday mornings as we sat in the middle of Mom and Dad's bed while they were counting all of the change from the week. Giving us chores was an excellent way for Mom and Dad to teach us the importance of hard work and becoming responsible and independent. They taught us well.

Fig. 129.1. Bobbitt's Hair Care Center. / Mildred Sexton personal collection.

130. Seventh and Eighth Grades

In grade seven, I went to the intermediate school located adjacent to the elementary school on Inborden School grounds. There was a shortage of classrooms and some of the intermediate classes were located in the high school building. I was enrolled in Mr. Eugene Richardson's class that was held in the front, right corner of the gym/auditorium. Much of the class time was dedicated to our watching other students practice for an assembly, listening to the glee club rehearse, watching the Topsy dancers practice their routines, and rooting for the physical education classes as they competed. It was not easy for Mr. Richardson to teach us with all of the activities going on around us. Mr. Richardson was really interesting to me because we were told that he was an Indian. I was curious and wanted to know about his culture, ceremonies, and way of life. Mr. Richardson was also the basketball coach, and he coached our girls' team and the boys' junior varsity team.

My last year at the intermediate level was spent in Mrs. June Swindell's eighth-grade class. I was twelve years old. Her classroom was located in the high school building. She not only taught eighth grade but also organized a dance group called Topsys. The group was a class act. I imagined them being as good as the Radio City Rockettes in Manhattan. Mrs. Swindell was also the music director of the schoolwide glee club. Although our resources were limited as a segregated school, Mrs. Swindell was very creative and resourceful. She directed the greatest plays and musicals. I remember playing one of the three little pigs going to the hop where the big, bad wolf wouldn't let us bop or do the slop. The slop was a popular dance during 1959 and 1960. We three pigs joined together bopping and slopping across the stage.

I think I was in the eighth or ninth grade when Miss Ruth Whitworth, the 4-H Club extension agent for Halifax County, invited me to go with her to 4-H Club meetings. The 4-H Club was segregated and there were White extension agents for the White children. Mr. D. J. Knight, a Negro, was in charge of all the Negro 4-H Clubs in Halifax County through A & T College. The Negro 4-H Clubs in North Carolina would have a 4-H Leadership Camp every summer at A & T College in Greensboro. One summer I traveled with Mr. Knight and Miss Whitworth to the camp at A & T. The girls and boys that attended the camp stayed in Scott Hall on separate floors. I met new friends at camp. When we returned home, we shared what we had learned with other 4-H Club members.

Our segregated 4-H Club exhibited projects at the Enfield Firemen's Fair in the fairground's exhibition building. The Fair was an annual event during the fall that everyone looked forward to. It was a time when we could buy candied apples, cotton candy, chili hotdogs, and French fries with lots of vinegar. It was a time when we could ride the Ferris wheel, carousel, swings, and other rides. It was a time to win stuffed animals or carnival glassware. It was also a time when segregation raised its ugly head again. There was a Negro fair night on Wednesday and a White fair night on Thursday. As a part of the fair's 4-H Club activities, the White and Negro exhibits were judged separately. D. J. Knight made sure we were on point and Miss Whitworth worked with him as our own 4-H agent. The best 4-H exhibits were awarded ribbons for first, second, third, and honorable mention. I won ribbons for my 4-H projects and sometimes a few dollars.

131. My Hometown of Entrepreneurs

My mother and father taught us to "Never forget where you come from." Any time I am asked where I am from, I proudly reply, "Enfield, North Carolina." I am often surprised at the number of people who have heard of this little rural town north of Rocky Mount with an exit marker on Interstate 95.

Our community was separated from the White communities. Negro neighborhoods were located throughout Enfield, and the Negroes knew where the boundaries were. The Negro communities had names such as Black Bottom, New Town, Tin Can Alley, New Road, East End, West End, and Cemetery Hill. I lived in New Town on the east side of the railroad tracks that ran right through the middle of Enfield.

Fig. 132.1. Addie Bobbitt back row, third from left, Area Beautician Club. / Mildred Sexton personal collection.

132. Black Businesses

The 1960s was a time of total segregation in the small town of Enfield. Negroes had their own businesses, churches, schools, and places of entertainment. The number of Black businesses was phenomenal. For example, barber shops were abundant. Lloyd Batchelor operated Batchelor's Barber Shop on Pope Street and Napoleon McWilliams was a barber in his shop. Buddy Sol and Queen Pittman had their beauty and barber shops together at the end of Hannon Street. Casper Hill had his barber shop on Cemetery Hill, and Louise Hill had her beauty shop on Whitaker Street. There were a number of beauty shops and among them were Ada McWilliams' Beauty Shop on Whitaker Street, Belle Cofield's Beauty Shop on Railroad Street, Rosa Lee Cofield's Beauty Shop on Dixie Street, and the William H. Mitchell Beauty Salon on Franklin Street. My Dad built Bobbitt's Hair Care Center on Whitaker Street. His building not only accommodated his barber shop but also was built to include my mom's beauty shop. Prior to my going to high school, my mom went to beauty school in Wilson, North Carolina. There were many days I rode with her on the train to her classes.

There were numerous Negro businesses where food and general items could be purchased. Dancy's Café was known for great food. The Dog House located on McDaniel Street specialized in hot dogs. Garfield Whitaker's Store was located on the last road on the east end of Enfield.

Other establishments were Ethel Hunter's Store and Edmond's Store. Garfield and Sue McWilliams's Store was on the New Road. George Brunson's Café on Pope Street was popular for the best fried chicken in town and for its live entertainment. Irene's Café, located on Whitaker Street, had the best desserts. Her sweet potato pie and pineapple cake were the best sellers.

Lightening's Store, operated by Mr. Carlyle, was on Dennis Street in Black Bottom. Mr. Carlyle served that Negro community for years. Pittman's Grocery was operated by Curtis Pittman and family in the little store at the fork of Whitaker and Franklin Streets. The Cofield-Exum Grocery Store, Service Station, and Garage on McDaniel Street was owned and operated by Julia Cofield Exum and her husband, Joseph Exum. Levi's Café was on Pope Street. Harry Cofield owned the Little Palace Restaurant on McDaniel Street where many special events and parties were held. The Sledge Store and the Smithy's Store were on McDaniel Street. There was the Teddy and Maud Store that was considered a convenience store. Elwood Whitaker's Store on Whitaker Street was also a convenience store where Daddy treated my brothers and sister and me to ice cream on Sundays. Most times, Mr. Elwood would give us cookies or candy as an extra treat.

There was no lack of places for Negroes to go to be entertained or just to have an evening out. One of these establishments was John Berry's Club in Black Bottom. The Rainbow Grill on Pope Street was run by Reed Johnson and Tyler Vaughan, a well-known contractor. It was the weekend hot spot where Negro teenagers hung out. Sweetie's porch was one of the entertainment spots. The White Swan Inn was owned and managed by Mutt Davis on Highway 1001, Scotland Neck Road. It was located approximately two miles outside of the Enfield city limit. It was a night club with a big city atmosphere. Otis Redding and James Brown were among many singers and bands that performed at the White Swan Inn before they became famous artists.

The Negro community members only knew the isolated world of segregation, and in it they found ways to provide for their families by becoming entrepreneurs. Willa Cofield Johnson's father, Thomas Cofield, owned Cofield Funeral Home and Cofield Laundry on Pope Street and her family also operated Cofield's Flower Shop. Dick Wilkins was the driver at Curtis Cofield's Coal and Wood Yard that served Negro families throughout Enfield. David Clark operated the Gulf Gas Station on McDaniel Street. Other businesses were Edward's Coal Company, Dave Bell's Carpentry, Jip McWilliams's Painting Service, and Nathaniel Harvey's Painting Service.

Powell's Garage was owned and operated by Robert Powell on McDaniel Street. Rudd's Radio and TV Repair Shop was also on McDaniel Street. Mrs. Marrow and her husband operated Rudd's Cleaners. Williams's Funeral Home was located on McDaniel Street and operated by Linwood Williams. Frank Hunter had a Car Body Shop and George Thornton had a taxi service. Hosea Cotten's very successful Radio and Television Repair and Furniture Store were located on the east end of Whitaker Street. There was Hudson's

Plumbing Service and John Berry's Plumbing in Black Bottom. Bobbitt's pool room, Bobbitt's Upholstery, Bobbitt's Bail Bondsman and Taxi Service were all run by James Bobbitt, along with his barber shop in downtown Enfield on Whitaker Street. Dr. Bryant was the Negro doctor in Enfield during World War II and for some years after. His wife, along with Mrs. Llana Joyner, operated the first Negro kindergarten beside St. Paul Baptist Church on McDaniel Street. Negro owned and operated Bricks Federal Credit Union was also located on McDaniel Street. All these Negro entrepreneurs made it possible for their customers' money to remain in the Black community. The numerous Negro businesses ensured that our segregated community was self-sufficient.

133. MY HIGH SCHOOL YEARS

134. Starting My Teens: 1960–61

The year 1960 was the beginning of my teen years and many life-changing experiences. I was the oldest child at home, and when I started high school, I was given the responsibility to take care of my younger brothers and sisters after school and on Saturdays when my parents were at work. My parents taught me to be responsible, productive, and self-sufficient. They taught me that I had to work for whatever I wanted to become in life. I entered ninth grade ready to work hard. For the first time, I had a team of teachers consisting of English, mathematics, history, biology, and physical education teachers, and an elective teacher.

Mr. Charles Cameron was my homeroom and biology teacher. He was also our class sponsor until we graduated in 1964. I loved biology and the sciences so much that I minored in biology when I attended college. Mr. Cameron occasionally let me teach his class. Mr. Cameron's home was located approximately forty-five minutes from Enfield in Raleigh, North Carolina.

Oftentimes, when individuals came from a distance to Enfield to teach, they roomed with other teachers or lived with families instead of moving into their own homes. Mr. Cameron lived with the Eatmons on Hannon Street, the same street where I lived. Not only did I see him during the school day, but also at the Eatmons or in the neighborhood as he traveled from place to place.

There was no escaping his involvement with my parents because my dad cut his hair, and he would visit our home from time to time.

I was really introverted and shy as a child entering into high school. As I began to develop into a teenager and young lady, Mrs. Willa Cofield Johnson, my English teacher, became my mentor and role model. I loved having Mrs. Cofield Johnson as my English teacher. I began to mature in her English class. I gained an appreciation for English and majored in English while in college.

My confidence increased when I became involved in the civil rights movement, and I began to feel I could do anything I desired.

Willa Cofield Johnson and Reed Johnson, her mortician husband, built their house on Whitaker Street. I knew even in elementary school that when I became an adult and had my own job, I would build a beautiful house just like theirs. Willa and Reed's house was the last house on Whitaker Street, just before the beginning of the White neighborhood that had sidewalks on both sides of the street. There were no sidewalks in the Black Whitaker Street neighborhood. I never questioned why the White neighborhood had sidewalks and the Black neighborhood did not. But I was always happy to get to the sidewalk in the White neighborhood because there was no more dust to eat and breathe as cars sped by.

Mr. Guion Davis from Rocky Mount was one of my ninth-grade team teachers. I was in his algebra class, and he always seemed jovial and down to earth. He was also one of my basketball coaches along with Mr. Witherspoon. Mr. Davis was not intimidating while he taught and coached. Both men were outstanding teachers and excellent basketball coaches. When they coached our Inborden Wildcats team in 1960–61, our girls' basketball team won its first of three championships.

Playing basketball from grade nine (1960–61) through grade twelve (1963–64) was one of the most exciting experiences of my high school years. Our female Wildcats ranked first in the Negro NCPAA Conference. I was a member of that championship basketball team as was Cynthia Cousins Samuelson (one of the coauthors of this book), Joyce Mills Schmidt, Gwendolyn Cofield, Bertha Bullock Fields, Carol Hunter Hunt, and many others who played on the championship team from 1960 to 1963. Cynthia and I always made the All-Conference and All-Tournament teams. My position on the team was as a forward. For three consecutive years, the Lady Wildcats captured trophies for Inborden High School when we won the NCPAA Conference championships. Unfortunately, we lost the championship game in 1964 to our number one rival, Eastman High School.

Our school was completely segregated, which meant our team, the Inborden Wildcats, only competed against Black schools in our county and other neighboring counties. In *The Reflector*, the school newspaper that Willa Cofield Johnson created, there was a column titled "Inquiring Reporter." When the student news reporter asked a group of students including myself, what we thought about the possibility of our Negro basketball team playing a White basketball team, my response was not too optimistic or promising. I stated, "It will never happen!" (Fig. 134.1)

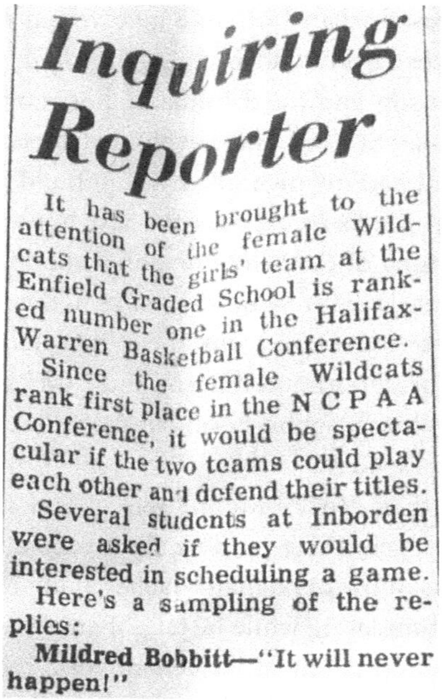

> **Inquiring Reporter**
>
> It has been brought to the attention of the female Wildcats that the girls' team at the Enfield Graded School is ranked number one in the Halifax-Warren Basketball Conference.
>
> Since the female Wildcats rank first place in the N C P A A Conference, it would be spectacular if the two teams could play each other and defend their titles.
>
> Several students at Inborden were asked if they would be interested in scheduling a game. Here's a sampling of the replies:
>
> **Mildred Bobbitt**—"It will never happen!"

Fig. 134.1. Inborden High School newspaper *The Reflector*. / Mildred Sexton personal collection.

Mrs. Ina Alexander Mitchell was my French I team teacher. She was Miss Alexander when she taught me. She was so kind and soft-spoken that I never heard her raise her voice or belittle anyone. Her spirit and her relationship with others were comforting. She maintained classroom order through kindness, gentleness, and exhibiting a quiet demeanor. For her class, the French name Monique was assigned to me. I loved the English language, and I had to really discipline myself to embrace French. Now I thank Mrs. Mitchell for teaching me the basics, because the language came in handy when I was in France.

Mr. Anthony Farmer was my social studies teacher. He instilled in us the importance of keeping up with what was going on in the world locally, nationally, and internationally. We were responsible for completing weekly current events assignments and remembering many dates and events. Mr. Farmer was a great teacher. He taught me a lifelong lesson about perfection. My parents were more than pleased with my success my first year in high school. I ended ninth grade with all A's on my report card with the exception of the B that I received in history for the last quarter of Mr. Farmer's class. When my parents wanted to know why there was a B on my report card, I asked Mr. Farmer. He shared with me that no one is perfect. As I matured, I began to realize that he was right. No one is perfect. Yet whenever I see that report card, that B sticks out like a sore thumb. But that B did not deter me from always wanting to do my very best.

My electives were glee club and physical education. Alice Poston was my physical education teacher. Mrs. June Swindell, my former eighth-grade teacher, was also the music director for the glee club. As her students, we worked really hard to get our parts right. I learned so much about the origin of the songs we sang that the words to "Give Me Your Tired, Your Poor" are still in my memory. The lyrics are touching and teach a lesson about our responsibility to all people and our humanity toward each other. The words I remember are as follows:

Give me your tired, your poor,
Your huddled masses yearning to breathe free
The wretched refuse of your teeming shore
Send these, the homeless, tempest-tossed, to me
I lift my lamp beside the golden door!

Of course, these words are inscribed on the Statue of Liberty. They led me to think about how my ancestors came unwillingly to America and about the stories of slavery that my mother shared about her grandparents and great-grandparents. This knowledge of slavery impressed upon me that we were not far removed from those times and the horrible treatment that they endured. I also thought about how my great-grandparents were the children of slaves who lived their lives being limited to all that exists in this world and who never had the opportunity to experience freedom.

When I was thirteen my parents allowed me to go to the White-owned Levon Theater with a friend. The movie was segregated. That was the norm for us. It was almost a privilege for us to be able to go to the movie at all. The Whites sat downstairs and the Negroes sat upstairs. We could not reach the balcony through the movie house itself. The stairs to the balcony were on the outside of the theater. We bought our tickets at an outside window. There was a separate concession for COLOREDS ONLY where we were able to purchase popcorn, drinks, and candy. My favorite movie candy was called Milk Duds. Back then, I did wonder why we were seated upstairs because anything could have gotten airborne and landed on the White people downstairs. But knowing the do's and don'ts of racism during that time, it was smart not to throw anything downstairs.

Because our race lived in a vacuum of segregation in Enfield, there was a whole world out there about which I had little to no knowledge and experience. My parents put forth the effort to change that. My mother exposed us to poets like Langston Hughes and James Weldon Johnson, and I learned their poems. I admired W. E. B. Du Bois and James Baldwin. When the thirty-fifth president of the United States was to be inaugurated in Washington, DC, on January 20, 1961, my parents wanted me to attend the inauguration. John F. Kennedy was a Democrat. He was the youngest president elected to that office, and he had many innovative ideas. I was elated that I would get to hear Marian Anderson sing "The Star-Spangled Banner," and one of my favorite poets, Robert Frost, was going to recite "The Gift Outright." My parents purchased a long, heavy green coat for me as well as other warm clothing. My classmate, Esther Fenner, was going to the inauguration as well. We planned to leave on the charter bus Thursday night, January 19, at midnight. As the day went on, the weather became more and more of a challenge. By nightfall, it began to snow and the trip was cancelled. I was really disappointed and so was Esther. On Friday, January 20, 1961, I had to watch President Kennedy's inauguration on television.

135. News of Current Events: 1961–62

In the fall of 1961, when I was fourteen years old, I entered tenth grade. My teachers were the very same ones as in ninth grade. Mr. Davis taught me geometry and chemistry. Mrs. Mitchell taught French II. Mr. Anthony Farmer was my social studies and history teacher. It was a weekly requirement that his students were to read the newspaper or listen to the news. Then we were to choose a story to share with the class as our current events assignment.

My parents saw the importance of keeping up with what was going on in the world. In my household, it was understood that we watched the news and read the newspapers the *Journal and Guide*, the *Enfield Progress*, and the *News and Observer*. Our television evening news reporter was Douglas Edwards. He was the news anchor for "Douglas Edwards Views the News." In the morning, there was Slim Short on Channel 9 with local news. There was unrest across the United States due to segregation and integration. In the news, there were demonstrations, sit-ins, boycotts, and deaths of Negroes. Police who were armed with weapons and dogs also used firehoses to deter Negroes from assembling. At age fourteen, I thought that there was really something wrong with how Negroes were not allowed to vote and were prevented from going into any place they wished to enter.

Fig. 135.1. Bobbitt's Hair Care Center, built 1967. / Mildred Sexton personal collection.

During the spring of my sophomore year in 1967, my dad made history when he built Bobbitt's Hair Care Center at 125 Whitaker Street on a lot sold to him by Bud Marshall (Fig. 135.1). Bud was the White farmer and landowner who owned the farm where I was born. My dad was the first and only Black man to build a building in downtown Enfield. Although he was able to negotiate and mingle with White people, my dad was still a Black man who had to survive in a segregated environment. In other words, he knew his place. Very little is said about his major accomplishment.

Dad provided employment for John Tillery, who was married to my mom's cousin, and Harold Person, who was married to Dad's sister, Joyce. Dad had a total of six barbers in his shop over many years including my brother, Edward, and his wife, Sula Hoyle. Dad was a quiet, humble man. Everyone who sat in his chair heard words of wisdom and encouragement. Dad's goal was to make sure his shop was paid for and he was able to make that dream come true the year before he passed.

136. The Protests Begin: 1962–63

In 1962–63, I was fifteen years old and in the eleventh grade. Mr. Davis, one of my favorite teachers, taught me trigonometry and physics in the same class with the seniors. Cynthia Cousins Samuelson was a senior and we sat side by side at a science table in these two classes. Gwendolyn Adams was my bookkeeping teacher. Mrs. Willa Mae Cofield Johnson was my English teacher again. She was one who set goals and offered as many opportunities to her students as she possibly could.

One day Mrs. Cofield Johnson called me to her desk and said that she wanted me to participate in the Delta Sigma Theta sorority's Jabberwock Pageant. I was so excited to have the opportunity to dress in my very first formal gown for such an important event. The gown was pastel blue with a matching blue bow for my hair. During the spring, I wore the very same gown to my junior prom without the bow. The pageant was to raise monies for the Delta Sigma Theta College Scholarship Fund. Scholarships were awarded to young ladies who were entering college for the first time or to support students who were already enrolled in a higher education institution. Those participating sold advertisement spaces or had a patrons' list in support of them in the Delta Sigma Theta Jabberwock program. I sold popcorn at my dad's shop and sought donations from family and friends. I had the third highest amount of money raised for the event. As an eleventh grader, I was awarded a college scholarship from the sorority for participating in the event. The scholarship was sent directly to North Carolina College during my freshman year. It was an honor to be asked to participate in the Jabberwock event. I made a promise to myself to become a member of Delta Sigma Theta sorority. I kept that promise and became a Delta (Fig. 136.1).

Willa Cofield Johnson was also the sponsor and advisor for our National Honor Society (NHS). It is a nationwide organization that gives recognition to high school students based on their academic achievement, leadership, service, and character. Mrs. Cofield Johnson worked diligently to make sure our initiation week was challenging, enjoyable, and memorable.

Initiation night was scary in the beginning but ended with a great celebration. I now equate it to being initiated into a sorority even though there were males in our group. The Negro students who were being initiated into the National Honor Society were segregated.

During the latter part of my junior year in 1963, Mrs. Cofield Johnson invited me to join the civil rights movement in Enfield as a member of the youth leadership group protesting racial inequalities. We met at her home and at the Cofield Funeral Home and Flower Shop. Reed Johnson, Willa Cofield Johnson, Lillie Cousins Smith, and other advocates were a part of our meetings. I remember Mrs. Alice Evans, a person of influence at Mt. Olive Holiness Church on Hannon Street, being a very active participant in the movement. I began to realize, based on what I learned in the youth civil rights meetings, that there had to be a change. There was no reason why I should not participate in the civil rights movement if Black lives could benefit.

Toward the end of May, the youth marched in downtown Enfield and encouraged the Negroes not to patronize the segregated movie theater. I

Part III: The Impact

Fig. 136.1. Inducted into Delta Sigma Theta sorority. / Mildred Sexton personal collection.

remember participating in the demonstrations at the movies. The protests happened mostly on Saturdays. My parents never said one time not to participate in the movement even with all the dangerous threats the Whites in Enfield directed toward our parents and other Black citizens. Although they were not demonstrating on the picket lines, many of our parents supported us. They did their share when it was time to boycott the White businesses. All of the parents who allowed their children to join the movement should have been given medals of honor.

I missed quite a bit of the protests that summer because I was in New Jersey. I had always heard that there was no segregation in the North, but every event I attended in New Jersey was segregated. I worked for a White family at their summer home taking care of the four children who were left in their grandparents' care while their parents went on vacation. When I was told to eat in the kitchen with the children while everyone else ate in the dining room, I questioned the Northerners' perception of segregation and integration. Enfield was not the only place where I was subjected to segregation and had to sit in a "Colored Only" area. Segregation was in the North as well as in the South.

137. The Nine O'Clock Whistle

At noontime every day except Sunday, the whistle would blow in downtown Enfield alerting workers that it was lunchtime. As a youngster, I really did not know why the whistle was blown every Saturday night at nine o'clock. I was told it was blown to alert everyone that the stores were closing at 9:00 p.m. I remember Saturday as the day that Blacks in rural areas came to town and spent the day shopping and socializing. The Negroes, young and old, that lived in town would also mingle with friends who came in to shop for the day. When I entered high school and began to understand the racial divide, it became obvious that the nine o'clock whistle was rooted in segregation.

There were two different worlds in Enfield. There was the Negro world and the White world. The most prominent, racist, demeaning symbol that screamed segregation and hatred in Enfield was the NINE O'CLOCK WHISTLE. Blowing the whistle was a powerful Jim Crow tactic that served as a reminder to Blacks to adhere to the mandate of the nine o'clock curfew. That mandate was that at 9:00 p.m. all Negroes should clear the streets and get out of town or go home. The whistle reinforced the divide between the races and created an atmosphere of isolation and second-class citizenship for all the Negroes.

What a subtle way to be put down by White authority! Just imagine hearing that sound week in and week out and there was nothing Negroes could do about it. The sound of the nine o'clock whistle was a blatant symbol of racism. The reality was that Negroes became deaf to the sound and dismissed its meaning and purpose in order not to feel intimidated. When the nine o'clock whistle blew and my dad's barber shop was filled with customers, he would pull down the shades and everyone would remain in the shop until their hair was cut. Oftentimes, many of the people who were not getting haircuts would come into the shop when the whistle blew and stay until my dad closed the shop. The shop usually closed around midnight most Saturday nights.

When I returned to Enfield at the end of the summer of 1963, the civil rights protesters were still boycotting and demonstrating. The last Saturday in August, the youth were picketing in a peaceful demonstration in downtown Enfield. We were protesting and boycotting the White businesses and stores that did not hire Blacks. The nine o'clock whistle was blown in the belief that when the Negroes heard the whistle blow, they would scatter and go home. On that day, that did not happen. Instead of dispersing, the marchers sang more strongly and forcefully, and the protest songs became more intense and powerful. Even the Negroes who had come to town just for shopping that day joined in and raised their voices in song. Water hoses were used to stop the march. The strong force of the water knocked down those who were picketing. Many students and adults were injured, and many were put in jail.

My regret is that I did not remain with the march on that Saturday. The force of the water did not knock me down, and I did not go to jail. I escaped both by leaving the group and running to Dad's shop. Others joined me as we ran into the barber shop. I could hear the singing and the screaming as hoses washed protesters off their feet. I had friends and relatives go to jail that day and many of them were injured. When I fled into my dad's barber shop, I missed out on a very impactful event.

If you grew up in Enfield, the sound of the nine o'clock whistle rubbed racism in the face of every Black person who heard it. The nine o'clock whistle was a powerful and demeaning symbol of racism and segregation personified. What an insult! The whistle blasting on the day the youth were participating in a march downtown certainly served as a catalyst to solidify the Black community behind the civil rights movement in Enfield.

138. Picketing and Threats: 1963–64

In 1963–64, I was sixteen years old and a senior at Inborden High School. My twelfth-grade English teacher was again Mrs. Willa Mae Cofield Johnson. She had been my English teacher from the very first day I entered high school. Alice Poston continued to be my physical education teacher, and she also became my basketball coach. Mr. Davis did not return my senior year, and I was so grateful that I had met all the science and mathematics requirements before he departed.

That fall there was an effort to organize a peaceful demonstration to boycott the annual Enfield Firemen's Fair. We were picketing and protesting outside the fairgrounds when a policeman asked me whether I was James Bobbitt's girl. I said, "Yes." With a knife in his hands acting as if he was cleaning his fingernails, he told me that I needed to go home. I did go home after the sky opened up and it rained and rained. We all went home.

I remember my father received threatening phone calls. I know the calls always had something to do with his barber shop and Mom's beauty shop. One night, Daddy put all of us in his car and took us with him to the shop. We stayed there most of the night. It was a very tense time. In fact, in 1964, the Black newspaper the *Carolina Times* reported that the Enfield police posted advertisements on their bulletin board announcing Ku Klux Klan rallies. During the same year, the Halifax County Voters Movement sought the rights of Blacks to have protection from the KKK at home, in their businesses, and in public places.

Even though my father had served in the United States Army during World War II and was honorably discharged in 1946 with the rank of Sergeant First Class, he returned to his life in segregated Enfield with no voting rights. Prior to 1964, my parents did not have a voice as to how these United States of America should be run, because they could not vote. When the movement moved on to voter registration, I became involved in many school and community activities. I remember John Salter and the meetings of the Halifax County Voters Movement to make plans at the Cofield Funeral Home. Although the Ku Klux Klan threatened to bring harm to those attempting to register, my parents registered and voted on the first opportunity that came their way.

During the 1963–64 school year, our English teacher, Willa Cofield Johnson, worked to help our class. I remember how she helped us create our own book of memories because Inborden High School did not have a yearbook. Being segregated limited our resources and there was no yearbook for any graduating class. We were already getting secondhand textbooks and rarely new ones. At that time, we had to pay book fees and having a yearbook would have been an extra expense for our families. Mrs. Cofield Johnson was always on the cutting edge of figuring out ways to offer opportunities like the memory book to students in her class.

My senior prom somewhat balanced all that was disheartening during the course of the year (Fig. 138.1). Unlike my junior prom, I attended my senior prom with three of my best friends. My girlfriend and I were escorted to the prom and treated royally by two handsome gentlemen who were juniors at Inborden High School. We did not have to worry about the boyfriend-girlfriend relationships. We danced with whomever we wanted and mingled freely as we went from table to table. The four of us had an awesome time.

139. A Time of Courage

Willa Cofield Johnson experienced consequences for her role in the movement. Without notice, our English teacher was no longer teaching at Inborden High School. Of course, we students were privy to the rumors and gossip that she had been fired. We had lots of questions among ourselves, and we surmised that she had been fired because of her participation in the civil rights movement. It was a sad time for me because she had exposed me to many

Fig. 138.1. Mildred at senior prom, 1964. / Mildred Sexton personal collection.

opportunities and glimpses of the world outside Enfield. In addition, she was an excellent English teacher.

It took courage for me to join the civil rights movement and to sign an affidavit in support of Mrs. Cofield Johnson in the *Willa Johnson v. Joseph Branch* lawsuit. The affidavit I signed mainly addressed her character and the efforts Willa Cofield Johnson put forth to help her students. The affidavit bears my name as Mildred Bobbitt. It states that Mrs. Cofield Johnson was an excellent teacher who presented the material to her students in a variety of interesting ways. She taught me skills that enabled me to do well on my Scholastic Aptitude Test for admission to college. I also wrote about how she sponsored the Honor Society and found unique ways to celebrate our induction. One of the highlights of the induction was that she took us on a weekend trip to Colonial Williamsburg in Williamsburg, Virginia, and to Hampton Institute in Hampton, Virginia. Becoming a member of the Honor Society was a key factor in my scholastic success.

After I signed the affidavit, I was denied an opportunity that was directly related to my connection to the case and my participation in the civil rights

Fig. 139.1. Mildred's Inborden High graduation picture. / Mildred Sexton personal collection.

movement. The consequence was that when I applied to two White colleges, my Inborden High School transcripts were not forwarded to those colleges even after the colleges requested them. The college I was really hoping to attend was East Carolina College in Greenville, North Carolina, which was considered a White college at the time.

My parents were my saving grace. They shared my pain and disappointment without condemning the establishment that broke my spirit. They assured me that the consequences did not define who I was or who I would become. My parents taught me that I am the creator of my destiny and oftentimes when others attempt to be stumbling blocks, their actions create a more powerful and positive destiny for the individual.

For a time after graduating from high school in May 1964, I was disappointed, hurt, and somewhat discouraged (Fig. 139.1). I eventually applied very late to North Carolina College and was accepted. In the fall, I went to North Carolina College, a predominately Black college, and majored in English and biology. I often think that if I had attended East Carolina, I would not have met my husband and many great opportunities would have been missed. So I am thankful that the course of my life was changed as a result of my bittersweet senior year at Inborden High School.

140. MY LIFE CONTINUES

141. North Carolina College: 1964-68

Although I was ninety-plus miles away from Enfield in the fall of 1964, my life continued to be segregated. I was starting my studies in Durham at North Carolina College on a Black campus. I had always been a part of that segregated world, and I was very comfortable in that environment.

For the first time, I experienced being in the presence of Whites in an educational setting. I had never had a White teacher before. Some of my professors were White and many of them taught at Duke University as well as at North Carolina College. My White and foreign chemistry teacher was my greatest challenge. He was an immigrant whose accent was really hard to understand. I would have been a much better chemistry student if I had understood what he was saying. Although I made a passing grade in chemistry, at the end of my sophomore year, I switched my primary concentration from biology to English.

I completed four successful years from 1964 to 1968 at North Carolina College, including four sessions of summer school. During all four years that I was a student, civil rights meetings were going on. Stokely Carmichael was a prominent civil right advocate who was frequently seen on campus. I did not participate in any civil rights activities until a tragic, historical incident happened on the balcony of the Lorraine Motel in Memphis, Tennessee, on April 4, 1968. I was one month from graduating when the assassination of Dr. Martin Luther King Jr. devastated the nation and turned it upside down. The students reacted immediately and organized a march on the morning after King's assassination from the campus to the Durham City Hall in downtown Durham. I knew it was my duty to join the civil rights march on Durham. I was very familiar with the civil rights struggle after participating in the Enfield movement. On April 5, 1968, I was right there participating in the

Fig. 141.1. Mildred Bobbitt, 1968 North Carolina College graduation. / Mildred Sexton personal collection.

Fig. 141.2. Mildred Bobbitt, 1968 North Carolina College graduation. / Mildred Sexton personal collection.

march. It was very peaceful and well organized, with a large number of students from North Carolina College taking part in the demonstration.

Although the march was peaceful, the following day on April 6, some of the Durham demonstrators caused an arson eruption. The city officials sought help from the National Guard to put an end to the violence. As a result of the arson incident, a curfew was implemented in Durham. Due to the violence in the city, the president of North Carolina College made the decision to close the campus and send all of the students home.[6]

We were just weeks from graduation. The big question was "What about our graduation?" The seniors received a letter in the mail that gave us a date to return to campus. Once on campus, we gathered at the bursar's office and received letters regarding our eligibility for graduation. My letter stated that I was a candidate for graduation on May 12, 1968. My friends Sandra Wallace, Mary Todd, and Lillian Avent got letters that stated the same. The four of us celebrated our last few days on campus together. When graduation day arrived, my parents, sisters, brothers, and my future husband attended my graduation. On Mother's Day, May 12, 1968, I graduated from North Carolina College with a bachelor's degree in English and a minor in biology (Figs. 141.1 and 141.2).

142. My Return to Enfield: 1968-70

Prior to graduating, I took the National Teachers' Examination and scored really well. I was very fortunate that Clemon Williamson, the principal of Inborden High School, shared with my dad that there was a job waiting for me if I returned to Enfield. I returned home and began teaching at Inborden High School in August 1968. At that time, Inborden High School was still segregated.

Black students from Inborden Elementary and High Schools began to integrate the White Enfield Graded School during 1964–65 while I was at college. My brother Edward was among the first to integrate Enfield High School (Fig. 142.1). Edward described his experience integrating the White school in a letter to me as follows:

> I was one of the first high school students to have the choice to go to Enfield Graded. I chose to go along with six other high school students.
>
> I did not want to leave my friends at Inborden High School, but something inside of me said I had to go.
>
> I, along with others, was not welcomed at the all-white school. We were taunted, called names, and were the object of other cruel acts. Some were mistreated more than others. I remember in math class on my report card I received an E+, which was unheard of. Mathematics was always my best subject. The teachers were unfair and unjust to all of us.

In May 1968, my brother and five other students made history in Enfield by becoming the first Blacks to graduate from integrated Enfield High School. Then Edward moved on to my dad's alma mater, Harris Barber College in Raleigh.

My sister, Dalphne, began first grade in 1964 at segregated Inborden Elementary on the very same day that I had gone to college (Fig. 142.2). In the fall of 1965 as a second grader, she entered Enfield Graded School. Being among the first to integrate the White school was not a fond memory for Dalphne. She recounted her experiences in the following excerpts from a letter to me:

> I was only seven years old when I was transferred to the Enfield Graded School. I remember very little about my experiences. That which I do remember is unpleasant. I was in second grade and the only Black student in the class. My stomach hurt all of the time, especially in the morning when it was time for me to go to school. I was treated differently and I knew I was different. Mom sent extra clothes to school with

Fig. 142.1. Edward Bobbitt integrated Enfield High School as a ninth grader. / Mildred Sexton personal collection.

Fig. 142.2. Dalphne grade 2, Enfield Graded School. / Mildred Sexton personal collection.

me because quite often the teacher would not let me go to the bathroom. So it was not unusual for me to wet my clothes.

I had very thick and long hair. Mom would always do my hair in two braids with my hair parted down the middle and a fat braid on each side of my head. One day, Mom noticed that one of my braids was missing. She asked me what happened to my braid. I lied and told her that a girl cut it off at school hoping Mom and Daddy would not let me go back to that school. That evening, Mom was sweeping our room and she swept my braid from under the bed. She was really, really angry. Mom and Dad realized that Enfield grade school was not a healthy environment for me. They took me back to Inborden Elementary School. I was so happy to be back with my friends.

Dalphne was many grades behind my brothers and sister and me. The year that I returned to Enfield as a teacher, she was in the fourth grade at Inborden Elementary.

When I began teaching at Inborden High School in August 1968, I was hired provisionally because I had not done student teaching. I was observed twice during the 1968–69 school year by the Black administrative instructional director of the Halifax County Central Office School Board. At the end of my first year teaching, I received full certification. My first-year teaching salary was barely $3,000. I remember my dad saying, "You mean to tell me I sent you through four years of college to make this amount of money!" He said he could make more than that amount in one month cutting hair. Nevertheless, I was impressed with my salary. I could make a car payment, purchase what I needed, and help my brother, Edward, who was in barber school by that time.

I loved working at my high school alma mater. Clem Williamson was a great principal. The students loved him and the environment was peaceful with a well-disciplined atmosphere. He loved to tease and joke with the students and staff, but everyone knew what the expectations were. I was the only teacher on the high school staff who had graduated from Inborden High School. At that time, I had the unforgettable opportunity to teach my sister, Joyce. My brother, Larry, managed to escape having me as his teacher.

I had great mentors during the two years I taught at Inborden High School. Lois Smith was my number one mentor and friend. She shared with me her very effective classroom discipline routine. Although the students saw her as a very strict and no-nonsense teacher, she was highly respected and loved by them. Lois Smith taught biology, which was my favorite subject.

I taught English and physical education. I guess my biology minor had qualified me to teach physical education. I loved teaching English, but I had my apprehensions when it came to teaching physical education. Although I was athletic when I was a student, I preferred teaching English and biology. I also coached the girls' basketball team. During the two years I coached, we had a perfect record of no wins. Although I had played basketball in high school, I was not a good coach. The girls really put forth effort to win their games, and I truly felt as though I let them down. When Inborden High, Enfield Graded, and Enfield High School were fully integrated, I was saved from coaching a third year.

143. Integration of Enfield Schools: 1970–71

Inborden High School lost its identity when Enfield schools integrated in August 1970. I had ended my second year teaching at segregated Inborden High in May 1970. My brother Larry was in the last class of students to graduate from segregated Inborden High School (Fig. 143.1). The old Inborden High School buildings became an elementary and middle school, housing pupils from kindergarten through eighth grade. A cafeteria was built and the

Fig. 143.1. Larry Bobbitt—member of the last class to graduate from segregated Inborden High School, 1970. / Mildred Sexton personal collection.

agricultural building was renovated and converted into a media center. That meant that everyone who had ever graduated from segregated Inborden High School no longer had a physical building as an alma mater, and little by little, the traditions of our Black high school faded away.

Inborden High School as we knew it no longer existed. As early as 1964, small groups of Black students had integrated Enfield Graded School. But this forced integration in the fall of 1970 was another first for our small town. When all the Black students who attended Inborden High School integrated Enfield High School across town in the West End, we Black teachers transferred with them. I was among the group of Black teachers forced to integrate Enfield High. My sister, Joyce Bobbitt, transferred to Enfield High School as an eleventh grader. No one knew what to expect and how we as Black people would fare in this new White environment.

When this significant influx of minorities came into their school, White flight happened. White people moved into the rural areas and opened private schools for their children. They organized their very own Christian Academy for Whites only. Many of the White parents who remained in Enfield transported their children to the White private schools. The few White students who remained at Enfield High appeared to adjust well to the Black students entering their school.

I taught ninth-grade English. My classes were made up of Black students only. This was the face of integration in Enfield with the majority of the classrooms still segregated by race. The White students were obviously being sheltered whenever possible. The White teachers who remained were cordial and we were all able to work together. At the end of the school day, we all returned to our segregated neighborhoods, segregated churches, segregated clubs, and segregated activities.

144. Black Soldiers in the 1960s

The employment opportunities for Negroes in Enfield were very limited. During the 1960s, one of the career pathways for young Negroes to become economically self-sufficient was the military. There were those who volunteered to enlist in the Army, Navy, Marines, or Air Force. There were also many who were drafted. The 1960s was not the best time to be in the military because of the Vietnam War. Those who chose the military as a career and retired after serving twenty years or more made a smart and successful choice if they were able to serve in Vietnam without being a casualty or being affected by the hardships of war.

Many of our young Enfield Negro men returned home from the Vietnam War injured and suffering emotionally and physically. Some of our Black men who were as young as eighteen were exposed to Agent Orange and others came home with physical wounds or posttraumatic stress disorder (PTSD). Some lost their lives. Those soldiers who spent time on the front line for our country and then returned home faced the same prejudices and racism they had experienced prior to going to Vietnam.

My brother, Edward, and his best friend, Wendell Taylor, who was our neighbor on Hannon Street, both graduated from high school in 1968. Wendell joined the US Army and participated in the Vietnam War. During his second tour in Vietnam, he lost his life. The news was devastating for all who knew him. That was a sad time for our families on Hannon Street and throughout Enfield.

145. True Integration: 1970–74

I taught at segregated Inborden High School from August 1968 to May 1970 and at Enfield High School from August 1970 through the spring of 1972. The

Fig. 145.1. Alfred Sexton and Mildred Bobbitt at 1968 senior ball, North Carolina College. / Mildred Sexton personal collection.

last day of school in May 1972, I packed my car with all my belongings and moved to Richmond, Virginia. My very first true experience with integration was when I began working at Hanover School for Boys in Hanover, Virginia. I had Negro and White students in my classes from October 1972 to February 1974. I made great friends with both Blacks and Whites. The children from both races were well taught and loved.

I left Hanover School for Boys in 1974 when I married Alfred Landon Sexton Jr. of Hampton, Virginia. I had met him in 1966 during my junior year at North Carolina College (Fig. 145.1). We dated for seven years and became engaged in September 1973. We married on February 23, 1974, at St. Paul Baptist Church in Enfield where I had attended church while growing up. Rev. Frank L. Bullock officiated at our wedding. The only people invited to our marriage were my parents, my sisters and brothers, my husband's immediate family, the best man, Robert Hamlin, and the maid of honor, Carol Hunter. Robert had been Alfred's best friend from childhood and Carol had been mine.

When I entered the church, my dad stopped me and said, "You are having a wedding today!" To my surprise, every pew in the large church was filled from the back of the sanctuary to the choir loft up front. Even the balcony was overflowing. My dad probably invited everyone who had ever sat in his barber chair. Many others had received invitations to the wedding reception to be held at the Little Palace Restaurant owned by Harry Cofield. In a small town like Enfield, others had simply invited themselves. My eighth-grade teacher, Mrs. June Swindell, played the organ and sang. I cried all the way down the aisle. Her playing and singing at my wedding were the best gift ever. Although I do not remember any other time when an individual of another race entered St. Paul Church, my White coworker from Richmond attended our wedding. I could not have planned a more successful wedding filled with people who loved me.

146. MY PROFESSIONAL CAREER BLOSSOMS

147. My Tenure in Hampton City Schools

After leaving Hanover School for Boys in 1974, I taught in the middle schools in Hampton, Virginia, from 1974 to 1990. Virginia was known for its massive resistance to integrating schools. In fact, schools in Virginia had been shut down as a means of resisting the inevitable. By the time I came to Hampton in 1974, the schools were integrated. In 1980 I received my master's degree in English from Hampton Institute (now Hampton University) and taught communication skills as an adjunct professor at Hampton Institute from 1980 to 1988. In 1990, I received my Certificate in Administrative Studies (CAS) from Old Dominion University in Norfolk, Virginia.

In the 1991–92 school year, I became assistant principal at Spratley Middle School. Dr. Billy Cannaday was the superintendent at that time, and during the 1994–95 school year, I became principal. Until June 2003, I was the principal at Spratley Middle School, where year-round school was implemented. I was invited to serve as an ex-officio member for several years on the National Year-Round Board of Directors, headquartered in San Diego, California. I was also a regional representative on the Virginia Middle School Association board of directors and served for a number of years as their president.

In 2003, I received my doctorate in education (EdD) from Virginia Tech and became Director of Compensatory Programs, specifically, Title I, Hampton City Schools. In 2004 I became executive director of Elementary School Leadership, supervising sixteen principals as a member of the superintendent's leadership team. I continued to work with compensatory programs. As members of the Hampton City Schools Leadership Team, we were instrumental in building two PreK-8 schools. Our names, along with the names of the Hampton City Council and the names of the Hampton City School Board, are engraved on the cornerstones of George P. Phenix and Hunter

B. Andrews PreK-8 schools. Superintendent Dr. Allen Davis was instrumental in my transferring into central administrative positions. Dr. Linda Shifflette was the superintendent when I retired from Hampton City Schools in 2011.

148. Conclusion

In retrospect, the clarity of who I am today is apparent. After leaving Enfield, North Carolina, my world became totally integrated. I met wonderful children and coworkers of all races. In understanding my journey in an integrated world, the clarity of retrospection has become my point of reference. I am not saying racism no longer exists, but I can now identify and recognize it because my world changed. My life moved in a different direction than my ancestors could ever have imagined. I have experienced not only the world of segregation but also an integrated world.

The 1960s and 1970s were filled with political chaos locally and nationally. The youth of my generation demanded that there be civil rights for all throughout the United States. I took part in the volatile civil rights rebellion when I participated in the civil rights movement in Enfield, North Carolina. My generation took action and made demands for laws to be changed in the hope of creating a better world for everyone.

The children born in our community after 1970 have no idea about how life was in those segregated times. They can go to a movie and sit anywhere they want to sit. They do not have to sit at the back of the bus or give up their seats to a White person. They can sit anywhere they wish on a train, bus, plane, or any other kind of public transportation. They can move around freely and not be intimidated by racist signs such as FOR WHITES ONLY or FOR COLORED ONLY. They do not have to go to a separate restroom or be denied outright when they ask to use a restroom. They do not have to stand outside a restaurant and purchase food through a window for Coloreds Only. They can go into any restaurant, take a seat anyplace, and be served a meal. They do not have to pack food when traveling because they can purchase food anywhere. When traveling long distances, they do not have to find a safe and protected place to park and rest because they can stay in any hotel or motel. They can choose to live in neighborhoods where I could not reside in the 1960s.

All these segregated situations and circumstances felt normal to me in the world where I grew up. I had no idea that my life was so sheltered and separate prior to the l960s because my world was all Negroes. When Dr. Willa Cofield invited me to become a part of the civil rights movement, the course of my life changed. The decade from 1960 to 1970 was a time that affected my world and changed the culture of the United States, the state of North Carolina, and my little birthplace of Enfield. Long after the civil rights movement ended, the nine o'clock whistle in Enfield was finally silenced.

149. EPILOGUE

150. Enfield Today

Nowadays, whenever I visit Enfield, there are always reminders of times past and what my hometown was like when I was a child. The most obvious is the fact that there are so many places that have disappeared, especially Black businesses. Interstate 95 rerouted all the traffic that previously ran through the heart of our small town on Highway 301. The town has not been the same since the 1960s.

Due to the lack of jobs in and around Enfield, after graduation many of my peers moved north to seek employment in the larger cities. Although attending college and trade or vocational schools opened more opportunities for Negroes in the South, it did not matter what type of training one received, the employment options were limited to serving the Negro race. In Enfield, professional opportunities were limited to jobs as educators teaching in Negro schools and barbers, beauticians, doctors, and nurses working in Negro establishments. Education and training were advantageous economically to Negroes in the South but not nearly as advantageous as White people's opportunities. As a result, during the 1960s, many young men and women from Enfield moved to Washington, DC, Maryland, New Jersey, and New York.

The schools in Halifax County were reorganized from 1981 to 1983. High school students from Enfield and Scotland Neck were transferred to the newly built Southeast High School. Enfield High School became the middle school, housing grades six through eight. Inborden School became the elementary school, housing prekindergarten through grade five. In January 2008, a new elementary school and middle school were opened on thirty-five acres of land located on Highway 481 in Enfield. The old Enfield Middle School was renovated and transformed into an apartment building. In July 2017, Inborden Elementary School was renamed Inborden Elementary S.T.E.A.M. Academy.[7]

From the early 1960s to this day, the sidewalk on Hannon Street continues to be one of only two paved sidewalks located in a former Black neighborhood. During segregated times, there were sidewalks throughout the White neighborhoods. Because of integration and White flight, Black families populate the majority of the former White neighborhoods today. The houses in the White area of town were much larger and more beautifully built. Many of them were two-story brick homes. Brick houses were very rare in Enfield Black neighborhoods. As of 2019, there were only six or seven homes occupied on Hannon Street compared to the twenty-two or more occupied homes during the 1960s. Our home, the Pierces' home, and the Penders' home are the only three houses occupied by family members who grew up on Hannon Street. The former Black neighborhoods no longer resemble the well-kept and prosperous places I knew as a child, teenager, and young adult. There are three homes on Hannon Street that need to be demolished because they have deteriorated and are falling down. Two of the once most beautiful houses on the street are among the three left to be demolished.

There are still Black businesses in Enfield that survived the 1960s and exist today. My brother Larry manages and works in the barber shop that my father built on Whitaker Street. Larry's wife, Linda, works in the beauty shop. Many of the Black baby boomers who migrated to other parts of the country for employment have returned to Enfield as retirees or to open new businesses. Mr. Richardson returned to Enfield to open a dry-cleaning business. Larry Perkins, who left Enfield at age sixteen, has returned to give back to the community. He has renovated the old Meyers Grocery store building on Whitfield Street and opened the Collective Center, sponsoring talks, events, and profiling talent. Special events such as weddings, family reunions, and other activities that are held there do not have to end by nine o'clock on Saturday nights. Although in 2019 the whistle continues to be blown at midday, it is not blown at 9:00 p.m. on Saturday nights. However, the memories of the indignity of that demeaning Jim Crow tactic exists in the minds of many. Maybe the silencing of the whistle now serves as a memorial to the strength and perseverance of those who still remember.

NOTES

Part I: The Nine O'Clock Whistle

1. Williams, M. W., and George W. Watkins. *Who's Who among North Carolina Negro Baptists*. Publisher unknown, 1940. 227.
2. Stevenson, Robert Louis. "The Swing." *Childcraft: Poems of Early Childhood*. 2nd ed., vol. I. J. Morris Jones, editor-in-chief. Chicago: Field Enterprises, 1954. 132.
3. Brownlee, Fred L. *New Day Ascending*. Boston: Pilgrim Press, 1947. 149–50.
4. Eastman School. http://www.eastmanalumni.org.
5. Brownlee, Fred L. *New Day Ascending*. Boston: Pilgrim Press, 1947, 152.
6. Morton, Ruth. Men of the Soil. New York: American Missionary Association, 1945, 10.
7. Brownlee, 151–53.
8. Anderson, James. *Race and Politics in North Carolina, 1872–1901*. Baton Rouge: Louisiana State University Press, 1981. 114.
9. Anderson, 115–16.
10. Anderson, 126.
11. *Enfield Progress*, May 24, 1963.
12. "Negro Teenagers Picket Enfield Theatre." *Enfield Progress*, May 24, 1963.
13. *Enfield Progress*, June 7, 1963.
14. North Carolina General Statutes Chapter 14. Criminal Law § 14-134.3. Domestic Criminal Trespass. https://codes.findlaw.com/nc/chapter-14-criminal-law/nc-gen-st-sect-14-134-3/.
15. 261 N.C. 463,135 S.E.2d 14; 261 N.C. 467, 135 S.E.2d 17.
16. 379 U.S. 684 (85 S.Ct. 635, 13 L.Ed.2d 603).
17. Bennett Jr., Lerone. "The March," essay, *The Day They Marched*. Chicago: Johnson Publishing Co, 1963, 3.
18. SNCC Digital Gateway. SNCCdigital.org.
19. US Census, 1960.
20. *Enfield Progress*, May 29, 1964.
21. Interview by Cynthia Samuelson, *The Nine O'clock Whistle* documentary.
22. Salter, John. 1964. "An Upsurge in Carolina." *Southern Patriot*, June 1964. 2.
23. *Johnson v. Branch*, Appellate Brief and Appendix, Willa Johnson Aff., 15.
24. *Johnson v. Branch*, Appellate Brief and Appendix, Willa Johnson Aff., 15.
25. *Johnson v. Branch*, Appellate Brief and Appendix, Willa Johnson Aff., 15.
26. *Johnson v. Branch*, Appellate Brief and Appendix, Willa Johnson Aff., 16.
27. *Johnson v. Branch*, Appellant's Brief and Appendix, Plaintiff's Exhibit, 34–35.
28. *Johnson v. Branch*, US Court of Appeals, 4th Circuit. App. Br., 34–35.
29. *Johnson v. Branch*, US Court of Appeals, 4th Circuit. App. Br., 34–35.
30. *Johnson v. Branch*, US Court of Appeals, 4th Circuit. App. Br., 34–35.
31. *Johnson v. Branch*, US Court of Appeals, 4th Circuit. App. Br., 36.

32. *Daily Herald*, May 13, 1964.

33. The HCVM may have used SNCC flyers, as the latter organization's name appears at the bottom.

34. Barksdale, Marcellus. "The Indigenous Civil Rights Movement and Cultural Change in North Carolina: Weldon, Chapel Hill, and Monroe, 1946–1965." Diss., Duke University, 1977, 94.

35. Civil Rights Movement Archive. www.crmvet.org.

36. *Roanoke Rapids Daily Herald*, May 4, 1964.

37. *Alston v. Butts*, Complaint, Civil Action #875. U.S. District Court, Eastern District of North Carolina.

38. *Alston v. Butts*, Deloris English, Aff., May 13, 1964.

39. *Alston v. Butts*, Mrs. Barbara Eatmon, Aff., May 13, 1964.

40. *Alston v. Butts*, Lottie Pittman, Aff., May 13, 1964.

41. *Alston v. Butts*, Reed Johnson, Aff., May 13, 1964.

42. *Alston v. Butts*, Ernest Leach Jr., Aff., May 13, 1964.

43. *Alston v. Butts*, Mrs. Vivian Mima Johnson, Aff., May 13, 1964.

44. *Alston v. Butts*, Dr. Salter Cochrane, Aff., May 13, 1964.

45. *Alston v. Butts*, Preliminary Injunction, U.S. District Court, Eastern District Court of NC, May 14, 1964.

46. *Alston v. Butts*, Lillie Cousins Smith, Aff., May 13, 1964.

47. *Alston v. Butts*, Harry Boyte, Aff., May 13, 1964.

48. *Alston v. Butts*, Thomas J. Andrews, Aff., May 13, 1964.

49. *Alston v. Butts*, Plaintiff Motion, US District Court, Eastern District of NC, May 13, 1964.

50. *Alston v. Butts*, Plaintiff Motion, US District Court, Eastern District of NC, May 13, 1964.

51. *News and Observer*, May 14, 1964.

52. *News and Observer*, May 14, 1964.

53. *Statesville Record and Landmark*, May 14, 1964.

54. Salter, John. Report to SCEF Board. June 6, 1964.

55. Salter, John. *Southern Patriot*, June 1964.

56. Salter, John. *Southern Patriot*, June 1964.

57. *Southern Patriot*, June 1964.

58. *Johnson v. Branch*, App. Br., Willa Johnson, Aff., 17.

59. *Johnson v. Branch*, App. Br. and Appendix, 1.

60. *Johnson v. Branch*, App. Br., Ina Alexander Mitchell, Aff., 30.

61. *Johnson v. Branch*, App. Br., Erie Barton, Aff., 29.

62. *Johnson v. Branch*, App. Br., Ethel Speight, Aff. 28; Margie Ford, Aff., 22.

63. *Johnson v. Branch*, App. Br., Mildred Bobbitt, Aff., 23–24.

64. *Johnson v. Branch*, App. Br., Votie B. McWilliams, Aff., 25.

65. *Johnson v. Branch*, App. Br., June Scott, Aff., 32.

66. *Johnson v. Branch*, App. Br., Willa Johnson, Aff., 18–20.

67. *Johnson v. Branch*, App. Br., 8.

68. *Johnson v. Branch*, 33–34. Hirschkop, Philip J., William M. Kunstler, Samuel S. Mitchell, and Prof. Chester J. Antieau. 1964. *Willa Johnson v. Joseph Branch*, No. 10,281. United States Court of Appeals for the Fourth Circuit.

69. *Johnson v. Branch*, App. Br., Eddie Copeland, Defendant's Direct Examination, 81.

70. *Johnson v. Branch*, App. Br., Robert Coppage, Direct Examination, 96.

71. *Johnson v. Branch*, App. Br., Percy Thorne, Direct Examination, 92.

72. *Johnson V. Branch*, App. Br., Deposition of Frances Arnold, 116.

73. *Johnson v. Branch*, App. Br., L. M. Williams, Cross Examination, 90.

74. *Johnson v. Branch*, App. Br., Consent Order of July 31, 1965, 39.

75. *Johnson v. Branch*, App. Br., Amicus Notice by T. Wade Bruton and Ralph Moody, 8.

76. 9/28/1964 filed copy of official Court Reporter's transcript of Hearing of Sept. 28, 1964 (Ward Allen, Court Reporter).

77. 9/28/1964 filed copy of official Court Reporter's transcript, p18–44.

78. 9/28/1964 filed copy of official Court Reporter's transcript, 20.

79. 9/28/1964 filed copy of official Court Reporter's transcript, 21–22.

80. 9/28/1964 filed copy of official Court Reporter's transcript, 27.

81. 9/28/1964 filed copy of official Court Reporter's transcript, 27.

82. 9/28/1964 filed copy of official Court Reporter's transcript, 27.

83. 9/28/1964 filed copy of official Court Reporter's transcript, 41.

84. 9/28/1964 filed copy of official Court Reporter's transcript, 26.

85. *Johnson v. Branch*, App. Br., Lillie M. Smith, Aff., 25–27.

86. 9/28/1964 filed copy of official Court Reporter's transcript, 30.

87. 9/28/1964 filed copy of official Court Reporter's transcript, 31.

88. 9/28/1964 filed copy of official Court Reporter's transcript, 43.

89. 9/28/1964 filed copy of official Court Reporter's transcript, 44.

90. 9/28/1964 filed copy of official Court Reporter's transcript, 46.

91. 9/28/1964 filed copy of official Court Reporter's transcript, 33.

92. 9/28/1964 filed copy of official Court Reporter's transcript, 34.

93. 9/28/1964 filed copy of official Court Reporter's transcript, Second Hearing, 31.

94. 9/28/1964 filed copy of official Court Reporter's transcript, 50.

95. 9/28/1964 filed copy of official Court Reporter's transcript, 49.

96. 9/28/1964 filed copy of official Court Reporter's transcript, 48.

97. 9/28/1964 filed copy of official Court Reporter's transcript, 7, 56.

98. Fortunately, I met all three of the criteria to qualify for assistance during the 1964–1965 school year from the NEA DuShane Legal Defense Fund.

99. *Carolina Times*, August 17, 1948.

100. Barksdale, "The Indigenous Civil Rights Movement and Cultural Change in North Carolina," 93.

101. *Carolina Times*, January 7, 1950.

102. *Roanoke Rapids Daily Herald*, December 8, 1964.

103. *Roanoke Rapids Daily Herald*, December 8, 1964.

104. *Roanoke Rapids Daily Herald*, December 8, 1964.

105. *Roanoke Rapids Daily Herald*, December 8, 1964.

106. *Roanoke Rapids Daily Herald*, December 8, 1964.

107. *Roanoke Rapids Daily Herald*, January 3, 1965.

108. Mrs. Edna Griffin was a member of the NEA panel that interviewed Willa Johnson in March 1965.

109. "Edna Griffin NEA Expert Testimony Heard In Federal Court," report given at NEA convention, New York, June 30, 1965.

110. *Johnson v. Branch*, App. Br., Phillip Constans, Plaintiff Direct Examination, Transcript of March 18, 1965, 73.

111. *Johnson v. Branch*, App. Br., Phillip Constans, 74–75.

112. *Johnson v. Branch*, App. Br., Phillip Constans, 76.

113. *Johnson v. Branch*, App. Br., Phillip Constans, 77.

114. *Johnson v. Branch*, App. Br., L.M. Williams, 88.

115. *Johnson v. Branch*, App. Br., L.M. Williams, 88–89.

116. 10/19/1964 filed copy of official Court Reporter's transcript, 31.

117. United States District Court for the Eastern District of North Carolina, Wilson Division, 242 F. Sup 721; 1965 U.S. Dist., LEXIS 6286, 13.
118. 242 F. Sup 721;1965 U.S. Dist., LEXIS 6286, 13.
119. 242 F. Sup 721;1965 U.S. Dist., LEXIS 6286, 14.
120. United States Court of Appeals for the Fourth Circuit, 364 F 2D 177;1966 U.S. Ap LEXIS 5918; 9 Fair Empl. Prac. Cas (BNA)1074, 1.
121. 9 Fair Empl. Prac. Cas (BNA)1074, 2.
122. 9 Fair Empl. Prac. Cas (BNA)1074.
123. 9 Fair Empl. Prac. Cas (BNA)1074, 4, 3.
124. 9 Fair Empl. Prac. Cas (BNA)1074, 4.
125. 9 Fair Empl. Prac. Cas (BNA)1074, 4.
126. 9 Fair Empl. Prac. Cas (BNA)1074, 5.
127. 9 Fair Empl. Prac. Cas (BNA)1074, 5.
128. 9 Fair Empl. Prac. Cas (BNA)1074, 5.
129. 9 Fair Empl. Prac. Cas (BNA)1074, 5.
130. 9 Fair Empl. Prac. Cas (BNA)1074, 5.
131. Gilmore, Al-Toney. *All the People.* Washington, DC: NEA, 2008, 54.
132. Gilmore, Al-Toney. *All the People.* Washington, DC: NEA, 2008 (handwritten note on title page).

Part II: Next in Line

1. The Enfield Savings and Loan Association became the Enfield Branch of the Southern Bank and Trust Company.
2. The Civil Rights Act of 1964, signed by President Lyndon Johnson, made segregation in public places illegal and prohibited discrimination on the basis of race, ethnicity, religion, sex, or national origin.
3. Dorosin, Mark, et. al. "'Unless Our Children Begin to Learn Together . . .': The State of Education in Halifax County." Chapel Hill: UNC Center for Civil Rights, 2011. Print.
4. Hampton Institute became Hampton University in 1984.
5. Booker, Simeon, with Carol McCabe Booker. *Shocking the Conscience: A Reporter's Account of the Civil Rights Movement.* Jackson: University Press of Mississippi, 2013. Print.
6. John Lewis was one of the Freedom Riders. He became a member of the House of Representatives in 1987 representing Georgia's fifth Congressional district. He served in that capacity until his death in 2020.
7. O'Brien, M. J. *We Shall Not Be Moved. The Jackson Woolworth's Sit-In and the Movement It Inspired.* Jackson: University Press of Mississippi, 2013. Print.
8. The first Citizens' Council was a White supremacy group that was created in Mississippi in July 1954 following the May 1954 *Brown v. Board of Education* decision to end segregation in public schools. The councils subsequently spread throughout the South.
9. "Six Dead After Church Bombing." *Washington Post*, September 16, 1963. Web. Accessed March 18, 2018. http://www.washingtonpost.com/wp-srv/national/longterm/churches/archives1.htm.
10. "Six Dead After Church Bombing."
11. Simkin, John. "George Wallace." Spartacus Educational, n.d. Web. Accessed March 18, 2018. https://spartacus-educational.com/USAwallaceG.htm.

12. For additional information about the Quigless Clinic-Hospital, see Whitfield, K. M. "The Quigless Clinic: Its impact on the lives of African Americans living in Tarboro, North Carolina, in the 1950s." *Journal of the National Medicine Association* 101.2 (2009): 184–88. Print.

13. Johnson v. Branch, 242 F. Sup 721 (E.D.N.C. 1965). Print.

14. Academies were all-White private schools set up to keep White children from attending integrated schools.

15. Mildred Bobbitt Sexton, who was a key contributor for Willa's documentary film and book, reminded others of us on the documentary team that Interstate 95 had a major impact on the town of Enfield.

16. Brick School, located near Enfield, was established in 1895 by the American Missionary Association for Black students. The school closed in 1933.

17. "Foundations of Independence: Enfield." *Roanoke Rapids Daily Herald*, July 9, 2008: 8. Print.

18. "Senior Executive Service." US Office of Personnel Management, n.d. Web. Accessed April 27, 2019. https://www.opm.gov/policy-data-oversight/senior-executive-service/.

Part III: The Impact

1. Concerned Citizens of Tillery, Tillery Farms Homestead Mural Unveiling, Remembering Tillery A New Deal Resettlement souvenir program booklet compiled by the Concerned Citizens of Tillery, Tillery, North Carolina (November 12, 2016).

2. Strickland, Shantara Nicole (Under the direction of Dr. Katherine Mellen Charron). "For the Sake of Freedom: Landownership, Education, and Memory in Halifax County, North Carolina, 1900–1960."

3. "Born with a Caul or Veil." Crystalinks. www.crystalinks.com/caulveil.html.

4. Draughan, Addie Clark Bobbitt. *The Life Experiences of Mrs. Addie Clark Bobbitt Draughan: A Woman of Knowledge and Wisdom.* Self-published, 2012.

5. Barrett, Heather L. (May 2000). "Quigless Clinic" (PDF). *National Register of Historic Places—Nomination and Inventory.* North Carolina State Historic Preservation Office. Retrieved November 1, 2014.

6. Durham Civil Rights Heritage Project. http://durhamcountylibrary.org/exhibits/dcrhp/aftermath4.ph.

7. History of Inborden Elementary School, https://www.halifax.k12.nc.us/Page/683.

ABOUT THE AUTHORS

Willa Cofield is a retired educator with a deep devotion to community uplift. She previously held positions at the North Carolina Fund, Livingston College, and the New Jersey Department of Education. She produced the documentary films *The Brick School Legacy* and, with Karen Riley, *The Nine O'clock Whistle*.

Cynthia Samuelson spent more than twenty-five years leading public and private information technology services organizations. She formerly worked for the Department of Defense, the Department of Transportation, and the National Endowment for the Arts.

Mildred Sexton retired after forty-three years as an educator, having worked for the Halifax County, North Carolina, public schools; the Virginia Department of Juvenile Justice; Hampton University; Old Dominion University; and the Hampton, Virginia, city schools.